LONGMAN LINGUISTICS LIBRARY

Explaining Language Change

Explaining Language Change

An Evolutionary Approach

WILLIAM CROFT

An imprint of **Pearson Education**

Harlow, England · London · New York · Reading, Massachusetts · San Francisco · Toronto · Don Mills, Ontario · Sydney
Tokyo · Singapore · Hong Kong · Seoul · Taipei · Cape Town · Madrid · Mexico City · Amsterdam · Munich · Paris · Milan

Pearson Education Limited
Edinburgh Gate
Harlow
Essex CM20 2JE
England

and Associated Companies throughout the world

Visit us on the World Wide Web at:
www.pearsoneduc.com

First published 2000

ISBN 0-582-35678-4 CSD
ISBN 0-582-35677-6 PPR

British Library Cataloguing-in-Publication Data

A catalogue record for this book is available from the British Library

Library of Congress Cataloging-in-Publication Data

Croft, William.
    Explaining language change : an evolutionary approach / William Croft.
      p. cm. — (Longman linguistics library)
    Includes bibliographical references and index.
    ISBN 0-582-35678-4 — ISBN 0-582-35677-6 (pbk.)
    1. Linguistic change. 2. Evolution (Biology) I. Title. II. Series.

P142.C76 2000
410'.1'8—dc21
                                      99-088742

Set in 10/12pt Times by 35
Produced by Addison Wesley Longman Singapore (Pte) Ltd.
Printed in Singapore

LONGMAN LINGUISTICS LIBRARY

General Editors:

R. H. ROBINS
University of London

GEOFFREY HORROCKS
University of Cambridge

DAVID DENISON
University of Manchester

Introduction to Text Linguistics
ROBERT DE BEAUGRANDE and WOLFGANG
DRESSLER

Psycholinguistics
Language, Mind and World
DANNY D. STEINBERG

Principles of Pragmatics
GEOFFREY N. LEECH

The English Verb
Second edition
F. R. PALMER

Pidgin and Creole Languages
SUZANNE ROMAINE

General Linguistics
An Introductory Survey
Fourth edition
R. H. ROBINS

**Generative and Non-linear
Phonology**
JACQUES DURAND

Modality and the English Modals
Second edition
F. R. PALMER

Dialects of English
Studies in Grammatical Variation
PETER TRUDGILL and J. K. CHAMBERS (eds.)

An Introduction to Bilingualism
CHARLOTTE HOFFMANN

Linguistic Theory
The Discourse of Fundamental Works
ROBERT DE BEAUGRANDE

A History of American English
J. L. DILLARD

Aspect in the English Verb
Process and Result in Language
YISHAI TOBIN

The Meaning of Syntax
A Study in the Adjectives of English
CONNOR FERRIS

Latin American Spanish
JOHN LIPSKI

A Linguistic History of Italian
MARTIN MAIDEN

The History of Linguistics
All edited by GIULIO LEPSCHY

**Volume I:
The Eastern Traditions of Linguistics**

**Volume II:
Classical and Medieval Linguistics**

**Volume III:
Renaissance and Early Modern
Linguistics**

**Volume IV:
Nineteenth Century Linguistics**
ANNA MORPURGO DAVIES

To come:
**Volume V:
The Twentieth Century**

Modern Arabic
Structures, Functions and Varieties
CLIVE HOLES

Frontiers of Phonology
Atoms, Structures and Derivations
JACQUES DURAND and FRANCIS KATAMBA (eds.)

To the memory of Keith Denning
1955–1998
Scholar, colleague, friend

Contents

Preface and acknowledgements

This book presents a framework for understanding language change as a fundamentally evolutionary phenomenon. It is part of a larger research program, outlined in 'Autonomy and functionalist linguistics' (Croft 1995a). In that article, I argued that there is a variety of theoretical positions that are unfortunately lumped together under the labels 'formalism' and 'functionalism'. These positions fall into two general classes. The first class comprises positions taken on the relationship between the conventional syntactic and semantic knowledge in the minds of individual speakers (their grammar). I argued for a position on this issue which I then called 'typological functionalism'. This position is defended in Croft (to appear b), which should be thought of as a pendant to this book.

The second class comprises theoretical positions taken on the nature of the relationship between a speaker's grammar and language use, manifested in the utterances produced by a speaker in discourse. In Croft (1995a), I argued for a position on this issue which I called 'integrative functionalism'. Specifically, I argued that: one cannot deny the existence of grammar, that is, knowledge of linguistic conventions in a speaker's mind; one cannot disentangle this knowledge from the act of using language; language function influences language form through the dynamics of language use and language change. The evolutionary framework of language presented here is intended to fulfill the promise of an integrative functionalist model offered in that article.

In fact, the main task of integration in writing this book was to acquaint myself with various aspects of pragmatics, discourse analysis, semantics, language acquisition, historical linguistics and several sub-areas of sociolinguistics, not to mention evolutionary biology, in order to work out the consequences of an evolutionary model of language. I hope that I have not committed too many scientific gaffes in the process, and that the framework presented here, programmatic though it is, will be of interest to specialists in those areas. Nevertheless, I believe that specialization has gone much too far in contemporary scientific research, and I hope that in this book, particular specialists will find interesting and important connections to ideas and facts in sub-areas of linguistics other than their own, as well as connections to ideas in evolutionary biology and philosophy of science.

The central thesis of this book originated with an idea which first occurred to me as a doctoral student taking a course in sociolinguistics from the late Charles A. Ferguson – that the proper linguistic equivalent to the genome was not a speaker's grammar but the utterance. I owe a great debt to him and to Joseph Greenberg and Elizabeth Traugott. Still, I would not have gotten anywhere without some biological thinking. I was first inspired by the evolutionary biology common core course at the University of Chicago taught in 1975–76 by Charles Oxnard (thank Chicago for general college education!). Susan Stucky introduced me to Mayr (1982) at Stanford. My thoughts were fertilized in the late 1980s by two biologists at the University of Michigan, Elena Tabachnick and Barbara Lundrigan, both of whom I thank for bringing me further up to date in developments in evolution and systematics. (Elena is to be thanked in addition for bringing Grant 1981 to my attention, and inspiring the title for §8.1.)

But the catalyst that led to this book was a fortuitous accident (evolutionary biologists are fond of emphasizing fortuitous accidents). I read a review of Harry Collins & Trevor Pinch's *The golem: what everyone should know about science*, and went to seek it out at the Manchester University library. Fortunately, Manchester is an open-stack library, and since I had just arrived in Manchester, I browsed the philosophy of science shelves. In this way I discovered that in *Science as a process*, David Hull, a biologist turned philosopher of science, had worked out a generalized theory of selection for the evolution of concepts as well as organisms, which gave me the framework that I needed. Meanwhile, the needs of the Department of Linguistics at the University of Manchester obliged me to teach courses in sociolinguistics, discourse analysis and grammatical change, which gave me the opportunity to flesh out my recreational reading in those areas, discover new and interesting ideas that fit in with the evolutionary framework, and present some of those ideas to students. I would like to thank the Department of Linguistics and the students in those classes. I would also like to thank the University of Manchester and the Humanities Research Board of the British Academy for funding sabbatical leave and research leave respectively, which allowed me to complete this book.

I have also benefited from audiences at the University of Manchester, Università di Pavia, Lunds Universitet, Cambridge University, Stanford University, the Max-Planck-Institut für Psycholinguistik in Nijmegen, the Conference on Functional Approaches to Grammar in Albuquerque, the XII International Conference on Historical Linguistics in Manchester, and from three anonymous referees for an anonymous journal, who were exposed to earlier versions of parts of this work. Thanks go to many others who individually commented on or discussed various parts of this work with me, including Mira Ariel, Melissa Bowerman, Joan Bybee, Herb Clark, Bernard Comrie, Sonia Cristofaro, David Denison, Guy Deutscher, Martin Durrell, Ray Gibbs, Joseph Greenberg, Martin Haspelmath, Bernd Heine, Masja Koptjevskaja-Tamm, Tania Kouteva, Yaron Matras, Lesley Milroy, Jim Milroy, John Ohala, J. C. Smith, Elizabeth Traugott, Peter Trudgill, Åke Viberg, Nigel Vincent and Tess Wood. I hope that those whose names elude me at this moment will accept my apologies. I would also like to thank Henry, Melissa, Mira and especially Carol for the emotional support they gave me while I was writing this book.

Last, but not at all least, was the inspiration of the late Keith Denning, my best friend in linguistics. As doctoral students together at Stanford, and later as nearby colleagues in Michigan, we talked incessantly about typology, historical linguistics and sociolinguistics and the great need for our field to integrate all of these approaches to the dynamic and variable essence of language. Keith was generous, funny, enthusiastic, and passionately dedicated to his students and to the study of language. This initial attempt at integration was inspired to a great extent by Keith. He was the first person I would have wanted to read this book. I still can't believe I won't hear his voice giving me constructive criticism on this book. I dedicate this book to his memory.

Chapter 1

Introduction

This book presents an evolutionary framework for understanding language change, interprets major current theories in the context of this framework, and makes certain new proposals for aspects of the theory of language change. Although this is an ambitious agenda, there has been much interesting work in the theory of language change in the past two decades, and I believe the time is ripe for an attempt to integrate the various advances and insights into the nature of language change.

1.1 On theories of historical phenomena

Why do languages change? This is a difficult question to answer. But part of the difficulty lies in our view of the thing about which the question is being asked, namely, a language.

Language change is a historical phenomenon. Hence the study of language change – historical linguistics – must satisfy certain basic requirements. The first requirement is that one must clearly distinguish historical entities from the types they represent. A historical entity is a spatiotemporally bounded individual, that is, it is a specific entity that exists in a specific place for a specific period of time. This is basically the distinction between a token of something and the type it belongs to. The distinction is clear when describing physical phenomena: a droplet of water is a collection of tokens of the molecular type H_2O. Tokens of water can come into existence and pass away via various chemical processes. There are general chemical laws to describe the chemical processes undergone by water.

The distinction is not so clear when dealing with entities such as languages. Certainly, it is recognized that particular languages exist during a particular time and place. Proto-Germanic arose somewhere in northeast Europe (or farther east) at a certain time, expanded its range, and came to an end with its breakup into what ultimately became English, German, Swedish, etc. More precisely, Proto-Germanic was identified as the language of a finite speech community, whose origin, spread and breakup determined the spatiotemporal boundaries of the historical entity of Proto-Germanic. Its daughter languages, that is the languages used by certain other speech communities, in turn arose in certain locations, perhaps migrated or spread, and will eventually die out or break up themselves.

But this historical view is often set aside for a different characterization of a language. In this characterization, a language such as German is a system of rules and forms, divided into a phonology, morphology, syntax, semantics and so on (in varying ways depending on one's grammatical theory). This system is treated as an idealized entity, abstracted away from any particular speaker's mental knowledge or its uses in particular discourse contexts. Is this entity a token or a type? It is neither. The German language system is not a token because it has been removed from its historical context: one is not analyzing the mental knowledge of actual speakers, or actual occurrences of use. The German language system is not a type because it is still a specific entity: German is still a specific language; its rules do not apply to language in general but to the particular language of German. To the extent that its rules apply at all, it is only to an abstract yet particular entity that has only an ideal existence.

One consequence of the idealization of a particular entity is that it gives the impression that there could be laws governing processes of change in the German language system, that is, the impression that one of the tasks of historical linguistics is to predict what changes to the German language system will occur and at what time, just as one predicts what will happen to molecules of H_2O when subjected to electrolysis. Yet this is patently not the case: we cannot predict what changes will happen to the German language system. H_2O is a type; the German language system is not a type. This fact has led some linguists to argue that historical linguistics cannot be a science because it cannot provide a predictive explanation (Lass 1980:xi).

I suggest that a reason why historical linguistics – and perhaps linguistics itself – as practiced by some might not be a science has to do with what the object of study is taken to be. When linguists analyze language as an abstract system, they are not looking at a historical entity, nor are they looking at a type about which predictions can be made. In fact, they are not looking at anything that is real at all, either as a type or as a token. An empirical science must examine real, existing entities, and then construct generalizations about what types are involved, as well as principles and constraints governing the structure and behavior of those types.

In the study of linguistics, the real, existing entities are utterances as they are produced in context, and speakers and their knowledge about their language as it is actually found in their minds. From these basic tokens, we can describe more complex tokens, such as a specific language or a speech community; and then we can construct types, such as 'language' or 'grammar' (mental representation), over which constraints and generalizations can be made.

I am not arguing that in doing so, we can construct a predictive model of language change. In all probability we will not be able to make detailed predictions, any more than historical sciences of natural phenomena, such as meteorology, astrophysics or geology, are able to do. There are two possible reasons for this, one 'optimistic', one 'pessimistic'. The 'optimistic' one is that we simply do not know the facts in particular cases in enough detail to predict the changes; if we did know, we would be able to make predictions (cf. Keller 1990/1994:159).

The 'pessimistic' one is that we would never be able to predict the change because there is at least some element of randomness in the process, as is the case with the randomness of mutation in biological reproduction and the random factors for survival of individual organisms.

I am inclined towards the pessimistic view with respect to language change, which implies that even with perfect knowledge of the initial state, we would not be able to predict a language change. But not all explanations of historical phenomena need predict the outcome of individual cases. With some types of processes, what really matters is probabilities of change: the cumulative effect of the probability leads ultimately to an overall change. Historical explanations can be, and often are, probabilistic. Probabilistic explanations are particularly effective when the object of study is a population: a gene pool or a population of organisms, for example – or a population of speakers, or of utterances. Both speakers and utterances form populations, and that is what allows probabilistic mechanisms of language change to be effective explanations.

Processes can be roughly divided into two types (see Hull 1988:410). One involves INHERENT CHANGE: a single object that exists over time changes in some way or other. An example of inherent change is human physiological development over its lifetime. Another example is human linguistic development, that is, the development of mental structures that we interpret as representing linguistic knowledge, over the lifetime of the speaker.

The other type of process involves REPLICATION: the creation of a new entity that preserves in large part the structure of its parent entity (or entities). An example of replication is the creation of the DNA of the offspring of an organism, replicated in MEIOSIS. Another example of replication is the production of a linguistic utterance, which replicates grammatical structures of previously occurring utterances of the language, according to patterns of knowledge in the minds of their producers. Another example which is often thought of as replication, but is much more indirect, is the learning of grammatical knowledge on the part of a child, compared with the grammatical knowledge in the minds of its parents and/or caregivers.

One of the problems with treating language as an idealized abstract system is that it makes language change into an inherent process: a single object – the abstract language system – changes over time. But the real, existing entities of linguistics are utterances and speakers' grammars. The evolution of both of those entities, particularly utterances, occurs through replication, not inherent change.

Replication can result in change at two levels. At one level, change can occur because the structure of the replicate is not exactly the same as the structure of the original. For example, I may pronounce *bad* in an utterance with a slightly higher vowel than in earlier utterances which I heard and internalized. I will call this ALTERED REPLICATION. Altered replication produces variants of a structure. At the other level, change can occur by the shift in the frequencies of variants of a structure. For example, more and more utterances occur with a higher vowel in *bad* than with the lower variants. Perhaps *bad* with the lower vowel variants will eventually die out. This sort of change is called DIFFERENTIAL REPLICATION (Hull 1988:409).

The position taken in this book is that the study of language is about empirically real entities, not idealized abstract systems. The real entities of language are utterances and speakers' grammars. Language change occurs via replication of these entities, not through inherent change of an abstract system. In chapters 2–3, I will argue that the primary replicators are in fact utterances, not speakers' grammars; but the point that matters here is that a theory of language change must be a theory of replication of empirically real entities, either grammars or utterances.

1.2   Desiderata for a theory of language change

We are now in a position to outline some desiderata for a theory of language change.

First, a theory of language change must avoid the reification or hypostatization of languages. If one speaks of 'forces' causing a language to change, such as Sapir's concept of drift (Sapir 1921), then one is speaking as if language change is an inherent change applying to an abstract system. Descriptions such as '[a phoneme's] performance represents an extreme phonetic possibility as when it is an /i/ badly pressed by an invading /e/ with surrounding diphthongs which block all way of escape' and 'Isolated phonemes do not rush into structural gaps unless they are close enough to be attracted' (Martinet 1952/1972:147, 159) are examples of reification taken to excess. Languages don't change; people change language through their actions (Croft 1990:257). Keller describes this desideratum as the principle of methodological individualism: 'the explanation [of a language change] is based on acting individuals, not languages, structures, processes, or collectives' (Keller 1990/1994:121).

Second, a theory of language change must explain why languages do NOT change in many ways, sometimes over many generations of speakers (see Milroy 1992b:10–13). Many theories of language change focus their attention on mechanisms to bring about change. But if those mechanisms were the only mechanisms around, then languages would be changing constantly in all of their respects. Yet they are not. A theory of language change must provide for mechanisms that act as forces for stability as well as for change, and ideally get the proper balance in order to account for rates of change. Another way of putting this desideratum is to say that a theory of language change must provide mechanisms of NORMAL (identical) REPLICATION as well as altered replication (and also mechanisms for nondifferential replication as well as differential replication).

Third, a theory of language change must distinguish the two processes of change, that is, it must distinguish altered replication from differential replication. To use the terminology more typically found in linguistics, the two processes are INNOVATION or actuation – the creation of novel forms in the language – and PROPAGATION or diffusion (or, conversely, loss) of those forms in the language. Both processes are necessary components of the process of language change. The distinction between these two processes, and the fact that both are necessary components of language change, is very rarely recognized in models of language change (but see Jespersen 1922:166–7). Because of this, some apparently contradictory positions have been taken on the nature of language change.

Some linguists argue that only innovation is a language change. Joseph writes, 'language change always takes place in the present, i.e. it always occurs in some speaker's (or group of speakers) present' (Joseph 1992:127; see also Joseph & Janda 1988). Joseph can only be speaking of innovation, as propagation of a novel form does take place over long periods of time, exceeding the life spans of individual speakers. Others argue that only propagation constitutes a language change. James Milroy writes, 'a change in the output of a single speaker might be regarded as the locus of a change in the system, whereas of course a change is not a change until it has been adopted by *more than one* speaker' (Milroy 1992a:79, emphasis original; see also Labov 1982:46). Others do not recognize the distinction, leading to misunderstandings such as that in the following passage:

> How can one 'understand' or get at 'the intention behind' or discover the 'meaning' of a shift from SOV to SVO, or a monophthongization, or a vowel-shift, etc., in any 'cognitive' or empathetic way, or 're-enact' them, or attribute them to 'reasons' and 'beliefs'? Especially as linguistic changes . . . typically unfold over very long periods of time, most often beyond the lifetime of any human 'actor'. (Lass 1997:339)

Lass is criticizing hypotheses about the innovation of a language change – hypotheses appealing to speaker intentions – by citing a fact about the propagation of a language change – propagation typically extends over many generations. Lass may be correct that innovation does not involve intention; but not for the reason he gives. Lass is not alone in this misunderstanding; but neither do the advocates of such explanations (in this case, Anttila 1989) tend to distinguish innovation and propagation, thereby inviting the erroneous criticism.

One consequence of recognizing that innovation and propagation are distinct but jointly necessary processes for language change is recognizing that language change is both a synchronic and a diachronic phenomenon. Innovation is a synchronic phenomenon, as Joseph notes in the quotation above: it occurs in speaker action at a given point in time. Propagation is a diachronic phenomenon: it occurs sometimes over a very long period of time, even centuries. On the other hand, sociolinguistic research has demonstrated that one can observe propagation occurring in less than the lifetime of a speaker (see e.g. Trudgill 1988).

Fourth, a comprehensive framework for understanding language change must subsume structural, functional and social dimensions of language change, or their equivalents. Most current approaches to language change address only one or another of these dimensions. Sociohistorical linguistics examines almost exclusively the social dimensions (although Labov 1994 discusses the phonetics and phonology of vowel shifts and mergers in some detail). Traditional philological and structuralist approaches focus on structure and to a lesser extent on function. Generative theories focus on structure exclusively, though largely because they deny function or social factors any interesting or central role in language change. Grammaticalization theory focuses on structure and function, with a stronger emphasis on the latter. To the extent that function and social factors play a role in language change – and there is strong evidence that both do – they must be integrated in a single framework.

Last, a comprehensive framework for understanding language change must subsume both INTERNAL and EXTERNAL causes of language change. Theories of internal causes are varied, and most attention has been focused on them. Externally caused changes, that is, changes caused by contact such as borrowing and substratum phenomena, tend to be discussed relatively little in theories of language change, and are typically placed in separate chapters from internal causes in textbooks on historical linguistics. Contact-induced change appears to have an obvious source – the other language. Nevertheless, mechanisms for the innovation and propagation of contact-induced change, preferably mechanisms comparable to those posited for internal changes, must be established.

The framework presented in this book satisfies all five desiderata for a theory of language change, and thus can be counted as a comprehensive framework for understanding language change. However, it is only a framework; it is hoped that future work will be able to flesh out theories of specific types of changes in this framework. The last section of this chapter briefly outlines the framework.

1.3   An utterance-based selectional theory of language change

The framework for understanding language change to be presented here is based on a generalized theory of selection for all types of evolutionary phenomena, originally developed in biology and applied to the history of science by David Hull (Hull 1988; see Dawkins 1976). The generalized theory of selection, described in chapter 2, distinguishes variation (altered replication) from differential replication. It specifically provides a model of selection, which Hull argues is the mechanism for differential replication for most types of biological evolution and also conceptual evolution in the history of science. Hull also emphasizes that replication and selection involve historical entities (tokens), not types (except for very general types such as 'gene', 'species', 'population' and so on: see chapter 2). The generalized theory of selection thus satisfies the first three desiderata enumerated in §1.2.

The framework presented in chapter 2 can be used to interpret the major extant theories of language change; they are surveyed in chapter 3. However, in chapter 2, I also present the first of four major theses about the nature of language change set forth in this book. I propose that UTTERANCES, more precisely the replication of linguistic structures in utterances in language use, play a central role in the theory of language change. A widely held view treats language change as occurring in the process of 'replicating' a grammar in child language acquisition. There are however serious empirical problems with this view, discussed in §3.2. For this reason, the Theory of Utterance Selection, which is more or less compatible with most aspects of sociohistorical linguistics, grammaticalization theory and the invisible hand theory (see §3.3), is pursued here.

In the Theory of Utterance Selection, CONVENTION is placed at center stage. Normal replication is in essence conformity to convention in language use. Altered replication results from the violation of convention in language use. And selection is essentially the gradual establishment of a convention through language use.

Convention does not generally take center stage in linguistic theory, formalist or functionalist. The reason is that conventions are essentially arbitrary (see §4.2.4). Saussure considered arbitrariness to be central to the understanding of language: '[The arbitrary nature of the sign] dominates all the linguistics of language; its consequences are numberless' (Saussure 1916/1966:67–8). Yet neither formalists nor functionalists have shown much interest in arbitrariness per se. Functionalists are chiefly interested in the nonarbitrary, functionally motivated aspects of grammatical structure. Formalists find arbitrariness useful in criticizing functionalist analyses, but they are chiefly interested in general, formal universals that have an innate basis. But a central aspect of a speaker's use of language is convention. When I say *Who did you meet yesterday?*, I put the interrogative pronoun *Who* at the beginning of the sentence because that is the convention of my speech community, I know the conventions of my speech community, and my use of language will serve its purpose best most of the time if I conform to the conventions of my speech community. It may be that the initial position of *Who* is partly motivated by pragmatic universals of information structure, or partly specified by an innate Universal Grammar. In fact, one (or both) of those factors may be the motivation for the origin of the convention. But that is not why I have put it there in that utterance. As Saussure wrote: '[arbitrary conventions] are nonetheless fixed by rule; it is this rule and not the intrinsic value of the gestures that obliges one to use them' (Saussure 1916/1966:68). Convention – whether conforming to it, violating it, or establishing it – plays a key role in language use and in language change. (It also plays a key role in our knowledge of language; see Croft to appear b.)

Convention is a property of the mutual knowledge or COMMON GROUND of the speech community. Of course, common ground is found in the minds of speakers, albeit shared with other members of the speech community. Thus, there is an interplay between convention and individual speakers' knowledge, or COMPETENCE as it is usually called. There is also an interplay between conventional and nonconventional aspects of language use, which plays a critical role in the understanding of how replication of linguistic structures in utterances occurs. All of these concepts are discussed in some detail in chapter 4.

The second major thesis of this book pertains to the nature of grammatical (and lexical) change. The causal mechanisms for innovation involve the mapping from language structure or form to language function, that is, meaning in context (Croft 1995a; see §4.3 for some discussion of other senses of the word). This mapping occurs at two levels or interfaces. One is the mapping from phonological structure to phonetic reality (articulatory and auditory). The other is the mapping from grammatical (morphosyntactic) structure to its semantic/pragmatic/discourse function in context. Neither mapping has been found by linguists to be simple to represent. But nor is it simple for speakers to represent these two levels of mapping. In chapters 4–6, I argue that altered replication is essentially a result of speakers adjusting the mapping from language structure to external function. I focus chiefly on grammatical change, with a few references to sound change.

The mechanisms for innovation in language change involve both structure and function. The mechanisms for propagation, on the other hand, are essentially social, namely the various factors discussed by sociolinguists (see §3.4.3, §7.4.2). In other words, there are two distinct mechanisms operating in language change – this is my third major thesis (see also Croft 1995a:524; 1996a: 116–17). The mechanism for innovation is functional, that is, involves the form–function mapping. The mechanism for propagation is a selection mechanism, in the evolutionary sense (see §2.3), and it is social. Thus, the integration of structural, functional and social dimensions of language change is achieved largely by integrating the two distinct processes of change, innovation and propagation/selection.

The last major thesis about language change presented in this book pertains to the relationship between internal and external (contact-induced) sources of language change, which is more complex than is usually assumed. In chapter 4, I argue (following sociolinguistic theory) that a speech community is defined in terms of domains of use, not in terms of collections of speakers. All people in a society are members of multiple speech communities, whether those communities are conventionally described as representing a single language or multiple languages. In other words, all speakers command multiple varieties or codes, and thus some of the mechanisms for internal sources of change are the same as those for external sources of change. These mechanisms are discussed in chapters 6–7. The blurring of the line between internal and external changes also allows us to integrate the study of language contact and genetic linguistics. The naturalness of this view becomes more apparent when one recognizes that language 'speciation' is more like plant speciation than animal speciation. This view of language speciation is discussed in chapter 8.

Chapter 2

An evolutionary model of language change

The formation of different languages and of distinct species, and the proof that both have been developed through a gradual process, are curiously parallel . . .

Charles Darwin, *The descent of man*

2.1 Introduction

The relationship between language change and biological evolution has been debated since the emergence of linguistics as a science in the nineteenth century, at around the same time as the emergence of evolutionary theory. The debate has increased in recent times. One can identify three separate ways in which biological evolution has been connected to linguistic evolution in recent discussion.

First, interest has revived in the evolution of language, that is, the evolution of the human linguistic capacity (Pinker & Bloom 1990; Hurford, Studdert-Kennedy & Knight 1998; Kirby 1999). The evolution of human linguistic capacity is directly a biological process: some genetic change among ancestral primates led to the creation of a social and cognitive capacity for language or a language-like system for communication, and some process selected those primates with that capacity, leading to humans as a speaking species. This topic, while interesting, is also extremely speculative, and will not be surveyed in this book: this book is concerned with language change itself, not the evolution of a certain biological capacity of human beings.

Second, interest (and controversy) has arisen over the so-called genetic origin of contemporary human languages. Here the evolutionary connection is one of historical association. The internal structure of genetic families such as Austronesian are compared to the distribution of biological traits, such as alleles in mitochondrial DNA, or blood types (Bellwood 1991). It is assumed that, for the most part, transmission of biological traits through offspring is historically paralleled by transmission of language from parents to children, and hence family trees of human communities based on biological traits should roughly parallel family trees constructed on linguistic evidence.

Of course, all know that this parallelism in the history of languages and of human biological traits is not necessary. Languages are not transmitted via an individual's DNA; biological traits are. Rather, languages are transmitted to new speakers through exposure to their use. A group of people may abandon

9

their language and adopt one of another group to whom they are not biologically closely related. For more recent families such as Austronesian, where the demographic history is better known, the relative contribution of language shift vs parent-to-child transmission can be more easily sorted out. In Austronesian, for example, it is clear that Melanesians are biologically closer to Papuans, and presumably have shifted to the Austronesian languages that they now speak (cf. Melton *et al.* 1995; Redd *et al.* 1995).

Relationships have also been observed between proposals for historically deeper linguistic families such as Amerind (Greenberg 1987) or even Proto-World (Bengtson & Ruhlen 1994) and proposals for historically parallel biological phylogenies (Greenberg, Turner & Zegura 1986; Cavalli-Sforza *et al.* 1988). These are much more controversial, chiefly because of challenges to the linguistic classification; the classification based on some biological traits (in particular mitochondrial DNA) is also questioned. Again, this relationship between biological evolution and language change will not be surveyed in this book: this book is concerned with the mechanisms of language change, not the origin and spread of specific families of languages.

The third connection between language change and biological evolution is found where the theory of biological evolution itself has been adopted, or adapted, in order to construct an evolutionary theory of language change (see e.g. Keller 1990/1994:141–52; McMahon 1994:314–40; Lass 1990, 1997 passim; Ritt 1995). Evolution is recognized as a process that occurs with certain types of entities. The process is probably best understood as it occurs with populations of biological organisms; that is evolutionary biology. The hypothesis is that language change is an example of the same process, or a similar process, occurring with a different type of entity, namely language. It is this hypothesis that forms the starting point of this book.

A number of approaches have been taken to an evolutionary model of language change. The first approach is literal: language is a genetic capacity, and hence obeys certain principles of biology. This approach is associated with Chomskyan linguistics, because Chomsky argues for the biological basis of quite specific linguistic properties (e.g. certain syntactic structures and constraints). The literal approach also makes developmental claims: for instance, the hypothesis that the human language capacity in all its detail emerges in maturation.

However, the main goal of the literal approach is to claim a biological basis for the universal properties of languages. The ways in which contemporary human languages are divergent, and have diverged or will diverge in history, cannot be accounted for in the literal approach. A literal approach to language diversity would amount to claiming that the differences among languages reflect genetic differences among their speakers. This is patently false, as can be seen from the aforementioned fact that a person can learn a second language, and learns whatever language is spoken in their surroundings. For this reason, the literal approach generally turns to questions of the evolution of the human linguistic capacity, that is, what gave us the genetic basis for the properties common to all languages, whatever those may be.

The second approach is essentially analogical: there are analogies between certain biological processes as described by evolutionary theory and certain processes of language change that call for description. Hence, linguists seeking better descriptions and analyses of those processes can borrow or adapt the descriptions and explanatory mechanisms that evolutionary biologists have proposed. However, no deeper claim is made about the relationship between the theory of evolution in biology and the theory of language change in linguistics. There are simply analogies or metaphors between a process in one domain of scientific study and a process in another domain; in particular, one should not push the analogy too far. In the analogical approach, the relationship between evolution and language is essentially opportunistic – an opportunity for linguists to utilize some already developed theoretical constructs.

An example of the analogical approach appears to be the use of the biological metaphor in creole studies, e.g. Whinnom (1971) and Mufwene (1996a, to appear). Whinnom suggests that the biological concept of hybridization can be applied to language contact 'provided that the analogies are properly applied' (Whinnom 1971:91). Mufwene compares languages to species and the factors that determine a language's survival or extinction as ecological factors, but states:

> I do not want to suggest that language evolution is in all, or most, respects like species evolution . . . There are, however, some similarities between the concepts of *language* and *species*, which I find informative and would like to use cautiously to shed light on the process of language evolution. (Mufwene to appear, fn. 1)

It appears that Lass's adoption of an important concept in recent evolutionary theory, exaptation (Lass 1990), and its application to historical linguistics, is another example of the analogical approach to the relation between biological evolution and language change (see §5.3 for further discussion). Lass writes: 'while claiming that the notion of exaptation seems useful in establishing a name and descriptive framework for a class of historical events, I remain fully aware (even insistent) that languages are not biological systems in any deep sense' (Lass 1990:96). He adds, for instance, that 'There is as far as I am aware no storage or coding mechanism for linguistic transmission equivalent to DNA' (ibid.).

However, Lass makes it clear in the following paragraph that he is not taking an analogical approach. It is not that languages ARE biological systems. It is that languages and biological systems are instances of a more general phenomenon: 'rather than extending a notion from biology to linguistics, I am suggesting that the two domains . . . have certain behaviors in common by virtue of evolving' (Lass 1990:96). In fact, Lass is taking a third, generalized approach. This approach proposes a generalized theory of evolutionary processes, which applies to the evolution of species and their traits in biology, to language change in linguistics, and to other domains as well: 'I am convinced . . . that there is such a thing as a theory of "historically evolved systems"' (Lass 1997:316). In the generalized approach, there is a profound relationship between biological evolution and language change, which is worth exploring in greater detail. The two are not identical by any means. But they both display salient properties that demonstrate that they are instantiations of the same generalized theory that crosses disciplinary boundaries.

Even in the generalized approach, the evolutionary biologists are again in the forefront. Lass cites Dawkins in support of this approach. Dawkins' popular book *The selfish gene* (Dawkins 1976), besides making specific proposals about the nature of biological evolution, suggests that his model can be applied to cultural evolution as well. He proposes the notion of a MEME to represent a sociocultural unit that can evolve via differential replication. David Hull, a biologist who became a philosopher of science but not without continuing to make contributions to systematics and evolutionary theory, develops a generalized theory of selection which subsumes both biological and conceptual evolution (Hull 1988, especially chapters 11–12). In this chapter, I will argue that Hull's model can be applied to language change, and allows us to construct the foundations of a theory of language change and the major mechanisms that bring it about.

If the generalized approach is to be taken seriously, then Lass's claim – that there is no equivalent of DNA in linguistic evolution – raises a difficult question. If Lass's claim is true, then are linguistic and biological evolution really instances of the same thing? Does DNA play an essential role in the theory of evolution developed by biologists – developed in far greater detail than the theory of language change in linguistics? If so, then the role in evolutionary theory that is played by DNA in biological systems must have a counterpart in linguistic systems. Lass argues against the literal approach, that is, that there is a genetic basis to the phenomena of linguistic evolution: language change does not occur through biological genetic mutation and selection. But that does not necessarily mean that there is no functional equivalent to DNA in linguistic evolution. Hull writes, 'People reject selection models in conceptual change out of hand because they have a simplistic understanding of biological evolution' (Hull 1988:402). The trick is making the right instantiation of the theoretical constructs of the generalized theory.

In this chapter, I will argue that there is an equivalent to DNA in linguistic evolution, and that it is the utterance. Both the existence of an equivalent to DNA and the entity I am proposing as the equivalent will at first strike the reader as surprising, perhaps even bizarre. But an essential role in the generalized theory of selection is assigned to a function most typically centered on DNA in biological evolution. I will argue that this function is most typically centered on the production and comprehension of utterances in language change. It should be clear from the wording of the preceding sentence that the DNA–utterance analogy is going to be rather indirect and not the one that Lass rightly rejects. In fact, what will emerge from the application of Hull's theory to language change is a theory that is thoroughly based on what happens to language in use, from the origin of an innovation to its adoption as a convention of the speech community, and which unifies internal and external causes of language change. The remainder of this book will explore some of the consequences of this theory. But first we must explicate the two most fundamental notions in the generalized theory, the population theory of species and the generalized theory of selection.

2.2 Populations and phylogenies

One of the major advances of the so-called evolutionary synthesis is the replacement of the essentialist theory of species by the population theory of species (Dobzhansky 1937, Mayr 1942, cited in Hull 1988:102; see also Mayr 1982). The population theory of species is sometimes traced back to Darwin, but Darwin was not entirely clear in his definition of species (Mayr 1982:265–69; Hull 1988:96, 213 fn. 2; see Mayr 1982:272 for other precursors). The population theory is also inextricably tied up with the question of systematics, that is, the taxonomic classification of organisms into varieties, species, genera, families and higher taxa. Here the contrast is between classification and phylogeny; we must discuss this question as well.

In the ESSENTIALIST view of a species, each species has immutable essential structural properties that identify it (Mayr 1982:256). That is, the essentialist view is that a species instantiates an abstract type. The essentialist view ran into problems due to various sorts of structural variation among species, including high degrees of structural variation among individuals in a population and also among different life-stages in an individual in a population (for example, a caterpillar and the butterfly it turns into, or a species that changes sex over its lifetime; Hull 1988:430). The essentialist view also ran into problems with populations which could not be distinguished by structural features but were distinct reproductive communities (Mayr 1982:271; see below). But the greatest problem for the essentialist view of a species is that a species evolves, and in so evolving, can lose 'essential' structural properties. Identifying this problem is one of the major contributions of Darwin to evolutionary biology.

The POPULATION theory of species is completely different from the essentialist theory (Mayr 1982:272). A species consists of a population of interbreeding individuals who are REPRODUCTIVELY ISOLATED from other populations. This property – interbreeding, and lack thereof between species – is the 'essential' property the individuals have in common. There is no essential species type. Individuals can vary in enormous ways in physical structure (and behavior), but as long as they form a population in the evolutionary sense, they are members of the same species. Conversely, individuals may be structurally extremely similar, but if they come from two distinct reproductively isolated populations, they are members of different species. This is a radically different view of the species as a conceptual category. The category definition is based on a specific set of individuals, and category membership is defined in terms of how the individuals interact with each other, not by any specific traits associated with all and only the individuals in the category.

Not every individual need breed with every other individual in order for the set of individuals to form a population; only reproductive isolation is necessary: 'extensive interbreeding with the population system is not an essential property of biological species; non-interbreeding with other population systems is' (Grant 1981:91). Although reproductive isolation is treated in theory as a sharp dividing line, it is not entirely so in fact (Hull 1988:102–3). There are cases in which populations which were separated and then brought into contact again developed a stable hybrid region in between the two distinct populations. Hull gives the example of the hooded crow and the carrion crow in Europe: separated by glaciers which then receded, the species populations remain distinct, but there is a stable band of hybrids in a zone not exceeding 75 to 100 kilometers in width (Hull 1988:103). Hence there is interbreeding where there is contact, but there is little gene flow between the two populations. Conversely, reproductively isolated populations of plants can merge: 'estimates of the proportion of plant species in general that are of hybrid origin run as high as 30 or 40 percent' (Hull 1988:103; cf. Grant 1981:203).

In the essentialist view of species, a species is a type, defined by a set of properties, that is not located in space or time but in an abstract domain of biological traits. In the population view, a species is a spatiotemporal individual, not an eternal essence. The population of organisms constituting a species is circumscribed by the region in time and space collectively occupied by the individual members of the species. The beginning of a species is defined by its branching off in a speciation process, and its end by either its extinction or its fission into two or more new species in speciation: 'Just as the name "Gargantua" [an individual gorilla] denotes a particular organism from conception to death, "*Gorilla gorilla*" denotes a particular segment of the phylogenetic tree' (Hull 1988:215).

A species, like an individual organism, is a historical entity in the population view. In the essentialist view, a species is not a spatiotemporal individual: it is a type or kind, whose instantiations may be particular individuals, but the kind is not spatiotemporally bounded itself. But species are not types; they cannot be types. The essentialist view treats a historical entity as if it were a type. In the population view, only entities as abstract as species (in general), and certain theoretically defined subpopulations of a species such as demes (in general) or geographical races (in general) are kinds. Any particular species, deme or geographical race is a spatiotemporal individual. In other words, a population is a fundamentally historical entity. This point is a very important one in understanding both the relationship between populations and classification and between populations and selection (see §2.4.1).

If the population theory of species is distinct from the essentialist theory of species, then one would expect to find cases where there are mismatches in the world between species defined in terms of reproductively isolated populations and species defined in terms of essential structural properties. In fact, this is the case (see e.g. Hull 1988:104). SIBLING SPECIES are two reproductively isolated species whose structural descriptions overlap to such an extent that on an essentialist definition, they would be the same species. For example, five different species of the flower *Gilia* in the Mojave Desert are so similar that they were once classified as a single species, but the five species are highly intersterile (Grant 1981:61–2). POLYTYPIC SPECIES, on the other hand, are species that are structurally so heterogeneous that an essentialist would be hard put to categorize them as a single species, yet they form an interbreeding population (in terms of gene flow; Mayr 1982:287–92).

A population may split into two or more parts, often through geographical isolation. The term VARIETY is generally used for a subpart of a species population. Varieties may cease to interbreed. In fact the two populations may diverge in structure and behavior such that they could no longer interbreed even if brought together again. At this point one would say that the original species has split into two daughter species. (I follow Hull 1988, and Hennigian systematics in general, by assuming the old species no longer exists after such a split, thereby avoiding the pseudoproblem of deciding which of the daughter species is 'really' the continuation of the parent species.) 'Varieties are merely incipient species. Not all varieties become species, but all species at one time were varieties' (Hull 1988:96).

If one constructs a historical account of the splitting (and also merging) of populations of organisms, the result would be a PHYLOGENY. A phylogenetic classification is intended to reflect the history of the organisms being classified. A phylogenetic classification is not the same as a taxonomic classification, the familiar classification of species into genera, families and so on. A taxonomic classification is based on similarities and differences among traits. It is basically founded on an essentialist view of species. A phylogenetic classification is historical. Yet the two have often been confused, even by biological systematists (taxonomists). There are two reasons for this confusion. The first is the apparent similarity between a phylogenetic tree and a taxonomic tree: 'The relationship between a branching phylogenetic tree and the successive subdivisions of a hierarchical classification could not seem more patent. Yet, it is not' (Hull 1988:98).

The second is due to a practical problem in determining phylogenies. It is not always practically possible to discover patterns of gene flow in populations. In particular, it is impossible if the species is extinct and one must rely on fossil evidence. Instead, one examines traits, and uses the differences in traits among populations to hypothesize a historical scenario of the successive splitting (and merging) of populations. Since one is using traits to project a phylogeny, it is tempting to use a taxonomic classification to project the phylogeny. But a proper phylogeny requires the differentiation of traits based on their history. If two taxa share a trait, it could be a retained trait from the parent population (a SYMPLESIOMORPHY), or it could be a shared innovation of the two taxa (a SYNAPOMORPHY). Only a shared innovated trait can justify grouping the two taxa together phylogenetically. A shared retained trait simply indicates that the two taxa may be grouped together phylogenetically with other taxa at a greater time depth. And of course the shared traits may be shared accidentally, that is, the trait arose independently in each population, and hence they do not form a phylogenetic group (see Lass 1997:113–14 for a brief introduction to these terms and concepts in a historical linguistic context).

In sum, populations and phylogenies represent historical entities and evolution, while the essentialist view of species and taxonomic classification represent a view of species and groupings of species that is not historical or evolutionary, and at best provides indirect evidence for historical phenomena. In developing an evolutionary theory of language change, or of any historical process involving populations and their divergence (or merging), the concepts of populations defined by interaction of individuals (or lack thereof) and phylogenies are the relevant ones.

All of the phenomena described above are directly relevant to linguistics. A genetic linguistic classification, the family tree model, is intended to be a phylogeny of languages (although some linguists retain certain essentialist views; see §8.1). Shared innovations are crucial to establishing a genetic linguistic grouping; shared retentions represent at best some higher genetic grouping. There is of course the possibility that apparent shared cognates are accidental. Historical linguists have also adopted the convention of giving daughter languages different names from the parent language, and generally assume the daughter language is a 'new' language (compare the naming of daughter species in Hennigian systematics alluded to above).

The mismatches occurring between the essentialist and population definitions of species are also found in languages. These are the standard examples of the problem in defining language and dialect (see e.g. Chambers & Trudgill 1980, chapter 1).

Sibling languages are two linguistic varieties that are structurally so similar that they are considered to be 'dialects of the same language', yet are perceived by the speakers – or at least by one group of speakers – as distinct languages. Examples of sibling languages (of varying degrees of controversiality) include Macedonian and Bulgarian, Danish and Norwegian, Serbian and Croatian, Hindi and Urdu, and Malay and Indonesian. Dixon (1980:33–40) points out that many instances of neighboring languages in traditional, small, decentralized, nonliterate societies such as Australian aboriginal societies involve what I call sibling languages. In some cases the perception of the sibling languages as distinct is not reciprocal: many Bulgarians tend to see Macedonian as a dialect of Bulgarian, but the reverse does not hold. Of course, this reflects different perceptions about the social and political separateness of the communities that speak these linguistic varieties.

Polytypic languages, on the other hand, are linguistic varieties that are structurally so diverse that linguists would characterize them as different languages, yet their speakers perceive them as dialects of the same language. Examples of polytypic languages include the Chinese so-called dialects: they are mutually unintelligible (Li & Thompson 1981:2), but the writing system and political unity tends to imply identification as a single language (Norman 1988:1–3). Another example of polytypic languages is found in diglossia

(Ferguson 1959/1972), where there are two related but mutually unintelligible varieties, the L[ow] variety being a vernacular and the H[igh] variety a written standard, as in German-speaking Switzerland or the Arab countries. Speakers perceive H and L as a single language, L often being perceived as a substandard or imperfect version of the H variety. The same is true of postcreole continua, where the creole basilect and standard language acrolect are mutually unintelligible, as with Jamaican creole and Standard Jamaican English (DeCamp 1971:350). The structural diversity of traditional dialects of English, German, Italian and other western European languages may be instances of a lower degree of polytypy, depending on the degree to which their speakers identify themselves as speakers of English, German, etc., albeit nonstandard speakers.

Turning to the crux of the matter, the conflicting definitions of species, we find a parallel clash of definitions of a language. The linguistic or STRUCTURAL definition of a language – if two varieties share enough structure in common (phonology, grammar or morphosyntax, lexicon), then they should be classified as part of the same language – corresponds to the essentialist definition of a species. Comparison of linguistic varieties based purely on structural properties leads to assessments of language vs dialect based on essentialist criteria. The structural definition of a language possesses the same flaw as the essentialist definition of a species. As I argued in §1.1, the structural definition of a language makes a type out of a historical entity. As with species, languages evolve over time, undermining the structural definition; and sibling languages and polytypic languages demonstrate further problems with the structural/essentialist definition of a language.

What is the linguistic equivalent of the population definition of species? Chambers & Trudgill (1980) offer a social definition of language as an alternative to the structural definition (see also Haugen 1968/1972). They define an AUTONOMOUS VARIETY as one that is perceived by its speakers as a distinct language, no matter how similar it is structurally to some other variety. A HETERONOMOUS VARIETY, on the other hand, is perceived by its speakers as being the same language as that of an autonomous standard variety, no matter how structurally distinct those varieties are. We may apply Chambers & Trudgill's definition to the cases of sibling languages and polytypic languages. Serbian and Croatian are examples of sibling languages. Serbian is autonomous from Croatian because Serbian speakers perceive their language as distinct from Croatian and vice versa. Modern Arabic is an example of a polytypic language. The colloquial varieties of Modern Arabic are heteronomous, because speakers of the modern colloquial varieties perceive their colloquial variety as a version of Arabic.

Chambers & Trudgill's social definition of language closely corresponds to the population definition of species. However, their definition is based on speaker perceptions (and the existence of a standard variety). The genuine equivalent to the population theory of species for a language must be in terms of actual communicative interaction. This does not imply that every speaker of a socially defined language speaks with every other speaker of that language, any more than every organism of a species mates with every other organism of that species in its lifetime (see above). It merely implies that every speaker perceives every other speaker as someone he or she should be able to communicate with by using what they perceive as the same language.

The last remark illustrates a parallel with one of the qualifications of the population theory of species: not all members of a population must necessarily interbreed in order to be deemed members of the population. Not surprisingly, there are parallels with the phenomenon of different degrees of reproductive isolation (the European crow example described above). Chambers & Trudgill note that there is a 'hybrid' area in East Anglia between the Northern English vowel [ʊ] and the Southern English [ʌ], one of the most salient phonological markers of Northern vs Southern English (Chambers & Trudgill 1980:129–37). In the hybrid area, one finds MIXED and FUDGED varieties (lects in their terms; see §7.4.4). Mixed varieties possess [ʊ] in some words and [ʌ] in other words; fudged varieties use a phonetically intermediate vowel such as [ɤ] in some words. The mixed and fudged varieties form a transition zone between the Northern and Southern English varieties. Similar transition zones are found with bundles of ISOGLOSSES (geographical boundaries between one linguistic feature and another). For example, the boundary between French and Occitan is defined by a number of lexical and grammatical features. But the isoglosses for each feature do not match perfectly: there is a transitional zone across the middle of France where varieties possess some 'French' features and some 'Occitan' features (Chambers & Trudgill 1980:111, Map 7–6, after Jochnowitz 1973).

If we pursue an evolutionary theory of language following the lead of the evolutionary theory of biology, then we must take the population (social) definition of a language as the basic one. A structuralist linguist may feel uncomfortable about the social definition of a language. But the fact is that the social definition is the correct one from a historical perspective, in terms of causal mechanisms of language speciation. The social definition makes predictions of likely historical developments whereas the structural definition does not. Sibling species are likely to diverge morphologically as their reproductive isolation continues (see Hull 1988:66–7, discussing Mayr's theory of speciation). Likewise, sibling languages are likely to diverge structurally as their communicative isolation persists. A polytypic species may break up if the gene flow is interrupted, or possibly become more homogeneous or at least maintain itself as a single language. A polytypic language may break up if its social unity is broken – this appears to be what is happening in the distinct modern Arab nations. Or it may survive as a single language as in China, possibly becoming more homogeneous, as with the loss of the traditional dialects of western European languages. Social and communicative isolation leads to structural divergence; social and communicative intercourse leads to a maintenance of the status quo, or even convergence (which itself is a result of tighter social cohesion and mobility).

The last few paragraphs have surreptitiously introduced the linguistic equivalent to reproductive isolation: COMMUNICATIVE ISOLATION. Conversely, linguistic interbreeding is communication. The population definition of a language thus appears to be very similar to the notion of mutual intelligibility used to distinguish languages from dialects. However, mutual intelligibility tends to be defined in terms of potential communicative interaction, whether or not the speakers belong to the same speech community. Communicative interaction depends not only on the degree of structural similarity of the varieties spoken, but also on the social behavior of the speakers. Serbian and Croatian are mutually intelligible to a high degree, but many speakers do not communicate with the opposite community due to the recent political changes in former Yugoslavia.

One must distinguish the real potential of communicative interaction of two members of the same speech community who happen not yet to have conversed with each other, with the abstract potential of communicative interaction of members from different speech communities who would not normally talk with each other, except in a dialectologist's experimental situation. An analog to the latter situation in biological populations is, for example, plant species which could produce hybrids if they interbred, but do not interbreed because one species is pollinated by certain bees in the early morning and the other by other bees in the late afternoon (Grant 1981:113). Only the real potential of interbreeding/communication matters for the population definition of a species/language.

It is worth describing the two other sorts of biological populations mentioned earlier in this section in a little more detail. A SPECIES is a population of interbreeding individuals. A GEOGRAPHICAL RACE is a subpopulation of a species which is defined geographically, and often has structurally diverged to a slight extent, but presumably not so far as to prevent interbreeding. A DEME

> consists of organisms in sufficient proximity to each other that they all have equal probability of mating with each other and producing offspring, provided they are sexually mature, of the opposite sex, and equivalent with respect to sexual selection. To the extent that these conditions are met, the organisms belonging to a deme share in the same gene pool. Of course, in natural populations, some mating occurs between adjacent demes, and not all organisms within a single deme have precisely equal probability of mating, but the isolation between demes is met often enough and well enough for demes to play an important role in biological evolution. (Hull 1988:433)

These different types of populations are also relevant to the notions of language, dialect and speech community, defined in terms of communicative interaction and social identity rather than in the essentialist terms of linguistic structure. A language and its speakers should be defined in population terms just as species generally are. A geographical race is a traditional geographical dialect: defined geographically, slightly divergent structurally, but not enough presumably to prevent communication (i.e. intelligibility) or to provide a separate sociolinguistic identity, assuming we are not dealing with sibling languages.

A deme is related to one definition of the complex notion of a speech community. In fact, the term speech community as it is broadly used is the proper linguistic equivalent of a biological population (see §4.2.3). A speech community can be defined as broadly as all of English no matter where it is spoken, at an intermediate level such as Hiberno-English, or as narrowly as a particular fairly cohesive social network such as the ones analyzed by the Milroys in Belfast (Milroy 1987). A SOCIAL NETWORK corresponds most closely to a deme: a group of people who are most likely to communicate with each other, and not so much with those outside the network. One can describe the results of the Milroys' research in Belfast rather well by paraphrasing the Hull quotation and making the appropriate substitutions of sociolinguistic terms for biological ones (see chapter 7):

> a social network consists of speakers in sufficient proximity to each other that they all have equal probability of communicating with each other, if they have some reason to linguistically interact. To the extent that these conditions are met, the speakers belonging to a social network share in the same language. Of course, in natural speech communities, some communication occurs between adjacent social networks, and not all individuals within a single social network have precisely equal probability of communicating with each other, but the isolation between social networks is met often enough and well enough for social networks to play an important role in language change.

Species are formed only when a population reproduces sexually. Asexual organisms do not form species: each asexual organism is reproductively isolated (Grant 1981:64; Hull 1988:215). Communicative interaction is 'sexual': language is produced when a speaker communicates with a hearer. Even writers presuppose an audience. Hence, languages and their speakers form populations in the biological sense.

The metaphor found in the word 'intercourse' (sexual or linguistic) is not an accident. This parallel should make the DNA–utterance equivalence to be introduced in §2.4.1 a little more plausible. But first we must review certain recent developments in the theory of selection in biology.

2.3   The generalized theory of selection

The theory of selection provided by the neo-Darwinian synthesis has been the subject of criticism and modification in recent decades. The neo-Darwinian theory of selection is basically that organisms that are better adapted to the ecological conditions of the environment will have a greater likelihood of survival and reproduction – i.e. are selected. One criticism directed towards the neo-Darwinian theory of selection is the role of adaptation in selecting individuals in the population. Other mechanisms for selection besides the standard adaptive one have been proposed. One such mechanism is exaptation: some trait which evolved for one purpose, or evolved for no apparent purpose at all, is exapted to serve some other function which bestows a competitive advantage on its possessor (Lass 1990; see §5.3). This particular application of evolutionary theory to historical linguistics seems quite appropriate, and Lass takes it to be a strong argument for the position that each instantiates a generalized theory of evolution.

We will concern ourselves here with another, perhaps more profound, critique of the theory of selection, that concerning the unit of selection. In the standard view found in the neo-Darwinian synthesis of evolutionary theory in biology, it is the organism that is the unit of selection. Selective processes, of whatever sort, operate on the level of the fitness of the organism. Although it is genetic material that is ultimately replicated and then generates a new organism in reproduction, it is the organism which is ultimately selected in the evolutionary process, by virtue of its (successful or unsuccessful) interaction with its environment.

This view, the organism selectionist view, was challenged by (among others) Dawkins (1982a, 1982b). Dawkins argues that the gene, not the organism, is the unit of selection. Selection can be described only in terms of favoring or disfavoring gene frequencies in populations: 'According to Dawkins, in sexually reproducing organisms only short segments of the genetic material have what it takes to be selected. Organisms are simply survival machines constructed by genes to aid them in their single-minded quest for replication' (Hull 1988:211).

However, the complications in biological selection do not end there. Others have argued that selection may occur at other levels as well. It has been argued that selection might occur at the species level, or even at higher taxonomic levels. For example, it has been suggested that a species may possess a population structure that favors its evolutionary survival (Hull 1988:420–1, citing Vrba 1984). It has also been suggested that the geographical range of a higher taxon makes it more likely to survive a mass extinction, no matter how many species are contained in the taxon (Hull 1988:220, citing Jablonski 1986, 1987).

Still worse complications ensue when we abandon our zoöcentric view of evolution and ask ourselves at what level of organization does natural selection operate for cloned groups of plants and single-celled organisms:

> botanists distinguish between tillers and tussocks, ramets and genets. For example, many sorts of grass grow in tufts (tussocks) composed of numerous sprouts (tillers) growing from the same root system. Which is the 'organism,' each tiller or the entire tussock? More generally, botanists term each physiological unit a ramet, all the ramets that result from a single zygote, a genet. Sometimes all the ramets that compose a single genet stay attached to each other; sometimes not. (Hull 1988:417)

The basic problem is that the divisions between the levels of organization for organisms is not at all clear, once we go beyond animals: 'The hierarchical boundary between organisms and groups of organisms is no sharper than that between genes and organisms, in fact much less so' (Hull 1988:418). Hence, one should not base a theory of selection on a particular alleged level of biological organization.

But there is another way to look at selection. Hull argues that there has been a convergence in the two approaches in the gene vs organism selectionist debate as they have refined their positions. Hull quotes an organism selectionist, Mayr, and then a gene selectionist, Dawkins:

> as Mayr (1978:52) has emphasized tirelessly, 'Evolution through natural selection is (I repeat!) a two-step process' . . . According to the terminology that Dawkins (1982a, 1982b) now prefers, evolution is an interplay between replicator survival and vehicle selection. (Hull 1988:217; see also pp. 412–18)

The two steps involve two processes, replication of individuals and selection of individuals through interaction with their environment. However, in the paradigm case, these two individuals are not the same: it is genes that are replicated and organisms that are selected – which ensures the survival of their genes.

Hull argues that the debate between gene selectionists and organism selectionists is largely a matter of emphasis as to which process is more important. But both processes are necessary, and it appears that prominent advocates on both sides of the debate accept this: 'Since the . . . dispute over the units of selection broke out, all sides have come to accept the distinction between replicators and interactors, albeit not necessarily in the terms I am urging' (Hull 1988:413). And, in fact, this is the crucial conceptual advance in understanding the nature of evolution.

Hull himself has contributed to this debate. He borrows the term REPLICATOR from Dawkins and chooses a different term, INTERACTOR, from Dawkins' term 'vehicle' (which Hull believes renders the role of the interactor more passive than it actually is, and is a consequence of Dawkins' gene selectionist bias; see Hull 1988:413). From this, Hull constructs a general analysis of selection processes. The basic components of Hull's theory of selection are quoted below (Hull 1988:408–9; emphasis original):

(1) 'REPLICATOR – an entity that passes on its structure largely intact in successive replications'
(2) 'INTERACTOR – an entity that interacts as a cohesive whole with its environment in such a way that this interaction CAUSES replication to be differential'
(3) 'SELECTION – a process in which the differential extinction and proliferation of interactors CAUSES the differential perpetuation of the relevant replicators'
(4) 'LINEAGE – an entity that persists indefinitely through time either in the same or an altered state as a result of replication'

There are a number of important consequences of Hull's theory that will be described here. The first is that a replicator must not simply replicate its structure. The replicated structure must also be able to replicate its own structure: 'If all a gene did was to serve as a template for producing copy after copy of itself without these copies in turn producing additional copies, it could not function as a replicator' (Hull 1988:409). That is, one must be able to have a replication of a replication of a replication ... This leads to the creation of lineages of indefinite age.

Replication also allows for an indefinite sequence of differences in replication that can eventually lead to very different structures from the original replicator. Replication must preserve structure largely intact, otherwise we would not call it replication; but it can involve alterations to that structure. Once the structure is altered in replication, that alteration can be further replicated. The result can be a replicator that is quite different from the original replicator. 'The important principle is that in a chain of replicators errors [alterations – WAC] are cumulative' (Dawkins 1982b:85).

The second feature is equally important. Hull emphasizes that causality is involved in the selection process. In fact, there are two different causal mechanisms. The first mechanism, implicit in (1) and not discussed in any detail by Hull, causes replication, both identical (NORMAL) and ALTERED REPLICATION. The paradigm example of the mechanism of normal replication in biology is the process of copying genes in reproduction, with mutation and recombination being mechanisms for altered replication.

The possibility of altered replication gives rise to variation, by creating new replicators with a different structure from the original. The second mechanism, referred to in (2) and (3), causes differential replication, that is, perpetuation of (different) replicators: this mechanism propagates some variants at the expense of others.[1] Differential replication is hypothesized to result from the interaction of interactors as a group with their environment, specifically, the survival of some interactors (and hence their replicators) and the extinction of others. The paradigm example of differential replication is the increase in frequencies of certain genes due to the favored survival and reproduction of the individual organisms possessing those genes in their ecological environment.

Hull makes a third important proposal in his theory: that his general analysis of selection processes applies not just to the gene-organism level in biological evolution, but may apply to other levels as well: 'Just as genes are not the only replicators, organisms are not the only interactors. Just as variable chunks of the genetic material function as replicators, entities at different levels of the organizational hierarchy can function as interactors' (Hull 1988:417). If the population structure of a species can be heritable, then species might be able to function as replicators. Genes may be interactors as well as replicators, since they interact with their cellular environment at the molecular level. Although Hull expresses some doubts as to whether organisms and species can function as replicators, he suggests that it is possible, and cannot be ruled out absolutely (for organisms, see Hull 1988:409, 415; for species, see ibid. 219 and 419). Hull's main point, though, is that a generalized model of selection must be cut loose from the hierarchy of levels of biological organization.

On the other hand, change can occur without selection, and selection need not result in change:

Once the distinction between replication and interaction is made, one can distinguish four possibilities: changes in replication frequencies due to interaction (directional selection), no change in replicator frequencies because the effects of the relevant variations happen, by chance, to balance each other out (balancing selection), changes in relative frequencies that are not due to any environmental interactions (drift), and replication sequences in which there are neither changes in replicator frequencies nor significant environmental interactions (stasis). (Hull 1988:443)

This classification of selective and nonselective changes will be relevant for understanding the mechanisms of language change (see §3.3.2).

The fourth, and most important, aspect of Hull's general theory is that selection operates only on spatiotemporally bounded individuals: 'only an individual has what it takes to be selected' (Hull 1988:215). Spatiotemporally bounded individuals are actual individuals, by definition, and so selection operates only over actual individuals: 'In selection processes of all sorts, selection takes place among actual, not possible, alternatives' (Hull 1988:473). 'Individual' is taken in the broad sense here, so that spatially discontinuous entities (such as populations) are individuals as well, as long as the collection of entities is spatiotemporally bounded. Thus, taking the population view of species, a particular species is an individual: it has a beginning and an end temporally and it is also bounded spatially. Particular organisms and genes are also individuals; so is a collection of plants growing from a single root stock; so are other population-based entities such as demes.

Hull's purpose in devising a generalized theory of selection is not merely to sort out certain controversies in evolutionary biology. Hull wishes to apply the generalized theory of selection to sociocultural evolution. He suggests that a misinterpretation of biological evolution has impeded application of evolutionary models to sociocultural evolution:

If biological evolution were the neat process of genes mutating, organisms being selected, and species evolving, then sociocultural change is nothing so simple. One purpose of this chapter has been to show that biological evolution is not so simple either. In this chapter I have shown how general the characterization of selection processes must be if they are to apply to biological evolution. (Hull 1988:430)

Hull then applies his generalized theory of selection to conceptual change in the history of science. The first step is to discard an essentialist theory of concepts. In order to understand how scientific theories evolve, concepts must be treated as spatiotemporal individuals, in fact, lineages of ideas replicated from one scientist to another. For the understanding of conceptual change, what matters is the history of the concept, not its content. Two similar concepts with distinct lineages are distinct concepts, even if they seem alike from an essentialist point of view. The 'same' concept as 'discovered' by another scientist without knowledge of the conceptual lineage of the first scientist is, in Hull's view, a different concept, belonging to a different conceptual lineage. The phenomenon of 'reinventing the wheel' in science is not really reinvention, if the second scientist came up with the idea independently. The concept of the phoneme was invented several times, but only once did it catch on and was replicated in subsequent linguists' research and publications.

Conversely, two concepts that are of a different type are the same concept from a historical point of view if one is a later replication of the other and thus in the same lineage. As with organisms, ideas can change with each replication from scientist to scientist, even though they form a single lineage, since replication is not always identical. For example, the Prague school notion of markedness and Greenberg's notion of markedness in typology are quite different on essentialist grounds (Croft 1996b); but they are one historical concept in Hull's theory because Greenberg's notion was intellectually derived from the Prague school notion, as Greenberg acknowledges in his work (Greenberg 1966:11, 13). This view of concepts is radically different from the traditional essentialist one, where concepts have an immutable, eternal identity.

As my examples have indicated, Hull argues that it is the concept as a spatiotemporally bounded individual that is the replicator, that is, the equivalent to the gene in the classic biological gene-organism selection process (Hull 1988:441). The scientists are the interactors. The environment that scientists interact with is their empirical observations and their fellow scientists. Their interaction with their environment causes the replication of concepts (new or modified ideas), and their differential propagation (the amount of attention those ideas enjoy among scientists) causes the differential perpetuation of the relevant replicators (the ideas embodied in scientists' theories). It is possible that conceptual lineages may converge if the two scientists criticize each other and refine their ideas in response to those criticisms. Again this is parallel to biological evolution; it occurs frequently among plants and other organisms (see chapter 8).

This is Hull's theory of conceptual evolution – scientific change – in a nutshell. It applies the generalized theory of selection to conceptual evolution in a novel way, redefining concepts as historical individuals and treating concepts rather than scientists as the basic components of scientific change. In fact, Hull's theory of conceptual evolution can be seen as an instance of the theory of language change to be argued for in the next section: it can be considered a theory of semantic change in a certain specialized register, scientific language. We now turn to the more general theory of language change.

2.4 The generalized theory of selection applied to language change

2.4.1 The paradigm instantiation of selection in language change

We begin by presenting some definitions that closely resemble the definitions of these terms used in nonformal linguistic theories, formal linguistic theories and philosophical theories of language, but differ from them in certain critical respects.

An UTTERANCE is a particular, actual occurrence of the product of human behavior in communicative interaction (i.e. a string of sounds), as it is pronounced, grammatically structured, and semantically and pragmatically interpreted in its context. This definition more or less conforms to the standard philosopher's definition of utterance-token with the additional specification of its phonological and morphosyntactic peculiarities. An utterance is differentiated from a sentence, as the latter term is understood by philosophers, formal language theorists and syntacticians. A sentence is defined in essentialist terms; it is not a spatiotemporally bounded individual. An utterance as defined here is a spatiotemporally bounded individual. Thus, unlike sentences, only actually occurring tokens count as utterances in our sense. It is critical to the theory of language change that utterances be actually occurring language; recall that selection operates only over actual, not possible, alternatives. Since an utterance is an actually existing entity, all levels of its structure are included, in particular its specific pronunciation and meaning in context as intended by the speaker and interpreted by the hearer (see §4.3.2).

A LANGUAGE is the population of utterances in a speech community. This definition appears to be quite deviant from the structuralist notion of a language as a system of contrasts of signs. However, the structuralist notion of a language as a system of signs is the embodiment of essentialist thinking (see §1.1, §2.2), and a population approach is necessary for attacking the problem of the nature of language change (and, for that matter, language itself; see §1.1). Thus, our definition of a language actually more closely resembles the formal language theory definition of a language as a set of sentences. But it differs from the formal language theory definition in two important respects. First, a language is a population of utterances, not sentences (see the preceding paragraph). Second, our definition does not denote the set of all and only the sentences or utterance types that are generated (in the technical sense of that term) by a formal grammar. It is only the set of actual utterances produced and comprehended in a particular speech community. Again, this restriction conforms with the biological definition of a population: it is a spatiotemporally bounded set of actual individuals, not a set of 'possible' individuals – whatever that would mean.

A GRAMMAR is the cognitive structure in a speaker's mind that contains her[2] knowledge about her language, and is the structure that is used in producing and comprehending utterances (the nature of this knowledge will be discussed further below). The grammar of each speaker is acquired on the basis of the subpopulation of the language that she is exposed to.[3] Thus, each speaker will have a slightly different grammar. This definition is also based on the formal language notion of grammar but deviates from it just as our definition of language does. First, the grammar is not generative in the technical sense of 'generate' as characterizing a set of admissible sentences. This is because the grammar does not generate the language as described in the preceding paragraph in the formal language theory sense of 'generate'. It cannot do so, because the language is not all possible sentences or even all possible utterances (whatever that would mean). On the other hand, the grammar (in our definition) does generate the language in the informal sense of 'generate': it is what a speaker uses in producing (some of) the utterances of a language.

Second, the grammar consists of all our mental capacity in the use of language. Some theorists, notably generative linguists, argue that the processing mechanisms involved in producing and comprehending utterances are separate from the repository of grammatical knowledge (competence) in the mind. Others, notably cognitive linguists, argue that a single, more or less integrated cognitive structure both 'contains our knowledge of the language' and is used for actually producing and comprehending utterances of the language. For our purposes, it does not matter whether the two are separated or not: what matters is that the whole mental apparatus is included in our definition of grammar. Hence, our definition of grammar does not correspond to only the competence module postulated by formal syntacticians; it must include any processing modules as well. Whatever one's linguistic theory is, however, it must be clear that our definition of a grammar is a real, individual, psychological entity, not an abstraction that does not have a psychological (or physical) existence. In other words, a grammar as defined here is also a spatiotemporally bounded individual.

Now we may apply the generalized theory of selection to language. Recall that Hull argues that one should not expect interactors and replicators to be found at only one level in the organization of life. Nor should we expect the same in language. In fact, though, Hull points out that the paradigm case of an interactor is the organism, and the paradigm case of a replicator is the gene, which is found in DNA. Likewise, we will begin with the paradigm cases of interactor and replicator in linguistic selection.

It seems fairly uncontroversial that the paradigm case of a linguistic interactor is the speaker, including of course the speaker's grammar as we have defined it. The speaker interacts as a cohesive whole with her environment. The speaker is a cohesive whole as a member of a speech community, communicatively interacting with other members of the speech community. The ENVIRONMENT is thus the other members of the speech community, the social context of the speech event, and the goals of the speech event itself (see §3.4 and chapter 4). The grammar used by the speaker is a real existing mental structure: it must be able to interact with a real physical/mental/social environment. The speaker interacts as a cohesive whole in that the appropriate level of description of social interaction and communication is that of individual humans as social/cognitive beings, not any smaller unit.

What is the paradigm replicator? Recall that in the basic level in biological selection, the replicator is a GENE, and genes are found in DNA, which is replicated in sexual reproduction in sexual organisms. In Hull's theory of conceptual change, the replicator is a concept, which is replicated whenever a scientist uses the concept, in particular in interaction with students and other scientists. However, identifying a gene in DNA is not a simple task, nor is identifying a concept. Hull writes, 'If ever anyone thought that genes are like beads on a string, recent advances in molecular biology have laid that metaphor to rest' (Hull 1988:218; see Hull 1988:442; Mayr 1982:794–807; Dawkins 1982b:85–6 for more details), and 'in both biological and conceptual evolution, replicators exist in nested systems of increasingly more inclusive units. There are no unit genes or unit ideas' (Hull 1988:449).

Here we arrive at the proposal made in §2.1. The entity corresponding to DNA, over which the replicators are defined, is the utterance. The replicators themselves – parallel to genes – are embodied linguistic structures, anything from a phoneme to a morpheme to a word to a syntactic construction, and also their conventional semantic/discourse-functional (information-structural) values. The replicator is the particular linguistic structure as embodied in a specific utterance. An utterance, or more precisely some aspect of the utterance, embodies a linguistic structure: a passive clause, say, or a closed syllable, or a particular encoding of a predicate–argument relation. The linguistic structures as embodied in utterances are not beads on a string either. They exist in nested systems of more inclusive units, and with further complications (overlapping, discontinuity, intersection, etc.) that are well known to students of linguistic structure (see §2.4.3).

Most important of all, the replicator is a spatiotemporally bounded individual, i.e. a token. It HAS structure – '[i]n order to function as a replicator, an entity must have structure' (Hull 1988:409) – but it should not be identified with the structure as an abstract essence (type). The formal structure of e.g. the passive construction, or its semantic/discourse function, or the phonetic expression of a phoneme, can change in replication. In order to clearly distinguish the embodied replicator from the structure that it possesses, we must give it a name. Following a suggestion by Martin Haspelmath, I propose that the paradigm linguistic replicator be called a LINGUEME, on analogy with Dawkins' meme. Thus, the paradigm replicator in language is the lingueme, parallel to the gene as the basic replicator in biology; an utterance is made up of linguemes, and linguemes possess linguistic structure.[4]

The genes found in one organism are organized into chromosomes. Biological genes occur at different LOCI in the chromosomes. The alternative forms of a gene that can occur at a single locus on a chromosome are called ALLELES. The total set of genes in a population of organisms, including all alleles that occur in the same locus in different organisms, is the GENE POOL of the population. The equivalent concepts in language play an important role in the evolutionary framework for language change. The equivalent to alleles of genes are VARIANTS of a lingueme, that is, alternative structures used for a particular structural element, such as alternative phonetic realizations of a phoneme, alternative words for the same meaning, or alternative constructions used to express a complex semantic structure such as comparison. The locus for a set of variants is essentially the VARIABLE in the sociolinguistic sense of that term, that is, 'two ways of saying the "same thing"' (Weinreich, Labov & Herzog 1968:162; see §3.3.1, §6.2). Just as only one allele is found in a given locus in a piece of DNA, only one variant can occur in the appropriate structural position in an utterance. The total set of linguemes in a population of utterances (the language), and hence in the grammars of the speakers taken as a whole, is the LINGUEME POOL.

The term 'lingueme pool' may suggest that there is no organization or structure to the inventory of linguemes in a language. But the term 'gene pool' in biology does not deny the fact that genes are organized in chromosomes in a very complex and highly structured fashion. Although it is true that the evolutionary framework for language change implies a looser organization of a language system than the structuralist and generative models do (see §8.1), a lingueme pool does have a high degree of structural organization (see §2.4.3).

The grammar – the speaker's knowledge about the language – is acquired through hearing other utterances embodying these linguistic structures. Knowledge of language is essentially the ability to replicate linguemes in the appropriate social-communicative contexts.[5] A speaker may not know all of the linguemes in the language's lingueme pool, of course, so her grammar may not be able to replicate every lingueme.

When a speaker produces an utterance, she replicates a linguistic structure – actually, a large number of linguistic structures. In fact, the production of an utterance involves an extremely complex recombination of elements from a great range of utterance parents, far more complex than the two-parent recombination of DNA in the reproduction of sexual organisms in biology. When another speaker hears that utterance and produces another one, the structures are replicated again – recall that 'in order to function as a replicator, an entity must have structure and be able to pass on this structure in a sequence of replications' (Hull 1988:409).

The act of replicating the appropriate linguemes in social-communicative contexts – saying what you want to say to your addressee, in the way you want to say it – represents the use of the conventions of the speech community. Conforming to a convention is a regularity in linguistic behavior in a particular speech community (see §4.2.4). The regularity is of course the structure that is passed on in lingueme replication. The set of linguistic conventions represented by the replicable structures of the linguemes in the lingueme pool of a language is the evolutionary equivalent to the language system (see §1.1). But the evolutionary concept of a language system is not essentialist. The conventions vary and change as a result of altered replication and selection. And conventions are defined by the speech community: an identical lingueme structure in another language is not the same convention in the evolutionary framework (cf. Rohde, Stefanowitsch & Kemmer 1999).

By this point, the idea that an utterance is the linguistic equivalent to DNA should not sound as bizarre as it may have sounded in §2.1. It seems counterintuitive; at first glance, a more appropriate analogy appears to be between the grammar as the genotype and the utterance as the phenotype (but see §2.5). But the proposal here is also parallel to Hull's application of the theory of selection to conceptual change, where the concept rather than the scientist is the replicator. In fact, Hull hints at this proposal in a remark on the tokens of scientific terms in their use in scientific discourse: 'Term-tokens themselves change in replication sequences, e.g. sequences of allelomorph-allelomorph-allelomorph gave way to allele-allele-allele. This sort of transition is the subject matter of historical linguists' (Hull 1988:505; see also Keller 1990/ 1994:147; Mufwene 1996a:85).

One might object that utterance replication is not really replication, since the utterance does not replicate itself; it must be replicated by a speaker, using the knowledge of her language embedded in her mind. This is not all that different from replication of genes in biology, however, particularly in sexual reproduction. Replication of the genome in biological reproduction is fundamentally a cell-level process, and it is mediated by among other things RNA molecules. In sexual reproduction, however, replication of the genome is also a population-level process, mediated by the behavior leading to and including the mating of two organisms. If an organism does not mate and produce offspring, its genome will not be replicated. Likewise, replication of linguemes in utterances is fundamentally a cognitive process, mediated by activation of some mental structure and articulatory motor routine. (This mental structure / motor routine is of course acquired from exposure to prior occurrences of the linguemes in language use.) And replication of linguemes is equally fundamentally a social process, mediated by the speaker in conversational interaction. If a speaker doesn't speak, she will not replicate any linguemes.

I will call this theory of selection in language change the Theory of UTTERANCE SELECTION for language change. I conclude this section with three important observations about the claims made by the Theory of Utterance Selection.

First, the Theory of Utterance Selection does not preclude the existence of selection processes in language change at other levels of the language, the individual and society. The Theory of Utterance Selection does however assume that utterance selection is the primary locus of language change, and hence that most language changes can be accounted for in terms of utterance selection. Selection processes at other levels of organization will be discussed in appropriate places in this book (see §3.2, §8.6).

Second, the hypothesis that utterance selection occurs does not entail a particular set of causal mechanisms for replication or selection of linguemes in utterances. Of course, a proper utterance selection theory of language change will propose certain causal mechanisms for replication and selection, and attempt to account for observed facts of language change with those mechanisms. Some causal mechanisms will be sketched in the next section, and most of chapters 5–7 will be devoted to presenting the case for those mechanisms.

Third, the Theory of Utterance Selection for language change puts linguistic convention at center stage (see §1.3). Normal (i.e. identical) replication of linguemes in utterances is conforming to the linguistic conventions of the speech community. Altered replication of linguemes in utterances – the creation of variants – is a causal consequence of not conforming to the linguistic conventions of the speech community. The reasons for nonconformity are the causal mechanisms of altered replication. And the selection of linguemes is equivalent to the establishment of a linguistic convention in a speech community. The reasons for selection of a lingueme are the causal mechanisms of selection.

2.4.2 *The causal mechanisms of evolution in language change*

As Hull and others have pointed out, evolution is a two-step process: altered replication of the replicators, and selection of interactors. Language change is also a two-step process, as was pointed out in §1.3: innovation and propagation. The core of any substantive theory of language change is the causal mechanisms proposed by the theory for both steps in the process. Chapter 3 will survey and discuss various approaches to this problem. In this section, I will outline the proposals for the model of language change advocated here; they will be presented in detail in the remainder of this book.

As mentioned above, convention plays a critical role in the Theory of Utterance Selection. Normal replication is simply conformity to linguistic convention. Altered replication is the result of not conforming to linguistic convention. However, a wide range of mechanisms may lead to a speaker not conforming to linguistic convention in an utterance. These mechanisms may be social or interactional, that is, be the causal consequence of interlocutors attempting to achieve certain goals in language use. They may also be psychological, involving purely internal psychological processes (including perceptual-motor processes) and not (directly) involving social interaction.

I will argue in §3.4 that there is not as sharp a line distinguishing these classes of mechanisms as various adherents claim; in particular, all of them take conformity to convention as a baseline for analyzing altered replication. In chapters 4–6, I will argue for mechanisms of altered replication that make crucial reference to the relationship between forms and their conventional meanings or functions. In this sense, the mechanisms for altered replication are functional; but they are not functional in the sense of being teleological, and not necessarily in the sense of being the means towards an interactional goal (see §3.4).

Altered replication leads to the existence of variants descended from a single lingueme. These variants usually begin as variants of a single linguistic variable, that is, different ways of saying the same thing, different at the phonological, lexical or grammatical (morphosyntactic) levels. Once variant linguemes occur, then they may be differentially replicated, leading to propagation or elimination. In the generalized theory of selection, differential perpetuation of replicators is a causal consequence of the differential extinction and proliferation of interactors and the differential perpetuation of the relevant replicators. This process is selection, and we must seek the causal mechanisms of selection of linguistic structures.

What exactly is selection in language? Clearly, it is not (just) the differential extinction and proliferation of speakers themselves that lead to the differential perpetuation of the linguistic structures found in utterances. Linguistic forms, and languages themselves, can die without their speakers having to die. Instead, the speakers give up their language and shift to another; or gradually stop using one form and favor another. Thus, it is something about the grammars that leads to the differential perpetuation of utterance structures, that is, of the variants in a linguistic variable.

In this book I will argue, following sociohistorical linguistics, that the selection process is essentially a social one, and not a functional one in the sense of (external) function that I use to characterize innovation (see §1.3, §3.3.1 and chapter 7). The variants in a linguistic variable have social values associated with them. Speakers select variants to use – that is, to replicate – in particular utterances on the basis of their social values: overt or covert prestige, the social relation of the speaker to the interlocutor, etc. (the mechanisms that have been proposed by sociolinguists will be discussed in chapter 7). This causes the differential perpetuation of the relevant replicators, that is, the differential survival/extinction of linguistic structures in utterances. In other words, it is social factors, not functional factors, that play the same role in selection that ecological factors do in biology.

How is it that the differential extinction and proliferation of interactors causes the differential perpetuation of replicators? The perpetuation of a particular linguistic structure in utterances is directly dependent on the survival of the cognitive structures in a grammar that are used by the speaker in producing utterances of that structure. The survival of cognitive structures is their ENTRENCHMENT in the mind (see Langacker 1987:59; see §3.4.2). I suggest that the interactive activation model used by cognitive grammar and by Bybee (1985) offers us a cognitively plausible model of linguistic variables, and provides a mechanism by which cognitive structures can 'survive' – become entrenched in the mind – or 'become extinct' – decay. The shift in proportions of the variants of a linguistic variable in usage is brought about by shifts in degrees of entrenchment of those variants in the grammars of speakers.[6] This shift is a result of the social value of those variants for individual speakers, but the global effect is an adjustment of their activation value, or a shift in their entrenchment, in a speaker's grammar.

2.4.3 Linguistic lineages and utterance structure

In the model of linguistic selection given in §§2.4.1–2.4.2, a lineage is the spatiotemporally bounded individual resulting from replication of a lingueme. The first linguistic lineage that probably comes to the reader's mind is a word ETYMOLOGY. A word etymology is a summary of all the replications of the word, which usually is replicated in an altered state over a long enough period of time – sound change, semantic change, syntactic change, etc. Recall that Hull points out that a lineage can go on indefinitely, in principle at least, although the species which contains it may terminate through its breakup into daughter species. Likewise, a word etymology extends indefinitely, even though it may be traced back through different languages – Old English, Proto-Germanic, Proto-Indo-European, and further back. Likewise, the lineage can be traced forward even to a creole such as Torres Strait Creole English (see §8.5). A grossly simplified example of such a lineage is Proto-Indo-European *bhlē* 'blow' > Proto-Germanic *blē-w* 'blow' > Old English *blāwan* 'blow' > Middle English *blowen* 'blow, smoke, carry by wind, play a wind instrument, etc.' > Modern English *blow* 'blow, smoke, carry by wind, play a wind instrument, cause to explode, etc.' > Torres Strait Creole *blo* 'blow, puff, pant' (*American Heritage Dictionary New College Edition*; *Oxford English Dictionary*; Shnukal 1988:117).

A word etymology is probably the prototypical case of a linguistic lineage; but sounds and grammatical constructions form lineages as well. The phoneme /f/ is a lingueme that has been replicated in utterances millions of times over in the history of English and even further in the past (cf. Heringer 1988, cited in Keller 1990/1994:158–59; Ritt 1995). This replication can be differential: /f/ can change from [f] to [h] for instance. Historical linguists would notate this change as *f* > *h*; what this means is that there is a lineage of replications of a sound in which altered replication has occurred.

A type of lineage that has become of great interest in recent historical linguistics and diachronic typology are the lineages that result from grammaticalization of a word or construction, called GRAMMATICALIZATION CHAINS (Heine, Claudi & Hünnemeyer 1991:221–2). Grammaticalization chains are actually lineages for whole syntactic constructions, not just individual lexemes or morphemes (Bybee, Perkins & Pagliuca 1994:11; Traugott 2000). For example, the construction *[X is going to VERB]* has been replicated millions of times in the history of English. The replication has been altered over time in that, semantically, it has changed from motion + purpose to future meaning, and, phonologically, it has changed from . . . *going to* . . . to . . . *gonna* . . . Nevertheless, it still represents a single lineage replicated by many different speakers on many more different occasions of use over several centuries.

All of this may sound like a return to the prestructuralist view held by many dialectologists that every word has its history, a view attacked by structuralist linguistics, which argued that the linguistic system functions as a whole. However, both the 19th-century view and the structuralist view have an element of truth in them (§8.1, chapter 9). Lineages of different kinds of linguemes can be remarkably independent of each other. But they must all interact in order to form utterances, and that interaction implies the existence of a system.

The production of an utterance involves replication of phonemes, morphemes, words and syntactic constructions (and their semantic content). But utterances are themselves very complex, and the production of an utterance implies a complex organization of the grammar even in the Theory of Utterance Selection for language change. Replication of those various linguemes must be coordinated carefully in order to produce an acceptable utterance. In particular, replication of a syntactic construction requires replication of its component lexical items; replication of lexical items requires replication of their component morphemes; and replication of morphemes requires replication of their component phonemes. As Hull writes (see §2.4.1), 'in both biological and conceptual evolution, replicators exist in nested systems of increasingly more inclusive units' (Hull 1988:449).

It should not come as news to linguists that phonology, morphology, lexicon and syntax are independent levels in a hierarchy of greater inclusiveness;

indeed, these facts about lineages in linguistic evolution reveal that this basic structure of grammatical organization still holds in the evolutionary model of language change advocated here.[7] However, the linguistic picture is more complicated than this. The building-block model of linguistic organization I have suggested implies that the higher (more inclusive) levels of linguemes do not specify any information occurring at lower (less inclusive) levels in the structure that they replicate. But in fact they often – perhaps usually – do. As Hull writes in the continuation of the above quotation, 'There are no unit genes or unit ideas' (ibid.). That is, linguemes at higher levels of inclusiveness are more independent as replicators from their less inclusive levels than one might imagine. I will briefly survey a few examples from English, with reference to the more general class of phenomena they illustrate, to show how common this is.

2.4.3.1   Phonological and lexical patterns

Old English had a phonological process by which intervocalic fricatives were voiced; voiced fricatives were not separate phonemes, but allophones of the voiceless fricatives between voiced segments (Hogg 1992:92). The voicing distinction in fricatives became phonologized as a result of the loss of the gemination distinction between [s:]/[z], [f:]/[v], etc. (Lass 1992:59–60), and so the *f*/*v* alternation was no longer allophonic. Yet the *f*/*v* alternation was retained for example in *life/lives, knife/knives, wife/wives,* etc. after the loss of the allophonic rule in general. What has happened here is that the plural form of these nouns has been identically replicated even though the replication of intervocalic fricatives at the phonological level was altered (and also the conditioning environment was lost with the loss of the following vowel). These examples demonstrate that these lexical items, in particular the plural forms, have a degree of integrity in replication that prevented the loss of the allophonic alternation when the phonological system of English changed. In other words, lexical replication can be almost completely independent of phonological replication, to the point of specifying phonological patterns independent of the lineages of the individual phonemes themselves.

Of course, for those speakers who say *roofs* rather than *rooves,* altered replication of the phoneme in this lexical item has led to altered replication of this particular lexical item (due to paradigm leveling; see §6.2.1). This example demonstrates the unremarkable fact that phonological replication can be independent of lexical replication, to the point of specifying the phonological content of lexical items. This fact is unremarkable because it follows from our reductionist structuralist assumptions that the properties specified by the lower levels of linguistic organization completely determine those properties at higher levels of organization.

The more remarkable examples of *life/lives,* etc. demonstrate that higher levels sometimes specify information at lower levels. This fact simply shows that linguemes are not organized as beads on a string, or as building blocks, easily dividable into units. But neither are genes, as units of selection. There is nothing problematic about this approach, in biology, conceptual change, or language change:

> As in the case of Williams's (1966) definition of a evolutionary gene and Dawkins's (1976) parallel definition of a replicator, the 'size' of a conceptual replicator is determined by the selection processes in which it is functioning. From the point of view of replication alone, units are not needed. Entities can pass on their structure largely intact even if this structure is not subdivided into smaller units. (Hull 1988:443)

If the proper representation of *lives* required it to be subdivided into smaller units, then it would be pronounced *lifes*, at the time that the phonological rule was lost or afterwards. (The instantiation of the voiced allophone of the Old English /f/ phoneme is now presumably merged with the lineage for /v/ independent of /f/.) Instead, at least at the time of the loss of the voicing alternation, *lives* was a single unit lingueme including specification of the voicing of the fricative.

2.4.3.2 Phonological and morphological patterns

The same sort of phenomenon demonstrates that morphological patterns are independent of phonology. This can be shown by phonological alternations affecting only specific morphological forms. An example of this is the phonological alternation between [s], [z] and [ɪz] found in the English plural suffix (*books, rods, boxes*) and also in the 3rd person singular present suffix (*looks, flies, misses*). The widespread existence of so-called morphophonological rules (phonological patterns that are restricted to specific morphological or lexical classes) demonstrates that lexical items and morphemes quite frequently specify phonological properties as part of the structure that they replicate, rather than leaving it to the phonological level to specify.

Linguists have generally accepted the existence of morphophonological rules, although in fact the analysis of morphophonological rules has always called for extra theoretical constructs of dubious value (abstract underlying segments in generative phonology, multiple-level lexicons in lexical phonology, and so on). The most neutral representation of this sort of cross-level specification in structural analyses is to describe a phonological rule as referring to a morphological class or a morphological boundary. We may call this analysis UPWARD SPECIFICATION: the phenomenon is described at the lowest level (in this case a phonological process), but the rule in addition specifies properties of higher levels (morphological class). The representation entailed by the description of linguemes is DOWNWARD SPECIFICATION: a morpheme or class of morphemes specifies some of its phonological properties. Downward specification is the proper description of the locus of replication of the properties of the lingueme because the lingueme is an entity existing at the higher, more inclusive, level. We will see that downward specification is useful for syntactic representations as well (see also Croft to appear b).

2.4.3.3 Phonological and syntactic patterns

There are also cases where particular syntactic constructions possess special phonological patterns unique to them. English possesses phonologically special contracted forms of the English auxiliaries and *not* as in *I'm going* and *He won't go*. These contractions are not manifestations of general (i.e. exceptionless) phonological patterns. Moreover, they can only be described at a syntactic level, since they violate the phonological integrity of individual words and also violate syntactic boundaries such as that between subject noun phrase and predicate phrase in *I'm going*. Less dramatic but far more common examples of phonological properties specified by syntactic constructions are sandhi phenomena and any phonological processes that cross word boundaries. These examples demonstrate that syntactic constructions are replicators which may specify phonological structure as well, rather than simply inheriting the phonological properties from lower levels of organization.

2.4.3.4 Lexical and morphological patterns

Lexical items can function as units specifying morphological properties rather than simply being built up from morphemes. For example, alongside the plural *brothers*, which involves the independent replication of the stem and the plural suffix, there also exists *brethren*, in which the lexical item has survived with an otherwise relic plural (cf. *children*) and also was replicated with a specialization to one meaning of *brother* (see §7.3). Another example is *shadow*, which formerly was an oblique case form of *shade*, but has been independently replicated from *shade*, with a distinct meaning and no specialized case function (*Oxford English Dictionary*). A more complex example is *hole/hollow* [n.], which may have resulted from a split of alternative inflectional forms of the Old English noun *holh* 'hollow' (ibid.). Less dramatic but far more widespread examples are the sorts of semantic variation found in the meaning of derivational affixes: compare the meaning of the *-er* suffix in *runner* (a person who runs on a regular basis), *walker* (the object used by people who have difficulty walking), *broiler* (a chicken that one broils), *fiver* (a five-pound note, in Britain), and so on. In these cases, the lexical item as a whole specifies the role whose referent is picked out by the *-er* derivational suffix.

2.4.3.5 Lexical and syntactic patterns

Syntactic constructions can also be replicated with the specification of properties of their component lexical items independent of the replication sequence of the lexical item itself. Idioms such as *tell time* specify the meaning of the verb *tell* as 'count', even though the verb *tell* as a word lineage no longer occurs with that meaning. Many, in fact most, idioms are what Nunberg, Sag & Wasow (1994) call 'idiomatically combining expressions', where the meaning of the lexical items involved is specified as part of the structure replicated by the construction. And such idioms are very common (ibid.).

2.4.3.6 Morphological and syntactic patterns

Finally, syntactic constructions can be replicated with the specification of properties for specific morphemes such as their semantics, position or form. English lacks much morphology, but one example of a morpheme whose meaning is specified in the construction is the passive participle in the perfect construction *[Sbj have Verb-en (Obj)]*. The passive participle morpheme in this construction does not have the passive voice meaning that it otherwise has (as in *the boys were taken home*; *the window is broken*; *a word borrowed from Italian*). Its perfect meaning in combination with the auxiliary *have* is specified by the construction and is a result of the independent replication of this construction, including its morphological affixes, from the morphological units that appear to make it up.

In sum: more inclusive linguemes as replicators often specify the structure of less inclusive linguemes that they contain. This fact demonstrates that the distinctions between these allegedly hierarchical levels are not always clear. We find evidence for this fact any time we observe the reduction from an independent word to a bound morpheme, the fusion of two morphemes, the morphologization of an exceptionless phonological rule, or the semantic specialization of words in idioms or morphemes in particular words and constructions.

This fact has also occasionally been used to argue against the independence of these linguistic levels. But this fact does not invalidate the independence of these levels in replication in many other cases, that is, where phonological, morphological, lexical, syntactic and semantic changes occur in a wide range of utterance contexts. As Hull writes, 'Yes, conceptual evolution can occur at a variety of levels, and, no, the levels are not sharply distinguishable. But by now it should be clear that exactly the same state of affairs exists in biological systems' (Hull 1988:424). There is no incompatibility in the hierarchical organization of phonology, morphology, lexicon and syntax, and recognizing that linguemes can specify replicable structure at multiple levels in the hierarchy. (Of course, a theory of grammatical representation must allow for this possibility, preferably as transparently as possible; see Croft to appear b.)

2.5 A unified model of linguistic variation and change

Hull's general analysis of selection processes presupposes a fundamental distinction between replication and selection, with selection causing differential perpetuation of the relevant replicators. Hull's model provides a theoretical grounding to the distinction between the innovation and the propagation of a language change. The Theory of Utterance Selection for language change applies Hull's general analysis of selection processes to language change, hypothesizing that utterances play the central role. The paradigm instantiations of the generalized theory of selection in biology and language are given in (5).

(5) *Generalized theory of selection*	*Paradigm instantiation of selection in biology*	*Paradigm instantion of selection in language*
replicator	gene	lingueme
replicators in a population	gene pool	lingueme pool
structured set of replicators	string of DNA	utterance
normal replication	reproduction by e.g. interbreeding	utterance production in communication
altered replication	recombination, mutation of genes	mechanisms for innovation (chs. 5, 6)
alternative replicators	alleles	variants
locus for alternative replication	gene locus	linguistic variable
interactor	organism	speaker (including grammar)
environment	ecological environment	social-communicative context
selection	survival and reproduction of organisms	entrenchment of convention by speakers and its propagation in communication

Hull's model also implies, or at least suggests, that there are two distinct sets of causal mechanisms in evolutionary change, one for replication and one for selection. One of the central theses of this book is that there are distinct causal mechanisms that bring about the innovation and the propagation of language change (see §1.3). Functional factors – the phonetic and conceptual factors appealed to by functionalist linguists – are responsible only for innovation, and social factors provide a selection mechanism for propagation.

In gene-based biological selection, perpetuation of the replicators – genes – is achieved by reproduction by the interactor – the organism. But reproduction is possible only if the interactor – the organism – survives in the environment long enough to reproduce, and in sufficient numbers that its offspring will in turn reproduce. And reproduction may result in altered replication of the gene. In utterance selection, perpetuation of the replicators – linguemes – is achieved by production of utterances by the interactor – the speaker. But production is possible only if the interactor – the speaker – survives long enough to produce utterances with that lingueme, and in sufficient numbers that knowledge of the lingueme will become entrenched in another speaker's mind and she in turn produces utterances with that lingueme. And production may result in altered replication of the lingueme.

There are two significant disanalogies between biological and linguistic evolution, both hinted at in the last two paragraphs. These disanalogies might be taken as evidence against the applicability of Hull's generalized theory of selection to language change. However, both disanalogies are irrelevant to the generalized theory of selection, and hence to the theory of language change that follows from it.

Many biologists have assumed that functional adaptation is one of the primary determinants of biological selection at the organism level (see Hull 1988:221, 300, 426 for defense of this view against recent critics). Altered replication of genes, on the other hand, is a more or less random process involving (rarely) mutation and (much more commonly, in sexual species) recombination of DNA (gene selectionists would also argue for adaptive selection at the gene level). In linguistic evolution, under the hypothesis proposed in Croft (1995a), external functional motivation that is presumably adaptive for the purpose of communication (see chapter 4) is the cause of altered replication, not selection. This position is contrary to that taken by many linguists seeking functional explanations in language, who assume that functional explanations in linguistics are analogous to adaptive explanations in evolutionary biology (see e.g. Kirby 1997; Nettle 1999; Haspelmath 1999). However, the empirical evidence indicates that linguistic selection is governed largely if not exclusively by social forces that have little or nothing to do with functional adaptiveness for communication.

The disanalogy in the role of adaptive mechanisms in biological evolution and language change is not relevant to the generalized theory of selection. Any generalized theory of selection that is applicable to evolutionary phenomena in a wide range of domains of experience must abstract away from the causal mechanisms involved in selection in any particular domain: 'The specific mechanisms involved in biological and conceptual evolution are quite different. Conceptual change does not depend on DNA, competition for mates, and what have you' (Hull 1988:431). Thus, we should not expect a specific mechanism like adaptation, even broadly construed, to be a causal mechanism in evolution in another domain, let alone the causal mechanism for the same step in the process.

The second significant disanalogy between biological and linguistic evolution has to do with the relationship between the replicator and the interactor, other than the causal relationship leading to altered replication of the replicator. In biology, an organism is described as having a phenotype – the physical and behavioral properties of the organism – which is expressed, i.e. at least partially determined, by its genotype – the genes in its DNA. In linguistics, we say that a grammar generates an utterance, or that a speaker expresses an utterance of the language. That is, it appears that in some sense, the genotype – the replicator – 'produces' the phenotype – the interactor – in biology; but the grammar – the interactor – 'produces' the utterance – the replicator – in linguistics (cf. Keller 1990/1994:148). This disanalogy has probably contributed to the notion that language change occurs through speakers' grammars (child language acquisition) rather than through language use (see chapter 3).

There is a good reason why this is a false analogy between biology and linguistics. The generalized theory of selection does not apply only to the levels of the gene and the organism in biology. It is independent of the levels of organization of biological entities: 'The fact that all three processes – replication, interaction, and evolution – occur at a variety of levels in the traditional organizational hierarchy is one very good reason to abandon this hierarchy for the purposes of capturing evolutionary regularities' (Hull 1988:428). Thus, the fact that the genotype is expressed in the phenotype, but a grammar generates an utterance, has no bearing on the mechanisms or processes involved in replication, interaction and evolution. In fact, selection might occur at higher levels of linguistic organization as well, and so the specific relationship between grammar and utterance is not a necessary part of the evolutionary mechanisms of language change.

These disanalogies do not weaken the generalized theory of selection and evolution proposed by Hull. Hull's theory does not predict the spurious 'analogies'. All it specifies are certain causal relationships between replicator, interactor and environment. It does not specify what kind of causal mechanisms are involved, nor does it specify other sorts of causal relationships that may hold between the three entities involved in selection. Other cross-disciplinary theories will be necessary to account for these differences in causal relationships and mechanisms between biology and language.

Hull is not making random, convenient or opportunistic analogies between biology and conceptual change, and nor am I doing so in applying his generalized theory of selection to language change. Hull's generalized theory of selection stands above disciplinary boundaries. Hull illustrates its instantiation in biological evolution and applies it to conceptual evolution, thereby producing a theory of conceptual change in science. I am applying the same theory to language change, thereby producing the Theory of Utterance Selection for language change.

Notes

1 In Croft 1996a, I misinterpreted Hull's concept of differential replication as referring to the creation of different replicators in replication. Although one passage (Hull 1988:409) suggests this interpretation, other passages now make clear to me that differential replication refers to selection only. Dawkins (1982b:85) uses the term 'differential replicator survival' as the effect of adaptation, that is, selection. The consequence of this reinterpretation is that the mechanisms for altered replication (the creation of variants) need not involve interaction with the environment in the generalized theory of selection, although in fact they might do so (see §3.4.4).

2 Throughout this book, I will conform to the convention of using *she* to refer to the speaker and *he* to refer to the hearer.

3 So-called ungrammatical utterances have only a heuristic status in this theory, as one of several methods used by linguists to find out the structure of a speaker's grammar.

4 The term 'gene' has an unfortunate ambiguity between token and type. A phrase such as 'gene frequencies' refers to frequencies of gene tokens. However, a phrase

such as 'the gene for hemoglobin', refers to the type: many different individuals have 'the gene for hemoglobin'. I am, unfortunately, going to continue this practice with 'lingueme'. In virtually all uses in this book, 'lingueme' will refer to tokens; if I am referring to a lingueme type, I will use the phrase 'lingueme type'.

5 We may remain fairly neutral as to what sort of mental representations of linguistic structures and their relationships is required by the ability to replicate linguemes; all that matters is the ability to replicate linguemes. For more specific proposals for mental representations conforming with the evolutionary framework, see §2.4.3, §8.1, chapter 9 and Croft (to appear b).

6 Tabor (1993) and Hare & Elman (1995) apply interactive activation models to problems of language change, within somewhat different theoretical frameworks than the one described in this book.

7 Construction grammarians may object to the syntax/lexicon distinction I am making here. Langacker (1987) argues for a syntax–lexicon continuum. However, I am casting the syntax/lexicon distinction in this passage as the distinction between a complex whole and its component parts. When Langacker and other construction grammarians argue for a syntax–lexicon continuum, they are arguing that syntactic knowledge should be represented as constructions which consist of pairings of syntactic form and semantic-discourse function, and which can occur at varying degrees of schematicity (e.g. *[V NP]* and *[kick [the bucket]]*). In this view, lexical items are merely simplex, maximally specific constructions; but constructions are organized in a network like the lexicon. The construction grammar model of grammatical knowledge as complex form–meaning pairings in fact fits well with the philosophical definition of linguistic convention described in §4.2.4.

Chapter 3

Some theories of language change in an evolutionary framework

3.1 Introduction

In chapter 2, I described a generalized theory of selection developed by Hull (1988) for biological evolution and conceptual change, and proposed an instantiation of that model as the Theory of Utterance Selection for language change. In this chapter, I will survey and critique other hypotheses on the nature of language change from the perspective of the generalized theory of selection.

One might ask, why should other hypotheses on the nature of language change be judged as instantiations of the generalized theory of selection? Isn't it possible that language change is a process that operates in some other way than evolution via altered replication and selection? It is certainly possible, though in fact not likely given the proposed alternatives. More significantly, if language change actually involves replication rather than inherent change, as I argued in §1.1, the generalized theory of selection can in fact subsume any theory of language change.

The simplest and least interesting alternative theory is that language change is totally random. This theory can easily be subsumed under the generalized theory of selection. Randomness is the mechanism underlying both altered replication and differential replication. (Recall that differential replication can occur without selection; this is DRIFT in the technical evolutionary sense of the term – see §2.3.) I am inclined to believe that randomness does play some role in language change. That is to say, randomness may be one of the causal mechanisms underlying altered replication, and perhaps even selection. But there is enough evidence of regularity in language change, in both innovation and propagation, to lead historical linguists to assume that language change is not solely a random process.

Another alternative theory is that language change is accomplished purely by design, like a man-made artifact. The speech community, or its designated representatives, collectively decides how its language will change and then implements the change. The empirical evidence against this theory is overwhelming. At most, some innovations are explicitly legislated; but this is only a tiny fraction of known language changes. And even those innovations that are explicitly legislated must be propagated, and that is undoubtedly a selection process: human beings do not automatically follow rules in the same way that an artifact's structure is a direct result of its design and manufacture. Nevertheless, language change by design is still describable in terms of the theory of selection: design is the causal mechanism for both altered replication and differential replication; speakers obeying the will of the legislators of language change would be the interactors causing replication to be differential.

Yet another alternative theory is that language change is a natural process, that is, it follows from causal laws not unlike those that governed the formation of the universe or the evolution of the earth's climate (to select two examples of a physical historical process). This approach assumes a very narrow view of what a 'natural' process is. Selection, in biological evolution at least, is a natural process. It applies to change occurring via replication as well. I have argued that language change is the result of a replication process (§1.1). As Hull emphasizes, it involves (two) causal processes, one bringing about altered replication and the other, differential replication.

Differential replication may be caused by an interactor interacting with its environment, in which case selection is involved; or it may occur without selection, in which case it is drift, as mentioned above with respect to randomness. One could argue that the generalized theory of selection is inappropriate to describe language change because all language change is simply drift; no selection is involved, no matter how one instantiates the selection process. In other words, language change results from some 'natural' mechanism of differential replication, either of utterances or of grammars, that does not involve selection as defined in §2.3. Such a theory would claim that no selection occurs, and would propose one or more nonselectional, causal mechanisms of differential replication. (The random change theory is a limiting instance of such a theory.)

In fact, I know of no such theory of language change. Although there are some processes of language change which might be equivalent to drift, many of them are problematic and most theories allow for other sorts of replication or selection processes (see §3.3.2). Nevertheless, such a theory can be described in the framework of the generalized theory of selection, and compared to other theories of language change. The crucial point is that the generalized theory of selection provides a framework for describing and comparing such a 'natural' theory of language change; this is the premise of this chapter.[1]

Theories of language change can vary in two essential dimensions: what entities are treated as replicators and interactors; and what causal mechanisms are involved in altered replication and in selection. Of course, not all possible theories have been proposed, and I will focus my attention on the major existing alternative approaches.

One of the most fundamental differences in current theories of language change is in what is hypothesized to be the replicator at the lowest or basic level of selection (all of these theories take the grammar as the primary interactor). The Theory of Utterance Selection takes the utterance as the primary replicator. Three other theories are also UTTERANCE-BASED THEORIES: sociohistorical theory, the invisible hand theory and grammaticalization theory. One of the most widely accepted theories of language change, however, takes the speaker's grammar as the primary replicator as well as the primary interactor.

Altered replication takes place in the transmission of linguistic knowledge from one speaker to another. The canonical example of transmission, that is grammar replication, is from parent to child. Hence, the locus of language change is assumed to occur in child language acquisition. The CHILD-BASED THEORY of language change has been entertained since at least the late 19th century, and is the central assumption of generative theories of language change. The child-based theory will be discussed in §3.2, and the other utterance-based theories will be discussed in §3.3.

Choice of the utterance or the grammar as the primary replicator is the most fundamental dimension on which theories of language change differ. Theories may also differ on the types of causal mechanisms that are proposed for differential replication and/or selection. The causal mechanisms proposed in the child-based and utterance-based theories will be referred to briefly in §3.2 and §3.3 respectively. A general survey of causal mechanisms, including mechanisms not associated exclusively with either child-based or utterance-based theories, will be presented in §3.4 and discussed further in chapters 4–7.

3.2   The child-based theory of language change

The child-based theory of language change treats the speaker, or more precisely the speaker's grammar, as the replicator as well as the interactor. I will outline the general child-based theory in the evolutionary framework described in chapter 2, and then turn to a critical discussion of some of its major variants, in particular generative models of language change.

The child-based theory was debated by several linguists at the end of the 19th century (see Jespersen 1922:161–2). Its first major explication in generative linguistics is Halle (1962), and it is widely assumed by generative linguists. However, it is also found in contemporary nongenerative structuralist linguistics, e.g. in the abduction theory of Andersen (1973).

Language change is conceived as a change in the grammars of different speakers. The speaker's grammar is the replicator. The replication process is first language acquisition, prototypically the transmission of grammatical knowledge from parent to child. Altered replication comes about through the learning process. The child is exposed to the utterances produced around her, and may intuit a grammar that is different in some way from the grammar of her parents or caregivers. The speaker is also the interactor, not as a social being but as a mortal biological organism. Selection occurs merely through the succession of generations of speakers. That is, differential extinction and proliferation of interactors – the death of older speakers and the survival of younger speakers – causes the differential perpetuation of the relevant replicators – their grammars.

A priori, from the perspective of the generalized theory of selection, the child-based view is mostly unproblematic. It is not impossible for the replicator and the interactor to be identical, although Hull suggests that it is more natural for them to be different: 'when different functions must be performed by a single structure or entity, none are performed very well' (Hull 1988:409). The selection process is merely the biological fact that people who are born earlier tend to die earlier. The one problematic aspect is the replication process. It is difficult to describe the language learning process as a replication of the grammar of the parent by the child. The replication process is very indirect: the parent's grammar produces utterances, which provide the input for the formation of the child's grammar.

Of course, utterance replication is also indirect, being mediated by the grammar of the speaker who is replicating the linguemes. However, the structure being replicated is directly observable by speakers in the case of linguemes. It is not clear what structure is being replicated intact in grammar replication. Only if one makes the assumption that much of our grammar, quite specific aspects of it in fact, is genetically programmed, and hence is probably implemented at the cellular level in similar ways, can we reasonably describe the transmission process as replication. Exactly this assumption is made in generative linguistic theory. The universal aspects of core areas of grammar are hypothesized to be innate, by the 'poverty of the stimulus' argument (that the input is sufficiently complex and irregular that the language could not be learned without a significant innate component). The innate part of our grammatical knowledge in this theory is indeed replicated – in the biological sense of genetic replication. (It should be noted that the generative assumption that many specific aspects of grammatical structure are identical across languages is disputed on empirical grounds, especially by typologists.)

This genetic replication pertains only to those aspects of (core) grammar that are universal, that is, invariant. A theory of language change is concerned with the variable parts of grammar, that can and do change over time. In recent versions of generative grammar (Chomsky 1981 onwards), variability is accommodated by a series of grammatical parameters. The parameters themselves and their possible values are invariable and innate, but the actual value for a particular speaker is set in the language acquisition process. The parameter setting for the child may be the same as that for the parent, or it may be different. The parameter settings are determined by the input, that is, language use around the child.[2] (Hence, there is still a significant usage-based component to this model.)

The child-based model makes a number of empirical predictions. The first is that the sorts of changes to the adult system that children make in first language acquisition should be of the same type as are found in language change, since they are in fact the source of language change. The second is that the sorts of changes that children make in first language acquisition will be maintained through to their adulthood, so that the changes become the altered language of the new generation (cf. Bybee & Slobin 1982a:29). The third is that language change should be relatively abrupt, because the change occurs in a single generation, that is, in the lifetime (in fact, the childhood) of a single speaker or generation of speakers. The fourth is that a speaker will either have the 'old' grammar or the 'new' one. All four predictions are false. Modifications have been made to the model in order to accommodate some of the anomalies, but serious problems still remain. We will now survey the predictions, their outcome, and the modifications made to the theory to accommodate them.

3.2.1   Changes in language history and child language

The types of changes attested in historical language change are not identical to those found in language acquisition (Dressler 1974; Drachman 1978; Vihman 1980; Hooper 1980; Slobin 1997a:313–14; Bybee & Slobin 1982a:36–7; Aitchison 1991:168–73). Dressler and Drachman discuss a relatively wide range of phonological processes, while Vihman undertakes a systematic survey of three phonological processes in a set of children acquiring various languages and in a set of language families. Vihman found that consonant harmony is quite widespread in child language, but extremely rare in adult language. Drachman adds that vowel harmony is quite common in adult language but rare in child language. Vihman examined long word reduction, and discovered a pattern of retention of word-final syllables in child language absent in adult patterns. More impor-·tant, while children eliminated whole syllables, historical language changes usually involved eliminating the vowel nucleus only (sometimes the consonants would be reduced as a consequence of consonant cluster reduction).

The third process Vihman examined was consonant cluster reduction. She found a frequency hierarchy of consonant types to be reduced in clusters in child language that was completely the opposite of the frequency hierarchy of reduction in language change. Drachman noted other dissimilarities, including strengthening of consonants in child language vs weakening in language change (cf. Dressler 1974:97; but see Andersen 1988; Trudgill 1989; §7.4.4), and a rearrangement of consonants in a word to fit with the place of articulation hierarchy in child language, not found in adult language. In fact, the main impression from the literature is that those processes of child language reduction that are found in language change are rare and sporadic in the latter.

In morphology, Hooper (1980) compares 'errors' in child language and innovations in adult language. She argues that children and adults make similar errors/innovations. Thus, children may be the source of morphological change, but adults could equally well be the source. And Bybee & Slobin note that younger children's errors were often unlike language change; when they were like language change, they were the same as older children and adults (Bybee & Slobin 1982a:36–7). Aitchison further notes that less frequent words are the more likely to be regularized, but less frequent words are also unlikely to be known to children (Aitchison 1991:169–70).

In syntax, there has not been as much investigation of this issue. Early proposals that the source of double negation in English was due to children producing double negatives (Kiparsky 1968) have been discredited; the child pattern is more likely to be due to constructional blends or a wider pattern of double marking of morphological categories (Aitchison 1991:170). In unpublished work on zero (lexical) causative formation in English, Melissa Bowerman and I have observed a similar pattern to those found by Bybee & Slobin, namely that children produce errors almost never found among adults, and the other errors they produce are also produced by adults:

(1) *Common children's innovations in overgeneralization that are rare in adults*
   a. You SAD me [= make me sad]
      (John C., 2;2–2;4, collected by Melissa Bowerman)
   b. Don't EAT it me [= feed it to me]
      (Rachel G., 2;0, collected by Melissa Bowerman)
   c. Small company's new golf ball flies too far; could OBSOLETE many golf courses.
      (fictitious news item in a magazine ad; Pinker 1989:154)

(2) *Innovations in overgeneralization relatively commonly found in adults as well as in children*
   a. Water BLOOMED these flowers. [= make bloom]
      (Christy B., 5;10, from Melissa Bowerman's corpus)
   b. He said that the Agnew and Watergate affairs have tended to DETERIORATE confidence in the American system. [= cause to deteriorate]
      (newspaper article, from Bowerman 1982:19)

(3) *Innovations in overgeneralization occasionally found in both adults and children*
   a. I'm trying to GUESS Aunt Ruth what I have [= want Aunt Ruth to guess]
      (J, 4;8, from Lord 1979)
   b. If she SUBSCRIBES us up, she'll get a bonus [= gives our name to a cable TV company, resulting in our subscribing]
      (Pinker 1989:154)

Aitchison (1991:173) and Vihman (1980:315) suggest that one of the reasons that changes brought about by children are different from those brought about by adults is that children have not yet fully acquired the motor and cognitive processing skills to produce utterances. Adults have mastered these skills, and innovate for other reasons (see §3.4.3).

3.2.2 Changes in child language as the child matures

It is not the case that 'errors' or innovations in a child's grammar survive into adulthood. Instead, children's errors which presumably manifest a grammar (or lexicon) different from that of their parents tend to disappear in later phases of language acquisition. That is, the child's grammar and/or lexicon tend more and more to conform to the conventions (norms) of the speech community in language acquisition. In fact, one of the chief puzzles that theories of language acquisition attempt to solve is the ability of the child to 'unlearn' the novel forms she produces without any explicit correction. This puzzle is the so-called no negative evidence problem (Bowerman 1988; Pinker 1989).

Of course, at some point, children do grow up to become members of the speech community who are in a position to innovate changes that are then propagated to the next generation of children. But by the time children achieve the status of being innovators or sources of language change (Milroy & Milroy 1985), they are rarely producing the sorts of novel structures that characterized their language acquisition process. Children achieve the status of innovators by adolescence, but cease making acquisition errors well before then.

Labov suggests that 'older ... cadres of adolescents and pre-adolescents' (Labov 1982:46–7) are the (youngest) agents of transmission of change, at least in urban First World communities. Kerswill (1996) surveys a number of studies of variation and change for 'infants and young children' (age 0–6), 'pre-adolescents' (age 6–12), and adolescents (age 12–17). The studies surveyed by Kerswill focused on phenomena which were variable in the adult speech community, and also on urban vernaculars, so they do not follow the assumptions of a homogeneous grammar of the child-based theory (see the discussion of the fourth prediction below). Nevertheless, Kerswill's survey of the evidence suggests that Labov's observation is essentially correct.

Young children are moving towards adult norms in acquisition. Younger children make innovations that are more deviant from the adult norms, while older children approximate them more closely (Kerswill 1996:189; see also Bybee & Slobin 1982a:36–7). Children acquiring language move first towards the norms of their caregivers and then as they grow older, towards the norms of adolescents and preadolescents (Kerswill 1996:192–4). It is worth noting in this context that one usually finds native-like acquisition of a community language by children even when their parents are nonnative speakers of that language (Weinreich, Labov & Herzog 1968:145, fn. 36; Labov 1982:47). It appears that preadolescents 'are changing their speech in slight but systematic ways, accommodating to their peers and to older children' (Kerswill 1996:196). Adolescents were found to be able to acquire a new dialect – that is to say, they accommodate to it, rather than acting as agents of transmission of their native dialect forms. Kerswill suggests that dialect acquisition can occur successfully up to the age of around 16; Chambers (1992) however suggests a lower age of around 12 (see §3.3.1 for a critique of the critical age hypothesis).

Similar results were obtained by Ravid in a series of studies on acquisition and language change in Modern Hebrew: 'Thus young children do not cause Language Change: It is the population of older children and naive ... adult speakers who both provide the pool of possible variation necessary for change and induce change' (Ravid 1995:170).

But most of the overgeneralizations and irregularities studied by language acquisition specialists have been 'unlearned' by the time that children have become preadolescents, let alone adolescents. In fact, there is relatively little literature on late acquisition, that is, beyond age 6. However, a brief glance at the outlines of the acquisition of various languages in Slobin (1985, 1992,

1997a) suggests that much of the acquisition process has been completed by that age. References to overgeneralizations or first uses (presumably not entirely 'error'-free) at later ages are quite rare in those volumes. Warlpiri embedded clauses come in around age 7 (Bavin 1992:326). Inflections combining change of stem and addition of suffix in Scandinavian are learned around 2;6 to 8 (Plunkett & Strömqvist 1992:477). Not all aspects of the Modern Greek case–number declensions are learned by 6;4–6;6 (Stephany 1997:200, 203, 216, 222), and some (optional) proclitic sandhi rules are not fully acquired by age 9 (ibid. 212); innovative word formation is reported for a 6-year-old (ibid. 255; the context was not entirely natural however). The binding patterns of the Korean reflexive *caki* 'self' differs from adult use for 'even school-age children' (Kim 1997:347, based on experimental studies). Errors at adolescence are even rarer. Some aspects of the Japanese honorific system are not acquired until junior high school, if at all (Clancy 1985:383). Sporadic 'errors' for certain English syntactic constructions occur as late as 12 (Melissa Bowerman, personal communication). Ravid suggests that some aspects of pronominalization, relative clause formation and gerunds are not 'fully mastered' until around age 12 (Ravid 1995:14).

It appears that although some 'errors' of acquisition still occur at ages 6–12, they are very rare, and if any such 'errors' are produced in adolescence, they may not differ in kind from adult innovations at that point. As Kerswill writes, 'At the preadolescent stage, we can assume that most areas of language are fully mature, with the exception of the command of an adult range of speech styles' (Kerswill 1996:191).

3.2.3 Abrupt vs gradual language change

If language change occurred through children intuiting a different grammar from their parents and caregivers, then one would expect language change to be abrupt, occurring in a single generation. In fact, many generative models of language change have argued that language change is abrupt (e.g. Lightfoot 1979). However, the facts where available have indicated that language change is a gradual process: different linguistic features shift at different times, and the different variants coexist, sometimes in the same text (see Tabor 1993:451 and references cited there). For example, Plank argues that there is a larger number of properties relevant to the syntactic development of English modals than those described by Lightfoot (1979), and shows that they change at different points in the history of English and over different periods of the history of English (Plank 1984, esp. Table 2). Denison argues that the shift of Old English impersonal verbs was also very gradual, in fact apparently via diffusion from one verb to another (Denison 1990). Allen (1995) argues that the loss of dative experiencer subjects was also gradual, and not that strongly connected to the loss of the case marking system (Allen 1995:347). Allen (2000) examines Early Middle English texts and found no evidence of an abrupt shift from OV to VO word order in that period; in fact, the coexistence of both orders must be accommodated. These facts have been observed not only in historical corpora. The variation found in the language produced by contemporary speakers in a speech community gives evidence of gradual language change as it is actually taking place (§7.4.3; see Chambers 1995:193–206 for discussion and a survey of the literature).

This empirical problem has been recognized by Lightfoot in his more recent model of language change (Lightfoot 1991). Lightfoot advocates a more sophisticated generative model which preserves the essence of the generative child-based theory but offers a more plausible model of the gradual propagation of an innovation. As in the classic child-based theory, an innovation (a parameter resetting) occurs in the process of a child learning a grammar based on input – but not necessarily just the parents' input. Each child that resets a parameter and thus produces novel variants thereby alters the mix of linguistic forms that other children and future children will encounter in their language learning process. As more and more children reset the parameter, there are more and more occurrences of the novel variants in future children's input, triggering more parameter resettings, until all speakers have grammars with the new parameter setting. Thus, what appears to us as a gradual process of language change, with old and new variants cooccurring over a long period of time, is in fact a gradually changing mix of speakers each with a single variant in their grammar.

Lightfoot's theory succeeds in modeling the gradual propagation of a change. But Lighfoot's theory still suffers from other problems. The first problem is shared by Lightfoot's and other parameter-setting models. In these theories, parameter resetting occurs across time and individuals through changes in language use (i.e. changes in triggering experiences) around the child. But what causes those changes in language use (that is, the changes in the triggering experiences)? Lightfoot argues that there are changes in language use that do not involve the change in underlying grammars at first, but can lead to parameter resettings:

> these options [a change in Old English word order] tended to be exercised more and more over a period of several hundred years. This no more reflects a difference in grammars than if some speaker were shown to use a greater number of passive or imperative sentences. Rather, it reflects the kind of accidental variation that is familiar from studies in population genetics. Nonetheless, changes in the primary linguistic data, if they show a slight cumulative effect, might have the consequence of setting a grammatical parameter differently. That is what seems to have happened with English verb order. (Lightfoot 1991:67–8)

In this passage, Lightfoot suggests that accidental variation can lead to grammatical change. This does not explain why the change is directional. In other passages, Lightfoot suggests that expressiveness is the causal mechanism for changes in language use: 'a particular construction type may become more frequent, perhaps as a result of taking on some expressive function (a greatly underestimated source of linguistic change)' (Lightfoot 1991:160); 'new constructions are introduced which, by their unusual shape, have novelty value and are used for stylistic effect' (ibid. 171). This is a widely appealed to mechanism for innovation (see §3.4.3, §6.2.3, §6.3.2); but it is not the mechanism of innovation associated with the child-based model.

Another problem with Lightfoot's model, and the child-based model in general, is that there is evidence that the propagation of a language change is not necessarily due to the higher mortality rate of older speakers, leaving younger speakers with an altered version of the language. The reason that younger speakers have an altered version of their elders' language is due to the fact that they choose to emulate their peers' linguistic innovations rather than the elders' language. It is a priori possible for younger speakers to emulate older speakers, in which case the language of the older speakers would be maintained, in violation of the mortality hypothesis for the propagation of a language change. It is simply a social fact of at least First World urban societies that most of the time, younger speakers do not emulate their elders.

The fact that it is social processes, not mere mortality, determining the difference in younger speakers' language is demonstrated by the exceptions to this rule. These exceptions are known as AGE-GRADED VARIATION. In age-graded variation, younger speakers adopt the language of their older peers when they themselves reach that age. The most typical case is certain variants used by adolescents, which are abandoned for the adults' variant when adolescents leave adolescence. An example of age-graded variation is the stigmatized variant [ʔ] for the phoneme /t/ in middle-class Glasgow English (Chambers 1995:190–3, from Macaulay 1977). The glottal stop is used by 10-year-olds at approximately the same high rate as lower-class speakers of their age and older. But 15-year-olds' use of the glottal stop drops suddenly to near adult middle-class levels, which are much lower than lower-class adult usage.

In addition, Lightfoot's (1991) theory suffers from another empirical problem, discussed under the next empirical prediction of the child-based view.[3]

3.2.4 Grammar(s) and variation

In Lightfoot's theory, there is a rigid differentiation between changes in language (use) and changes in a speaker's grammar: changes in language use do not lead to changes in the adult's grammar (but see §3.3.1); grammatical change occurs only in language acquisition. Lightfoot assumes that individual speakers have either the old parameter setting or the new one in their grammars. This would predict that although there is variation in a speech community, individual speakers are uniform in their usage. This is in fact not the case, as countless sociolinguistic studies have demonstrated. Speakers use several, possibly all, variants of a linguistic variable; and they use them consistently in ways that reflect the variable's social functions (see e.g. Weinreich, Labov & Herzog 1968:101, who call this 'structured heterogeneity'; Hymes 1972, who calls the speaker's ability 'communicative competence'; and Gumperz 1982, who observes the same ability in code-switching).

In one case, the choice of dative or nominative case for experiencer (psych-) verbs, Lightfoot proposes that individual speakers are diglossic (Lightfoot 1991:136–8). However, as Traugott & Smith (1993:437) note, this analysis has nothing to do with the sociolinguistic phenomenon of diglossia, in which distinct (in fact, mutually unintelligible) varieties are used by the same speaker in socially distinct domains (see §2.2, §8.4.2). Instead, Lightfoot's hypothesis is more like a general claim of multilingualism, and is evidently proposed in order to maintain the existence of discrete nonvariable grammars in Lightfoot's theory (see also Allen 1995:315–20 and Harris & Campbell 1995:86–7 for critiques of Lightfoot's diglossia account on various grounds).

If one assumes that all variation is due to multiple homogeneous grammars in a speaker's mind, then one would have to posit an enormous number of discrete grammars for any actual speaker's competence. There is a much larger number of variable forms in a speaker's linguistic competence than the few variables examined by historical linguists because of their significance to current linguistic theories. Moreover, the variants do not align in utterances in such a way that an utterance is the output of one of a small number of grammars. For example, in the Guyanese postcreole continuum, the variables for the individual lexical items for the sentence 'I gave him one' are as follows (Bell 1976:136, cited in Wardhaugh 1992:82):

(4) a. (I) = [aɪ, a, mɪ]
     b. (aux) = [Ø, dɪd, dɪ, bɪn]
     c. (gave) = [geɪv, gɪv, gɪ, giː]
     d. (him) = [him, ɪm, iː, æm]
     e. (one) = [wʌn, wan]

The variants in (4a–e) are ranked socially from 'highest' to 'lowest'. One might assume there are four grammars. But in fact eighteen versions of 'I gave him one' were recorded.

Admittedly, this is an example of a POSTCREOLE CONTINUUM (see §8.4.2), where one would expect a greater degree of variation than in a community with a written standard such as English. Yet this is only one sentence, and even in a more focused speech community, where norms are tighter, the amount of variation within individual sentences is very great. At any rate, the Guyanese speaker's competence needs to be modeled by linguistic theory as well. The number of homogeneous grammars required to model the Guyanese creole speaker's competence would be simply enormous. A simpler and more plausible model of the representation of the grammatical knowledge of a speaker is a single grammar made up of a system of grammatical variables, with associated social values as well as semantic values, that would produce the actual attested utterances. This is the model of grammatical knowledge proposed by sociohistorical linguistic theory (see §3.3.1 and §4.2.3).

In sum, the child-based theory of language change hypothesizes that the basic replicator in language change is the grammar, not an utterance, and altered replication occurs via acquisition of a grammar by the child that is different in some way from the old generation of speakers. But the child-based theory is not supported by the empirical evidence, and modifications of it, such as Lightfoot's model of gradual language change in the child-based model, do not avoid the empirical difficulties of the original version. On the other hand, some of the empirical evidence brought to bear on the child-based theory in this section in fact lends support to other theories of language change, in particular the sociohistorical theory. In the next section, I will argue that the sociohistorical theory and certain other theories of language change are utterance-based theories of language change, and discuss them in the context of the Theory of Utterance Selection.

3.3 Utterance-based theories of language change

The child-based theory of language change has dominated in generative grammar; but outside generative grammar a number of other theories have been proposed. Three of the most prominent ones – sociohistorical linguistic theory (which has a number of variants), the invisible hand theory, and grammaticalization theory – can be productively interpreted as utterance-based theories of language change. All three theories offer important insights that will be utilized in this book. However, there are important elements missing from all three theories.[4]

This section will focus on how the three theories can be interpreted as theories of utterance selection in the evolutionary framework for language change advocated here. Attention will be focused on how these theories are theories of the innovation and propagation of linguemes, and how speakers function as interactors with respect to their environment in the differential replication of linguemes in selection. Reference will be made to the causal mechanisms of normal replication, altered replication and selection proposed by advocates of the three theories; but a more systematic discussion of the causal mechanisms is reserved for §3.4.

3.3.1 Sociohistorical linguistic theory and the role of adults in language change

The sociohistorical linguistic theory was first explicated in detail in the seminal paper by Weinreich, Labov & Herzog (1968; see references therein for earlier work by the authors; see also Bright & Ramanujan 1964). It is also called 'variationist sociolinguistics', to contrast it with other areas of sociolinguistics that are not specifically directed to variation and its role in language change.

Central to the sociohistorical linguistic theory is the concept of the (socio)linguistic VARIABLE as an entity in the grammar. A linguistic variable represents two or more 'ways of saying the "same thing"' (Weinreich, Labov & Herzog 1968:162; see §2.4.1). The linguistic variables most commonly illustrated are alternative phonetic realizations of the same phoneme. The concept is in fact more general, involving any two (or more) alternative manifestations of a single common property in the grammar, e.g. alternative syntactic expressions of a single semantic function. The variants of a linguistic variable are the replicators in this model (see §2.4.1).

Two important theoretical claims are implicit in the concept of a linguistic variable as used by sociolinguists. First, language change does not involve an abrupt shift from A to B, but instead involves a period of variation between A and B; in this phase, A and B are variants of a single linguistic variable.[5] Second, individual speakers typically use more than one variant of the linguistic variable. Both of these claims have strong empirical support, as was illustrated in the critique of the child-based model in §3.2. A third claim is that the pattern of distribution of the variants of a linguistic variable in language use across the speech community and over time is dependent on social factors, including socioeconomic class, gender, age and ethnicity. More recent work (Milroy 1987; Milroy & Milroy 1985) has focused on social network relations among individual speakers as social determinants of linguistic variation and change (see chapter 7).

The variants of a linguistic variable as they occur in language use in a speech community are linguemes (§2.4.1). The variants are replicators, and the speakers are interactors. Speakers replicate competing variants differentially for social reasons, leading to selection. The causal mechanisms underlying selection are the social motivations for speakers using one variant over another. These mechanisms will be discussed in §3.4.2 and §7.4.2.

However, sociohistorical theory has had difficulties with the mechanism for innovation. Weinreich, Labov & Herzog named it the ACTUATION problem and posed it thus: 'Why do changes in a structural feature take place in a particular language at a given time, but not in other languages with the same feature, or in the same language at other times?' (Weinreich, Labov & Herzog 1968:102). Explaining innovation posed in this way is most likely an impossible task. One cannot predict future specific events and their timing (or location) in this way (see §1.1). One can try to predict types of possible and impossible changes under given specified conditions (cf. Milroy 1992a:76; Keller 1990/1994:120). But that still leaves the problem of where the innovations come from; that is the problem that needs to be answered.

After identifying innovation, Weinreich *et al.* then call the distinction between innovation and propagation 'untenable' (Weinreich, Labov & Herzog 1968:129). But the central problem of the sociolinguistic theory of language change, for all its empirical success in explaining propagation, is that it always presupposes the existence of multiple variants. Instead, attention has been focused on the patterns of linguistic variation, or structured heterogeneity, in the speech community. The pattern of structured variation is described as the grammar of the speech community (Weinreich, Labov & Herzog 1968:188; Milroy 1992a:78). Effort has been devoted to providing the social motivation for the existence of structured heterogeneity: after all, it is a universal and utilitarian feature of human languages. Nevertheless, the question remains how specific variants arise and become part of the variable linguistic system. That is, a mechanism for innovation is also required.

Theoretical discussions of variation almost never explain how the variants arise. This is true of all of the examples in Weinreich, Labov & Herzog (1968), for instance. Labov's step-by-step description of how a language change begins, starts with a novel variant already prevalent in 'a restricted subgroup of the speech community' (Labov 1972b:178). Milroy & Milroy's theory of speaker innovation (Milroy & Milroy 1985) explains how a novel variant gets transmitted into and then through a speech community (see §7.4.1); but the novel variant is already there, present in another social network with which the 'innovator' (actually the transmitter) has social ties. If a restricted subgroup, or neighboring social network, possesses the novel form but the speech community in question (at first) does not, then we are dealing with a case of external innovation (see §6.1). Kerswill summarizes the model of innovation commonly assumed in sociohistorical theory:

> I take the view that both linguistic variation and change within a language com-
> munity are a matter of dialect contact. Speakers are continually in contact with
> others who have different backgrounds and use different language varieties from
> themselves – even when there is no 'dialect contact' in the more usual, restricted
> sense, which involves migration and mobility. (Kerswill 1996:179)

In fact, the source of new variants is often external; but this can be argued to be propagation across dialect (or language) boundaries (see §§8.3–8.5). But the question remains as to where the dialect diversity that is the source of variants came from in the first place.

Some proposals for innovation mechanisms have been made. Labov argues for what he calls a mechanistic mechanism for innovations in chain shifts of vowels (Labov 1994:221; see §3.4.4). Milroy recognizes the need for explaining innovation in an utterance-based model as the production of innovative struc-tures (altered replication) by speakers:

> [innovation] must be speaker-based. Linguistic change originates with speakers
> and is implemented in social interactions between speakers . . . But as language
> use . . . does not take place *except* in social contexts . . . our analysis and interpreta-
> tion . . . must take account of society, situation and the speaker/listener. (Milroy
> 1992a:77, emphasis original; cf. Milroy 1992b:164–72)

However, he does not propose any specific mechanisms for innovation.

A major stumbling block for many linguists in accepting sociohistorical linguistic theory as a theory of language change is the belief that an adult's grammar, once acquired, is fixed. If an adult's grammar is totally fixed, then neither innovation nor propagation can occur via adults. More precisely, an innovation might occur in adult language use; but it could never result from a change in the adult's grammar (see §3.2). The innovation results from 'per-formance'; and it could not alter another adult's grammar.

If this is true, then it appears that the only way in which innovation can take place is via children acquiring the language. I believe that at least some support

for the child-based theory, despite the empirical problems outlined in the preceding section, is due to the fact that the alternative, language change via
adults, is believed by many to be impossible. Also, the fact that much sociohistorical theory does not really address the problem of innovation contributes
to doubts about its validity as a theory of language change in adults. But the
hypothesis that an adult's grammar is fixed is based on a series of assumptions
about the nature of a grammar, the nature of language acquisition, and the
nature of native ability. Some of these assumptions are not logically necessary
and others are empirically questionable.

There are two assumptions about the nature of a grammar that are questionable, and if dropped, make it much more plausible that an adult's grammar
can change. The first assumption is that an adult's grammar is homogeneous.
That is, there is no variation in grammatical patterning, and any observed
variation is to be attributed to multiple grammars in the speaker's mind. I
argued against the tenability of this position in §3.2. There is a great deal of
variability in an individual speaker's linguistic behavior, too much to be captured in a plausibly small number of individually homogeneous grammars in a
speaker's head. Moreover, this variability is structured, that is, the variants
have social values conventionally associated with them that determine their
appropriate use to a great extent. These facts point to the organization of a
grammar as a system of linguistic variables in the sociolinguist's sense. If a
grammar is a system of variables, each with multiple variants, then the possibility that those variants gradually shift in their relative positions even for an
adult seems much more plausible.

The second assumption is that a grammar is not an instrument of communication – more precisely, the fact that a grammar is an instrument of communication is irrelevant to grammatical change (change in phonology, morphology
or syntax). The alleged irrelevance of communication to a grammar results
from assumptions about the organization of a grammar which have been questioned in recent theories of syntax. A speaker's grammatical knowledge must
of course represent the formal structures conventional in the speech community, that is, its phonology, morphology, lexicon and syntax. But a speaker's
grammatical knowledge also includes the conventional meanings and discourse
functions associated with those forms (Croft 1995a:492–3). This is true even of
those theories of grammar that assume the 'autonomy' of syntax (Newmeyer
1992:764–5). Such theories split the formal structures of linguistic signs and
their semantic and discourse functions into separate components or levels. But
even these theories must have linking rules that link forms to their functions.
These linking rules have increasingly played a central role in such theories (see
e.g. Jackendoff 1990). Also, the lexicon – the one grammatical component that
directly links phonological, morphosyntactic and semantic information for linguistic signs – has come to play a major role in current generative theories.
Other recent theories of grammar have encoded the conventional linking between
syntactic form and function directly in constructions; these theories include
cognitive grammar (Langacker 1987), construction grammar (Fillmore & Kay

1993; Goldberg 1995; Croft to appear b), and Head-driven Phrase Structure Grammar (Pollard & Sag 1993). Moreover, the definition of convention in philosophy of language is in terms of a form conventionally used for a particular function (see Lewis 1969 and §4.2.4).

In other words, in any theory of grammar, both form and function – meaning and discourse function – and their conventional relationship must be represented somehow. And meaning and discourse function, by which I include the social factors proposed by sociolinguists to describe linguistic variables, are directly sensitive to language use. Language use involves applying the conventional meanings and social values of linguistic forms to the current discourse situation and the experience to be communicated. As I will argue in chapters 4 and 6, there is flexibility in the application of forms to current contexts of use. Hence, when we observe changes in the frequency of use of a form, it almost certainly indicates changes in the conventional meaning and/or discourse function of grammatical units and constructions (cf. Bybee, Perkins & Pagliuca 1994:4). If linguistic variables are a part of the grammar, as I argued above, then changes in use are changes in grammatical knowledge. In other words, changes can occur in the grammar of adults in the course of language use.

Another assumption, about the nature of language acquisition, has played a central role in the hypothesis of a fixed adult grammar. This assumption is the critical period hypothesis: there is a critical age beyond which nativelike acquisition of a language is impossible, specifically around adolescence. Aitchison provides a series of arguments against the biological basis for this hypothesis (Aitchison 1989:84–9; see also Aitchison 1991:167–8 for these arguments in a historical linguistic context). The biological basis for the critical period, the development of lateralization of the brain for language, has been shown to exist already for infants. Various cases of impaired language acquisition (children deprived of language, Down's syndrome, left-brain damage) appear to be due to other brain damage, not to a critical age for language acquisition. There appears to be a gradual process of slower ability to acquire nativelike proficiency in a language so that adolescents and adults cannot achieve nativelike mastery of a new language; but there is no sudden cutoff. In fact, the apparent sudden cutoff of language 'learning' at adolescence probably represents the transition in social status of a speaker: the child speaker begins as an emulator of other social groups (and hence a learner), but in adolescence becomes a member of the social group whose speech is being emulated (and hence a full-fledged 'native speaker'; see below), as noted above.

More significantly for the fixed adult grammar hypothesis, linguistic ability can evolve beyond the so-called critical period. Aitchison reports sporadic cases of nativelike acquisition of a language by an adult speaker (Aitchison 1991:168). It is also clear that a speaker's lexicon continues to change through adulthood (Aitchison 2000), and speakers continue to acquire additional social and stylistic registers through adulthood (Kerswill 1996:191, quoted in §3.2).

Conversely, an adult native speaker can lose at least some of her native ability when it is not reinforced by language use in the community around her.

Speakers isolated from their native communities lose phonological abilities in their native languages (Major 1993) as well as grammatical proficiency (de Bot, Gommans & Rossing 1991) to varying degrees. A significant factor in this process is basically lack of use: de Bot *et al.*'s study of Dutch immigrants in France concludes that 'proficiency in Dutch does not change over time when there are many contacts with Dutch, but it deteriorates linearly over time in the case of few contacts' (de Bot, Gommans & Rossing 1991:91). It may be that the retention of phonological details from adolescence noted by Labov and others (e.g. Labov 1982:68) is due at least in part to reinforcement through continued interactions with other speakers of the same age cohort with the same phonologies. Nativelike ability can be regained, at least to some extent, if the speaker is placed in the native speech community again (Major 1993:473; no precise measurements were made however).[6] But this is the point: linguistic ability is sensitive to exposure to language use in the surrounding community; it is not completely fixed at adulthood.

The fixed adult grammar hypothesis assumes that late language learners cannot achieve native speaker ability. But what is a native speaker? Certain assumptions about the status of native speakers are also questionable, and if abandoned undermine the fixed adult grammar hypothesis. While it does appear to be difficult for late learners of a language to acquire nativelike ability, this does not logically entail that native speakers' ability is fixed. The difficult-to-acquire nativelike ability to use a language is not simply mastery of grammatical details, but also mastery of the choice of appropriate variants of a linguistic variable, and mastery of the shifting currents of social values of the speech community that affect the choice. Nativelike ability includes nativelike ability to vary and shift one's language use appropriately. As Harris & Campbell put it, citing various types of empirical evidence for the flexible view of adult grammars: 'The grammar of an adult can change . . . These facts show that the grammar of an adult is best viewed, not as an inflexible completed object, but as an adaptable, constantly growing set of generalizations' (Harris & Campbell 1995:49; cf. Jespersen 1922:165).[7]

Finally, language variation and change in a speech community may not be dependent on nativelike ability. In certain language contact situations, those involving shift of a segment of the community to a nonnative language, the nonnative speakers are able to shift the language in the direction of their former native language with respect to phonological and grammatical structure (see §8.3.1). In effect, the late language learner achieves 'native' speaker social status, and her form of speech is the one that is emulated by future language learners (and users). In sum, there simply is no sharp line in terms of either psychological ability or social status between native speakers and nonnative speakers. We must abandon the assumption that there are 'native' speakers whose grammars are fixed and always determine the conventions of the speech community, as opposed to 'nonnative' speakers, whose grammatical knowledge is 'imperfect' and variable and who only try to approximate the conventions established by the 'native' speakers.

All of these considerations make it more plausible to treat adult grammars as flexible, determining convention to the extent that the speaker is in a social position to do so, and varying in response to exposure to the use of the language around them in various social situations. Thus, both innovation and propagation of language change plausibly occur in language use by adult speakers. This hypothesis underlies any utterance-based theory of language change.

3.3.2   The invisible hand theory

Keller (1990/1994) develops an invisible hand theory of language change which is another type of utterance selection theory. Like Milroy, Keller argues that the action of individual speakers is the cause of language change (Keller 1990/1994:121). More precisely, Milroy argues for the role of individuals in the innovation of language change; as we will see, the same is essentially true of Keller.

Speakers do not produce innovations with the intention of changing the phonological and grammatical system of their language. Speakers set out to achieve certain social goals with their interlocutors. The communication of information using language is a means to those goals. Sometimes speakers innovate linguistically – violate conventions – in the course of pursuing these goals. If the innovation leads to a language change, the language change is an unintended causal effect of an intended human social action. This is what Keller calls a PHENOMENON OF THE THIRD KIND: an unintended result of an intended action (Keller 1990/1994:57). Keller's phenomenon of the third kind is to be distinguished from phenomena of the first and second kind, natural phenomena and artifactual phenomena. ARTIFACTUAL PHENOMENA are those that occur by (intentional) human design; these correspond to teleological mechanisms proposed for language change. NATURAL PHENOMENA occur as purely natural processes, without human intention involved; these correspond roughly to 'mechanical' mechanisms proposed for language change.

Keller's three-way classification of mechanisms for the innovation (and propagation) of language change is an important one, and will be more or less adopted in discussing different mechanisms of language change in §3.4 below. For now, what is to be noted in Keller's theory is that he proposes mechanisms for the replication of utterances in language use, namely phenomena of the third kind. He divides his mechanisms, which he calls maxims, into static and dynamic maxims. The static maxims (chiefly, conformity to convention; see §3.4.2) are mechanisms for normal replication, and the dynamic maxims (see §3.4.4) are mechanisms for altered replication.

Keller invokes the invisible hand in order to account for the propagation of an innovation in a speech community: 'an invisible hand explanation explains its explanandum, a phenomenon of the third kind, as the causal consequence of individual intentional actions which are based on at least partially similar intentions' (Keller 1990/1994:71). If just one speaker innovates, then of course the innovation will not be propagated. But in Keller's model, any speaker in the appropriate situation (or ecological conditions, as he calls it), will behave in essentially the same way. The collective result of a mass of individual speaker actions will be the propagation of an innovation.

The invisible hand process for the propagation of an innovation is not a selection process, in the framework of the generalized theory of selection. A selection process requires the selection of one variant over another by the interactor, as a causal consequence of the interactor's interaction with its environment. In Keller's model, the only process is the creation of a novel variant by an individual speaker (the phenomenon of the third kind). Differential replication of the novel variant is simply the causal consequence of most and eventually all speakers producing the same innovation in the same ecological conditions. Thus, the invisible hand process is an example of evolutionary drift (§2.3, §3.1): 'drift is differential replication in the absence of interaction' (Hull 1988:410). The invisible hand process can be contrasted with the sociohistorical theory, which does involve a selection process. In the sociohistorical theory, speakers choose one already existing variant over another already existing variant as a result of social factors in their environment (class, gender, social network ties, etc.; see §7.4.2).

A model of differential replication based on drift cannot be an empirically complete theory of the propagation of language change. There are clearly many language changes which are propagated in accordance with the principles of the sociohistorical theory. Indirect evidence against an invisible hand model of propagation can also be ascertained. If the propagation of a language change occurred as the collective result of a mass of individual speaker actions in similar ecological conditions, then one would expect the change to be propagated quite rapidly through a speech community, once those ecological conditions are established. But many changes take place over a long period of time, sometimes over many centuries. One could argue that the ecological conditions changed very gradually over that period. But that would have to be demonstrated, and it seems that one would predict much more rapid change for an invisible hand process in most cases.

There is another pattern of occurrence of innovations that argues against an invisible hand theory of the propagation of language change. One fairly often observes the empirical pattern of random occurrences of the innovation before the change 'takes off' (propagation). Sociolinguists have observed that some innovation has occurred too sporadically to be analyzed in a sample from a speech community, only to find upon returning to that community some years later that the innovations were now widely used as variants subject to the usual social factors. Trudgill observed the sporadic occurrence of a labiodental variant of /r/ in Norwich in 1968; it had become a proper variant of a sociolinguistic variable by 1986 (Trudgill 1988:40–1). Milroy observed sporadic cases of a glottal variant of /t/ in the Belfast vernacular, which he suggests may be the leading edge of an innovation, presumably adopted from other English varieties with the glottal variant (Milroy 1992b:171–2).

One also finds random occurrences of an innovation for a long historical period before the innovation is picked up and propagated (assuming there is enough data to detect the early occurrences). One example of this historical pattern appears to be the evolution of the English connective *since* (earlier *siþþan*) from a temporal meaning to a causal but not necessarily temporal meaning (Hopper & Traugott 1993:76–7; see §3.3.3). It turns out that the newer causal meaning is attested in quite early sources of Old English:

(5) *Temporal meaning*
þa   siþþan   he irre   wæs &   gewundod he ofslog   micel
then after/since he angry was and wounded   he slaughtered much
þæs   folces
of.that troop
'Then after/since he was angry and wounded, he slaughtered many troops.'
(ca. 880, Orosius 4 1.156.11)

(6) *Causal meaning*
Ac ic þe   wille nu   giet getæcan ðone weg siððan ðu   ongitst þurh
but I thee will   now still teach   that way since   thou seest   through
mine lare   hwæt sio soðe gesælð   bið &   hwær hio bið
my   teaching what that true happiness is   and where it   is
'But still I will now teach you the way since you see that true happiness comes through teaching, and where it is.'   (ca. 880, Boethius 36 104.26)

But the change in meaning – that is, more than a sporadic appearance of causal *since* – appears to have been conventionally established only in the 15th century (Hopper & Traugott 1993:77). Hopper & Traugott allude to a similar phenomenon in the rise of the past tense of *will* (modern *would*) as a marker of later time: there is an occurrence in Orosius but the phenomenon did not spread until Middle English (ibid. 37–8). One would not expect to find the pattern of random occurrences, especially over a very long time period, followed by propagation, in an automatic propagation model such as the invisible hand. Instead, this pattern implies that innovation and propagation are independent, distinct processes. This pattern, the S-curve, is expected when propagation is a result of selection (see §7.4.3).

Thus, most language changes are not propagated by the invisible hand process. One might still ask whether there are some language changes that involve the invisible hand. Keller discusses just two examples, the pejoration of the German word *Frau* and its replacement in less pejorative contexts by *Dame*, and the loss of the meaning 'angelic' from the word *englisch* 'angelic, English' and its replacement in that meaning by *engelhaft*. Both examples involve the narrowing of use of a term (*Frau* restricted to pejorative contexts, *englisch* restricted to 'English') and its replacement in another function. In both cases, Keller argues that speakers choose another word in the relevant use,[8] and this results in the narrowing of use of *Frau* and *englisch*. The collective, unintended result of all speakers eventually choosing another word is the narrowing of the context of use of the original word.

The invisible hand explanation might be valid as an example of drift in the case of pejoration: it does appear that pejoration is propagated fairly rapidly in a number of cases (witness the successive terms used for the descendants of slaves in the United States: *Negro, colored, black, African-American,* . . .). However, it is not clear that all cases of pejoration are as automatic as this implies. For example, the term *toilet* has undergone pejoration in American English (*bathroom* is the preferred euphemism, at least in my generation), but not in British English. Again, one could argue that the ecological conditions are different (bodily functions are not as taboo in Britain?), but that remains to be demonstrated.

Even if the invisible hand explanation works for pejoration, it can account only for the narrowing of the old term to pejorative contexts; it cannot explain the adoption of the new term for nonpejorative contexts. All speakers would coincidentally have to choose *Dame* (or *bathroom*) for the neutral meaning lost from the original term due to pejoration. This is implausible, because there are normally several alternative choices that could be made, and yet normally just one is established as a convention.[9] It is much more likely that the new term is propagated through a social selection process. The same comments apply to the elimination of homonyms (see also §3.4.1 on homonymy avoidance).

This critique of Keller's examples does not rule out entirely the possibility of drift via an invisible hand process as a propagation mechanism for language change. It does imply that drift via an invisible hand process is a relatively minor propagation mechanism, however.[10]

3.3.3 *Grammaticalization theory*

GRAMMATICALIZATION theory (Lehmann 1982, 1985; Heine & Reh 1984; Heine, Claudi & Hünnemeyer 1991; Heine 1994; Hopper & Traugott 1993; Traugott & Heine 1991; see §6.3) is a theory of how constructions and lexical items develop grammatical functions, including the development of further grammatical functions by already grammaticalized forms. More recent work in grammaticalization theory has emphasized that it is whole constructions, not individual lexical items or morphemes, that undergo grammaticalization (Bybee, Perkins & Pagliuca 1994:11; Traugott 2000). As such, it does not cover (regular) phonological change, many morphological changes, or lexical semantic changes (other than the acquisition of grammatical functions by lexical items). Grammaticalization theory does purport to account for most grammatical change, perhaps all grammatical change depending on whether the theorist considers other processes such as reanalysis and analogical change to be part of grammaticalization or not.

For the grammatical changes covered by grammaticalization theory, it presents a model to characterize all aspects of the change undertaken by a grammatical form or construction: phonological, morphological, syntactic and semantic. Grammaticalization theory argues that such changes tend to occur together, and all in the same direction, essentially towards reduction and tighter integration of form (to the point of fusion or elimination), and with respect to function from more 'concrete' to more 'abstract' (see §6.3.2).

Grammaticalization theory also accommodates the (empirically well-attested) fact that constructions with the same historical origin, but at different degrees of grammaticalization on formal and/or functional dimensions, may coexist in a speech community at a given moment in time. For example, the source construction *[be going to VERB]* (meaning move with intention to VERB), the functionally grammaticalized *[be going to VERB]* (meaning future time reference), and the formally further grammaticalized *[be gonna VERB]* (usually with contracted *be*), all coexist in contemporary English. The last two examples illustrate the fact that grammaticalization theory, like sociohistorical theory, allows the existence of alternative ways of saying the same thing. In fact, Heine *et al.* suggest that

> grammaticalization has to be conceived of as a panchronic process that presents both a diachronic perspective, since it involves change, and a synchronic perspective, since it implies variation that can be described as a system without reference to time. (Heine, Claudi & Hünnemeyer 1991:261)

Grammaticalization theory can easily be interpreted as taking utterances as the basic unit of replication. The panchronic nature of grammaticalization can only be understood by treating grammaticalization as a phenomenon of language, that is, a spatiotemporally bounded population of utterances of a speech community that is also bounded in space and time. Grammaticalization chains are lineages of linguemes (see §2.4.3), either particular morphemes or more complex constructions, including both normal and altered replication.

The mechanisms proposed for grammaticalization all refer to innovation, and all involve the speaker (as the instrument of replication). Altered replication, resulting in an incrementally more grammaticalized lingueme, is argued to fall under a range of processes. Heine *et al.* emphasize the role of metaphorical extension, and account for it in terms of a creative or expressive function (e.g. Heine, Claudi & Hünnemeyer 1991:78 and Heine 1994:259; see also Lehmann 1985:314–17). Traugott emphasizes the role of invited inference, where interlocutors pragmatically reconstruct a different meaning for a particular word or construction from the context of use (see §5.4.3). Keller proposes an invisible hand account for the formal dimensions of grammaticalization, based on work by Helmut Lüdtke (Keller 1990/1994:108–14). These mechanisms will be discussed further in §6.3.2.

Grammaticalization theory does not propose a model of selection, but it does not purport to offer one. As a theory of utterance selection, however, grammaticalization theory is compatible with selection mechanisms proposed by other utterance-based theories such as sociohistorical theory.

3.4   Types of causal mechanisms in language change

In discussing the child-based and utterance-based theories of language change, we have already had to make reference to a number of proposed mechanisms for both innovation and propagation. In this section, I will offer an overview of the types of mechanisms that have been proposed by various historical linguists. Some of these mechanisms will be discussed in further detail in later chapters describing particular processes of language change, such as grammaticalization, reanalysis and language contact. In this section, I will focus on the categorization of the mechanisms in the evolutionary model, that is in terms of normal replication, altered replication and selection. Before doing so, we must discuss a cross-cutting classification of mechanisms, essentially that offered by Keller (see §3.3.2) in terms of artifactual phenomena, natural phenomena, and phenomena of the third kind.

One of the popular misconceptions of evolutionary processes is that they are teleological, that is, they are to be explained in terms of the organism aiming towards some goal. Part of the reason for this misconception is that it is difficult to comprehend that selection is not a teleological process. One does not have to build in the goal of the process; one simply must have a mechanism which causes different interactors to have a differential rate of survival. One such mechanism is adaptation, that is, certain properties of the organism interact with certain properties of the environment such that the likelihood of the organism surviving is increased (or decreased). The result of adaptation is directed selection, such that a greater proportion of organisms with adaptive properties survive.

But adaptation is not teleological. It is not even deterministic. The possession of adaptive properties only increases the probability of survival, it does not guarantee it. In a population of organisms over enough generations, however, the laws of probability will dictate a directed change favoring the better adapted organisms.

These observations about the theory of selection suggest two important points for language change. First, a theory of language change need not appeal to teleological mechanisms in order to account for directionality in language change. Second, language change, even directional language change, is a probabilistic process, not a deterministic one.

There has been some confusion as to what sort of explanations are really teleological. The problem arises because of a third type of mechanism or explanation: those that involve intentional behavior on the part of the speaker. Many linguists criticize intentional mechanisms (usually called functionalist explanations) along with teleological mechanisms, apparently assuming that all intentional mechanisms are teleological (e.g. Labov 1994:549, McMahon 1994:330).

Some intentional mechanisms are teleological, when a speaker is claimed to innovate in order to alter the linguistic system in some way. These mechanisms are what Keller calls artifactual: the linguistic system is designed (by the speaker) to have the structure it does, and to change as it does. Teleological intentional mechanisms are as problematic as other teleological mechanisms (see §3.4.1).

But other intentional behavior is not teleological: the speaker is aiming towards some other goal in language use, and produces an innovation in the process. Hull argues that intentionality in the conduct of science by scientists does not preclude an evolutionary model of conceptual change, pointing out that even in natural selection, intention plays a role:

> For example, a rabbit strives to elude a fox chasing it just as surely as the fox strives to catch it. However, with respect to selection, neither organism is striving to change its future course of evolutionary development, although their behavior may well have this effect. (Hull 1988:471)

That is, intentional processes may not intend to produce linguistic innovations; they occur as unintended side-effects of actions with other goals. As Keller puts it, in response to Lass 1980:

> One way to argue against the possibility of a functionalist explanation of language change is to say that it is not intended. Roger Lass writes, for example, that 'Change does not involve (conscious) human purpose' [Lass 1980:82]; for this reason, among others, he regards functionalist explanations as impossible. It is true that the change . . . is not intended . . . However, 'conscious human purpose' is always 'involved'. One can say that the explanandum [the language change – WAC] is a non-functional effect of functional actions. (Keller 1990/1994:89–90)

Intentional processes give rise to what Keller calls a phenomenon of the third kind: an unintended result of an intended action (Keller 1990/1994:57; see §3.3.2).

I will use the term INTENTIONAL to describe mechanisms that are not teleological but involve the intention of a speaker to achieve some other goal in language use. Teleological analyses have been called 'functional' explanations of sound change, both by proponents (e.g. Martinet 1952/1972; Anttila 1989:181–94) and by critics (e.g. Labov 1994, chapter 19; Lass 1997:352ff.). However, intentional mechanisms have also been called 'functional' explanations. I will refer to teleological mechanisms as SYSTEMIC FUNCTIONAL explanations, since their purported goal is to create, restore, or maintain certain properties of the linguistic system. FUNCTIONAL explanations proper refer only to nonteleological intentional mechanisms.

Still other causal mechanisms for language change that have been proposed are claimed to be neither teleological nor intentional, even in the sense described here. The language change is not even an intended means to achieve some other goal of the speaker. It is simply a change that just happens as a consequence of the act of production (and in some theories, also comprehension) of an utterance. Such mechanisms are sometimes called mechanical, when they apply to motor production in phonetic articulation (e.g. Labov 1994:221). But they can be proposed for higher-level cognitive processes in language use, and so a broader term than 'mechanical' is necessary. I will use the term NONINTENTIONAL to describe this class of causal mechanisms. These correspond most closely to Keller's category of natural processes.

The term 'nonintentional' is somewhat of a misnomer as well. Theories of language change using nonintentional mechanisms do assume that speakers are carrying out an intentional action in language use, namely conforming to the linguistic conventions of their speech community. (Ohala recognizes this in his nonintentional mechanism for sound change, calling it a 'very innocent teleology' [Ohala 1989:191, 1993:262].) The altered replication is an unintended consequence of the speaker trying to carry out her intentions in producing the utterance. The difference between intentional and nonintentional mechanisms for language change is whether or not the innovation is a means towards the intended goal. In intentional mechanisms, the innovation is a means towards the intended goal; in nonintentional mechanisms, it is not.

Teleological mechanisms are highly suspect, and I believe that the balance of evidence, discussed in §3.4.1, weighs against them. On the other hand, it is not obvious to me that one should exclude either intentional or nonintentional mechanisms, at least not on an a priori basis. Neither are teleological, and both can participate in replication and selection processes. In fact, it is not clear that one can always differentiate intentional and nonintentional processes, at least at the grammatical level. In chapter 4, I argue that convention is not sufficient by itself for successful communication. Without a sharp line between conventional and nonconventional language use, it is not always clear whether a speaker is innovating a means to achieve communication, or 'despite' it.

3.4.1   Teleological mechanisms in language change

TELEOLOGICAL MECHANISMS are those in which changing (or preserving) the linguistic system is the explanation of the innovations, either as the intended goal of the speaker in her behavior, or as some mysterious law that linguistic systems submit to in their evolution.

Applying this definition of teleological mechanisms shows that some changes described as nonteleological are in fact teleological. For example, in her historical linguistics textbook, McMahon discusses the deletion of intervocalic /s/ in Ancient Greek. This apparently phonologically conditioned process is blocked just when the /s/ is the only means to distinguish present and future tense forms of verbs. McMahon writes:

> Either a teleological or a non-teleological explanation can be invoked here. According to the teleological one, the sound change is blocked . . . because the future and present would be formally identical if the /s/ were lost. The non-teleological account proposes that /s/ was lost in all cases, but was later reintroduced . . . since this reintroduced the formal present–future distinction. (McMahon 1994:332)

The teleological account is indeed so, since the purported goal is to maintain the present/future distinction in the linguistic system. The 'non-teleological account' is in fact two processes. The first is the purely phonological loss of intervocalic /s/, presumably genuinely nonteleological. The second is the reintroduction of /s/, in order to maintain the present/future distinction. This process is also teleological. In fact, the only difference between the two accounts is the relative timing of the two processes.

The Ancient Greek example is a case of a teleological mechanism to avoid homonymy (in this case, of the present and future forms). Avoiding homonymy can be described in a purely teleological fashion: to preserve phonological, lexical and/or grammatical distinctions in the grammatical system, such that there is a one-to-one mapping from forms to meanings. Homonymy avoidance can also be described as intentional rather than teleological, however: that is, in order to avoid misunderstanding in communication (Martinet 1952/1972:144; see below and §3.4.4).

The converse of avoiding homonymy is the creation and/or maintenance of uniformity of stem forms and inflections in morphological paradigms. The process by which this is achieved is called ANALOGY. Analogy is not a mechanism for innovation but a class of changes. McMahon divides analogy into (more or less) general processes and sporadic processes. General analogical processes are analogical extension, such as the spread of the English plural allomorph /-s/ at the expense of other forms (McMahon 1994:71–2), and analogical levelling, in which the number of stem allomorphs is reduced, as in the following German example (McMahon 1994:74):

(7)

	Old High German	Modern German
present	kiu[s]an	küren
past singular	ko[s]	kor
past plural	ku[r]un	koren
past participle	(gi-)ko[r]an	gekoren

Analogical extension leads to uniformity of affix and analogical levelling leads to uniformity of stem. The teleological explanation for this phenomenon is iconicity, more specifically isomorphism (see §5.6): speakers aim to preserve uniformity of the mapping from form to meaning in morphological paradigms. Sporadic analogical changes (including contamination, back formation and folk etymologies) are accounted for in the same way: an association of meanings leads to a change in form towards greater similarity. For instance, there are some examples in which adjacent numerals come to share initial consonants: Proto-Indo-European *kwetwer/*penkwe evolved to English *four/five* (generalizing the labial stop of *penkwe) and conversely, Latin *quattuor/ quinque* (generalizing the labialized velar of *kwetwer).

Another purely teleological mechanism is the idea that speakers attempt to preserve symmetry in a linguistic system. Martinet argues that certain types of phoneme segment innovations represent 'the filling of "holes in the pattern"' (Martinet 1952/1972:159). Martinet gives the example of the vowels of the Hauteville dialect of Franco-Provençal:

(8) i   ü   u
      e   ö   o   ẽ
      ɛ   ɛ̃   ɔ̃
           a   ã

This system is asymmetric. Martinet argues that there was a shift such that ɛ was lowered to æ and a moved back, giving a symmetrical oral vowel system. The movement of two vowels is an example of a CHAIN SHIFT. If the a moved first, it would be a DRAG-CHAIN, so to speak dragging the ε down. If the ε moved first, it would be a PUSH-CHAIN, so to speak pushing the a back. (In this example, it is not clear which change occurred first.) However, the nasal system is still asymmetric. There was a chain shift such that $\tilde{e} > \tilde{\varepsilon}$, $\tilde{\varepsilon} > \varepsilon$, $\varepsilon > \mathit{æ} > a$ and $a > \mathit{ɔ}$ (Martinet 1952/1972:145; he includes the $\varepsilon > a$ shift in the chain). The result is another symmetric system:

(9)   i   ü   u
    e   ö   o
      ε ɔ $\tilde{\varepsilon}$ $\tilde{ɔ}$
        a $\tilde{a}$

Teleological mechanisms such as Martinet's are problematic in theoretical and empirical respects. How do symmetric systems become asymmetrical in the first place? This objection can be countered by the hypothesis that other changes are nonteleological, and that other parts of the linguistic system can change, affecting the phoneme segment inventory. (One might still ask, why is the linguistic system overall not perfectly balanced so that asymmetry would never arise?)

There is a much more serious empirical problem: there is a relatively high tolerance of homonymy, allomorphy and asymmetry in linguistic systems. There is a very high degree of ambiguity of words and especially grammatical morphemes (see chapter 4). For example, there are many languages which do not make a present/future distinction (such as Japanese), hence the potential homonymy of the Greek present and future forms cannot be a strong motivating factor. Also, Lass points out that there is already homonymy between indicative and subjunctive active 1st person singular present forms; and intervocalic /s/ survived in the first aorist, although it was not 'needed' to distinguish the aorist from other forms (Lass 1997:356). Lass also points out an example of sound changes in the history of English *tell/told* in which more allomorphy is created than lost (Lass 1980:71–3). (However, it should be pointed out that no systematic cross-linguistic survey of the frequency of homonymy and allomorphy in morphological paradigms has been made, to my knowledge.)

Labov surveys a number of studies of variable deletion of phonological segments that also occur as markers of inflectional categories, such as English /t/~/d/ (past tense), Spanish and Portuguese /s/ (noun plural, 3rd singular subject agreement), Spanish /n/ (3rd plural subject agreement), Ladakhi /s/ (perfect) (Labov 1994, chapter 19). According to the systemic functional analysis, the segments are less likely to be deleted when they indicate the inflectional category in question. The studies that Labov surveys give no consistent evidence for a teleological mechanism. From a typological perspective, it can be observed that many languages lack tense marking, plural marking and subject agreement; hence there is no strong 'need' for a language to maintain these inflectional categories. Moreover, many languages lose tense, number and other inflections. If homonymy avoidance was a significant factor, these inflections would not be lost.

With respect to symmetry, many phonological systems allow for gaps in their segment inventories, as in the following inventory from Beja (Cushitic), taken from Maddieson (1984:316):

(10)

–	t	–	ʈ	–	k	kʷ	ʔ
b	d	–	ɖ	–	g	gʷ·	
–	–	ʤ	–	–	–	–	
f	s	ʃ	–	–	–	–	
m	n	–	–	–	–	–	
w	–	–	–	j	–	–	

These gaps conform to phonetically motivated typological generalizations, and it is not clear that there is a tendency for phonological systems to fill gaps.[11]

In syntax and lexicon, there are very many cases of overlapping forms (partial synonymy) in grammaticalization, which implies the nonexistence of push-chains (this argument is made by Haspelmath 1997:89; see also Vincent 1978:412 and references cited therein). For example, Haspelmath's study of the typology and grammaticalization of indefinite pronouns revealed many overlapping forms in the basic functions that Haspelmath identified, such as the Finnish indefinites used in interrogative constructions (Haspelmath 1997:294):

(11) Soitt -i   -ok **joku?**
      call   -PAST.3SG -Q   someone

(12) Soitt -i   -ok **kuka** **-an?**
      call   -PAST.3SG -Q   who   -INDEF

'Did someone/anyone call?'

Finally, there is good reason to believe that at the morphosyntactic level, true gaps, that is, expressive gaps, are extremely rare and do not drive language change. Let us consider one specific case to illustrate the empirical problems of systemic functional explanations of language change. On the face of it, the innovation of new 2nd person plural forms in various dialects of English (*you guys, you all / y'all, youse, you'uns, you lot*, etc.) appears to be filling a gap in the pronoun paradigm of English that was created by the replacement of the familiar (formerly singular) *thou* by the formal (formerly plural) *you* in all of its 2nd person uses. The creation of new 2nd person plural forms would be an example of a drag-chain process leading to the selection of a new symmetric grammatical system.[12]

But it is not the case that there is no way for a speaker of English to refer to multiple addressees. A speaker of English could always use some form to denote multiple addressees, either the highly grammaticalized *you*, now also used for the singular (cf. Lass 1997:360), or an ungrammaticalized locution such as the quantified *all of you* or the appositional *you people*, or a term of address such as *ladies and gentleman*. Grammaticalization would account for the new nonstandard forms as instances of a grammaticalization chain: certain semantic domains (admittedly, for reasons not yet fully explained) naturally give rise to innovations that are more grammaticalized, that is, phonologically and syntactically more integrated. Plurals, especially pronoun plurals, are prime candidates for grammaticalization because of their highly 'grammatical' semantic character. What we see in colloquial varieties of English is altered replication via grammaticalization, and selection presumably occurring for social reasons other than adherence to the standard (note the variety of 2nd person plural forms in the different dialects, and also that some speakers use multiple forms).

The systemic functional and grammaticalization accounts make different predictions for the cross-linguistic distribution of this grammaticalization process. The systemic functional account would predict that the creation of new plural personal pronoun forms would occur generally in systems with a gap at that point in the pronominal paradigm – ideally, always and only in such systems. The grammaticalization account predicts that this process can and does happen independently of whether such a gap exists. There are many pronominal systems across the world's languages that have gaps in pronominal number. Ingram's (1978) summary of pronominal systems based on Forchheimer's (1953) survey indicates approximately 20% of languages have gaps in number.[13] The relatively high number of pronoun systems with gaps suggests that systems with gaps are not that unstable, as the systemic functional explanation would predict. On the other hand, there are cases where new plural forms arose where old ones existed, and the new plural morphemes are even added onto the old plural forms (as has happened in many Turkic languages for the 1st and 2nd person pronouns; see §5.5.3).

The commonness of both of these latter processes, REPLACEMENT and REINFORCEMENT as they are standardly called in historical linguistics, counts strongly against the systemic functional hypothesis. As I have noted several times above, there are usually several ways to say the same thing available in a grammar. Thus, linguistic systems are not that elegantly symmetrical in the first place.

But perhaps the greatest objection is that there is no plausible theory motivating a teleological mechanism. Sometimes a teleological mechanism is implied to hold of language as an abstract system. But a language does not change as an abstract system; the abstract system of language should not be reified (see §1.2). Instead, innovations must be brought about ultimately as a result of actions by speakers. Yet there is no obvious motivation for speakers to innovate in order to make the grammatical system more symmetrical, or to preserve distinctions for the sake of preserving distinctions. Speakers have many goals when they use language, but changing the linguistic system is not one of them.

Teleological mechanisms, defined here as language changes for the sake of altering the linguistic system itself, are as suspect in the theory of language change as they are in the theory of biological evolution or of conceptual change in science. However, it should be pointed out that some changes that have been interpreted as teleological could in fact be nonteleological but intentional. One such sort of change is the avoidance of homonymy. Avoidance of homonymy may follow from interlocutor intention, that is, the purpose of not being misunderstood. The discussion above demonstrates that the tolerance of ambiguity by interlocutors is actually quite high, as will be seen in discussing the nature of communication in chapter 4. Although not being misunderstood may contribute to language change as an intentional mechanism for innovation (see §3.4.4), avoiding homonymy plays at best a marginal role. Analogical processes may also occur via nonteleological mechanisms. In §6.2, following Bybee (1985), I will suggest a nonintentional mechanism for analogy based on the organization of morphological and syntactic information in the mind.

In sum, there appears to be little reason for a theory of language change to invoke teleological mechanisms.

3.4.2 *Mechanisms for normal replication*

Having argued against teleological mechanisms, I now turn to intentional and nonintentional mechanisms for normal replication, altered replication and selection.

Theorists of language change who have proposed mechanisms for language change have generally not distinguished between altered replication (innovation) and selection (propagation). Fewer historical linguists have addressed the issue of normal replication, that is, the state of affairs where there is no change. Nevertheless, at least two frameworks for intentional mechanisms of language change have proposed a range of mechanisms that can be interpreted as covering all three processes.

Jakobson proposed a functional account of language behavior (Jakobson 1960/1971), which has been subsequently appealed to for intentional mechanisms of language change. In particular, later linguists have continued to rely on three of Jakobson's functions of language use:

(13)   a.   *Referential function*: communication of information
        b.   *Poetic function*: creativity/expressivity
        c.   *Phatic function*: solidarity/conformity with social norms

There is a good reason from our vantage point that these three functions are the ones that continue to be used in linguistic theory.[14] Somewhat imperfectly, they represent the three processes involved in utterance selection. The referential function is related to conformity to convention (normal replication). The poetic function is a commonly invoked intentional mechanism for violation of convention (altered replication). The phatic function leads to the establishment or acceptance of a convention (selection).

Keller (1990/1994) proposes a more detailed model of speaker's intentional behavior that subsumes and improves upon Jakobson's. Keller does not represent his theory of language use as a reformulation of Jakobson's. What Keller does seek to do is provide an interactional characterization for the three Jakobsonian functions. Keller begins with a hypermaxim analogous to Grice's Cooperative Principle:

(14)   'Talk in such a way that you are most likely to reach the goals that you
       set for yourself in your communicative enterprise . . . at the lowest possible
       cost' (Keller 1990/1994:106, 107)

This hypermaxim describes the goal of linguistic interaction as having nothing to do with normal replication, altered replication or selection, in line with
a nonteleological account of language change. Keller then proposes a set of
maxims that carry out the hypermaxim just as Grice's maxims carry out the
Cooperative Principle. It is following those maxims which has the effect of
normal replication, differential replication, or selection. Since Keller's list of
maxims is fairly extensive, I will use them as the starting point for the discussion of mechanisms for the three processes underlying utterance selection.

Keller replaces Jakobson's referential function with what he calls Humboldt's
maxim:

(15)   'Talk in such a way that you are understood' (Keller 1990/1994:94), or
       more precisely, 'Talk in a way in which you believe the other would talk
       if he or she were in your place' (ibid. 99)

This maxim basically has the (unintended) consequence of conforming to linguistic convention: the hearer is highly likely to understand the speaker if she
conforms to the linguistic conventions of the hearer's speech community.

Keller states, 'this is one of the most fundamental maxims of communication' (Keller 1990/1994:99). This is because conformity to convention is normal
replication (see §4.2.4 and §7.3 for further discussion of convention). It is an
intentional mechanism, in our definition of the term, and is based on social
interaction – mutual knowledge of the conventions.

But mutual knowledge also entails individual knowledge of the conventions
of the language. We may now define a grammar (in the sense defined in §2.4.1)
as an individual's knowledge of conventions. The term COMPETENCE is also
used to describe an individual's knowledge of conventions. Competence and
conventions are not the same and should not be confused. Competence is an
individual psychological phenomenon, while convention is a social interpersonal phenomenon. Competence can vary; it depends on how well an individual knows the conventions of the community. Conventions are also variable,
but in a different way: conventions vary in the degree to which they are established in a speech community.

Competence can also drive language use partly independent of social convention. For example, it is not just that the use of the word *kleenex* is a
convention of American English that I am conforming to. Using the word
kleenex is a habit I have developed, as an American English speaker. Psychological habit is the ENTRENCHMENT or routinization of behavior (Langacker
1987:59); and the more a behavior is entrenched, the less control a person has
in using it. For example, I produce the word *kleenex* even in Britain because it
is entrenched in my mind, even though it is not the British English convention
and I know it is not, and hence not the best way to communicate with my

interlocutors; and even though I am not intentionally identifying myself as an American by using *kleenex* (see §3.4.3, §7.4.2). This phenomenon cannot always be attributed to lack of knowledge of the conventions of the speech community. It is merely an entrenched behavior of members of a speech community, indicating geographical origin, age group, sex, socioeconomic status, etc. to a degree that members do not fully control.

To the extent that production of a form is due to entrenchment as a purely automatic psychological process, then it represents a nonintentional mechanism of normal replication. As was argued in §3.3.1, entrenchment – grammatical knowledge – is sensitive to exposure to use. Entrenchment is reinforced through use (comprehension as well as production), and decays through lack of use (as any rusty second language learner can attest). Thus, it is more accurate to describe entrenchment, or rather variation in entrenchment relative to exposure to language use, as a mechanism for selection. For this reason, we now turn to selection mechanisms (also, the large number of mechanisms for altered replication merits leaving their discussion until the end of this section).

3.4.3 *Mechanisms for selection*

Mechanisms for selection, intentional or otherwise, can be distinguished from the mechanism for normal replication. The mechanism for normal replication involves simple replication of the existing structure, thereby extending its lineage. Selection mechanisms involve selection among, that is, differential replication of, already existing variants. Mechanisms for selection can also be distinguished from mechanisms for altered replication. Selection requires previously created variants to operate on, choosing one over another. Mechanisms of altered replication create novel variants that did not already exist in that lineage (of course, the same novel variant may be coincidentally created in a different lineage). For utterance selection, mechanisms of selection are those that favor a particular form being adopted among members of a speech community.

Keller proposes a maxim that essentially replaces Jakobson's phatic function:

(16) 'Talk like the others talk' (Keller 1990/1994:100)

Keller includes other maxims which he calls variants of (16):

(17) 'talk in such a way that you are recognized as a member of the group' (Keller 1990/1994:100)

(18) 'talk like the people around you' (ibid.)

The variants in (17–18), of talking like those in 'the group', usually meaning those around you, is equivalent to the social psychological theory of ACCOMMODATION (Trudgill 1986; Giles & Smith 1979; see §7.4.2). In the more general maxim in (16), the 'others' that Keller alludes to need not be the group to which one's interlocutor belongs. Instead, the others are the social group you wish to identify with. This maxim is equivalent to the theory that talking involves an ACT OF IDENTITY (LePage & Tabouret-Keller 1985; see §7.4.2).

Another mechanism that has been proposed for selection is PRESTIGE (Labov 1966). Prestige is often invoked in class-based approaches to sociohistorical linguistics. Variants associated with the higher socioeconomic classes, the standard variants, are propagated down the social class hierarchy. These approaches also recognize the existence of COVERT PRESTIGE (Labov 1966; Trudgill 1972), where a lower class vernacular variant is propagated through an inversion of overt class values. These intentional mechanisms for selection are discussed in chapter 7.

Reinforcement and decay of entrenchment represent a nonintentional mechanism for selection. If a speaker replicates one form instead of another as a function of exposure to use (measured for example by token frequency) rather than as an act of identity or accommodation, then differential replication has occurred independent of any intentional goal of the speaker. In fact, differential replication may occur despite any intentional goal of the speaker. To give an anecdotal example: on occasions I have produced a British English form in the United States, even though American English is my native variety. The British English was incomprehensible to my interlocutors, and was not likely to be even an unconscious effort to identify with my country of residence. I simply could not remember the American English form. Lack of exposure to the American English form combined with exposure to the British English form led to replication of the latter despite intentional selective pressures to the contrary.

3.4.4 Mechanisms for altered replication

Keller provides a series of maxims that more or less replace Jakobson's poetic function (Keller 1990/1994:101):

(19)   Talk in such a way that you are noticed.

(20)   Talk in such a way that you are not recognizable as a member of the group.

(21)   Talk in an amusing, funny, etc. way.

(22)   Talk in an especially polite, flattering, charming, etc. way.

This heterogeneous set of maxims provides an interactional purpose for the poetic function of language that is absent from Jakobson's formulation, and, in this respect, Keller's theory is an improvement on Jakobson's.

The poetic maxims, that is, increased expressiveness, are very widely invoked as a mechanism of differential replication, in theories as varied as the invisible hand theory, the child-based generative theory (Lightfoot 1991:160, 171; see §3.2), grammaticalization theory (Heine 1994:259 and Lehmann 1985:314–17; see §6.3.2), and others (e.g. Harris & Campbell 1995:54, 73 on what they call 'exploratory expressions').

Another one of Keller's maxims is at least as significant as expressiveness:

(23)   'Talk in such a way that you are not misunderstood' (Keller 1990/1994:94)

This maxim appears to complement Humboldt's maxim; but it is not the same. Speaking in order not to be misunderstood cannot be reduced to conformity with linguistic convention. One can speak cryptically or confusingly and still be conforming to linguistic convention. Conversely, one might use a paraphrase or circumlocution that is not the conventional expression for an idea, in order to not be misunderstood. This maxim represents a more prosaic intention than being expressive, but it may be more significant in language change, and Keller suggests it is central in understanding processes related to grammaticalization (see §6.3.2).

Keller posits one other maxim for differential replication, his version of the ECONOMY PRINCIPLE (Zipf 1935; Martinet 1952/1972:168; see Gabelentz 1901/1969:256, cited in Heine 1994:275):

(24)   Talk in such a way that you do not expend superfluous energy (Keller 1990/1994:101)

The economy principle has been frequently cited as a prime motivation for language change, in particular the erosion of form and the elliptical nature of speech. However, this maxim is problematic from the perspective of the interactional nature of language use in that it is not obviously oriented towards social interaction. For example, Keller had to explicitly build it into his hypermaxim (see 14). Keller justifies doing so because economy is a maxim referring to the 'cost' of talking, not 'profit' therefrom (Keller 1990/1994:107). It is possible, however, to see economy as being at least partially motivated by speaker interaction, and not just a psychological processing effect.

There is a plausible interactional motivation for economy. Economy may serve the interlocutors' goal of using as little time as possible in achieving their other interactional goals (this is Clark's immediacy premise; see §4.2.4). This joint goal is a common but not necessary goal of communication, of course. There are social contexts such as filibustering a legislative bill in the United States Senate, or keeping the floor in a conversation, where the opposite goal is desired. This exception proves the rule: minimizing the time involved in achieving the extralinguistic goals is a joint goal of some, perhaps most, but not all conversations. Hence economy cannot be assumed to occur in language use as an automatic consequence of psychological processing tendencies.

There is another interactional motivation for economy of effort. It was observed by Zipf and enshrined in the principle of economic motivation in typology (Greenberg 1966; Haiman 1983, 1985; Bybee 1985; Croft 1990, chapters 4–7; Haiman 1994), that erosion of form is highly correlated with frequency of occurrence in language use. For example, it is not an accident that in the general American speech community, certain wine varietals are called *Cabernet Sauvignon*, *Gewurztraminer*, *Zinfandel* and *Chardonnay*, but in the community of California wine connoisseurs where these varietals are a central topic of conversation, they are called *Cab*, *Gewurz*, *Zin* and *Chard*. The energy expended in an utterance becomes more superfluous, the more frequently it is used, hence the shorter the expression for it is likely to be(come). But what explains frequency of use? It is not frequency of occurrence in the world, but frequency of being talked about. Frequency of being talked about is a consequence of (joint) salience for the members of the relevant speech community. Hence joint salience determines frequency of use, which in turn motivates erosion of form (via the joint goal of minimizing time expended described in the preceding paragraph).

Expressiveness (or creativity), avoiding misunderstanding, and economy are all intentional mechanisms of altered replication. Nonintentional mechanisms of altered replication (innovation) have also been proposed in various theories of language change.

The first example of a nonintentional mechanism for differential replication is speech errors. This mechanism, proposed in the 19th century by Paul, is empirically untenable, because the sorts of novel forms created by speech errors are not the sorts of language changes that are empirically attested (Aitchison 1991:174–8). Aitchison points out that the majority of speech errors involve more than one word, and thus differ from most sound changes. Those involving a single word are typically malapropisms (choice of the wrong word), blends, and switching of segments. Although there are cases of changes due to folk etymologies, blends and metatheses, these are relatively rare processes in language change, and speech errors have little to say about the much more common sorts of sound change.

A number of nonintentional (mechanical) processes have been proposed for regular or Neogrammarian sound changes (so called because the Neogrammarians first postulated exceptionless sound changes). These explanations can be divided into two types, articulatory or auditory.

Articulatory mechanisms for altered replication of phonemes can be described as target-missing mechanisms: the speaker aims to produce a particular sound, but overshoots or undershoots the target, for essentially physiological reasons. Lindblom (1983) argues that most sound change involves undershoot. He attributes the tendency to undershoot to the economy principle: 'economizing occurs only insofar as it is purposeful' (Lindblom 1983:232). Hence Lindblom's mechanism for articulatory innovations is intentional rather than nonintentional.

Labov allows for overshoot as well as undershoot in appropriate contexts. In surveying chain shifts of vowels, he proposes a series of principles, at least some of which could be accounted for by purely articulatory mechanisms, rather than teleological symmetry preservation (Labov 1994:116, 280–5).[15] He suggests a causal mechanism for the fact that long vowels rise and short vowels fall, based on a hypothesis by Sievers (1881): 'in pronouncing a long vowel, speakers tend to overshoot the target, whereas in pronouncing a short vowel, they tend to undershoot' (Labov 1994:221). Since the mechanism involves overshoot as well as undershoot, it cannot be interpreted as an instance of the economy principle. Labov denies any other intentional or teleological interpretation (in terms of increasing contrast), instead suggesting it is a purely mechanical effect (ibid.).

Ohala has proposed a nonintentional causal mechanism for the innovation of at least some examples of sound change based not on articulation but on audition; hence he calls it a listener-based model of sound change (Ohala 1981, 1989, 1992, 1993). Ohala assumes that in articulation, a speaker is attempting to achieve normal replication of a phoneme based on her having learned the phoneme through audition. The hearer must analyze the mapping between a phonological entity and its phonetic realizations. But the phonology–phonetics mapping is complex – for example, there is a massive amount of coarticulation of segments (see Lindblom 1983:220). Phonetic realization is also highly variable: 'one of the most important discoveries of modern instrumental phonetics is the incredible amount of variation that exists in pronunciation, not only between speakers but also in the speech of a single speaker' (Ohala 1989:176). Because of the complexity and variability of the mapping, reanalysis of the mapping is always possible, leading to altered replication of the phoneme. Moreover, words consist of a fixed sequence of phonological units, so the complex phonetic coarticulation patterns repeatedly recur, further favoring reanalysis of the phonological units underlying the phonetic reality of a word (Ohala 1993:264; recall from §2.4.3 that words are independent replicators that can specify phonetic properties of their component linguemes).

Ohala describes two types of reanalysis, hypocorrection and hypercorrection. In HYPOCORRECTION, the listener reanalyzes a phonetic property of a segment as an inherent phonological feature of that segment and includes it in the phonological representation of that segment. Ohala cites vowel nasalization as a typical case. The nasalization of a vowel before a nasal consonant is a natural physical process, usually factored out. The listener may reanalyze the nasality as an inherent property of the vowel, leading ultimately to a phonemic nasalized vowel (Ohala 1989:186). Ohala attributes assimilation processes in general to hypocorrection.

In HYPERCORRECTION, a listener reanalyzes a phonetic property of a segment as having spread from another segment and factors it out of the phonological representation of the segment in question. Ohala accounts for dissimilation in this way, giving the following examples (Ohala 1989:189):

(25) a. Proto-Quechumaran *t'ant'a* > Quechua *t'anta* 'bread'
      b. Ancient Chinese *pjam* > Cantonese *pin* 'diminish'
      c. PIE $b^h end^h$ > Sanskrit *band^h*- 'bind'

Since hypocorrection and hypercorrection involve two opposite results, Ohala proposes constraints to differentiate the two (Ohala 1992, 1993). Hypocorrection commonly results in the loss of the conditioning environment, since the phonetic properties of the conditioning environment are reanalyzed as part of the altered segment. Hypercorrection never results in such a loss, since the property factored out of the altered segment is attributed to the other segment. Hypocorrection can create a new segment type but hypercorrection does not, since the reason a phonetic property is factored out is because the listener identifies the segment with another segment type existing in the language.

Hypercorrection is also typically restricted to factoring out of phonetic properties that require a longer period of time to be perceived.

Ohala's model does not call for any intentional processes other than the attempt to conform to the conventions of the speech community. Ohala criticizes explanations of sound change due to economy and other intentional and teleological factors, arguing that they are difficult to justify and moreover unnecessary, at least for the classes of sound changes that he has investigated (e.g. Ohala 1989:191–3, 1993:260–1).

It is not clear whether Ohala's research program to eliminate intentional mechanisms of innovation will succeed. Certainly normal replication – adherence to convention – is an intentional mechanism that nonintentional mechanisms cannot do without. Nevertheless, it is worth investigating the possibility that nonintentional mechanisms can account for a number of types of language changes, including grammatical changes. Vincent suggests that those features of language that are less in the speaker's awareness or control, such as sound change, will change mechanically, while those more in a speaker's awareness, such as grammatical change, may be teleological (Vincent 1978:416). I have argued against teleological mechanisms for innovation; but it may be that Vincent's hypothesis applies to nonintentional vs intentional mechanisms. That is, nonintentional mechanisms for innovation are more likely to be found at lower levels of organization such as sound structure, while intentional mechanisms are more likely to be found at higher levels.

While Vincent's hypothesis is quite plausible, one might nevertheless suggest that (barring direct evidence to the contrary) a good methodological strategy would be to seek nonintentional mechanisms first, and only turn to intentional mechanisms if those fail. In that spirit, I will propose that many grammatical changes may involve a nonintentional reanalysis of the mapping between grammatical form and conventional meaning or function. In chapter 4, I argue that even in normal replication of a word or construction, the mapping between form and function is extremely complex and variable. In chapter 5, I will suggest that reanalysis of the form–function mapping is always possible, and propose a set of form–function reanalyses for the innovation of a number of types of grammatical changes.

Table 3.1 on page 79 summarizes the mechanisms surveyed above (those argued against above are given in square brackets).

3.5 The concept of progress in biological evolution and language change

In §3.4, I have argued against teleological mechanisms of language change, and argued instead that nonteleological mechanisms, both intentional and nonintentional, are more appropriate mechanisms for language change, just as they are for biological evolution and conceptual change. In this section, I will address the question of whether there is progress in language change.

The idea of progress in evolution is associated with teleology. A teleological mechanism specifies some goal, and progress can be defined as movement

TABLE 3.1   Causal mechanisms of language change

	Teleological	*Intentional*	*Nonintentional*
Normal replication	–	convention (being understood)	entrenchment
Selection	–	accommodation acts of identity prestige (including covert prestige)	change in entrenchment
Altered replication	[preserve distinctions] [preserve symmetry/ gap filling] [preserver isomorphism]	expressiveness not being misunderstood economy	over/undershoot hypercorrection hypocorrection form-function reanalysis [speech errors]

towards that goal. But teleology and progress are independent of each other. If the goal is constantly changing in different directions, then following the goal will not lead to progress, where progress is defined as continuous movement in a single direction. (Progress is usually defined as movement in an allegedly positive direction; but the judgement of what is positive is so subjective that the more neutral description is better.) Conversely, a nonteleological process such as selection can be progressive, if it moves steadily in one direction – for example, increased adaptation to the environment.

Hence selection as a process could, a priori, be GLOBALLY progressive, that is, represent continuous movement in one direction. Selection is always LOCALLY progressive, that is, there is a change in a direction defined by the mechanisms of selection. But 'as I understand the current state of evolutionary biology, a respectable number of evolutionary biologists think that biological evolution is no more than locally progressive' (Hull 1988:464). Hull gives two reasons why biological evolution is only locally progressive. First, the environment is so variable, yesterday's adaptive improvement may be today's dysfunctional trait, and who knows what tomorrow will bring: 'because so many aspects of their environments change so rapidly and haphazardly, species seem to be forever chasing their changing environments' (Hull 1988:467). One way in which the environment is continually changing is the cycle of climate changes. Another way is the fact that the environment includes other organisms. For example, there has been extensive coevolution of flowering plants with their insect or avian pollinators, and also trees with mycorrhizal fungi that pass on nutrients to them; as one evolves (or goes extinct) so does the other.

The second reason that there is only local progress has to do with the nature of the selection process:

> Natural selection is a process capable of only local maximization . . . Compromises are constantly made in biological evolution. Chief among these is balancing the needs of personal survival with the needs of reproduction. If either side is shorted too drastically, the effect is the same – extinction. (Hull 1988:473)

However, Hull suggests that global progress occurred during an earlier phase of the history of the Earth. Hull is not referring to the evolution of a single organism as superior to other organisms; he vigorously (and entertainingly) criticizes this view (Hull 1988:461–2, 469–70). Instead, he is referring to the overall adaptation of organisms to the environment, assuming relatively fixed environmental constraints:

> Initially in the history of life, when so much of the environment was empty, selection was not very rigorous and everything increased but very slowly. As the earth filled up, selective forces became more rigorous and species packing increased until there was little room for improvement without a compensating loss occurring elsewhere . . . (Hull 1988:461)

Hull quotes Gould as stating that after the Cambrian explosion, 'inhabitants change continually, but the roles remain' (Gould 1977:19, quoted in ibid.), and himself adds, 'About the only instance in which evolution has had a direction during the past 500 million years is the surprisingly late exploitation of air as an adaptive zone' (ibid.). Of course, this only applies to a very general characterization of ecological niches; the examples of coevolution show that at a finer scale, there is still continuous change.

The notion of progress in language was prevalent in the 19th century, but is universally condemned today by professional linguists. (It survives robustly outside the realm of linguistics, in the notion of standard languages as superior to vernaculars, and the laments over the 'decline' of the standard whenever it changes towards the vernacular.) Part of the reason for the condemnation was the subjective evaluation of 'primitive' cultures as inferior to 'civilized' ones, or of modern languages as inferior to classical ones. However, the preceding discussion of the notion of progress in biological evolution should allow us to reopen the question and examine it without prejudice in either direction.

First, recall that progress is defined as directed change; no evaluative judgement is assumed here. It seems clear that there is virtually no global progress, that is, continued change in a single direction, in phonological and grammatical (morphosyntactic) change. The reason for this is parallel to the post-Cambrian state of affairs of life on Earth. All contemporary languages, and all earlier languages for which we have written records, are general-purpose communication systems at a coarse scale of description. It may be the case that before recorded history, language-like communication systems had not filled out the space of communicative possibilities, and global progress was possible. But once the space of communicative possibilities had been filled up (at this coarse view), no further progress could be made.

Instead, what we find is cyclic changes of linguistic subsystems, all of which are well enough adapted to effective communication that no one structural type has a decided functional advantage over the others. These changes are essentially locally progressive, that is, they involve directionality for a short period of time, but then turn back on themselves (completion of the cycle). For example, there is a typological classification of the morphological types of languages in terms of the number of concepts encoded in individual morphemes and words. In the 19th century, this classification was postulated to be globally progressive. Languages moved from an isolating type (one morpheme/concept per word) to agglutinative (multiple morphemes per word, each morpheme expressing a concept) to fusional (multiple concepts per morpheme). Evidence of the first shift, for example, is the development of compounds in an isolating language such as Mandarin Chinese. The ancient Indo-European languages were fusional: a form such as Latin *cantat* 'he or she sings' combines 3rd singular agreement, present tense, indicative mood in the suffix. But further examination of the facts demonstrated that fusional languages tended towards reduction of inflections, leading to a more isolating type, as has happened in English and French. Also, the process of morphological change turns out to be local in another sense, in that some parts of the grammar of a single language are at different stages in the cycle. For example, the contraction of English auxiliaries and negation is approaching fusion in some cases (*won't*, nonstandard *ain't*), while many word derivational affixes are more agglutinating (cf. *linguist-ic-al-ly*).

The reasons for these cyclic changes also appear to be parallel to the reasons for only local progression in biological evolution. The environment at a fine-grained scale is constantly changing. That is, parts of the language system are changing in ways that affect other parts of the language system, leading to further changes. The subsequent changes need not be 'compensatory' for the initial change – that would be a teleological explanation – but merely consequences of the original change in some way or another.

Research in the interconnections among grammatical systems (that is, cross-linguistic implicational universals in typology) have revealed some interconnections among grammatical systems that are manifested in chains of historical changes. For example, there are well-known implicational universals linking the word order of subject-verb-object, adposition-noun, adjective-noun and genitive-noun. In the Semitic languages of Ethiopia, an original verb-subject-object word order changed to subject-object-verb order, presumably due to contact with local languages. Once that change occurred, it appears that there was a gradual shift to adjective-noun order from noun-adjective order, then to genitive-noun order from noun-genitive order, then finally to postpositions from prepositions (Greenberg 1980; he also reports evidence of a similar pattern in the history of the Iranian languages). These subsequent shifts in word order were presumably triggered by whatever underlying factors account for the implicational universals of word order that link these patterns (Greenberg 1966/1990).

The second explanation for only local progress in biology is also invoked in diachronic typological research. Typologists have advocated competing motivation models of language change and the cross-linguistic variation that is the result of language change (see especially Haiman 1985). The competing motivations are essentially local maximizations of communicative value. The commonest example of competing motivation given in typology is that between economy and iconicity. Economic motivation, as discussed above (see 24), is the preference of shorter forms, or even zero expression, particularly for expressing concepts that are frequent in use. Iconic motivation is the overt expression of concepts, presumably motivated by the goal of not being misunderstood (see 23 and §5.6).

Competition between economy and iconicity can be illustrated in the development and loss of number inflections. Synchronically, one finds languages with economic encoding of the singular number, as zero, and overt (iconic) encoding of the plural (e.g. English); but one also finds languages with overt encoding of singular as well as plural (e.g. Latvian), and languages with economic encoding of both singular and plural, i.e. no inflection for number at all (e.g. Mandarin Chinese). Diachronically, one finds languages both acquiring and losing number inflections, both plural and singular. For example, a pronominal plural marker in Mandarin can be used with nouns referring to humans, and could extend to other nouns; but the plural marking of French nouns and adjectives is disappearing as a result of the loss of final consonants. There is certainly no global directed change towards the acquisition (or loss) of number inflections.

The use of language for communication provides an explanation of not only why language change is not globally progressive, but also why it is locally progressive. Language change is not globally progressive because all human languages have already progressed to being general-purpose communication systems, at the coarse-grained level. At a more fine-grained level, the environment for grammatical structures is constantly changing. This is because all changes are local, yet the language system is interconnected (see §2.4.3) and the local changes cause other grammatical structures to change. Moreover, even local changes are the result of competing motivations, which are only local adaptations to the problem of communication.

However, there are at least two possible examples of directional evolution at a more global level. If language is adapted to the environment of general-purpose communication, then if that environment changes significantly and permanently, then one might expect some evidence of global progress. One respect in which the environment has changed is the explosion of new objects, properties and processes with the technological advances of the past century. Any general-purpose communication system must involve the ability to name these new entities. The global progress (directional evolution) that has taken place is the massive increase of vocabulary in the languages used in the speech communities that possess the new technologies.

The second example of a possible global directional change is the advent of writing. Writing is a new medium of communication. Exploitation of the different perceptual modalities, time scale, audience interaction, etc. of literary comprehension (reading) and production (writing) may lead to significant language changes. These differences have been described in terms of oral vs literate style.

Two factors that are associated with the oral vs literate style dimension are degree of involvement or interaction, and degree of integration (Chafe 1982). Tannen argues that involvement can vary independently of medium (Tannen 1982:3). However, Tannen argues that integration is more closely identified with the difference in media:

> cohesion is established in spoken discourse through paralinguistic and non-verbal channels (tone of voice, intonation, prosody, facial expression, and gesture), while cohesion is established in writing through lexicalization and complex syntactic structures which make connectives explicit, and which show relationships between propositions through subordination and other foregrounding or backgrounding devices. (Tannen 1982:3)

Specific grammatical devices of integration used in writing include the following (Chafe 1982:39–45; Tannen 1982:8):

(26) a. nominalizations
      b. increased use of participles
      c. attributive adjectives
      d. conjoined phrases and series of phrases
      e. sequences of prepositional phrases
      f. complement clauses
      g. relative clauses

One might speculate that the advent of the written medium led to directed evolution in the development of these construction types. Typological research indicates, however, that all of these construction types are present in most if not all unwritten languages. Moreover, Biber (1986) presents a multivariate analysis of 41 linguistic features across a wide variety of spoken and written genres, and argues that there are three factors, identified as interactive vs edited text, abstract vs situated content, and reported vs immediate style, each of which only partly correlates with the spoken vs written distinction.

One possible difference between spoken and written language is the extent to which multiple iterations or embeddings of these constructions are found (Biber did not study this factor). In a study of English oral narratives, all of the constructions in (26a–g) were found, but generally only at one level of embedding (Croft 1995c; comparable evidence for Wardaman, an Australian aboriginal language, is presented in Croft to appear a). Multiple modifiers and nesting of subordinate clauses or phrases are extremely rare in oral conversation or narrative, and conjoined units, while found, are almost always broken into separate intonation units (an indication of a higher order of complexity in spoken language).

It is thus possible that there is directed change in the advent of the written register. However, expansion into the new linguistic niche results in the evolution at most of new degrees of syntactic complexity – multiple iterations and embeddings of structures – rather than in developing completely new grammatical structures.

In this section, I began with a more sophisticated analysis of the nature of progress (and lack thereof) in biological evolution than is popularly held. I have then applied this analysis of progress to language change. I have shown that the analysis of progress in biological evolution can shed important light on the nature of language change. These advances in understanding are possible only by looking at language as it is used in communication.

Notes

1   For example, a weaker hypothesis is that some though not all processes of language change are examples of drift, not selection, and conversely, some though not all cases of absence of language change are instances of stasis, not balanced selection. This hypothesis is not incompatible with the theory of language change advocated here; this might be the case for certain types of language change.

2   The structuralist/generative theory does not claim that this is the only means by which innovation can occur. The theory just described applies to internal means for innovation. It is also assumed that there are external means for innovations produced via language contact (see §6.1, chapter 8).

3   Clark & Roberts 1993 formulate an algorithm leading to language change in the language acquisition process that is somewhat different from that used by Lightfoot. However, their theory is only a theory of innovation and does not address the propagation problems that Lightfoot addresses. Clark & Roberts examine a set of syntactic changes that occurred in Middle French (ca. 1300–ca. 1500), which led to a change in parameter settings from Old French to Modern French. They employ a genetic algorithm model which allows for selection of parameter (re)settings by the child based on the input. Clark & Roberts argue that the various syntactic changes all follow from a single set of parameter resettings. Following the generative innovation model, they assume that the parameter resetting process occurs in child language acquisition, which implies that the change occurred in a very short period of time, not the two centuries it actually took. And they, like Lightfoot, still require some explanation for the variation in the input. They attribute that variation to a process external to the syntax, namely the rise of cliticized nominative pronouns (Clark & Roberts 1993:331, 338). But that process has syntactic consequences in their syntactic theory as well (regarding assignment of nominative case, and also whether clitic subject pronouns are counted in determining V2 order). Why are those consequences not carried out immediately and universally in the 'next generation'? Lightfoot's theory can be integrated with the Clark & Roberts' model of innovation of course, though it will still have the problems raised in the last two paragraphs.

4   This is not necessarily the fault of their creators. Grammaticalization theory is not intended to be a comprehensive theory of language change. The invisible hand theory is largely programmatic at this point. Even sociohistorical linguistic theory is largely a theory of selection, although a number of its practitioners have grappled with innovation.

5   A stage in a language in which there is variation between A and B need not lead to a shift to B; it is possible, and rather common, for a variant B to enter the language and then to be lost, leading to the continuation of A. Such a process can only be discerned when there are historical records of the A~B stage.

6   Unfortunately, such studies are in their infancy (de Bot, Gommans & Rossing 1991:87).

7   However, Harris & Campbell go on to say, 'it is true that children learning a language have a special role to play in furthering linguistic shifts' (ibid.; cf. Jespersen 1922:177–8). Harris & Campbell do not offer evidence for this claim; I have argued against this position (§3.2).

8   Keller argues that speakers choose *engelhaft* instead of *englisch* for 'angelic' in order not to be misunderstood as meaning 'English' (Keller 1990/1994:80–3, 93–5), and speakers choose *Dame* instead of *Frau* in order to be gallant to women (ibid. 76–7). This latter account is socially implausible, and cannot be extended to other cases of pejoration, e.g. racial terms. Instead, one could propose a different invisible hand explanation (Croft 1997:396–7): since most utterances with *Frau* are negative, a different term is chosen in order not to be misunderstood as maligning the group in question by association with previous negative utterances.

9   This is not always the case: consider the many slang words replacing taboo words for 'sex' and 'drunk'. Yet even these multiple terms can be differentiated socially and regionally, i.e. are variants of a sociolinguistic variable.

10 Keller in fact does not clearly distinguish between innovation and propagation of a change. He discusses the distinction briefly but suggests that it is 'not clear' how it applies to language change (Keller 1990/1994:146). In particular, some of his maxims of language use are in fact instances of the sociolinguistic mechanisms for propagation, i.e. represent selection as a cause of differential replication (see §3.4.2). However, Keller does not investigate this aspect of his model, and instead argues for the central role of the invisible hand in bringing about the propagation of a language change.

11 It has been suggested to me, by Martin Haspelmath and Peter Trudgill independently, that symmetry may play a role in changes in vowel systems only (cf. Lindblom 1986).

12 Actually, the retarding effect of the status of Standard English on language change has prevented the adoption of a new 2nd person plural form. Of course, the sociolinguistic model predicts that the establishment and the status of the standard would have this effect (see §7.4.2).

13 However, since Forchheimer and Ingram were interested in different kinds of pronominal systems, their sample overstates the proportion of different kinds of systems, particularly the 'asymmetric' ones. An areally and genetically more balanced survey performed by Matthew Gordon (personal communication) suggests that a more accurate percentage of pronominal systems with gaps in number is around 10% – still a significant minority.

14 Jakobson in fact had six functions of language, based on a model of language with six components: the addresser, the addressee, the context (including content), the message (the verbal form), the code (the linguistic system) and contact ('a physical channel and psychological connection between addresser and addressee') (Jakobson 1960/1971:21). For Jakobson, the context gives rise to the referential function. The addresser gives rise to the emotive function, i.e. her attitude towards the context. As Jakobson himself writes, 'we cannot restrict the notion of information to the

cognitive aspect of language' (ibid. 22), and so the emotive function can be subsumed under the referential function. The addressee gives rise to the conative function, which corresponds to the class of speech acts directing the addressee to do something. This function is subsumed under the more general theory of speech acts. Contact gives rise to the phatic function. Jakobson appears to be referring chiefly to speaker–hearer interaction in utterance acts, though he also cites Malinowski's more general concept. The code gives rise to the metalingual function, which in his examples involves speaker–hearer interaction in discourse. Finally, the message gives rise to the poetic function (which is in fact the main focus of Jakobson's paper).

15   However, Labov suggests that Martinet's push-chain analysis is the only plausible one known to him for the movement of back vowels to the front, since this process appears to coincide with the creation of a four-way height distinction among back vowels. Also, Labov proposes further principles (Labov 1994:280–5).

Chapter 4

A theory of language and meaning in use

4.1 Introduction

A usage-based theory of language change requires, of course, a model of language use. We must answer the question, Why do people talk in the way they do?, in order to discover why the way they talk sometimes changes – and why the way they talk often does not appear to change. This chapter offers such a theory, based on research in pragmatics, cognitive semantics and a variety of approaches in philosophy.

There are two significant aspects of the theory of language use presented in this chapter. First, language use is essentially a joint act between speaker and addressee. Language is a fundamentally social interactional phenomenon. So is language change. It is this hypothesis that allows us to use Hull's generalized theory of selection to develop the Theory of Utterance Selection. Selection of novel variants is a result of interaction of the interactor – the speaker – with her environment – her interlocutors and the knowledge and goals shared between the speaker and her interlocutors. Also, both intentional and nonintentional mechanisms of altered replication make reference to speaker goals in conversation (§§3.4.2–3.4.4). Second, meaning in language use is not static or fixed. Meaning is protean and cannot be reduced to simple logical formulae. In this and the following chapters, I will argue that the slipperiness of meaning is one of the chief mechanisms for innovation in language change.

4.2 Language, communication and convention

4.2.1 The function of language and communication

The function of language is often said to be to communicate information. Keller, however, argues that this view of the function of language is not correct. To see Keller's point, we must first define communication. Communication is the transfer of information; but it is not just any transfer of information. A speaker usually transfers more information than she intended, and, depending on how successful she is, also less. Grice proposed a now widely used definition of meaning that captures this difference: ' "speaker *A* meant something by *x*" is (roughly) equivalent to "*A* intended the utterance of *x* to produce some effect in an audience by means of the recognition of this intention" ' (Grice 1948/ 1989:220).

If we say that the function of language is to communicate, then we have a circular explanation: language is a means of communication, so of course its 'function' is to communicate (Keller 1990/1994:87). Keller argues that the function of an entity should be its role in a larger system. The function of language should be found in the larger system that language fits into – namely, interpersonal interaction in human communities. Hence, the function of language is some extralinguistic goal of the speaker. Keller formulates the function as follows: 'the human being has the goal to be socially successful, and influencing others by means of language is an essential element in the explanation of social success' (ibid. 86). Keller emphasizes at various points that social success comes in many varieties and is sensitive to the particular circumstances of the social context of utterance; hence this is not to be treated as a reductionist view of human behavior.

Keller's view is essentially not different from that of many analysts of discourse who emphasize the interactional nature of conversation. These analysts believe that undue attention has been focused on communication, and not enough on functions such as establishing or reinforcing group identity and solidarity. Nevertheless, it can be objected that one cannot use language to reinforce solidarity, or carry out other extralinguistic goals, without engaging in the communication of information, even if that information is not particularly informative. The apparent conflict in approaches to the function of language can be resolved by recognizing that communication with language is a means to carry out the interactional goals emphasized by Keller and others. Which one is the 'important' function depends on whether one considers the 'important' function to be the ultimate goal of the interlocutors – social-interactional – or the omnipresent means to any other goal achieved by language – communication of information.

More generally, language in use involves multiple levels of action on the part of the interlocutors, the lower levels being the means to achieve the higher levels, and the higher levels achievable only by carrying out the lower levels.

4.2.2   *The joint character of speech*

All utterances are not simply complex symbolic expressions; they are actions on the part of the speaker – and also the hearer. This is true of all levels of speech, from producing the sounds to the actions which the speaker wants to accomplish with the aid of the hearer.

The highest-level goal of language is social. Keller describes it as influencing others in order to achieve social success. A less self-interested way to put it than 'influencing others' is to describe language use as engaging in a joint activity such that the hearer and speaker share some goal. The crucial aspect of this definition is that the function of language is not carried unless both speaker and hearer act jointly. Of course, the actions carried out individually by speaker and hearer are not the same. But this is true of many joint actions: for example, the actions carried out by a flautist and harpsichordist playing a CPE Bach sonata are not the same. Clark defines a joint action as follows: 'Ensemble A-and-B is doing joint action k if and only if: 0. the action k includes 1 and 2; 1. A intends to be doing A's part of k and believes that 0; 2. B intends to be doing B's part of k and believes that 0' (Clark 1996:61). That is, each individual is carrying out their part of what they recognize and intend to be a joint action.

Speaking, or rather, speaking-and-hearing, is also a joint action. Most speech act analysts have ignored the action performed by the hearer because it appears to be relatively passive. But communication is not communication unless the hearer understands what is said, and the extralinguistic goals are not achieved if the hearer does not partake in them, or even if the hearer simply does not consider partaking in them. That is, language is not serving its purpose unless the hearer does his part.

A speech act cannot be successful, in fact cannot get off the ground, without the utterance – the string of sounds – being properly executed by the speaker. Equally important, the speech act will not get off the ground if it is not properly attended to by the hearer: if the hearer ignores the speaker, or background noise drowns out the utterance, the speech act has also failed. At the next level up, the formulation of the utterance in some language, the hearer also plays a role. The hearer must be able to identify the propositional act presented by the speaker. The speech act would not be completely successful if, for example, the hearer did not know the language or dialect being used by the speaker, or was not familiar with some of the jargon in the utterance.

The result of successful production and comprehension of the utterance at these levels is that the intentions of the speaker are mutually known, that is, part of the speaker and hearer's common ground (see §4.2.3). This is true of even simple assertions. Consider the following imaginary example of an assertion followed by two possible responses.

(1)   Student A: The transcripts need to be turned in before the next tutorial.
      Student B: Yeah.
      Student C: No they don't!

The response by Student B recognizes the intention of Student A that B accept A's assertion, and implicitly accepts it. B would not be able to accept A's assertion without recognizing A's intention, for instance if B misunderstood what A said. On the other hand, the response by Student C rejects A's proposal that her assertion be made part of their shared knowledge; but C's rejection of A's assertion could not be made unless C correctly understood A's intentions in communication.

Finally, the actions which speakers attempt to accomplish by their verbal statements are themselves joint. Their joint character is fairly clear since most of them require explicit responses on the part of the addressee: for example, a question calls for an overt response. But there are a variety of responses or uptakes that an addressee can make, ranging from full compliance to alteration of the proposed project to declination or even withdrawal from the project (Clark 1996:203–5). In any case, one cannot say the joint project is completed until some version of it is complied with, or withdrawal is accepted by the proposer. A joint project may take a number of turns to negotiate and finally achieve, as in the following example, taken from a conversation recorded and transcribed by a student at the University of Manchester:

(2) N: Have you got anything I can borrow?   *[pre-request]*
     T: erm..well I don't like you wearing any of my trousers (inaud.)
                                        [declination of anticipated request]
     N: 'ave you got any baggy ones?   *[alteration of pre-request]*
     T: erm..why don't you wear them black and white check leggings and
          then a smart blouse and my black blazer
                                        [alteration of project: suggestion]
     N: Yeah that's alright   *[compliance with altered joint project]*

The joint character of language use involves not only language as action but also language as symbol or sign (meaning), as will be seen in the rest of this chapter.

4.2.3   Speech communities and common ground

Language fundamentally involves people – plural, collective. We cannot talk about language use – speech acts in conversation and the nonlinguistic actions they serve – without talking about the people that use them. In particular, we must examine more closely the fact that the language that people use defines a speech community.

The proper model of a speech community is, or should be, a central issue in linguistic theory. A language, in the sense of a population of utterances as defined in §2.4.1, is the central defining concept; the delimitation of this population is by a speech community. Linguistic conventions, whose rise and fall must be accounted for by a theory of language change, are defined with respect to a speech community. Finally, the distinction between so-called internal and external causes of language change uses the notion of a speech community to provide the boundary between internal and external. Yet the analysis of speech communities found in sociolinguistics (which has examined the problem in greatest detail) and by Clark makes it clear that the notion of a speech community is much more complex than the naïve view, and this has important consequences for theories of language and language change. In particular, the analysis of speech communities underlies the analysis of propagation in chapter 7 and of phylogenetic relations among languages in chapter 8.

The naïve view of a speech community – immortalized by an oft-quoted passage from Chomsky – is that it is a collection of individuals who speak a single language among themselves, and are all native speakers of that language: 'Linguistic theory is concerned primarily with an ideal speaker-listener, in a completely homogeneous speech-community, who knows its language perfectly' (Chomsky 1965:3). If we apply the naïve view to the usage-based model of language change being proposed here, then the population of utterances are the utterances produced by the members of that speech community, the conventions of language are those that are found among those members, and the internal–external boundary is defined by the individuals of one speech community vs those of another.

The first obvious problem with the naïve view is presented by multilingual societies, i.e. societies where two or more distinct (often, mutually unintelligible) varieties are used by (at least some of) the same people. Generally when people use two (or more) distinct varieties in a society, sociolinguists use the term CODE. In multilingual societies, one can no longer use individuals to define the internal–external boundary. Instead, sociolinguists define a code as belonging to one or more social DOMAINS (Fishman 1972:50). Typical important social domains referred to by sociolinguists are family, friends, work, school, religion (Fishman 1965/1972). However, there are many subdomains: one knows different friends depending on the different sorts of recreational activities one does; different sorts of work may involve different codes. We will make the notion of 'domain' more precise below; but it is clear that an empirically adequate description of a single language based on the notion of a speech community will have to define a speech community relative to domains and not simply individuals. Of course, the code for each domain is used by the people who operate in that domain (often a subset of the society as a whole).

The first important consequence of this change in the definition of a speech community is that individual members of society are multilingual: they speak different codes by virtue of the different social domains they operate in. It may be that some members of multilingual speech communities are themselves monolingual; but this indicates that they do not participate in the social domain(s) which require use of the language(s) they do not speak. If (following sociolinguistic practice) we continue to use the term COMMUNITY to describe the speakers of a single code, then most members of multilingual societies are also members of multiple speech communities.

The second important consequence of this change in definition is that a code has a social meaning, determined by the context in which it is used, as well as a referential meaning, i.e. meaning in the usual sense of that word. In other words, conventional linguistic units such as words or constructions have not only a form (signifier) and meaning (signified) but a third dimension, the social domain/community in which they are used.

Another significant fact about codes in multilingual societies is that no code has the complete range of communicative power; there are things one cannot talk about in one or the other languages. For example, in the classic sociolinguistic study of the Buang in Papua New Guinea (Sankoff 1972), three languages were found in the community: Buang (the local language), Yabem (a language spoken by a larger group, into which the Bible was translated for all the tribes in the area), and Tok Pisin (a pidgin used for a variety of purposes). Buang was used for discussing traditional culture, and Yabem in the realm of Christian religion. A Buang could not really discuss Christian religion in Buang or traditional culture in Yabem. Another example is classic DIGLOSSIA, where two mutually unintelligible varieties are used, the spoken L[ow] variety and the written/formal H[igh] variety (Ferguson 1959/1972). In a diglossic situation, neither H nor L can properly serve in the domains for which the other is used. Of course, the codes could be mixed, and words and constructions could ultim-ately be borrowed, allowing the modified code to be used in other domains. But that would imply that the domains in which the language (say, Buang) is used is changing (mixing) or has changed (borrowing), and so the speech community (or communities) have changed. In a multilingual community, each code or variety is specialized for the domains in which it is used.

Multilingual communities are very common in the world; yet the norm for a speech community is usually taken in linguistic theory to be a monolingual speech community, and so a community is defined in terms of individuals rather than domains, and linguistic units are treated as two-sided signs, not three-cornered signs-in-a-community. Yet a closer examination of a monolingual speech community reveals that it is in fact much more like a multilingual community. The profound fact is: every language is a multiplicity of codes. Not everyone knows the language of sociolinguistics – or the language of classical music, or of wine-tasting, or of carpentry. Of course, there is a lot of overlap between the language of sociolinguistics and the language of wine-tasting – we call them both 'English' (or 'French', etc.). But what we call 'English' is really a multiplicity of codes, specialized to varying degrees, and known to 'English speakers' only to the extent that they are members of the relevant community:

> There is no limit to the ways in which human beings league themselves together for self-identification, security, gain, amusement, worship, or any of the other purposes that are held in common; consequently there is no limit to the number and variety of speech communities that are to be found in society. (Bolinger 1975:333)

To sum up: a linguistic code belongs to a (speech) community, and a community is defined by a domain. Every person is a member of multiple (speech) communities, hence every person speaks multiple codes, depending on which communities he or she belongs to. This is called his or her REPERTOIRE (Gumperz 1968/1972:230; Fishman 1972:47). Everyone has a slightly different repertoire. We still need a term to describe a group of socially interacting speakers as a whole, including all the communities they belong to. I will use the term SOCIETY to refer to a socially interacting group of speakers; hence, 'society' refers to the group commonly described as a 'speech community', even in much sociolinguistic research (see §7.2 for further discussion). Another way of stating the fundamental point is that every society consists of multiple communities. An effect of the massive degree of overlap in codes used in the communities of a single society is to break down the internal–external boundary in the theory of language change. This is one of the main reasons why languages are fundamentally variable. These facts will be discussed in chapter 6. Here, we will further explore the nature of communities and how that affects how individuals interact in using language.

A community is defined in terms of a domain of SHARED EXPERTISE: 'a cultural community is really a set of people with a shared expertise that others lack' (Clark 1996:102). Shared expertise is involved no matter how technical or how ordinary the expertise is. If you are a professional linguist, you share expertise with other professional linguists about the knowledge and discoveries and methods of the field. But you can have expertise in something less technical. For example, I have some shared expertise with my colleagues about how the University of Manchester works (at least from a professor's point of view). Another basic expertise which is shared among many people is living in a particular location, such as Manchester, or the San Francisco Bay Area. Another important shared expertise is our language: we know its grammar and vocabulary and how it is used to communicate. Yet another shared expertise of ordinary life is cooking: this allows you to recognize and name kitchen implements, various kinds of fruit and vegetables, spices, and how to use them all to create meals.

How do we divide shared expertise into domains, other than by the individuals who possess it? The shared expertise is obviously interconnected in various ways. Ultimately, however, it is defined by a social institution in the society (Fishman 1965/1972:19), for example the institution of the University of Manchester, a political entity such as San Francisco, or a less explicitly defined but nevertheless discrete cultural activity such as cooking in the home. Of course, there is also a lot of shared expertise that is common across domains: for example, shared expertise about spatial relations between objects will be shared across all domains which make reference to objects in the physical world. I will call this common shared expertise CORE EXPERTISE (see §7.2).

Shared expertise is the basis for mutual knowledge, which Clark calls COMMON GROUND. The common ground I share as, say, a classical musician or a cook, is of various types. The common ground is not just shared knowledge about general concepts, or specific practices (such as how to sauté vegetables), but also particular individuals that are important or salient to the community. Common ground also involves shared attitudes to a significant degree, certainly in the case of communities based on religious or political beliefs (Catholics, Republicans) but also in many other communities: shared attitudes strongly reinforce community solidarity.

Common ground is the fundamental basis of our social lives. We cannot interact without assuming some common ground with other people. Even with someone from the most distant and exotic culture, we can assume some common ground with our being human – physical properties, emotions, etc. – and living on the same planet – topography, climate, etc. (although we might erroneously assume too much common ground). It is common ground that enables us to communicate at all, as will be seen in the remainder of this chapter. But there has to be some shared basis for common ground. Community membership – i.e. shared expertise – is one of the most important shared bases for common ground. Communities are defined by functional domains – the functional domain is the shared expertise. The mutual knowledge that comes from community membership is called COMMUNAL COMMON GROUND. A speaker's knowledge must be specified by the community with which she shares that knowledge.

The most obvious linguistic manifestation of communal common ground is its COMMUNAL LEXICON. Communal lexicons are specialized vocabulary for a particular domain of shared expertise, such as the words *crotchet, sonata* and *quartet* in classical music (Clark 1998; see §7.2 for further discussion). Again, the three-cornered representation of a linguistic unit, describing it in terms of community, form and meaning, is necessary to describe communal lexicons.

There is also common ground shared more directly between individuals, based on their shared experience. Clark calls this PERSONAL COMMON GROUND (Clark 1996:112–16). It has two shared bases: what we experience together and what we tell each other. What we experience together is called the PERCEPTUAL BASIS by Clark (1996:112–13). The perceptual basis is simply that we are looking at (hearing, smelling, experiencing in general) the same thing, and we mutually know we are looking at that thing. That mutual knowledge is achieved via JOINT ATTENTION (see Tomasello 1995), and also via the common ground that you and I are human beings with normally functioning perceptual organs and brains – a person cannot establish joint attention with a mannequin, for example. What we tell each other is called by Clark the 'actional basis' (Clark 1996:114) – a rather peculiar term, which will be replaced here by DISCOURSE BASIS. Discourse basis involves joint attention – to what each of us is telling the other – and community membership (speakers of the same language), as well as the common ground of being human and rational.

Just as communal common ground is specific to particular cultural communities, personal common ground is specific to the persons with whom we shared the experience/conversation: e.g. a brother, a friend, a professional colleague, a fellow student, a partner. Not only are there communal lexicons, but there are PERSONAL LEXICONS as well. They are an indication of intimacy, and so are more likely to be found among family members, close friends, or partners. In other words, personal relations also have linguistic effects, creating tiny subcommunities, even of just two people (e.g. partners).

The redefinition of speech community revealed by sociolinguistic research will cause us to reexamine the notion of a language (see §7.2). The definition of speech community proposed by sociolinguists and elaborated by Clark links linguistic units more closely to their social context of use and also to the body of shared knowledge which is the foundation of the meanings they communicate (see §4.3.2). The codes used in the communities we belong to overlap, thus breaking down the boundaries between internal and external change is another potential source of language change (see chapters 7–8).

4.2.4   *Convention*

The definition of language as a population of utterances in §2.4.1 is not the more common definition of a language. The more common definition of language is as a system, more precisely, a conventional system for communication (where communication refers to the lower three levels described in §4.2.2). Conventions are manifested in the lingueme pool of a language (see §2.4.1). Conventions, commonly called 'norms' in sociolinguistics, are central to the understanding of language as a system and language in use. Convention is also central to any model of language change, because innovation is essentially language use beyond conventions (§3.4.4), and propagation is essentially the establishment of a new convention in a language (see §§7.2–7.3). In this section, we will present a definition of convention based on Lewis (1969) and Clark (1996).

Language is a joint action (see §4.2.2). Speaker and hearer share the same goal (at the lowest three levels of speech acts): communication. Speaker and hearer each do their part: the speaker communicates some meaning and the hearer understands the same meaning (or something like it; see §4.3.3). These are the two distinct individual actions that make up the joint action of communication. That is, speaker and hearer believe they intend to have the same, shared meaning when the speaker utters certain words in a certain grammatical construction. How does joint action succeed (when it does)? There is a problem here: the hearer cannot read the speaker's mind, and she can't read his. This is what is called a COORDINATION PROBLEM (Lewis 1969:5–8; Clark 1996:62–5). In speaking and understanding, speaker and hearer are trying to coordinate on the same meaning. To see how this is accomplished, we can first look at simpler kinds of coordination problems.

A simple type of coordination problem is a third-party SCHELLING GAME, a type of cooperative game from game theory (Schelling 1960, discussed in Clark 1996:62–3). In a third party Schelling game, two people are presented by a third party with a set of stimuli such as the following set of numbers, and are asked to choose one, with the idea that both people should choose the same number:

(3)   23 45 99 57

The players may succeed in a number of ways. They might both choose 99 because it is the highest two-digit number and it has the same two digits. They might both choose 23 because it is the 23rd of September. Or they might choose 57 because they both know that is the age of the person who set the game. What matters, however, is that each player believes that the solution each chooses is the most salient choice for both of them. If one player knows that the other doesn't know what day it is, then 23 is not a jointly salient choice. The essential strategy here is that the two players choose the jointly most salient possibility, that is, the choice that is maximally salient in the two players' common ground.

Third-party Schelling games can be tricky, since the players do not know how well the third party set up the game. Fortunately, communication is a first-party Schelling game: by choosing the words and the constructions, the speaker sets up the game of having speaker and hearer settle on the same meaning for the utterance. The participant who sets the problem is the speaker. The speaker wants the hearer to end up with the same meaning as the speaker has in mind. (We will take meaning to be some thought pattern in the mind; see below.) The speaker produces an utterance which she thinks will allow the hearer to understand the same meaning that the speaker intended. The hearer knows this. That is, the hearer knows that the speaker will have done her best to help him solve the coordination problem of understanding the same meaning that the speaker intended. The speaker and hearer can assume what Clark calls the solvability premises (Clark 1996:68):

(4)   The speaker:
    (i)   chose the problem (communicating something);
    (ii)   designed its form (chose the words and grammar of the utterance she produces);
    (iii) has a particular solution in mind (the particular meaning intended);
    (iv)   believes the participants can converge on that solution (that is, the meaning intended will become part of the common ground of the participants).

In addition, the participants in a conversation can assume two other premises, according to Clark (ibid. 69):

(5)   SUFFICIENCY PREMISE: the first party has provided all the information needed to solve the problem

(6)   IMMEDIACY PREMISE: the participants can solve the problem immediately, that is, with no delay

The sufficiency premise corresponds to the function of avoiding misunderstanding (§3.4.4). The immediacy premise is necessary because conversation is a time-constrained sequence of coordination problems: it is a string of words and sentences that comes at the hearer in very rapid succession. The immediacy premise partly motivates the economy principle (§3.4.4).

There are a variety of ways to solve coordination problems. In the third-party Schelling games, the solutions that I suggested were based on natural perceptual or cognitive salience: the perceptual distinctiveness of the two 9s in 99, or its cognitive salience as the highest two-digit number. More specialized cognitive salience is found in the date, or the age of the third party (assuming these facts are mutually known and contextually salient). Natural perceptual or cognitive distinctiveness is a COORDINATION DEVICE that can be used by people in order to win Schelling games. Of course, perceptual/cognitive salience is not perfect, but that's the way the world is, since people cannot read each other's minds. No coordination device is guaranteed to be foolproof – and this is one of the cracks in the system that gives language change a foothold.

Choosing one number out of a set is an extremely limited sort of coordination problem. Trying to figure out which of the infinitely possible range of experiences that a speaker is trying to communicate is a participant coordination problem of an entirely different order of magnitude. To say it again: people cannot read each other's minds (most of the time anyway). There are just too many things someone might want to communicate. Moreover, almost any gesture, particularly any string of sounds, could be used to mean anything. This is the arbitrariness of the linguistic sign. So there is no perceptually natural salient solution to the coordination problem of communication. What do people do?

Fortunately, people do want to communicate the same things, or similar things, over and over again. That is, communication involves recurrent coordination problems. And speech communities generally end up converging on a regular solution to a recurrent coordination problem. Speech communities arbitrarily pick one solution, say the string of sounds *butterfly* to mean the insect, and stick with it, so that everyone recognizes that *butterfly* is the solution to a recurrent coordination problem. In this way conventions arise.

A CONVENTION is defined by Clark as follows (Clark 1996:71):

(7) 1 a regularity in behavior (e.g. producing the string of sounds *butterfly*)
2 that is partly arbitrary (we could have used *Schmetterling* instead; that's what the German speech community did)
3 that is common ground in a community (we in the English language community all know we use *butterfly* . . .)
4 as a coordination device
5 for a recurrent coordination problem (talking about butterflies).

Lewis (1969) provides a more detailed definition of convention. How can a convention be a coordination device in a community? Lewis argues that it has to be a regularity in behavior that almost everyone in the community conforms to, almost everyone expects almost everyone else to conform to, and almost everyone would prefer any new member of the community to conform to. Lewis defines a convention as arbitrary when another solution (such as *Schmetterling*, or *papillon*) is of approximately equal preference to the members of the community. In fact, this example is not perfect, since *Schmetterling* and *papillon* are not of approximately equal preference because their phonology is not English. A better example would be to compare any of the myriad British English vs American English vocabulary differences, such as *intersection* vs *crossing* or *tissue* vs *kleenex*. In addition, a convention is arbitrary to the extent that if almost everyone conformed to the other solution, almost everyone would prefer that any new member of the community conformed to the other solution as well. That is, people don't care which solution is chosen – the solution is arbitrary – as long as almost everyone conforms to the solution chosen. It is the conformity that allows a convention to be a coordination device.

Hence, the combined Lewis & Clark definition of (linguistic) convention is as follows (the numbered parts of the definition in (8) are from Clark, while the qualifications under the letters are from Lewis):

(8) 1 a regularity in behavior (producing a string of sounds)
     2 that is partly arbitrary
        a. other regularities in behavior would be approximately equally pref-
            erable by almost everyone in the community
     3 that is common ground in a community
     4 as a coordination device
        a. almost everyone in the community conforms to it
        b. almost everyone expects almost everyone else to conform to it
        c. almost everyone would prefer any additional member of the com-
            munity to conform to it if almost everyone in the community
            already conforms to it
        d. almost everyone would prefer any new member of the community
            to conform to another regularity if almost everyone in the com-
            munity were already conforming to it
     5 for a recurrent coordination problem (communicating a meaning).

It is important to note that following a convention presupposes prior occurrences of the behavior. That is, the lingueme has already been used in the
community to communicate the meaning in question. Conventions are only
established after a lingueme has been propagated through a speech community. Innovation must always involve nonconventional coordination devices (see
§4.3.1). Propagation is essentially the establishment of a convention.

Linguistic conventions are coordination devices; they must still be used by
the interlocutors to solve the participant coordination problem of fixing on the
meaning intended by the speaker. Lewis (and Clark following him) argue that
a language system is a special type of joint action (or system of joint actions),
which Lewis calls a SIGNALING SYSTEM (Lewis 1969, chapter IV). In a signaling
system, the speaker's action is to produce a signal based on the state of affairs
she intends to communicate, and the hearer's action is to produce a response to
the signal produced. The signaling system can be defined as the following
individual components of a joint action:

(9) *Speaker*:   state of affairs → signal
     Hearer: signal → response

The state of affairs and the response are in some systematic relationship
which we may describe as the speaker and hearer converging on the same
meaning. This is not so obvious in the philosophical realist version of the joint
actions in (9) given by Lewis (and Clark). More accurately, a state of affairs
gives rise to a mental state in the speaker, and that mental state is the basis on
which she produces a signal. Conversely, the hearer enters into a mental state
based on the signal he understands, and then responds accordingly. This psychological version of the signaling system can be defined as follows:

(10) *Speaker*:   [state of affairs →]   mental state → signals
      Hearer: signals → mental state   [→ response]

In the psychological version, it is usually assumed that the speaker and hearer are coordinating on getting into the same mental state, which is usually spoken of as 'the meaning' of the signal, that is, the mental representation of the meaning of the signal. This is in fact not a necessary interpretation of this model. The mental states of speaker and hearer need not be identical, though it is assumed that they are systematically related. In §4.3, I will give reasons why the psychological version is more accurate, but also why a weaker link between the mental states of speaker and hearer is necessary.

At this point, we now have a precise definition of how a language system is a conventional system for communication: language is a conventional signaling system.

Linguistic convention is central to the theory of language change. Normal replication, altered replication, and selection are all defined in terms of convention (as conforming to convention, not conforming to convention, and establishing a convention, respectively). The detailed definition of convention given here is important as a starting point for understanding the processes involved in language change. It allows us to define nonconventionality in language use in the rest of this chapter, and to describe the establishment of conventions in chapter 7.

4.3   The open-endedness and flexibility of meaning in use

In this section, I will argue that meaning in use is not fully captured by the conventions of a language. All language use, but particularly innovative language use, involves nonconventional coordination devices. The conventional meaning of a linguistic expression cannot be as specific as a small finite set of semantic properties. Meaning is encyclopedic and subject to the conceptualization of the speaker. Both speaker's meaning and the meaning of an expression in a speech community are better described as a lineage of rich, context-specific meanings for which the expression has been used. Finally, meaning is negotiated jointly between speaker and hearer, just as other speech acts are (§4.2.2).

All of these assertions about the nature of meaning are controversial in some theories of semantics, although cognitive linguistic approaches to semantics have adopted most of them. However, in chapters 5–6, I argue that the openendedness and flexibility of meaning in use motivate speakers to reanalyze the relationship between form and meaning, and that much innovation in grammatical change involves form–function remapping. Hence, the lengthy discussion in the following sections is intended to persuade the reader that these assertions represent an accurate description of the nature of meaning.

4.3.1   Nonconventionality in language use

In order to succeed in their goals, speakers must communicate successfully; that is to say, speakers and their hearers must successfully solve a coordination problem when a speaker chooses an expression, conventional or nonconventional, to describe a situation. Nevertheless, convention is not sufficient to describe the relationship between form and meaning in language use. In fact, as I will argue in later sections of this chapter, there is no sharp distinction between conventional and nonconventional coordination.

To begin with, how does a linguistic convention get established in the first place? Since a convention involves conformity to a community behavior, there has to be a community behavior in place already. Hence the first use of a word or phrase with a particular meaning is not a conventional use by definition: it is not conforming to an existing community behavior. After the first use, or the first few uses, the word – the coordination device for this meaning – can spread through the community, that is, it is propagated. The first use, or the first few uses, are not conventional though – they do not satisfy the subconditions in clause (4a–b) of the Lewis & Clark definition given in (8).

But it is still communication. Hence it is a coordination problem, and the new word, or new use of a word, is a coordination device used to solve the coordination problem. The coordination problem must be solved by NONCONVENTIONAL COORDINATION DEVICES. Any coordination device will do, as long as it works, which means as long as it is jointly salient to the interlocutors. Lewis (and Clark) suggests three nonconventional coordination devices that are relevant to language use.

In the Schelling game in (3), I suggested that the coordination problem could be solved by using JOINT SALIENCE, perceptual and/or cognitive. This is the most important nonconventional coordination device available to human beings, used to solve all sorts of coordination problems other than linguistic ones (Lewis 1969:35–6; Clark 1996:81). To give one linguistic example: I coined the compound name *CD room* to refer to a small bedroom in our house used to store files, books, records and compact discs. The last are jointly most salient to us in that there are more of them than any other object in the room; they are found in that room only, thus allowing for a rapid solution to the room reference problem; and they are used the most often (i.e. it is the most common reason for my going into the room). Hence the choice of *CD room* instead of *file room* or *record room*, due to the perceptual and cognitive salience of that description of the room. This phrase has now become part of our personal lexicon, a convention conformed to by the two of us.[1]

Of course, this example involves conventional as well as nonconventional coordination. Success in solving the coordination problem with the phrase *CD room* requires conforming to the conventions for the words *CD* and *room* and the compound noun construction $[Noun_{mod} \; Noun_{head}]$. But it also requires joint perceptual/cognitive salience in order to establish reference. Only if a completely new word is coined, or if one is learning a language in the first place, is coordination completely nonconventional.

Another nonconventional coordination device is EXPLICIT AGREEMENT (Lewis 1969:33–5, 83–88; Clark 1996:80–81). For example, in the Schelling game, if the players had explicitly agreed always to choose the second number in the list, then they would have won every time. In language, the most obvious examples are with technical terms, as in this example: 'Word knowledge, properly viewed, divides into what I will call communal lexicons, by which I mean sets of word conventions in individual communities' (Clark 1996:107). Assuming we readers accept this proposal, we have explicitly agreed to the regularity of using the string of sounds/words *communal lexicon* to solve the recurrent coordination problem of talking about sets of word conventions in individual communities. As with perceptual/cognitive salience, explicit agreement requires conventional coordination as well, for the explicit agreement is couched in conventionally established language.

The last example of a nonconventional coordination device is PRECEDENT (Lewis 1969:36, 119–20; Clark 1996:81). Participants may solve a coordination problem by appealing to a precedent, without that precedent having been explicitly agreed upon, and without that precedent having evolved into a convention. For example, in a Schelling game in one of my classes where I asked the students to choose a place to meet in downtown Manchester, a pair of players succeeded by choosing the HMV record store, because they had met there before. Precedent operates only with the second and later uses of a word or form – it requires a precedent, after all – but before the use becomes established as a convention (if it ever does).

The role of nonconventional coordination devices in language use may appear to be a marginal one, found in the first novel uses of words and constructions, or in the language learning process. But, in fact, nonconventional coordination devices pervade the apparently ordinary, conventional use of language. Clark illustrates a large range of linguistic expressions where nonconventional coordination devices are necessary for the hearer to understand the meaning. There is good reason to believe that virtually all language use involves nonconventional coordination devices.[2]

One of the most pervasive sources of nonconventional coordination in language is indexicality and reference. Consider the instruction *Sit in that seat, please.* The noun *seat* is a conventional device to indicate a certain class of object. This convention does not however help the hearer identify which seat he is supposed to sit in. The demonstrative *that* is a conventional device to identify some object away from the speaker. At this point, joint perceptual salience (aided in part by a gesture) must enter the picture for the hearer to successfully establish reference.

A similar story must be told for so-called anaphoric pronouns, including null anaphora, definite reference and proper names, such as the italicized phrases in (11):

(11) A few pages of *Deacon*'s prose can be exhausting, let alone *500 __*. *That* is a pity, since *he* presents ideas that really should be aired as *the ideas* of evolutionary psychology bed *themselves* down in *the wider culture*. (*Independent*, 5.x.97)

To be successful, pronouns and null anaphora must refer to entities that the speaker believes are highly accessible to the hearer (Ariel 1990). Joint cognitive salience, usually determinable from the discourse basis of the interlocutor's personal common ground, is required to successfully establish reference. Even joint perceptual salience may suffice, on those occasions where a pronoun can be used as a first mention of a referent, where joint attention is already directed to the referent. Likewise, definite reference requires the combination of conventional information of the category of referent – provided by the noun and its modifiers – with cognitive salience of the unique instance of the category the speaker is referring to (e.g. which wider culture in (11)?). Even proper names may refer to different individuals (there are many people named Deacon), so joint perceptual/cognitive salience is necessary to establish proper reference.

Clark also notes the existence of indirect reference, as in the following example I overheard:

(12)   *Our flat* is going to the cinema – do you want to come along?

The expression *our flat* refers not to the physical part of a building, but instead to a jointly cognitively salient entity associated with it, namely the people inhabiting the flat. This is an example of metonymy, one of several conceptualization processes that is pervasive in language and thus requires pervasive use of nonconventional coordination devices.

Example (12) is in fact probably a conventional extension of the meaning of *our flat* in English, from buildings to their inhabitants. If both meanings are conventional, then the hearer is still posed a coordination problem: choosing the literal or the metonymic meaning. The resolution of ambiguity also requires nonconventional coordination devices. Ambiguity occurs when a regularity in behavior (the linguistic expression) is used to solve more than one recurring coordination problem (the meaning). A typical example of ambiguity is illustrated in (13), with some competing definitions given in (14):

(13)   'But what about Toad?' asked the Mole anxiously, as they set off together. 'We can't leave him here, sitting in the middle of the road by himself, in the distracted *state* he's in!' (*The Wind in the Willows*, p. 37; emphasis added)

(14)   **state** *n.* . . . . **3.** A mental or emotional condition or disposition . . . **6.** A social position or rank; estate. **7.** Ceremony; pomp; formality: *robes of state* . . . **10.** A body politic; specifically, one constituting a nation: *the states of Western Europe.* (*American Heritage Dictionary, New College Edition*)

I have selected just one word in the passage in (13). But in any utterance, most if not all of the words will be ambiguous, as inspection of the entries in a good dictionary for all the words in (13) would indicate. If many or all words are ambiguous, then the hearer is faced with the paradoxical situation described in the following passage (see also Croft 1993:362–4):

The polysemy of words is such that, in a given sentence, one can say that the word put back into its context, not the word itself, has a univocal meaning. But the context itself is constituted by other words, which also have many meanings. Thus an interaction between words is produced which ends up by attributing to *each one* the meaning which is compatible with the others. In turn, one attributes to these other the meaning compatible with that of the first. (Merleau-Ponty 1964/1973:91; emphasis original)

Merleau-Ponty does not mention in this passage that there is further context than just the other words in an utterance: there is the shared extralinguistic context, which will ultimately disambiguate the meanings of the words in the utterance (in most cases; see the following sections). But this context is available to the interlocutors only via nonconventional coordination devices, namely joint attention and shared expertise – the bases for common ground.

Finally, there are many constructions in English (and other languages), including quite basic constructions, which Clark calls 'contextual constructions', whose conventional meaning seems to include a requirement that the hearer use nonconventional coordination devices. Perhaps the best-known English construction of this sort is the compound noun construction and its close relative, the denominal adjective, both illustrated in this newspaper headline:

(15)   *Blood money setback* for *Saudi nurses* (*Guardian* headline, 7.xi.97; emphasis added)

The range of meanings linking the two nouns in the compound noun construction is almost completely free (Downing 1977). In (15), *blood money* is a conventionalized compound noun, but the combination with *setback* is novel and requires nonconventional coordination. Likewise, the nurses are not of Saudi nationality; they were working in Saudi Arabia. Joint salience solves this coordination problem – they were the only nurses with a Saudi connection who were in the British news at the time. To say that the meanings of the phrases are 'nurses with some connection to something Saudi' and 'a setback with some respect to blood money' does not tell us what these phrases mean, that is, the linguistic coordination problem they are intending to solve. The hearer has not solved the problem unless he has the right relationship between the two terms.

It is not only compound nouns that require context, so too do many other modifier constructions, such as the genitive construction and even the adjectival construction, as illustrated in the example **red** *pencil* (color produced by pencil, color of surface of pencil, color of stripes on surface of pencil, color of the eraser on the pencil, etc.). Other contextual constructions described by Clark include indirect descriptions (*You'll have to ask a zero*, that is, a person who you reach by dialing zero), denominal verbs and other derivational processes (*She Houdini'd her way out of the closet*, that is, cleverly escaped), and highly general verbs (*Since you're working on the spoon, I'll go ahead* (Carol T, 23.xi.97), that is, licking off the last bits of food on it).

Another aspect of modification that requires nonconventional coordination, not discussed by Clark, is pinning down the degree of a property (expressed by an adjective) possessed by an entity (expressed by a noun). How big is a *big book*? Is it bigger than a *small house*? Is a *small house* for a millionaire the same size as a *small house* for a working-class person? Gradable properties are expressed by pairs of antonymous adjectives, which implies the existence of a neutral reference point or region from which the antonymous adjectives depart in opposite directions. But the reference point is not absolutely fixed: it depends on our common knowledge of the range and distribution of possible values of the property for the particular object, and also on salient properties of the current context. In other words, perceptual and/or cognitive salience are necessary in order to establish the reference point which the hearer uses to determine what degree of a property the speaker is communicating about an object.

The degree to which ordinary language use, apparently conforming to linguistic convention, requires nonconventional coordination devices makes it clear that virtually all language use involves nonconventional coordination. In all but timeless generic sentences, people are using conventional expressions describing types or classes of objects, properties and events in order to talk about specific objects, properties and events. In other words, virtually every noun, verb and adjective in virtually every sentence requires nonconventional coordination in order to establish reference to the specific object, property and event being talked about. Moreover, the ambiguity of words requires the hearer to jointly resolve the ambiguity of most words in a sentence based on extralinguistic context, that is, again using nonconventional coordination devices. Finally, the context dependence of many constructions, in particular modifier constructions, constructions involving denominal derivation or noun compounding, and constructions with general verbs, requires nonconventional coordination simply to determine the exact content of the utterance.

4.3.2 Context, categorization and conceptualization

No word means the same thing twice.

Robert Musil, *The man without qualities*

In the preceding section, I demonstrated that convention, the chief property of human linguistic behavior that inhibits change, does not account for all linguistic behavior. Nonconventional coordination devices are called for in any innovative use of language, and in language learning. Most innovative use of language is also partly conventional, because it is based on the recombination of conventional coordination devices (words and constructions). But ordinary language use that does not appear to innovate also requires the pervasive use of nonconventional coordination devices. There is no sharp distinction between conservative and innovative language use. All language use is innovative, to some degree.

The chief reason why even conventional language use is innovative is that there cannot be a word or phrase to describe every experience that people wish to communicate. Every object and action and concept has a unique identity, although they share similarities with other objects, actions and concepts. Language – the conventional signaling system – attempts to solve this problem by identifying recurrent situations that people wish to communicate; that is clause (5) of the Lewis & Clark definition of convention. It is assumed that it is recurrent situation types that linguistic conventions describe. The full richness of the meaning to be conveyed in a particular context of use must be achieved by the interlocutors using nonconventional coordination devices. But this account of linguistic meaning is seriously flawed. The line between categories of recurrent situation types and the full richness of specific experiences to be communicated simply cannot be drawn. Hence convention is itself fluid to some degree – a degree that must be agreed upon by the interlocutors in particular occasions of use.[3]

Grice distinguishes two types of meaning on the basis of the supposed difference between the infinite richness of experiences that speakers wish to communicate and the available conventions of the language they use. The full meaning conveyed in a particular context is called the utterer's occasion meaning (Grice 1967/1989:90) or SPEAKER'S MEANING (Clark 1996:126). The recurrent situation type for a linguistic expression is the timeless meaning or sentence/word meaning (Grice 1967/1989:89), or, to use Clark's term, SIGNAL MEANING (Clark 1996:126).

The distinction between signal meaning and speaker's meaning is related to another distinction used to characterize linguistic meaning, that between the DICTIONARY and the ENCYCLOPEDIA. The dictionary approach to linguistic meaning is to argue that there is a small subset of information that is part of the linguistic (conventional) meaning of a word or construction; it is roughly equivalent to the standard view of signal meaning. The encyclopedic approach is that the meaning of a word (or construction) is all that we know about the situations for which the word or construction is used. The encyclopedic view of word meaning is not equivalent to the speaker's meaning, but rather to the sum total of the history of speaker's meanings of a word or construction in occasions of use. In the remainder of this section, I will argue that the description of signal meaning as a subset of properties is too simple, and instead offer an encyclopedic view of the signal meaning based on an individual's history of encounters with speaker's meanings. This model of meaning reveals a further source for variability and flexibility which may lead to language change.

Clark argues that although speaker's meaning is established in part by signal meaning – the conventions of the language – speaker's meaning is logically prior. For example, the meaning of contextual constructions is fixed in use. All novel use in language, such as metaphor, metonymy and indirect reference, has its meaning established only in context. But there is another more important way in which speaker's meaning is prior. A language learner acquires signal meaning on the basis of the history of speaker's meanings that they encounter, including their own uses of the signal (expression). And this acquisition process is not simple.

There is evidence from a variety of psycholinguistic experiments that the relevant features for a concept denoted by a word are variable across contexts (Barsalou 1987, 1993:31–5; Gibbs 1994:33–4; and references cited therein). For example, *piano* used in the context of producing music had different features as optimal cues for retrieval than *piano* in the context of moving furniture. When subjects provide definitions of a category, there is a remarkable degree to which definitions do not overlap between subjects and even in the same subject on different occasions. Moreover, the features and their ranking can be manipulated by manipulating context. The variability of concepts in context found in these experiments suggests no subset can be specified as 'the dictionary meaning'. Barsalou argues that what is much less variant is the sum total of knowledge of the object, which is presumably stored in long-term memory – in other words, the encyclopedic view of word meanings.

Similar evidence comes from language change. Proper names do not appear to have any meaning except to identify individuals, yet they can evolve to possess meanings drawn from contextual properties of those individuals, e.g. *napoleonic* (Haiman 1980a:350). A well-known example of peripheral contextual information coming to be a central part of the meaning of a word is English *bead* from *bede* 'prayer', since rosary beads were used in prayer. A more grammatical example is the shift of English *since* from an originally temporal meaning, with a contextual causative inference, to a causal connective (see §3.3.2, §5.4.3). Content – the 'dictionary' meaning – and context can shift and be interchanged, based on occasions of use.

Haiman (1980a) argues that all attempts to isolate a subset of our total knowledge of an entity and identify it as the dictionary meaning are ultimately untenable. Perhaps the most plausible division is based on essential information about a concept (dictionary meaning) vs accidental information (encyclopedic meaning; a distinction dating back to Aristotle). However, this distinction is valid only against a background theory of the entity in question, which determines what is essential and what is accidental (see Murphy & Medin 1985; Keil 1989; Gelman & Coley 1991). Such a theory would be built on our encyclopedic knowledge; moreover, theories differ from individual to individual and over periods of time. Consider for example the meaning of *meaning*: who among linguists and philosophers has the same essential concept for this word?

Likewise, objective meaning (dictionary) vs subjective meaning (encyclopedia) presupposes that there is a universal unchanging theory of what the objective properties of an entity are; and there is not. Lastly, Haiman draws on Quine's famous argument that the distinction between analytic statements ('true by definition') and synthetic statements ('true by empirical assessment') cannot be used to differentiate dictionary meaning from encyclopedic meaning (Quine 1951/1961). As Haiman summarizes Quine's argument: 'analyticity within a language can be defined only in terms of synonymy and definition, which in turn, however, can be defined within a language only in terms of analyticity'

(Haiman 1980a:349). Another way of putting it is that it is only in terms of some theory we have about phenomena that some statements describing those phenomena can be definitional.

Quine makes the further point that meaning/knowledge of words and statements is interconnected (cf. Gadamer 1972/1976:84–5). In our terms, the theory is in essence the organization of our encyclopedic knowledge taken as a whole; one cannot isolate the definitional part of it, let alone identify it as the dictionary meaning which characterizes the recurrent situation for a conventional linguistic expression. Thus, the meanings of individual words and constructions cannot be isolated mental representations, as is assumed in the dictionary view of linguistic semantics, but access points into a single network of encyclopedic knowledge (Langacker 1987:163). The flexibility of what knowledge is activated on particular occasions of use is manifested in the results of the experiments on concepts reported by Barsalou and Gibbs.

Even the encyclopedic knowledge model of meaning does not exhaust the richness of meaning. Searle (1979), Winograd (1980) and other cognitive scientists have argued that the sort of knowledge that is relevant to a linguistic expression's meaning cannot be enumerated in such a way that all contexts of use can be predicted. Searle argues that a basically infinite set of background assumptions is required to characterize the literal meaning of an utterance, and hence its appropriate use in context.

Consider example (16):

(16)   Give me a hamburger, medium rare, with ketchup and mustard, but easy on the relish. (Searle 1979:127)

We assume we understand what the literal meaning of this request is. Specifying it is much more difficult, however:

> Suppose for example that the hamburger is brought to me encased in a cubic yard of solid lucite plastic so rigid that it takes a jack hammer to bust it open, or suppose the hamburger is a mile wide and is 'delivered' to me by smashing down the wall of the restaurant and sliding the edge of it in. (Searle 1979:127)

Langacker makes a similar observation with a comparable example (Langacker 1988:16):

(17)   He is barely keeping his head above the water.

> imagine a race over the ocean by helicopter, where the contestants must transport a severed head, suspended by a rope from the helicopter, from the starting line to the finish; a contestant is disqualified if the head he is carrying ever dips below the water's surface. (Langacker 1988:16–17)

Searle points out that refining the semantic representation of the utterance to exclude all possible qualifications is impossible: one can always create new contexts in which the utterance is inappropriate and other minimally different contexts in which it is appropriate (Searle 1979:128).[4] For example, the philosopher's favorite sentence *The cat is on the mat* seems inappropriate when cat and mat are floating weightless in space; but if we are in a spaceship with cat–mat pairs floating around in just two configurations, mirror images of each other, the sentence could be an appropriate answer to the question, *Which is it now?* (Searle 1979:122–3) – if the interlocutors agree to it.

Searle's cat-and-mat example demonstrates the problem in describing a recurrent situation for a conventional expression. Is outer space context a recurrent situation for *The cat is on the mat?* Only if the interlocutors choose to conceptualize it as such. A situation does not simply present itself as a recurrence of some prior situation type, that is, as belonging to the same category as some prior set of situations: it has to be conceptualized as such by the interlocutors jointly.

It is a truism that situations can be categorized in many different ways. For instance, a speaker can categorize an individual whom she wishes the hearer to identify in a potentially infinite set of ways: *Tony Blair, neighbor, Labour leader, man, prime minister.* Each category is defined by the string of prior coordination problems which the string of sounds has been conventionally established to solve. For example, the string of prior coordination problems for which *Labour leader* has been used includes reference to Michael Foot, Neil Kinnock, John Smith; the string of prior coordination problems for which *prime minister* has been used includes reference to James Callaghan, Margaret Thatcher, John Major, not to mention a host of prime ministers in other countries.

A single coordination problem has several different solutions, that is, everything we talk about can be categorized in different ways. Which solution (category, word) the speaker chooses depends on joint salience. Britons in Britain can use the phrase *the prime minister* in certain contexts to refer to Tony Blair because their common ground makes Tony Blair – not the prime minister of Turkey or some other place, or the prime minister at some other time – the jointly most salient prime minister.

However, joint salience is not just there to be exploited by speaker and hearer; it can be created. By choosing a word to refer to something, we identify the current coordination problem as being the recurrence of certain coordination problems that have been solved before, and the hearer knows those problems and solutions as much as we do (clause (3) in the Lewis & Clark definition of convention). The speaker causes the hearer to compare the current situation to the prior ones, and thus makes (jointly) salient certain aspects of the situation by the choice of words.

In the cat-and-mat-in-outer-space example, speaker and hearer may or may not define the situation as a recurrence of the situation type conventionally denoted by *The cat is on the mat.* Once they choose to use the sentence or not in the outer space context, however, the interlocutors have altered the meaning of *The cat is on the mat* for themselves, by including or excluding the outer space context as an instance of the recurring situation type for that sentence.

The clearest cases of conceptualization is when there is overt dispute as to categorization, and hence meaning, of expressions. For example, by choosing to refer to it as a *fetus* or an *unborn baby*, one has identified the current coordination problem as a recurrence of two different situation types or categories. The term *fetus* can be used for any conceived-but-not-yet-born offspring of any animal (and thus dehumanizes it); while *baby* is used for already-born and specifically human offspring (see Bolinger 1980:138). Either term will successfully establish reference, that is, taps into jointly salient properties that allow the hearer to know what the speaker is talking about. But they are different properties and the properties chosen thereby become more salient.

Speaker's meaning is flexible and highly dependent on context. Inferring signal meaning from prior occurrences of speaker's meaning is possible only by building an encyclopedic representation of meaning – that is, reflecting the full range of common ground in the community using the conventional signal. Hence we cannot differentiate speaker's meaning from signal meaning in any particular context of use.

Instead, we must define meaning in two ways with respect to a different distinction. These two types of meaning are based on the distinction between a language as a population of utterances produced by a speech community, and a grammar as an individual speaker's knowledge about the conventions of the speech community. The COMMUNITY'S MEANING of a linguistic form – a lingueme – is the lineage of replications of its use, in their full encyclopedic, contextual value. The INDIVIDUAL'S MEANING of a lingueme is a mental structure that emerges from the individual's exposure to (necessarily partial) lineages of the community's meaning, including of course the use of the lingueme by that same individual. This is not to say that an individual speaker stores separately every individual meaning-in-context she has heard or produced. Particular meanings-in-context can crystallize into types in an individual speaker's mind, or be joined in networks of related meanings in her mind (polysemy; cf. Gibbs 1994:40–7). But an individual's meaning can be thought of as a sedimentation of the history of uses to which she has been exposed (including her own uses).

Both the community's meaning and the individual's meaning are always subject to change. Every new use alters the lineage of the community's meaning. Every new use to which a speaker is exposed (or which the speaker creates) alters the individual's meaning as well. A speaker's encyclopedic knowledge is based on finite prior situations of use, which includes an indefinitely large number of background assumptions about the conditions of categorization. These background assumptions do not all apply to the new situations we wish to communicate. Hence, the individual's meaning – our prior encyclopedic knowledge of the situation type – is not obviously or easily extendable to new situations where communication is desired. In fact, applying old words to new situations is often a creative, and even controversial, act, conceptualizing the new situation as a recurrence of an old one. And when the conventional signals are extended – or not extended – to new situation types, the individual's meaning is changed.

The hearer is expected to recognize the situation being communicated by the speaker as a recurrence of prior situations. Yet the hearer has his own history of uses of the lingueme, comparable to the speaker's only to the extent that they share common ground. And the speaker is conceptualizing the current situation in a particular way, so that the hearer is not only recognizing the situation, using conventional and nonconventional coordination devices, but also concurring with the speaker in her partially creative act of categorization. As we will see in the following section, the hearer's role in this process is not entirely passive.

The final level of complexity in relating the meaning of the current utterance to prior uses has to do with the structure of the utterance itself. An utterance is a recombination of replicated linguemes. The recombination of linguemes chosen by the speaker on a particular occasion of use represents her attempt to conceptualize the current situation as a (partial) recurrence of prior situations. Likewise, the hearer must also recognize / share in the conceptualization of the current situation as a recurrence of prior situations based on the lineages of those linguemes in his own histories of their uses. This final level is the locus of much grammatical change, as I will argue in chapters 5–6.

4.3.3   *Joint construal and the evolution of interpretation*

In §4.3.2, I emphasized the flexibility and even fluidity of meaning in use: 'language is made up of significations in the state of being born . . . language is in movement and is not fixed; and perhaps because one must recognize in the last analysis that there are "flowing significations"' (Merleau-Ponty 1964/ 1973:88). Nevertheless, I have tacitly assumed that for any particular occasion of language use, the meaning – speaker's meaning – is fixed, no matter how complex it is and how subtle the coordination problem is. In this section, I suggest that speaker's meaning in any particular occasion of use is not entirely fixed – thereby allowing a still greater degree of flexibility in language use that opens the door to language change.

There is a common model of communication which presupposes fixity of speaker's meaning that has been called the CONDUIT METAPHOR (Reddy 1993). In essence, the conduit metaphor assumes that the speaker packages her thoughts and/or feelings – which Reddy abbreviates as RM (repertoire member) – in a linguistic expression, and the hearer unpackages them upon hearing the expression. Linguistic expressions are conduits by which the RM moves from speaker to hearer. There is a vast number of everyday English expressions that use the conduit metaphor, some of which are given below (all examples from Reddy 1993):

(18)   *Language is a conduit for transferring an RM from one individual to another*
    a.   You know very well that I gave you that idea.
    b.   Your real feelings are finally getting through to me.

(19)   *Humans place their RMs within the external signal*
    a.   It is very difficult to put this concept into words.
    b.   He crammed his speech with subversive words.

(20)   *Signals convey or contain RMs*
    a.   His words carry little in the way of recognizable meaning.
    b.   Your words seem rather hollow.

(21)   *Humans find RMs within the signals and take them into their heads*
    a.   Please pay attention to what's there in the words!
    b.   We will see this thought several times again in the sonnet.

(22)   *Speakers/writers eject their RMs into an external 'space'*
    a.   Mary poured out her sorrows.
    b.   The essay brings out unusual thoughts on the matter.

There is an obvious error in the theory of communication behind this metaphor, and a number of important consequences that follow from rectifying this error. The obvious error is that thoughts or feelings cannot 'go' anywhere outside of the minds of humans, whether it is 'into' words or 'into' an external space. Reddy proposes what he calls the toolmakers paradigm (so called after the fanciful example he uses to illustrate it) that avoids this error. The Lewis & Clark model of convention and communication also avoids this error. The whole idea behind a coordination problem is that getting speaker and hearer to converge on the same meaning is a problem, precisely because our thoughts cannot leave our heads.

A less obvious error that follows directly from the primary one is that linguistic expressions do not contain meanings. Meaning is something that occurs in the interlocutors' heads at the point of language use (speaker's meaning), or something that represents a memory of a history of uses available to a speaker, albeit organized into senses and sense relations all embedded in a network of encyclopedic knowledge. Reddy emphasizes this fact, that for instance a body of texts does not have meaning; there must be a basis for readers to evoke a meaning in their heads through shared knowledge with the culture that produced the texts.

It is not so obvious that the Lewis & Clark model of convention avoids this error. Instead, in the preceding section I argued that one must interpret the notion of a recurrent situation in the definition of convention quite loosely in order to accommodate the fluidity of meaning. Linguistic conventions are not that rigid.

Another error that follows from the conduit metaphor model of communication is that successful communication is a perfect match of the speaker's intended meaning and the hearer's understanding via the 'transfer' of thoughts. Unsuccessful communication is a mismatch, resulting from the hearer's misunderstanding or possibly the speaker's improper packaging of her thoughts. Since thoughts do not travel, success in communication has to be construed differently.

In the simple Schelling game in (3), success seems to be easily assessed: the players perceive that they chose the same number, or they did not. But how do interlocutors figure out they have succeeded in communication? After the utterance is produced and the hearer has understood it, in his own way, how do speaker and hearer know they have the same meaning for the utterance, in particular the meaning intended by the speaker? They have no direct means of knowing. They have only an indirect means: if what the hearer says and does in response appears to follow naturally from a recognition of the meaning that the speaker intended. And the hearer knows that the speaker understood his response, and hence he understood her original utterance, on the basis of what her next response to him is. And so on.

But Clark observes that this process need not require a fixed interpretation of the speaker's first utterance as the speaker's original intended meaning for her utterance. First, a number of turns in conversation may be required to establish the jointly accepted meaning, and the hearer himself may contribute to the meaning being constructed (example (23) from Cheepen & Monaghan 1990:157):

(23)   1K: once those cameras start flashing particularly with the infants
      2C: it puts them off   *[hearer continuation of 1]*
      3K: it puts them off   *[acceptance of 2 by repetition]*
      4C: yeh   *[acceptance of 3 by a continuer]*

Meaning in use is defined by JOINT CONSTRUAL: 'For each signal, the speaker and addressees try to create a joint construal of what the speaker is to be taken to mean by it' (Clark 1996:212). Of course a joint construal, like any other joint activity, is not always easy to achieve. The standard case, where the speaker's original intended meaning is ultimately accepted (more precisely, is taken to be accepted, by continuing onwards), is found in what Clark calls verified construal and corrected misconstrual (Clark 1996:215):[5]

(24)   *Verified construal*
      1C: Buck's Fizz, is that a mixture of wine and orange juice?
      2A: Champagne.
      3C: Very classy [etc.]

(25)   *Corrected misconstrual*
      1S: what do you have to wear?
      2B: what..for football
      3S: yeah
      4B: em..lingerie
      5S: (laughs and ends up coughing) what do you have to wear seriously for football..what do you have to wear?

(26)   *Corrected misconstrual*
      1N: Oh..didn't you notice I put the dining room table back?
      2P: Dining room table? Why where's it been?
      3N: The kitchen table I mean..I cleared it yesterday
      4P: No

In (24), C's simple continuation after A's response implies that A's answer to C's question is sufficient evidence for C that A understood C's question. Examples (25)–(26) indicate misconstruals that are corrected by hearer and speaker respectively. In (25), B's response in 4 to S's question indicates that B did not take S's question seriously, and (after laughing) S asks the question again, adding *seriously* to her utterance. In (26), P's response to N's question causes P to correct herself. Corrected misconstruals are less infrequent than one might expect. Labov notes with regard to his Cross-Dialectal Comprehension project, '[this] study has demonstrated that the actual number of misunderstandings in everyday life is much greater than casual observations lead us to believe' (Labov 1994:565).

Note that in (25), B's joking response is probably a deliberate misconstrual; not every misconstrual is accidental. Nor is every 'misconstrual' rejected. In the more interesting cases, there is an alteration of the speaker's original intention which is accepted by the speaker as the basis for the continuation of the interaction. Clark describes two types, which are more or less illustrated with the following examples:

(27)   *Revised construal*
        1K: I just opened it [film] like you were going to.
        2M: In the dark?
        3K: Yeah. And it had rewound so
        4M: Didn't like my idea then, that's fine.
        5K: I'm sorry..I just..I was nervous and I thought about it and decided
               it would be a good idea rather than trying to figure out about
               sending something to Milton Keynes and spending a lot of money
               and (inaud.)

(28)   *Narrowed construal*
        1H: You need some kitchen roll
        2L: Can I have that as well?
        3H: Yeah just take it

In (27), K's utterance in 1–3 (including M's contribution to the utterance *in the dark*) is construed by M in 4 as an insult; in 5, K accepts that construal and apologizes. Here the revised construal pertains to an emotive aspect of the speaker's meaning. In (28), L construes H's general observation as an invitation to take the kitchen roll, probably a narrowed construal of H's original intention, and in 3, H accepts that construal by agreeing to L's request in 2.

In all of these examples, construal of the meaning of an utterance is not necessarily fixed by the speaker's original intention, but is jointly negotiated and agreed upon over the course of the conversation: 'understanding is not reconstruction but mediation' (Linge 1976:xvi). What may seem like marginal cases in these attested examples can be multiplied in other contexts. Any teacher who asks students to write essays based on class lectures and sees what is written quickly realizes the scope for altered construal in understanding. One might attribute this to students' uncertain grasp of the common ground of the community into which they are being introduced in the class. But any scientist who has given a lecture to colleagues, or discussed his or her own work with colleagues, will recognize that revised construal is a very common phenomenon:

> Science is a conversation with nature, but it is also a conversation with other scientists. Not until scientists publish their views and discover the reactions of other scientists can they possibly appreciate what they have actually said. No matter how much one might write and rewrite one's work in anticipation of possible responses, it is impossible to avoid all possible misunderstandings, and not all such misunderstandings are plainly 'misunderstandings'. Frequently *scientists do not know what they intended to say until they discover what it is that other scientists have taken them to be saying.* (Hull 1988:7; emphasis added)

In other words, a speaker's originally intended meaning may not end up being the jointly accepted meaning of the utterance. Other writers in other disciplines have made similar observations:

> For the speaking subject, to express is to become aware of; he does not express just for others, but also to know himself what he intends . . . Even we who speak do not necessarily know better than those who listen to us what we are expressing. (Merleau-Ponty 1960/1964:90, 91)

> The fact is that in most cases an author does not understand all the meaning of his work. (Eliade 1952/1991:25)

> language does not yet contain its meaning . . . all communication supposes in the listener a creative re-enactment of what is heard. (Merleau-Ponty 1962/1964:8)

Successful communication is not easy. But successful communication involves not the recovery of an original, 'correct' interpretation of the speaker's original intention, but instead an interpretation that evolves over the course of the conversation, and is assessed by the success or failure of the higher social-interactional goals that the interlocutors are striving to achieve.

One reason why this effort is not doomed to failure from the beginning is the fact that although we cannot read each other's minds, we do inhabit a shared world. Even with the Schelling game example in (6), assessment of success is due to joint attention in the shared perceptual field (the players point to which number each chose). Reddy recognizes that there exists 'an "a priori shared context", a prerequisite for achieving any communication whatsoever' (Reddy 1993:181). Interlocutors can achieve success in communication by means of joint attention to phenomena in the shared world and by virtue of shared expertise acquired through interaction with others in the shared world. Nevertheless, the establishment of a joint, shared meaning of an utterance does not happen automatically but involves an evolving interpretation, negotiated by the interlocutors through their continuing conversation. And one effect of the evolving interpretation is evolution of the mapping between form and function in language.

4.4 Conclusion

This chapter outlines a theory of language and meaning in use which can be used in the Theory of Utterance Selection for language change. In particular, the theory shows a number of ways in which language use gives speakers opportunity, indeed requires them, to innovate.

First, communication is subservient to other social goals of the interlocutors. Achieving those goals often means conforming to linguistic convention as closely as possible. But sometimes achieving those goals, or even achieving just the goal of communication, is better done by stretching or breaking linguistic conventions. This is one source of language change, albeit not a subtle or omnipresent one.

Language use, and the goals it serves, is a joint activity. It is facilitated by the interlocutors inhabiting a shared world, but hampered by the fact that the interlocutors cannot read each other's minds. (I say 'hampered', but one can readily perceive the advantages of this sort of world by imagining what it would be like if we could all read each other's minds.) Thus, the hearer may interpret the meaning of the speaker in a slightly novel way, and there is no direct check on the hearer's interpretation (although there are indirect checks in the form of negotiated construals and the natural course of the conversation). The interlocutors utilize various coordination devices, including joint perceptual/cognitive salience, precedent, explicit agreement and convention; but no coordination device is foolproof, and so the hearer may end up with a slightly different interpretation of the utterance.

Convention is the primary means by which linguistic communication is achieved. But convention is not sufficient to evoke for the hearer the full richness of the experience being communicated by the speaker. This is because every situation is novel in some way or another. The novel character of the situation may be subtle or it may be more dramatic (as in the cat-and-mat-in-outer-space examples). But the novelty of a situation means that all language use innovates to some degree.

Also, convention is not equal to competence. Members of the speech community have a different grasp of conventions, for instance in the range of situation types for which an expression is conventionally used. These interindividual differences may lead to innovations as well.

Finally, communities are defined in terms of domains of shared expertise. Any society is made up of multiple communities. There is a large degree of overlap in the codes used in any society, especially so-called monolingual societies. In this way, internal and external factors in language change are intertwined and this may facilitate language change.

All of these opportunities to innovate pertain to the expression of meaning in grammatical form. Hence, our theory of innovation in language change must be cast in terms of an alteration of the relationship between form and meaning. This theory will be outlined in the following chapters.

Notes

1 It may be objected that after the first uses of *CD room*, the phrase is still not conventional because it is not sufficiently arbitrary: no other solution to the coordination problem is approximately equal. The claim is in effect that the two of us compute the phrase *CD room* on the basis of joint perceptual salience every time we use it. This alternative is the pragmatic analysis, in contrast to the semantic analysis, where *CD room* is simply stored in our minds as a learned convention of our personal lexicon. There is little motivation for the pragmatic solution beyond initial uses of a term. For later uses of a word or phrase, the community behavior to which we are conforming is generally much more jointly salient than the perceptual and cognitive factors underlying the choice of the term in the first place.

2 Most of the following examples of the need for nonconventional coordination in ordinary language use correspond to the need for explicatures in specifying meaning in relevance theory (Sperber & Wilson 1995).

3 See Gibbs 1994, especially chapter 2, for a critique of conventional ('literal') meaning along similar lines.

4 Winograd (1980) makes a similar point in criticizing standard views of meaning as fixed entities, adopted by artificial intelligence researchers (see also Clark & Clark 1979:807).

5 Clark does not provide any attested examples of different sorts of joint construals. Examples (24)–(28) are taken from conversations collected and transcribed by students in classes on discourse analysis at the University of Manchester.

Chapter 5

Form–function reanalysis

5.1 Introduction

In chapter 4, I presented a theory of meaning in use that allows us to locate cracks in the system of conventions to which speakers are attempting to conform when speaking. These cracks are the points at which innovation can occur. The most important crack is the impossibility of separating conventional from nonconventional aspects of meaning in a particular context of use. In §4.3.2, I argued that one consequence of this is that the 'meaning' of a grammatical form (word or construction) is essentially the history of its uses by the members of the speech community, in other words, its lineage. Individual members have internalized knowledge of a partial history of the form, namely its contexts of use that they have heard or used themselves. This knowledge includes crystallization into senses and subsenses and networks of polysemy relations, and the slice of encyclopedic knowledge that the meaning represents.

Hence, when a speaker applies her grammatical knowledge to a particular context of use, she must select words and constructions that will conceptualize the current meaning to be conveyed in the way desired. More precisely, a speaker combines words and structures that have been used for a variety of prior situations in the hope that they will convey what she intends to communicate to the hearer in the current situation. The hearer in turn must rely on his knowledge of the words and structures in prior combinations in prior situations, and his experience of the current situation, and thereby construct what he thinks the speaker intended to communicate.

The recombination of words and constructions clearly adds a further layer of complexity onto the process of using language in a particular context. (This complexity of course is the result of the flexibility of recombining existing forms-cum-meanings to efficiently express an essentially open-ended set of contextual meanings.) For example, in producing a sentence such as the following, the verb *rob* and the argument-structure construction *[SBJ VERB OBJ of OBL]* are combined, along with the argument phrases, the tense-aspect-mood forms, etc.:

(1)   He robbed her of her bracelet.

Speakers put together the verb and the argument structure construction (choosing the argument structure in (1) instead of *He robbed the bracelet from her*). But the verb and the argument-structure construction never occur alone: the verb is always found in some argument-structure construction, and the argument-structure construction is always instantiated with a specific verb (*rob*, *deprive*, *relieve*, etc.).

In other words, the regularities in speakers' and listeners' internal representations of grammatical knowledge must be abstracted from histories of language uses in their rich communicative context. ABSTRACTION and ANALYSIS are the primary grammatical processes in language use. This is self-evident for hearers (and learners). It is true for speakers as well: speakers produce new utterances based on abstraction and analysis that they have done on previous utterances. We are presented with grammatical wholes and must analyze them into their component units, syntactic and semantic, in the process of learning and (re)using language. A central aspect of this process is abstracting a set of meanings for words and constructions, given the wide range of communicative contexts in which they can and do occur. The result of this process is a mapping from syntactic units onto components of meaning in the speaker's mind (see Croft to appear b). Nevertheless, because of the uniqueness and novelty of communicative situations, the recombination in utterances of pre-existing grammatical units and structures will involve some degree of novelty in the form-to-function mapping in each use of language, as was argued in chapter 4.

Moreover, a grammatical construction, that is, a complex syntactic unit, is a fixed combination of smaller syntactic units. The construction as a whole is mapped onto a complex semantic structure (directly in construction grammar and cognitive grammar, indirectly via mapping rules in other syntactic theories). There is of course a complex form–function mapping for the construction as a whole. But since the construction is a fixed whole, and so is the semantic structure it denotes, the syntactic units and their semantic denotata repeatedly cooccur in the same configuration across contexts of use. For this reason, there is a certain degree of potential indeterminacy or ambiguity in the attribution of semantic components to syntactic components in an utterance. That is, there is some leeway for speakers/listeners to reanalyze the form–meaning mapping in a grammatical construction.[1] This is FORM–FUNCTION REANALYSIS.

Form–function reanalysis is a nonintentional mechanism for innovation. Speakers' intended actions are towards conformity to convention, but the result is innovation, an unintended consequence. The unintended consequence of individual actions is due in part to the potential discrepancy between individual competence, which is constantly responding to use (§3.3.1, §4.3), and the conventions of the speech community. Most of the time, the grammatical forms produced are essentially the same as those produced before, albeit in novel combinations, in novel meanings in context, and also with variable pronunciations (see the discussion of the innovation of sound change in §3.4.4). The innovations may be due to random low-level neural processes, as would be modeled by interactive activation networks; or by higher-level restructuring of the knowledge of form–function mappings in the grammar. Either way, innovations result from speakers attempting to conform to convention.

An illustration of how innovations may occur randomly in language use can be found in an experimentally induced type of language use:

A list was compiled of 90 irregular [English] verbs, mixed in with three times that many regular verbs; thus two, three, or four regular verbs separated the irregular verbs. The subjects were asked to listen to the experimenter read the base form of the verb, and then to produce the past-tense form of that verb as quickly as possible. The subjects were told that the object of the experiment was to see how fast they could go through the list; and the experimenters were instructed to put as much time pressure on the subjects as possible, since the purpose was to induce errors. (Bybee & Slobin 1982b:268)

The result of this experiment, as reported by Bybee & Slobin, was various sorts of regularizations and also novel vowel-stem forms, as well as of course many correct productions. Thus, speakers produced innovations. But the innovations were a result of speakers attempting to produce 'correct' forms – conforming to linguistic norms – in (accelerated) real time. They were not the consequence of speakers trying – intending – to make past tense forms more similar to base forms, although that was in fact the result in many instances. The innovations are likely to be a stochastic outcome of spreading activation and interactive activation in the network of linguistic knowledge, in this case, the knowledge of morphological forms and their meanings (see §6.2.1). Similarly, the network of relations holding together the units of a grammatical construction and the semantic structures they conventionally denote can also be subject to interactive activation, leading to production of an altered form of the construction.

Form–function reanalysis is abductive (see Andersen 1973). That is, the representation of the form–meaning mapping in the speaker's and listener's heads is abducted (inferred or reconstructed) from prior and current experiences of the form–meaning mapping found with similar utterances in similar situations. This abduction occurs in language use, however, not in language acquisition (*pace* Andersen 1973), thereby conforming with what we know about how language change actually occurs (see §3.2 and §3.3.1).

The mechanism for innovation in form–function reanalysis is based on the form–meaning mapping in grammatical constructions. The form–meaning mapping clearly fits in with language use, since in communication, the form–meaning mapping plays the central role in jointly construing the information communicated by the speaker (§4.3.3).

The mechanism is based on a very simple model of grammatical structure. An utterance represents a construction that is made up of its component syntactic, lexical and morphological units; the grammatical units have semantic values, or at least are expected by the speaker to have semantic values; and the semantic values of grammatical units contribute somehow to the semantic value of the syntactic constructions of which they are a part.

There are of course more complex formal models of grammatical structure, and different degrees of abstraction that speakers might achieve. Functionalist linguists have questioned the need for the added complexity found in formalist syntactic models and also the maximal degree of abstraction such models assume (see Givón 1979; Langacker 1987; and Croft to appear b *inter alia*). I will return briefly to this issue in §5.6. The simple model described in the preceding paragraph represents a least common denominator that both functionalists and formalists recognize as constituting the grammatical structure which must be represented in a speaker's mind. It is certainly the minimum necessary to characterize the grammatical knowledge a speaker has/needs in order to communicate successfully. I will argue in the rest of this chapter that this simple model of grammatical knowledge actually accounts for many types of grammatical changes that occur in languages.

The types of innovations to be described as form–function reanalysis partially overlap with other definitions of reanalysis. Many authors assume that reanalysis requires a precondition of alternative surface structural analyses based on the existing structures of the grammar, e.g. ambiguity of case marking or alternative constituency analyses (Langacker 1977; Hankamer 1977; see §6.3.2.4). Form–function reanalysis is not of this type, since remappings between grammatical form and conventional function may violate existing unambiguous conventional mappings. Harris & Campbell also argue that the precondition of formal grammatical ambiguity for reanalysis is too strong (Harris & Campbell 1995:70–2).

Although Harris & Campbell have a broad definition of what sorts of grammatical changes can be defined as reanalysis (Harris & Campbell 1995:61–5), they exclude what other historical linguists would call later stages of a reanalysis, namely actualization, from their definition. ACTUALIZATION is the production of a previously unattested grammatical structure based on the reanalysis of the structure of the construction (whether syntactic or syntactic + semantic). For Harris & Campbell, reanalysis involves only the introduction of an alternative syntactic structure for a construction, even if there is not any visible change to the construction (i.e. an innovated structure). Haspelmath argues that one cannot determine when an unactualized reanalysis might have occurred, and so it is impossible to constrain the postulation of an unactualized reanalysis (Haspelmath 1998a:74–5). In the Theory of Utterance Selection for language change, replication of a lingueme occurs with each utterance employing that lingueme. Hence the time span from reanalysis to actualization is probably extremely short, probably to the point of being negligible for theoretical purposes. I include actualization as part of the reanalysis process, since I am concerned with the production of novel forms which occurs only with actualization.

Form–function reanalysis is syntagmatic: it arises from the (re)mapping of form–function relations of combinations of syntactic units and semantic components. The process may nevertheless have an apparently paradigmatic result, for example, a change of meaning of a syntactic unit (see for example §5.4).

One of the central goals, if not the central goal, of a language user's processing of grammatical structures is determining the semantic contribution each syntactic unit makes towards the meaning of the whole in a particular context of use. The argument I have just presented is that innovation in language change in many cases represents a reanalysis of this mapping, possibly as a stochastic low-level process in mental representations, emerging in language use. The next four sections will describe four types of form–function reanalysis: hyperanalysis, hypoanalysis, metanalysis and cryptanalysis.

5.2   Hyperanalysis (overanalysis)

Form–function reanalysis involves the remapping of the relationship between form and function in a grammatical construction. For any given construction made up of multiple (morpho-)syntactic units, the hearer attempts to identify what component of the content or function communicated in context is attributable to each syntactic unit, using prior knowledge of construction and word uses and the overall meaning communicated. Of course, all of these processes are occurring in parallel: a hearer has knowledge of the current context, a partial history of the construction's use, and partial histories of the uses of the words in the utterance. The hearer attempts to identify what component(s) of the meaning are conventionally denoted by the syntactic unit in question and what component(s) of the meaning are contributed by the context. The context for a syntactic unit includes other syntactic units in the construction, the construction itself (to the extent that it contributes conventional meaning not associated with any single unit), and the nonconventional context. As argued in §4.3, there is no sharp line between conventional (signal) meaning and the nonconventional components of speaker's meaning in an utterance. Hence, the meanings may be reassigned from one component to the other, or from nonconventional meaning to conventional meaning or vice versa.

In HYPERANALYSIS, the listener reanalyzes an inherent semantic/functional property of a syntactic unit as a contextual property (usually, a property of another syntactic unit of the construction). In the reanalysis, this inherent property of a syntactic unit is then attributed to the context (often another unit in the construction), and so the syntactic unit in question loses some of its meaning or function. Hence, hyperanalysis is a major source of semantic bleaching and/or loss in general. Hyperanalysis is analogous to Ohala's notion of hypercorrection in his listener-based model of sound change (see §3.4.4).[2] In §§5.2.1–5.2.2, I give two examples of plausible contexts for syntactic hyperanalysis.

5.2.1   Loss of governed oblique case

In many languages, the argument structure of certain verbs includes a governed oblique case or adpositional phrase. That is, the semantics of the verb requires an argument which is expressed as a (usually obligatory) oblique NP or PP. A good example is Russian, where verbs may govern 'objects' in the genitive, dative or instrumental case. Examples of verbs governing the genitive are given in (2) (Pulkina n.d.:82–7, 89–99):

(2) *Genitive*

trebovat'	'demand s.t.'	*bojat'sja*	'be afraid of s.t.'
prosit'	'ask s.t.'	*pugat'sja*	'be frightened of s.t.'
iskat'	'seek, look for s.t.'	*opasat'sja*	'fear s.t.'
ždat'	'wish (for) s.t.'	*stesnjat'sja*	'be shy of s.t.'
slušat'sja	'listen to s.t.'	*storonit'sja*	'avoid/shun s.t.'
stoit'	'be worthy of s.t.'	*lišat'*	'deprive of s.t.'
lišat'sja	'lose s.t.'	*izbegat'*	'escape, avoid s.t.'

English also has a number of governed PP arguments, three of which are illustrated in (3):

(3) a. I was *looking at* the redwoods.
     b. She was *listening to* the quartet.
     c. We were *thinking about* the election.

To some extent, there is semantic motivation for the choice of oblique case with particular verbs or semantic subclasses of verbs. For instance, the Russian genitive is used with arguments in which there is lack of physical contact or lack of complete affectedness of the genitive NP's referent, particularly as found in the oblique objects of verbs of seeking/requesting and the stimulus argument of emotion verbs. These patterns presumably reflect the semantic contribution of the genitive case, as extensions of its use in other contexts.

However, in many languages including Russian, governed oblique cases are highly conventionalized. There are instances in which the governed case does not fit the semantic motivations. The verbs *deržat'sja* and *prideržat'sja* 'keep, hold (onto) s.t.' and *kasat'sja* 'touch s.t.' involve contact in their physical meanings yet govern the genitive. The verb *dobivat'sja* 'seek s.t.' can also mean 'obtain, achieve s.t.', but governs the genitive in the latter senses as well although they represent successful completion of the act. These facts blur the link between syntactic unit (the genitive case) and its semantic contribution to the meaning of the whole. Also, the inherent meaning of the verb also specifies the semantic role of the governed oblique argument. That is, there is overlap between the semantic contribution of verb and oblique case.

These two conditions, semantic irregularity and semantic overlap, provide the conditions for hyperanalysis. The inherent semantic value of adposition/case can be reanalyzed as belonging solely to the verb meaning. The adposition/case is devoid of meaning, or rather is semantically unnecessary, and eventually is left out (actualization of the reanalysis). This appears to be a relatively common phenomenon, and can be observed in Slavic and in Germanic languages.

The genitive object in Russian is governed by particular verbs and also by particular constructions, such as the negative and the partitive (Timberlake 1977:157–8). Jakobson (1936/1984) argued for a general semantic characterization of the genitive/accusative distinction in terms of a 'limitation on the extent to which an object participates in an event' (Timberlake 1977:158). Although this semantic analysis is rather vague, it probably reflects the semantic distinction between accusative and genitive in these contexts. Timberlake notes that the genitive is being replaced by the accusative in Russian, particularly in less formal registers. This is a hyperanalysis of the oblique case. Timberlake also argues that this shift is occurring gradually, and the path of shift can be accounted for by the degree of nonlimitation of the object, e.g. higher individuation (Timberlake 1977:162–8). I would argue that the gradual shift to accusative marking reflects a gradual attenuation of the semantics of the governed genitive case by hyperanalysis.

Verbs govern nonaccusative objects in Germanic as well. Comparative indirect evidence suggests that nonaccusative objects are gradually being hyperanalyzed, and there are limited examples of shift to accusative case in English shortly before the breakdown of the case system.

In languages such as German and Icelandic, the case system is still in place and many verbs still govern oblique cases. However, there is indirect evidence for object status from syntactic behavior associated with objects, in particular passivization. The evidence is somewhat obscured due to the existence of impersonal passives in both languages, where the active subject is deleted or encoded as an oblique, but the active object / governed oblique is not encoded as subject (Zaenen, Maling & Thráinsson 1985:476):

(4) Ihm   wurde geholfen.
    he.DAT was   help.PASS-PTC

(5) Honum var hjálpað.
    he.DAT was help.PASS-PTC

Zaenen, Maling & Thráinsson (1985:476–8), following Cole *et al.* (1980:727–8), argue that the German construction in (4) is not a true personal passive, because the 'passive subject' *Ihm* fails various behavioral tests for subjecthood, such as EQUI control, relative clause reduction and conjunction reduction. Thus it is an oblique, or at least not a subject. On the other hand, the Icelandic construction in (5) is a personal passive, albeit with a so-called quirky case passive subject, since it passes similar behavioral tests for subjecthood. Thus it is a subject, and following the standard formulation of the passive rule, it should correspond to an active object. Hence there is evidence that the Icelandic object of 'help' and other governed obliques has been partly hyperanalyzed as a direct object.

Zaenen, Maling & Thráinsson hint at an explanation of this difference between German and Icelandic in a footnote (ibid. 471, fn. 22). German has a rich case system and relatively free word order, so word order does not inherently code for subject status. Icelandic retains the rich case system but has rigid word order. Hence word order can encode subjecthood, and in fact hyperanalysis of the grammatical relation must have taken place, allowing for the quirky dative NP to pass the behavioral tests for subjecthood in this passive construction.

In Modern English, the object of *help* is encoded as a direct object, and the passive formed from it is a personal passive (English lacks impersonal passives).

However, the reason for this is as much the loss of the case system as hyper-analysis. Evidence for hyperanalysis would be a recoding of nonaccusative objects as accusative objects before the loss of the case system in Early Middle English. There is some evidence of this, in that governed genitives are occasionally found in the accusative in Old English before the loss of the case system: 'although there are not a very large number of examples with accusative objects, they are nevertheless too frequent to be mistakes' (Allen 1995:135; examples are from Allen 1995:133, 135):

(6) Micel   wund   behofað micles   lædcedomes
     great.NOM would.NOM needs   great.GEN leechcraft.GEN
     'A great wound requires great medicine' ([*COE*] Bede 4 26.350.19)

(7) . . . swa heo maran lædcedom   behofað
     . . . so it greater leechcraft.ACC needs
     '. . . so it requires greater medicine' ([*COE*] ÆCHom I, 33 496.30)

Allen remarks that 'it seems rather surprising that genitive objects should have disappeared so early on, because the genitive was the most clearly marked of the cases in M[iddle]E[nglish]' (ibid. 217). A hyperanalysis account renders this fact less surprising.[3]

English also had passives that look like those of Germanic or Icelandic. Genitive objects rarely occurred in passives, leaving mostly examples with dative objects. These constructions were replaced by passives with nominative objects. Interestingly, the passives with nominative objects arose even when the dative/accusative distinction was still present, in at least some dialects (Allen 1995:357–64). Allen treats this as problematic, because this change would complicate the grammars of those speakers (ibid. 375). However, in a hyperanalysis account, it is a plausible remapping of the form–function relationship in these constructions; and grammar simplification is not an aim of language users (see §3.4.1).[4]

5.2.2 *Evolution of impersonals from locative agreement*

A second example of hyperanalysis is in the evolution of impersonal construc-tions from locative agreement in the southern Bantu languages (Croft 1995b). Most Bantu languages have a rich system of agreement with noun classes, so that for instance in the Chichewa example in (8), the verb *li* 'be' agrees with *chitsime* 'well' (Bresnan & Kanerva 1989:3):

(8) Chi- tsime chi-   li ku- mu- dzi
     CL7- well CL7.SBJ- be CL17- CL3- village
     'The well is in the village.'

In addition to the inherent noun classes, there are a set of noun class markers that originated as prepositions, traditionally labelled Classes 16–18; cf. *kumudzi* 'in the village' in (8). Not only may the locative class markers be prefixed to nouns, yielding a locative phrase, but if the locative phrase is fronted, the verb will agree with it (ibid.):

(9) Ku- mu- dzi ku- li chi- tsime
CL17- CL3- village CL17.SBJ- be CL7- well
'In the village is a well.'

This is a genuine case of agreement, not some sort of impersonal expression. The locative prefix on the verb must match the locative prefix on the locative phrase (see (10); ibid. 12), and a different class prefix is used for 'true' impersonals (see (11); ibid. 10):

(10) Ku- mu- dzi mu- ku- ganiz -a kuti ku-/*pa-
CL17- CL3- village 2.PL.SBJ- PROG- think -IND COMP CL17.SBJ-/*CL16.SBJ-
na- bwer -a a- lendo
REC.PST- come -IND CL2- visitor
Lit.: 'To the village, you think that there came visitors.'

(11) Zi- ku- ganizir -idw -a kuti a- tsibweni a- nga ndi
CL10.SBJ- PROG- think -PASS -IND COMP CL2- uncle CL2- my COP
a- fiti
CL2- witch
'It is thought that my uncle is a practitioner of witchcraft.'

While it is true that locative agreement in Chichewa is genuine agreement, other southern Bantu languages behave differently, and one can identify a gradual process by which one locative agreement prefix is reanalyzed as an impersonal. The details of this process are described in Croft 1995b; for present purposes, the relevant process is what licensed the first step from locative to impersonal. In Chichewa, as in a number of other Bantu languages, a subject phrase can be clause-final as well as clause-initial. This is true of locative subjects as well (Bresnan & Kanerva 1989:3):

(12) Mw- a- khal -a a- nyani m- mi- tengo
CL18.SBJ- PERF- sit -IND CL2- baboon CL18- CL4- tree
'In the trees are sitting baboons.'

The effect of this option, however, is to place the locative phrase in what superficially appears to be the same position as a normal nonsubject locative phrase (compare example (10)). This allows hyperanalysis to take place: the locative meaning is attributed the oblique function of its superficial position, the theme NP is in a nonsubject position, and the locative agreement on the verb now has no function, having been hyperanalyzed away.[5] This hyperanalysis has led to a completed change in Zulu. In addition to an invariant Class 17 locative verb form for existential contructions (13; Doke 1930:296), the same Class 17 form is used to resolved gender conflicts in conjoined subject NPs – which have nothing to do with locative meaning (14; Doke 1930:298):

(13) ku- khona izinja emazweni onke
CL17- be.present dogs countries.LOC all
'There are dogs in all countries.'

(14) ku-   yokubhubha aba- ntu   nezin-   komo
      CL17- will.perish   CL2- person and:CL10- cattle
      'The people and cattle will perish.'

5.2.3 Constraints on hyperanalysis

A desirable feature of any theory of innovation in language change is the postulation of constraints on the occurrence of the innovation. This is especially critical here, since as will be seen in the following sections, some of the mechanisms for form–function reanalysis go in opposite directions. Fortunately, the nature of form–function reanalysis permits us to construct a hypothesis as to what contexts would lead to hyperanalysis. In other words, a prediction can be made as to the contexts in which semantic bleaching and loss should occur.

In hyperanalysis, the conventional meaning or function of a less contentful syntactic unit is reanalyzed as belonging to a more contentful syntactic unit with overlapping conventional meaning but not vice versa. For example, the meaning associated with governed oblique case marking is hyperanalyzed because of the overlapping but more contentful verb meaning. Semantic bleaching or grammatical loss in other situations, if they exist, must be attributable to other mechanisms for innovation. For example, grammaticalization, which generally does not involve this kind of semantic overlap, has sometimes been described as loss of meaning (e.g. Heine & Reh 1984:15). However, it is better described as a CHANGE of meaning rather than a loss of meaning (see §6.3.2 and Traugott 1988, 1989), and so does not constitute a counterexample to the proposed constraint on hyperanalysis.

This hypothesis of a constraint on hyperanalysis can be tested in three ways. First, other examples of language change of this type may be examined to see if they satisfy the conditions just offered. Indeed, the constraint proposed here is inferred from occurring cases of language change. Second, a large sample of innovations in language use should demonstrate a preponderance of innovations of this type, where hyperanalysis is a plausible explanation. Finally, a psycholinguistic experiment can be constructed, along the lines of the past tense experiment of Bybee & Slobin described in §5.1. In such an experiment, it is predicted that innovations due to hyperanalysis should occur significantly more frequently in the contexts which favor it than in the contexts which do not. It is beyond the scope of this book to construct the second and third tests. In principle, however, we should be able to test theories for innovation both synchronically and experimentally.

5.3 Hypoanalysis (underanalysis)

In HYPOANALYSIS, the listener reanalyzes a contextual semantic/functional property as an inherent property of the syntactic unit. In the reanalysis, the inherent property of the context (often the grammatical context, but see §5.6) is then attributed to the syntactic unit, and so the syntactic unit in question gains a new meaning or function. Hypoanalysis is analogous to Ohala's notion of hypocorrection.

Hypoanalysis is the source of a process that has recently gained attention in historical linguistics. The process is called EXAPTATION by Lass (Lass 1990:98–9) and REGRAMMATICALIZATION by Greenberg (Greenberg 1991:303). Greenberg describes the process thus:

> increasing extension [of a grammaticalized element] leads to zero intension, so that the item has become desemanticized. There is, however, with expansive lexicalization a further possibility, namely its reinterpretation in a new function. We may call this process regrammaticalization. (Greenberg 1991:301)

In the rest of this section, I give four examples of plausible contexts for syntactic hypoanalysis (see §5.6 for another example).

5.3.1 Subjunctives and futures from present indicatives

Bybee, Perkins & Pagliuca discuss a case in which a verb form with subjunctive meaning has evolved from one with present indicative meaning (Bybee, Perkins & Pagliuca 1994:230–6). In Armenian, the progressive verb form has spread from present ongoing action contexts to habitual contexts, thereby ousting the simple indicative verb form in main clauses. The simple indicative form has survived in subordinate clauses. Many subordinate clause contexts are subjunctive, that is, the meaning of the construction implies a subjunctive meaning for the subordinate clause. In Modern Armenian, the simple indicative has been reanalyzed as a subjunctive and can be found as a subjunctive in main clause contexts (ibid. 232, from Fairbanks & Stevick 1958:118, 150):

(15) p'aymanóv vor ušadrutyámb varèk   mekenèn
     condition   that carefully   drive.2SG car
     'On condition that you drive the car carefully.'

(16) inč   lezvòv   gərèm   hascèn
     what language write.1SG address
     'In what language should I write the address?'

This change appears to have begun as a hypoanalysis. Instead of attributing subjunctive function to the sentential context, speakers have reanalyzed the subjunctive value as inherent to the simple indicative form, which occurs only in that context.

Haspelmath describes several other cases of subjunctives arising from old present indicatives where a new present indicative has spread to all main clause present functions (Tsakonian Greek, Modern Indic, Persian and Cairene Arabic; Haspelmath 1998c:41–5). Haspelmath also describes a number of cases of futures arising from old present indicatives, also through what I would call hypoanalysis (Welsh, Hebrew, Lezgian, Turkish, Udmurt and Kannada; ibid.

36–41). Again, a progressive is extended from ongoing action contexts to habitual contexts, leaving the future context for the old present (the original present is more like a nonpast tense form). What was originally a contextual property of the present or nonpast in future contexts has been hypoanalyzed as the function of the former present/nonpast. For example, the Hebrew imperfect form, accompanied by person agreement prefixes, is a future in Modern Hebrew (*?e-xtov* 'I'll write') but was used for present time reference in Biblical Hebrew (ibid. 37).

Haspelmath argues that the evolution of old presents to future and/or subjunctive meaning is not a case of grammaticalization. The hypoanalysis account agrees with that claim; semantic changes in grammaticalization are brought about by metanalysis instead (see §5.4.4, §6.3.2). Haspelmath further argues that telic present tense verbs are the first to be restricted to future meaning, because a telic event is more likely to be interpreted with future time reference in a present tense than atelic or stative events (cf. the English future use of the present as in *The train for London leaves at 9:30*, Haspelmath 1998c:49–51). This argument fits in with the hypoanalysis account: one would expect speakers to attribute the contextual meaning to the form in question first with verb classes where the contextual meaning is almost always associated with use of that form.

5.3.2   German umlaut

German umlaut is a classic case of exaptation (Lass 1990:98–9) or hypoanalysis, in that it began as a phonological process and then was hypoanalyzed to gain a plural function (among others). A history of the umlaut or *i*-mutation is found in Keller 1978. The late Germanic *i*-mutation fronted back vowels (Keller 1978:80–1). The *i*-mutation is phonemicized by the Carolingian period of Old High German (ibid. 159–64; this is an example of Ohala's hypocorrection, incidentally), and thus associated with *i*-plurals (ibid. 180). By the Middle High German, the *i*-mutation is morphologized (ibid. 279). In the Early New High German period one observes the 'analogical extension' of umlaut (ibid. 412, 560). It is this last stage that involves hypoanalysis. The semantically never-before-meaningful umlaut is attributed the contextual property of plurality and reanalyzed as a marker of plural inflection; the 'analogical extension' is the actualization of the hypoanalysis. Lass gives examples such as Modern German *Baum/Bäume* 'tree', as a novel umlaut; cf. OHG *boum/boum-e* (Lass 1990:99). Another example that Lass gives is Yiddish *shvits-shop*, which comes from English *sweat-shop* and hence is not descended from OHG, and has the plural *shvits-shep-er* (ibid.).

5.3.3   Nominalizers from Stage III articles

Another sort of hypoanalysis is Greenberg's regrammaticalization. Greenberg has argued that a grammaticalization process leads to the spread of etymological demonstratives to definite NPs (his Stage I articles), then to specific indefinite NPs as well (Stage II articles), then to nonspecific NPs (Stage III articles; Greenberg 1978/1990). By Stage III, the articles are found on virtually every occurring noun or NP. Hence it is simply associated with nouns. An example of a Stage III article is the so-called 'movable *k-*' of Nilo-Saharan (Greenberg 1981/1990). In some Nilo-Saharan languages, such as Ngambay Mundu, 'verbal roots beginning with vowels form verbal nouns meaning "act of..." by prefixing *k-*, as so often in Nilo-Saharan ... An example is *usa* "eat", *k-usa* "act of eating"' (Greenberg 1981/1990:479, citing Vandame 1963:66, 75). I suggest that this occurred due to hypoanalysis. The *k-* prefix is attributed the contextual property of nominality that is inherent to the nouns it is invariably found with, and then comes to be used as a nominalizer.

5.3.4 *Multiple exaptation/hypoanalysis:* do *and English 3rd singular present* -s

Lass observes the minimal remnant of English subject agreement found in the Standard English 3rd person singular present tense suffix *-s*, and writes, 'Now however this relic inflection [*-s*] not only has no "communicative" function ... it is a systemic excrescence ... But the exaptive impulse is strong' (Lass 1990:99). In fact, the exaptation/hypoanalysis has already occurred, in combination with the hypoanalysis of periphrastic *do*, in the traditional dialects of Somerset and Dorset (Ihalainen 1991; Trudgill 1990).

Commonly in earlier Standard English (and lasting into the 18th century), '[periphrastic] *do* is simply used as an unstressed tense marker' (Ihalainen 1991:148). It may be that hypoanalysis has led to its emphatic function in contemporary Standard English, presumably due to the attribution of a feature of the discourse context to the periphrastic *do*. In Somerset/Dorset traditional dialects, however, we find a combined reanalysis, so that the simple present *-s* is used for specific or single events, while *do* is used for iterative or habitual events (Trudgill 1990:95; Ihalainen 1991):

(17) a. I sees the doctor tomorrow [specific/single event, present]
      b. I do see him every day [iterative/habitual, present]

It appears that the semantically minimal *-s* acquires the contextual semantic property of marking present tense; this hypoanalysis leads to its use beyond 3rd person singular (as in (17a)). In addition, the semantically minimal *do* is attributed contextual properties of verbal aspect, and is reanalyzed as an iterative/habitual marker. As a consequence, present tense *-s* is attributed a semelfactive/nonhabitual semantic function. Again, we do not really know the usage contexts which might have led to this particular division of semantic labor between *-s* and *do*. But the use of *do* in 18th-century English plus the marginal grammatical status of *-s* probably gave rise to just the sort of complexity in the form–function mapping in language use that would invite hypoanalysis of these forms.

5.3.5 Constraints on hypoanalysis

Hypoanalysis is the opposite of hyperanalysis. If both processes operate unconstrainedly, then innovation can lead anywhere. However, the examples of exaptation and regrammaticalization that have been identified suggest that hypoanalysis can be constrained, just as I proposed that hyperanalysis can be constrained.

In hypoanalysis, it is hypothesized that a conventional meaning/function of context is attributed to a syntactic unit by virtue of the syntactic unit's restricted distribution or apparent redundancy with an overlapping more contentful expression. The crucial aspect of this constraint is the distribution of the syntactic unit across constructions. The syntactic unit simply does not have content in other constructions. Either it doesn't occur in other constructions, as with the Armenian simple present indicative; or it occurs in all contexts, and hence has no discriminatory semantic value; as in the Stage III article (noun marker) and other examples given above.

5.4 Metanalysis

METANALYSIS is the simultaneous occurrence of hyperanalysis and hypoanalysis. In metanalysis, the listener swaps contextual and inherent semantic values of a syntactic unit.[6] It appears that these two events occur simultaneously; that is, that there is no stage in which hypoanalysis has occurred but not yet hyperanalysis, or vice versa. For this reason, a distinct type of form–function reanalysis is proposed.

Metanalysis does not seem to be analogous to any type of phonological change in Ohala's model. Ohala does not describe such a process, and I cannot think of any clear examples of phonological analogs to metanalysis. Metanalysis appears to be the mechanism for innovation of the sort of grammatical changes that have gone under the name of invited or pragmatic inference (Hopper & Traugott 1993, chapter 4; see §5.4.3 and §6.3.2).

5.4.1 Reinforcement > replacement: the negative cycle

One particular type of reinforcement appears to be caused by metanalysis. It can be illustrated by the well-known negative cycle (Jespersen 1917). In the negative cycle, an emphatic element comes to be used with the negative marker and ends up usurping its negative function; in the final stage of the process, the original negative marker disappears. Jespersen illustrates the negative cycle with its pattern in the history of French (Jespersen 1917:7–8). In Classical Latin, there arose a negative marker *non*, as in *non dico*. In Old French, the parallel construction was syntactically the same (plus the subject pronoun): *jeo ne di*. However, at that point a variety of nouns came to be used with emphatic function associated with the negative construction, such as *point, pas, personne*, etc. These forms, which originally had a positive semantic value, came to cooccur obligatorily with *ne*, and hence became nonemphatic elements. This function came to be restricted to *pas*, as in Standard French *je ne dis pas*.

The process by which the emphatic forms became obligatory negative markers is caused by metanalysis. Before metanalysis, the negative meaning is attributed to the preverbal particle *ne*, and the emphatic function is attributed to the postverbal element (*pas, personne*, etc.). From the point of view of the postverbal element, negation is a contextual feature while emphasis is an inherent feature. However, as has been argued by a number of linguists (e.g. Schwegler 1988:36; Givón 1979, ch. 3), negative utterances are more likely to be emphatic in actual use than positive ones; that is, there is a high degree of correlation between negation and emphasis. This correlation sets the condition for metanalysis: since the emphatic element is found frequently in negative contexts, and negative contexts are frequently emphatic, there is a swapping of the two functions: the negative function is attributed to the emphatic element, while the emphatic function is attributed to the nonlinguistic context.[7] The actualization of the metanalysis is the use of the formerly emphatic element in nonemphatic negative contexts.

The final stage in the negative cycle, manifested in colloquial French *je dis pas*, is caused by hyperanalysis. The inherent negative value of the preverbal particle is attributed to the postverbal element alone, since its (newly acquired) negative function overlaps with that of the preverbal particle; and the preverbal particle is dropped. It is worth pointing out here that given the preceding stage of the process – two syntactic units mapping to the same semantic function – the theory does not predict which of the two units will undergo hyperanalysis. Nor should it, most likely. If in fact the etymologically emphatic marker underwent hyperanalysis and disappeared, then the result would not have been a change in this aspect of grammatical structure. Abortive changes certainly take place; we only know of them in cases where direct historical records are available (an example, the aborted shift of *seem* to an experiencer subject verb, is described by Harris & Campbell 1995:88–9).

Finally, we may note that French provides examples of metanalysis outside the context of the subsequent hyperanalysis of *pas* as the sole (colloquial) French negator. Two of the other emphatic elements that formerly occurred as negative emphatics survive as negative pronouns: *rien* 'nothing' < *'thing', *personne* 'no one' < *'person'. Having been metanalyzed by speakers, these forms were no longer restricted to use as emphatic markers; having acquired negative meaning, they came to be used in other negative contexts.

5.4.2 *Passives from 3rd person actives and reflexives*

Another example of metanalysis is found in the development of passives from 3rd person active forms. This is one of several common sources for passive constructions (Haspelmath 1990). An example of this development can be seen in Maasai (Greenberg 1959/1990). In Maasai, there are subject and object agreement prefixes, illustrated in (18) and (19) (Greenberg 1959/1990:413):

(18) a-   dɔl
      1SG.SBJ- see
      'I see him/her/them.'

(19) aa-   dɔl
      1SG.OBJ- see
      'He/she/they see me.'

The passive subject uses the object agreement forms but with a suffixed *-i*
that indicates that the verb is in the passive voice (ibid.):

(20) aa-   dɔl -i
      1SG.OBJ- see -PASS
      'I am seen.'

The suffix *-i* is a former 3rd person plural subject marker, so that
etymologically, the passive in (20) is 'They see me' (ibid. 415). This development can be interpreted as a case of metanalysis. As many linguists have
argued (e.g. Givón 1981; Shibatani 1985), the function of the passive includes
backgrounding of the agent, including elimination of the agent's specific identity.
Other constructions than the passive have this function as well. For example,
3rd person plural subjects of active transitives are often interpreted imperson-
ally: in English I can say *I called the ticket office and they told me that Friday's
performance was sold out*, even if it was only one person who told me. In
Maasai and other languages, the 3rd person subject affix was metanalyzed as a
passive affix. The passive contextual function of 3rd person plural impersonal
sentences was attributed to the 3rd person plural subject suffix, and the indefinite agent that the suffix originally denoted was attributed to the context.

It is possible that passives derived from reflexives via middles are also caused
by metanalysis. In a reflexive such as *Harriet washed herself* or *Theodore killed
himself*, the reflexive morpheme signals that the subject and the object are the
same referent, which means that the semantic role of the referent is both agent-
like and patient-like (or experiencer-like and stimulus-like, depending on the
verb). In a number of languages, the reflexive construction develops passive
functions, as in Spanish *Se cerraron las puertas a las diez* 'The doors were
closed at ten' (Schevill 1970:66).

Croft, Shyldkrot & Kemmer 1987 argue that the extension of reflexive constructions to passives follows a stage when the reflexive construction is used for
a variety of intransitive counterparts of transitive verbs where the intransitive
subject is an undergoer. Of course, only a subset of transitive events are such
that one can perform them on oneself: one cannot build oneself, sing oneself,
etc. The reflexive is first found with events typically undertaken on oneself
(unmarked middles), such as *vestirse* 'dress (oneself)' and *bañarse* 'bathe (oneself)' – note the optionality of the reflexive in English, suggesting a construal of
the event as intransitive. The reflexive middle is found both in verbs where the
intransitive subject is under its own control (so-called unergative) – Spanish

arrodillarse 'kneel' – and in verbs where the subject appears to undergo the action spontaneously (so-called unaccusative) – *quebrarse* 'break'. In both cases, the action could be carried out by an external force, and in fact may be implied even for the intransitive: saying *The window broke* does not commit me to a belief that the action occurred spontaneously. Finally, the construction *Se venden libros aquí* 'books are sold here' also implies an external agent, and it is a short step from this construction to an agentive passive.

At some point in this process, certainly by the point that the reflexive was used for unaccusatives such as *quebrarse* and for passives, the reflexive morpheme no longer denotes a participant coreferent with the subject. The formerly reflexive morpheme came to denote a verbal semantic property, something like 'subject both controlling and affected by the event' and eventually 'subject affected by the event, whether controlling or not'. The semantic shift can be analyzed as metanalysis. The contextual property associated with the reflexive is a class of events where acting on oneself is possible, and even typical (the unmarked middles). In metanalysis, the coreferential-subject denotation of the reflexive morpheme is swapped for the contextual property of affected-subject verbal semantic type. In fact, the coreferential-subject property, now merely a contextual factor, is weakened and removed by the time the former reflexive is extended to unaccusatives and passives.

5.4.3 Pragmatic inference and metanalysis

Metanalysis is basically an account of the innovation of invited inferences. PRAGMATIC INFERENCE represents a large class of semantic changes where some nonlinguistic contextual factor comes to be part of the meaning of the unit in question, and (a fact not emphasized in the literature) the former meaning of the unit is lost. A typical example is the connective *since* in the history of English (Hopper & Traugott 1993:74). *Since* began as a temporal connective meaning 'after'. In actual use, speakers frequently employ an 'after' clause when a causal as well as a temporal semantic relation holds between the main clause and the adverbial clause. *Since* underwent metanalysis: it is now largely used as a causal connective, although it retains some temporal uses (*She has been out of the country since February*).

Another typical example of pragmatic inference is the evolution of aspect markers into tense markers (see for example Bybee & Dahl 1989). Perfective aspect generally occurs in use with past time reference: it can be used for future time reference, but it is semantically incompatible with present time reference. Present tense usage is thus necessarily imperfective, though imperfective is compatible with past and future tenses. In many languages, the aspect markers have become tense markers, a change caused by metanalysis. The contextual past tense value of the perfective aspect becomes the inherent value of the marker, which loses its aspectual value. Similarly, the imperfective is metanalyzed to a present tense marker.[8]

5.4.4   *Constraints on metanalysis*

It should be clear from the examples that metanalysis is predicted to be possible when there is a high correlation between the relevant inherent and contextual meanings in language use. Under those conditions, the inherent and contextual meanings may be reversed. This is not a sufficient constraint to describe the facts of semantic change for which we are invoking metanalysis. The changes illustrated in this section are unidirectional. Is it possible to constrain metanalysis so that the changes are unidirectional?

In some cases it can plausibly be argued that the correlation is unidirectional, and hence the change will be unidirectional. For example, negative utterances usually have emphatic force, but emphatic sentences do not usually have negative force. Hence the emphatic force can be metanalyzed in negative utterances. Likewise, present tense is always imperfective; but imperfective aspect can be found with all tenses. Hence the imperfective meaning can be metanalyzed in present tense utterances. Passive utterances generally have 3rd person agents and affected subjects, but not all utterances with 3rd person agents or affected subjects are passive in discourse function (agent backgrounding, patient topic). Hence the 3rd person or reflexive affix can be metanalyzed in utterances with a passive discourse function. Finally, in the evolution of future tense markers from modals, future time reference is almost always irrealis in modality, but irrealis modality does not always imply future time reference. Hence certain irrealis modality markers can be metanalyzed as future tense markers.

Unfortunately, not all examples of unidirectionality in (putative) examples of metanalysis represent a unidirectional correlation. For example, the unidirectional change perfective aspect > past tense would imply that past tense correlates with perfective aspect more than perfective aspect correlates with past tense; but it is not obvious that this is true. If the contextual correlations in these examples are bidirectional, then metanalysis does not prevent the unattested change from past tense to perfective aspect. If so, an independent theory of the unidirectionality of semantic change will be necessary to account for these changes. Nevertheless, it may be that metanalysis will account for the unidirectionality of most if not all of the semantic changes found in grammaticalization (see §6.3.2).

5.5   Cryptanalysis

CRYPTANALYSIS is the result of reanalysis of a more subtle relationship between syntactic units and their semantic function. In cryptanalysis, the listener analyzes a covert semantic/functional property of a syntactic unit as not grammatically marked, and inserts an overt marker expressing its semantic value. Cryptanalysis, like metanalysis, appears to have no analog in Ohala's theory of phonological change. Cryptanalysis is the source of many cases of pleonasm and reinforcement, several of which are illustrated in the following subsections.

5.5.1 Pleonastic negation

A grammatical phenomenon that has attracted attention in both the standard literature and electronic discussions is pleonastic negation. A discussion on the LINGUIST list in 1993 focused on an innovation based on the cliché phrase *That'll teach you* and related phrases (see Horn 1978:176; Lawler 1974:358, 372). The (a) and (b) sentences in (21)–(22) mean the same thing, although the (b) sentences contain a negative that the (a) sentences lack:

(21) a.   That'll teach you to come early.
      b.   That'll teach you not to come early.
      a,b = You came early, some unhappy consequence ensued, and you should not come early in the future.

                                          (Laurie Bauer, LINGUIST 4.873)

(22) a.   I really miss having a phonologist around the house.
      b.   I really miss not having a phonologist around the house.
      a,b = There used to be a phonologist around the house, there isn't any more, and I wish there were one around the house now.

                                          (Dale Russell, LINGUIST 4.859)

Horn made the following remarks on this class of examples:

Now the negation that shows up pleonastically in *miss (not) VPing, surprised if it does(n't)* . . . , *prendre garde de (ne pas) tomber*, etc., is NOT, unlike the one in *so don't I*, ironic or sarcastic; . . . [it is] attributable to the difficulty of processing multiple negations ESPECIALLY WHEN AT LEAST ONE IS NON-OVERT. (Horn on LINGUIST 4.898; my emphasis)

The (a) sentences in (21)–(22) have in common a covert negative, as Horn notes. Now, polarity is something that is normally expressed overtly and grammatically in other sentences in English (and other languages). In (21a) and (22a), a listener recognizes the negative semantic component but there is no overt syntactic unit to which the negative semantic value can be linked; instead it is an entailment of some other syntactic unit. What has happened in (21b) and (22b) is that the hearer has reanalyzed the construction as 'needing' an overt syntactic unit to convey the semantic value, and actualized the reanalysis by inserting a pleonastic negative marker. This is cryptanalysis.

5.5.2 Paratactic negation

A very similar sort of cryptanalysis has occurred in the complements of certain negative-entailment verbs, specifically the translation equivalents of 'deny', 'forbid', 'hinder', 'doubt', etc. (Jespersen 1917:75, cited in Horn 1978:172). In English, the complements of such verbs do not have an overt mark of negation, although the special complement form *from Ving* is generally required with these verbs:

(23) She prevented him from entering the room. [*entails* 'he didn't enter the room']

In a number of languages, the complements of these verbs actually do contain an overt negator. Horn gives examples from Latin ((24); Horn 1978:173, from Lakoff 1968) and Basque ((25); ibid., from Lafitte 1962):

(24)   Potuisti prohibere ne fieret.
        'You could have prevented it from happening.'

(25)   Debekatu diot ez dezan holakorik egin.
        'I forbade him to do such a thing' [lit. '. . . so that he not do . . .']

Example (24) does NOT mean 'You could have prevented it from not happening'; nor does (25) mean 'I forbade him to not do such a thing'.

Espinal 1992 describes the phenomenon in Catalan as optional, which places the complements of these verbs at the same stage of this process as the English clichés in (21)–(22) (Espinal 1992:336, 333):

(26)   Tinc por que (no) arribin.
        'I'm afraid that they will arrive.'

(27)   Impediu que en Joan (no) surti elegit.
        'Stop Joan from being elected.'

Paratactic negation is also found in adverbial subordinate clauses introduced by 'before', 'until' and 'unless'. There is no covert entailed negation in these adverbial clauses. However, other adverbial subordinate clauses presuppose the proposition in the adverbial clause, while these adverbial clauses do not do so. This is illustrated by the following minimal pair offered by Levinson (1983:187):

(28)   a.   Sue cried before she finished her thesis.
        b.   Sue died before she finished her thesis.

Semantically, the state of affairs in the subordinate clause has NOT occurred at the time of the state of affairs described in the main clause (and may never occur), unlike other adverbial subordinate clauses. This is the covert negative value found in these adverbial clauses.

Vincent 1993 (among others) points out the presence of negation in these adverbial clause types in French (Vincent 1993:153):

(29)   avant que Pierre ne vienne
        'before Pierre comes'

Paratactic negation is also found optionally in adverbial clauses in Catalan (Espinal 1992:333):

(30)   Haurem d'intervenir abans que (no) arribi el nou gerent.
        'We'll have to take part in the discussion before the new manager arrives.'

Vincent also observes the existence of a special complementizer for 'before' clauses in Maltese (Vincent 1993:152–3, citing Sutcliffe 1936:207):

(31) wara li telqu
after COMP they.left
'after they left'

(32) qabel ma telqu
before NEG.COMP they.left
'before they left'

The 'before' complementizer *ma* is derived from the negative marker and possibly also the relativizer (Vincent 1993:162, n. 11). That is, the special complementizer is another example of paratactic negation.

Other examples of etymological negative markers in these adverbial clauses are described for West Flemish (33) and Standard Dutch (34) by Haegeman (Haegeman 1995:160):

(33) tenwoare 'unless' < t-en-woare [it-NEG-be.3SG.PST.SUBJ]

(34) tenzij 'unless' < t-en-zij [it-NEG-be.3SG.PRES.SUBJ]

When cryptanalysis has taken place in these examples, the semantic status of the negator changes. Before cryptanalysis, the negator expresses the semantic value of negation when that value is not entailed in linguistic context, but not when it is. That is, the negator is present only when no other element in the sentence indicates the negative meaning. After cryptanalysis, the negator expresses the semantic value of negation even when that value is covertly present in the linguistic context.

5.5.3 *Pleonastic double marking / reinforcement*

A more widely observed grammatical change that is due to cryptanalysis is reinforcement. A typical example is the addition of the nominal plural marker *-lar/-lär* to the 1st and 2nd person plural pronouns in many Turkic languages, where the two forms currently exist as variants (S, E and C refer to Southern, Eastern and Central subgroups):

(35)

Language	SG	PL		*Source*
Turkish (S)	1st *ben*	*biz*		(Lewis 1967:67)
	2nd *sen*	*siz*		
Uzbek (E)	1st *men, man*	*biz, bizlar*	'we [a group]'	(Sjoberg 1963:89–90)
	2nd *sen, san*	*siz, sizlar*	'we [a group]'	
Uigur (E)	1st *män*	*biz, bizlär*		(Nadzhip 1971:96–7)
	2nd *sän, siz*	*silä* [< *sizlär*]*, sänlär*		
Chagatay (C)	1st *men*	*biz, bizlär*		(Eckmann 1966:111–12)
	2nd *sen*	*siz, sizlär*		

The *-z* is etymologically a plural marker, but is found only in the 1st and 2nd person pronouns, as in Turkish. Its irregularity and rarity is sufficient to render the semantic value of plurality covert in the 1st and 2nd person plural pronoun forms, and invites cryptanalysis. This has taken place to various degrees in Uzbek, Uigur and Chagatay – indeed, in Uigur, the 2nd person plural has undergone further phonological reduction, while the etymological plural has become a polite singular marker (Nadzhip 1971:97).[9]

Other examples include novel plural forms based on irregular plurals such as English *feets*, and periphrastic comparatives based on the lexically restricted morphological comparative form, as in the English innovation *more harder*. Both of these innovations were produced by an adult native speaker, illustrating again that innovation can begin with adults.[10] Yet another source of cryptanalysis is acronyms. The British acronym *PFI* stands for *Private Finance Initiative*. But the fact that it is a government initiative is covert in the acronym, and cryptanalysis leads to utterances of the form *PFI initiative* (BBC radio news, November 1996).

5.5.4 *Spread of the definite article to proper names*

Another example of cryptanalysis is the application of the definite article to proper names. Proper names denote unique individuals in most contexts, and so are implicitly definite. In English the definite article does not combine with proper names in such cases: **The John came in.*[11] In some other languages, the use of a definite article is obligatory with proper names, e.g. Modern Greek *i Maria* [the Mary] 'Mary' (Harris 1976:162), Modern Hebrew *ha-rav yosef* [the rabbi Yosef] 'Rabbi Yosef' (Glinert 1989:16), and K'iche' Mayan *le a Lu'* [the HON Pedro] 'Peter' (Davies & Sam-Colop 1990:528). Again, the semantic value of uniqueness is covert in proper names, unlike the much larger class of common nouns, and the definite article is cryptanalyzed to overtly express covert uniqueness (definiteness).

5.5.5 *Cryptanalysis + metanalysis: the evolution of modals into subjunctives*

Bybee, Perkins & Pagliuca (1994:214–18) discuss a process by which a modal can evolve into a general subjunctive marker, spreading gradually into a wider range of subordinate clause contexts. The change appears to proceed in steps. In the theory of innovation proposed here, the change appears to be cryptanalysis followed by metanalysis.

The process has been described in some detail for the evolution of English *should* by Coates (1983:67–9) and Bybee, Perkins & Pagliuca (1994) (all examples in this section are attested). In main clauses, *should* denotes weak obligation:

(36) I just insisted very firmly on calling her Miss Tillman, but one should really call her President.

(37) Well perhaps I should choose a London map if I'm going to look at Clapham.

The first step is what Coates and Bybee *et al.* call 'modal harmony': *should* is used for weak obligation even where the main clause predicate already entails weak obligation for its complement (Coates 1983:68; Bybee, Perkins & Pagliuca 1994:215):

(38) It is essential that on this point the churches should learn from each other

(39) I suggested that they should put (a)round each carriage door a piece of beading

This step is a case of cryptanalysis: *should* is inserted in a context where weak obligation is covertly entailed in the context.

The next step is described by Coates as intermediate *should*: *should* is extended to 'quasi-subjunctive' meanings (where *should* is an 'empty' marker of irrealis mood) in subordinate clauses (Coates 1983:68):

(40) Is it legitimate that they should seek to further that aim by democratic and constitutional means?

(41) It was inevitable that Peter Ustinov should join the exclusive four-star club by writing, producing, directing and starring in one film

Coates observes that for at least some speakers of British English, *should* has become a general subjunctive marker; the example here, from Bybee, Perkins & Pagliuca (1994:215), is from a 1984 British TV broadcast:

(42) The police are expecting that the Libyans should make the first move.

The steps in the process to (40)–(41) and then to (42) represent a cycle of metanalysis and cryptanalysis. *Should* is not used in main clauses with meanings other than weak obligation. I find the following unacceptable with the meanings intended in (40)–(41) (I find (42) and extensions to factive complements questionable at best, so I cannot judge weaker meanings):

(43) #They should seek to further that aim by democratic and constitutional means.

(44) #Peter Ustinov should join the exclusive four-star club by writing, producing, directing and starring in one film

In other words, once *should* was cryptanalyzed as a modal indicator in subordinate clauses as in (38)–(39), this use of *should* also acquired an inherent value of complementation.

Since being a complement of this class of verb is a contextual feature, this process is an instance of hypoanalysis. But then how was the extension to other subordinate clause types as in (40)–(41) brought about? It appears that the modal value of weak obligation was hyperanalyzed as part of the main clause verb at the same time as the hypoanalysis as a marker of complements. In other words, subordinate weak obligation *should* underwent metanalysis: the inherent property of weak obligation was swapped with the contextual property of being a complement of this class of predicates. Since *should* now has the more general modal meaning of irrealis, it is then extended to other irrealis subordinate clauses. The metanalysis continued to the point that for some English speakers, *should* has become a subjunctive as in (42). This is followed by cryptanalysis of now-subjunctive *should* as a general subordinate clause indicator, extending even to factive complements of *funny, ironical, sad* (Coates 1983:69; not illustrated by her).[12]

The example of the spread of *should* and similar modal markers in subordinate clauses shows that the constraints on innovation mechanisms can end up specifying directionality in grammatical change, at least in some cases (see §6.3.2). In this case, the fact that metanalysis leads to the loss of modal meaning combined with the gain of subordinate indicator status means that the modal can continue to spread in subordinate contexts.

5.5.6   Constraints on cryptanalysis

Cryptanalysis is hypothesized to occur if the covert value in the construction is normally expressed by an overt function word or inflection in other contexts, as in the cases of implicit negation in the complement clauses of certain verbs. Cryptanalysis results in the insertion of the relevant function word/inflection. Cryptanalysis can also occur where the semantic value is overtly expressed, if the value is expressed by a synchronically opaque/nonproductive form in the construction in question, as with the Turkic pronoun plurals. In other words, the covertness of the semantic value leading to cryptanalysis is a matter of degree.

5.6   How far can we get with form–function reanalysis?

The preceding sections outlined four types of form–function reanalysis: hyperanalysis, hypoanalysis, metanalysis and cryptanalysis. In this section, I will address two questions. First, how many sorts of diachronic processes have been provided with a mechanism for innovation by form–function reanalysis? Second, how does form–function reanalysis relate to the functional motivations that have been offered for language change?

Form–function analysis can explain all examples of grammatical change (see for example the discussion of syntactic reanalysis in §6.3.2). A fairly wide range of types of diachronic processes can potentially be innovated by form–function reanalysis. Hyperanalysis is a mechanism for semantic bleaching and ultimately loss of a syntactic element. Hypoanalysis is the mechanism for regrammaticalization (Greenberg) / exaptation (Lass). Metanalysis provides a mechanism for at least some particular cases of replacement (in combination with hyperanalysis, as with the negative cycle). Metanalysis is also the mechanism underlying pragmatic inference, that is, the exchange of an inherent semantic property with another semantic property correlated to it in usage. Thus metanalysis is the mechanism underlying semantic change in grammaticalization (see §6.3.2). Finally, cryptanalysis is the mechanism for pleonasm and rein- forcement, and in certain special cases, a mechanism for extension.

Moreover, the hypotheses offered in §§5.2–5.5 for constraints on the mech- anisms for innovation, if correct, would provide some degree of directionality to these language changes.

The simple model of syntactic structure in the description of form–function reanalysis in §5.1 – a construction whose component grammatical units corres- pond to semantic units in the construction's meaning – builds in the notion of syntagmatic isomorphism, one aspect of iconicity. Isomorphism (Haiman 1980b, 1985) is the principle of a one-to-one mapping from units of syntactic form to units of conventional function. Haiman describes two types of isomorphism, syntagmatic and paradigmatic. Paradigmatic isomorphism applies to the in- ventory of symbolic units (signs) in the language (see §6.2). It is syntagmatic isomorphism that is built into form–function reanalysis.

In understanding the utterance, the hearer attempts to identify aspects of the meaning-in-context with particular morphosyntactic units of the utterance, and vice versa. I have argued that the complexity of this task leads to the reanalysis of the form–function mapping. One aspect of this reanalysis may be the absence of a function for a particular form. Form–function reanalysis will either exapt this unit (hypoanalysis) or eliminate it entirely (hyperanalysis). The result is that over time, syntactic units will be analyzed as correspond- ing to distinct semantic units. Thus, form–function reanalysis provides a nonteleological, in fact nonintentional, mechanism that increases syntagmatic isomorphism.

Isomorphism is only one aspect of (syntagmatic) iconicity, however. Haiman and others have employed the mechanism of iconic motivation to account for other linguistic patterns. Iconic motivation is the principle that syntactic struc- ture reflects a parallel semantic structure. For instance, there is considerable evidence that degrees of syntactic closeness of units reflects parallel degrees of semantic closeness between the entities that the syntactic units denote. One example of this is inalienable vs alienable possession. Where the two are distin- guished syntactically, inalienable possession – the semantically more intimate relationship – is expressed by a syntactically more tightly bound construction (Haiman 1985:102–47).

The model of form–function reanalysis presented in §5.1 does not predict that innovations will generally be in the direction of greater iconic motiva- tion.[13] However, this is not a weakness of form–function reanalysis, but a result of the deliberately minimal model of syntactic structure that was em- ployed in this chapter. If we hypothesize that speakers are doing more than just figuring out what part of meaning-in-context corresponds to what morphosyntactic unit of the utterance, then iconic motivation should follow from form–function reanalysis.

For example, speakers are figuring out what relations between elements of meaning-in-context are represented by what relations between morphosyntactic units in the utterance. If we make certain assumptions about the types of semantic relations that speakers are attempting to match to syntactic relations, then we could account for language changes that appear to be driven by iconic motivation.

It should be clear that form–function reanalysis is not incompatible with more complex synchronic formal models of syntax. Indeed, observed language changes conjoined with form–function reanalysis could be used to justify the existence of more complex syntactic structures. Conversely, more complex formal syntactic models combined with form–function reanalysis would lead to predictions of certain kinds of language changes.

Another functional motivation normally appealed to in language change is economy: that speakers will use shorter and/or simpler forms for more frequent contexts of use (see §3.4.4). Economic motivation underlies typological markedness, which involves two formal properties: the number of morphemes used to express a particular concept (structural coding), and the number of cross-cutting distinctions found for the concept in question (behavioral potential; Croft 1990).[14] Markedness is a manifestation of syntagmatic economy, and motivates the use of zero morphemes (which violates iconicity), a common manifestation of structural coding.[15]

Form–function reanalysis can account for at least one aspect of syntagmatic structural coding, the existence of zero morphemes for the most frequent value of a grammatical category. The association of the most frequent value with a zero form can be attributed to hypoanalysis. Consider a language with, say, no distinction of number for nouns. Text counts have demonstrated that reference to a single token of the type is much more frequent than reference to plural tokens. Now, all languages have paraphrases to indicate plurality or singularity, e.g. vague numerals such as English *a lot of*, for plurality. If hypoanalysis took place, the contextually most-frequent value – singular number – would be interpreted as an inherent (default) property of zero-marked form, and the optional marker of the marked category – plurality – would be grammaticalized as a plural number marker. Bybee (1994) offers a similar hypothesis. She observes that cross-linguistically, one typically finds zero perfective in the past tense and zero imperfectives or habituals in the present tense. She argues that the meanings of these zero forms arise from the default functions of the tenses: the present describes how things are and the past narrates what happened (Bybee 1994:244). Overt constructions are employed for nondefault, less common functions of the tenses, and hence zero present imperfective or habitual and zero past perfective arise via hypoanalysis (in our terms; see Bybee 1994:245).[16]

I have not discussed paradigmatic iconicity and paradigmatic economy here. Form–function reanalysis pertains to the simplest and most direct interaction between language use and a speaker's knowledge of her language, namely (re)analysis of the comprehension-production process. It is here that the continuous-feedback model of the knowledge–use relationship appears most directly. It should be evident that language use can in principle influence the paradigmatic organization of linguistic elements in the mind as well as their syntagmatic organization. Linguistic variables, for example, are clear examples of paradigmatically organized linguistic elements. In chapter 6, I will describe a mechanism that accounts for the innovation of at least some paradigmatic language changes.

Notes

1 Compare Ohala's argument that words consist of a fixed sequence of phonological units, so the complex phonetic coarticulation patterns repeatedly recur, inviting reanalysis of the phonological units underlying the phonetic reality of a word (Ohala 1993:264; see §3.4.4).
2 I choose the term 'hyperanalysis' instead of 'hypercorrection' in order to avoid the prescriptive implications of the latter term and its specialized use in sociolinguistics.
3 In fact, most governed genitive objects were replaced by prepositional objects by Modern English (Allen 1995:218). This change I would analyze as an example of intraference (see §6.2), where the oblique preposition enters the domain of the oblique case due to similarity in conventional meaning (less-affected or 'limited' objects).
4 The chief construction of interest to Allen and her predecessors is not discussed here, namely the shift from impersonal constructions, generally with dative experiencers, to personal constructions, generally with subject experiencer. While hyperanalysis probably plays a role in this process – after the dative experiencer is analyzed as a subject – another process combined with this is the remapping of participants into different grammatical relations and case roles. This process also involves a reanalysis of the mapping between form and function, possibly due to the extension of the nominative construction to the experiencer situation type (Haspelmath 1998a; see §6.3.2). However, the process involves more complex aspects of syntactic and semantic structure than can be discussed here; see §5.6.
5 Hankamer (1977:594–600) suggests that there is a large class of cases where two analyses are possible, one treating the structure as a reordering and the other treating the structure as changing grammatical relations. That is part of what is going on here. The hyperanalysis specifically involves the reanalysis of the prefix by attributing its content to the postposed locative.
6 I choose the term on analogy with the meaning of the prefix *meta-* in *metathesis*.
7 Note that metanalysis does not require that the contextual element that loses a function by transfer to the metanalyzed element be the same contextual element that gains the function lost by the metanalyzed element.
8 The mechanism for innovation need not be metanalysis, i.e. simultaneous hypo-analysis/hyperanalysis. For example, if a perfective becomes an aorist (perfective past tense) form, then it has only undergone hypoanalysis: it has gained an inherent past tense value, but has not lost the perfective aspectual value.
9 I do not know if the differentiation in meaning for the Uzbek forms reflects *-lar*'s original meaning – the grammar indicates only plurality, not collectivity, when *-lar* is attached to nominals – or a later semantic split.
10 I thank J. C. Smith for observing my production of these forms and pointing out their relevance to the analysis in this chapter.

11   If, however, there are multiple people in the context named *John*, then English uses a true definite article combined with a restrictive modifier to specify which one, e.g. *the John I knew from college.*

12   Bybee, Perkins & Pagliuca propose a general principle, which they call the harmonic principle: a form (e.g. subjunctive) will occur in harmonic contexts before it occurs in nonharmonic contexts. In a 25-language sample, they found that the presence of a subjunctive in a nonharmonic context implied the presence of a subjunctive in harmonic context (Bybee, Perkins & Pagliuca 1994:218–25). This finding suggests that the progressive metanalysis of subordinate markers is a more general diachronic process.

Another, similar candidate for cryptanalysis, mentioned by Bybee *et al.* (Bybee, Perkins & Pagliuca 1994:294) but not explored further, is sequence of tenses.

13   To be precise, local iconic motivation. There is no optimal structure of a general-purpose communication system such as human language, even taking just two simple principles such as iconicity and economy into consideration. Instead, we find competing motivations (Haiman 1985; DuBois 1985; Croft 1990; cf. §3.5). Competing motivations by themselves do not suffice to account for innovation, however. One must still invoke an argument along the lines of the one in §5.1 to explain why speakers might disturb the balance between competing motivations represented by the current linguistic system.

14   I also argue that neutralization phenomena are not markedness phenomena (Croft 1990:89–91; Croft 1996b).

15   There is also paradigmatic economy, the use of a single form for multiple meanings, presumably for efficiency in mental representation (storage of related meanings).

16   Hypoanalysis can only account for 'virgin zeros', i.e. a zero expression of a category that was not the result of phonological erosion of a prior existing form. Erosion to zero is also explained in terms of economy. One could postulate an explanation of erosion in terms of hyperanalysis. If the unmarked value, say singular number, is the most frequent one in the use of noun forms, then the property of singularity could be attributed to the context. The singular value would be hyperanalyzed away from the singular inflection, and the inflection is eliminated. However, this account does not strike me as being very plausible.

Chapter 6

Interference, intraference and grammaticalization

6.1 Interference

In §1.2, I referred to the fact that in addition to internal causes of language change, there are also external causes, due to language contact. Borrowings, such as English *rouge* from French, and calques, such as *it goes without saying* from *il va sans dire* (Hock 1986:397–9), are among the commoner examples of changes due to contact. The cause of these changes seems obvious: it is the other language, which some speakers have at least rudimentary knowledge of. The details of contact as a social process are discussed in chapter 8. But a mechanism for innovation still needs to be provided. How could a speaker produce a form, or a syntactic structure, or a semantic extension, from language Y while speaking language X? Why doesn't the speaker keep the two languages apart?

Weinreich (1968) offered a mechanism for innovation in contact-induced language changes: INTERFERENCE. He argues that contact-induced language change must originate with a bilingual speaker or speakers. The bilingualism may be minimal: all that is necessary is that the speaker has at least some knowledge of both languages (or both dialects; the mechanism is the same). Such a speaker thus has knowledge of both languages in her mind. These speakers are also able to create connections between the knowledge of the two languages.

For example, a speaker can identify a phoneme in the system of one language as roughly equivalent to a phoneme in the other language, because of phonetic similarity or identity in at least some contexts (Weinreich 1968:7). The range of phonetic realization of the counterpart phonemes in the two languages may differ, but if there is some overlap, there is the possibility of interference. Likewise, a speaker can identify a word or construction in one language as roughly equivalent to a word or construction in the other language, by virtue of semantic identity in at least some uses (ibid. 7–8). Again, the semantic range of the counterpart words or constructions in the two languages may differ, but if there is some overlap, there is the possibility of interference.

Weinreich calls this connection INTERLINGUAL IDENTIFICATION. Interlingual identification rests on the ability of the speaker to link the system-internal elements of two distinct linguistic systems by virtue of their external properties: phonetic in the case of phonological units, and semantic/functional in the case of grammatical/lexical units. Bybee, Perkins & Pagliuca call the external properties 'substance', in contrast with linguistic 'form' (Bybee, Perkins & Pagliuca 1994:1). In Bybee *et al.*'s terms, interlingual identification forms connections between forms in the two linguistic systems in the speaker's mind via a common external substance.

Interlingual identification does not imply that the two languages are represented as sharing a single phonetic or semantic representation in the bilingual speaker's brain. Interlingual identification is the establishment (possibly temporary) of a cognitive link between the corresponding linguemes of the two languages with respect to their identity in substance. The relationship between the mental representation of the knowledge of the two languages in the bilingual speaker's brain is complex and appears to vary depending on which language is dominant, proficiency, and social context of use (Romaine 1995:80–107). In fact, Romaine suggests that 'It may be that cross-linguistic influence [in bilinguals] is purely an "on line" phenomenon and has nothing to say about whether the underlying systems are separate or merged' (ibid. 93).

Interlingual identification motivates the transfer of properties of an element of one linguistic system to an element of the other, via the external substance that joins them. The effect of transfer is interference. A few examples are given here for illustration; further discussion of the linguistic patterns of interference is found in chapter 8.

The simplest sort of interference is the use of a word or string of words from one language in its entirety – phonology, morphology, syntax – in a sentence that is otherwise expressed in the other language, as in the following example of English and Panjabi (Romaine 1995:140):

(1)   baceã nũ tusĩ *force* nəi kər sakde.
      'You can't force children.'

The English word *force* is introduced in an otherwise Punjabi sentence because its semantic value in this context is equivalent to that for whatever is the appropriate Punjabi word that could be used in this context. This phenomenon is called code-switching, and is discussed in §8.4.1.

Weinreich cites an example of grammatical interference in Silesian Polish. Standard Polish employs the simple past form for past time reference, but neighboring German dialects use a 'have' perfect for past time reference, as in *ich habe es verkauft* 'I sold it'. In Silesian Polish, interference has led to a calque of this construction, using the Polish forms, as in *ja to mam sprzedane* 'I sold it' (Weinreich 1968:41, citing Vendryes 1921). The Silesian Polish form is 'intermediate' between colloquial German and Standard Polish: it uses the Standard Polish lexical and inflectional linguemes but the colloquial German constructional lingueme to express the meaning of past time reference. This sort of interference is characteristic of language shift and convergence (§8.3.1, §8.3.2).

Another type of interference is the production of intermediate or FUDGED FORMS (Chambers & Trudgill 1980:132–7), illustrated here for Norwegian (Trudgill 1986:63):

(2) a. Sunndal dialect: jub   'work'
     b. Oslo dialect: jɔbə   'work'
     c. 'Interdialect':   jubə   'work' (Sunndal migrant to Oslo)

Interlingual identification of meaning and of the phonetic realization of various phonemes has led to the production of a lexical form with the Sunndal dialect vowel and the Oslo dialect schwa together in the same lexeme. This phenomenon frequently occurs in dialect mixing and leveling (§7.4.3, §7.4.4, §8.4.2).

A grammatical example of an intermediate form resulting from interference is given here from a continuum between the high and low varieties of diglossia (see §8.4.1) in the Moroccan Arabic speech community (Heath 1989:32):

(3) a. Classical Arabic: hāðā l-yawm-a   'this day'
     b. Moroccan Colloquial Arabic: l-yum   'today'
                                       had n-nhaṛ   'this day'
     c. Educated Moroccan male: had l-yom   'this day'

In this case, interlingual identification of the meaning of the whole and of the grammatical elements making up the whole leads to the production of the form in (3c). The colloquial demonstrative *had* is retained, but the Classical Arabic word for 'day' is employed (in a fudged lexical form).

Interlingual identification via system-external linguistic substance provides a mechanism for innovation via interference. Most sociolinguists working on language contact phenomena have offered intentional mechanisms for introducing linguemes from one language into another language, in particular accommodation and acts of identification with a particular social group (see §7.4.2). These mechanisms are actually mechanisms for selection, however (see §3.4.3). A speaker cannot choose a form from one language over a form from the other unless she has made an interlingual identification of the two forms. Once interlingual identification of linguemes in the two languages is made in the speaker's mind, the counterpart forms in the two languages are rendered variants of a single variable, that is, two alternative forms for a single function for that speaker. Thus, choosing one variant over the other is a selection process, not an innovation process (see chapter 7). The variants are in theory strictly separated into two separate lingueme pools, but in reality they are available to the speaker at any time once interlingual identification has been made (see chapter 8). It is interlingual identification that 'creates' the variants, that is, gives the potential for replication of one variant in the other language as a novel variant lingueme of the variable in question.

Interference as a cognitive process is paradigmatic. The grammatical expressions of linguistic substance (function) from the native language, the 'foreign' language, or a fudged version thereof, are paradigmatic alternatives for expressing that function. This is true even though the superficial result may appear to be syntagmatic. For example, a shift in word order from SOV to SVO due to contact represents a paradigmatic replacement of an SOV construction in its various functions by an SVO version (a calque of the 'foreign' SVO construction), although the apparent result is a change in verb–object order. In this respect, interference contrasts with form–function reanalysis.

As noted above, sociolinguists generally treat the occurrence of variants resulting from interference as a consequence of an intentional mechanism of selection. However, it is possible that there is a nonintentional mechanism for the propagation of contact-induced language change. The mechanisms listed above do not exclude the possibility of SPONTANEOUS interference. Not every use of an individual grammatical element from another linguistic system may be the result of accommodation or an act of identity on the part of the speaker. A speaker may spontaneously produce a form from the other system as a probabilistic side-effect, by spreading activation along the cognitive links established in the mind via interlingual identification. And to the extent that interlingual identification is a natural cognitive process – after all, speakers generally know what words and sentences in one language correspond (roughly) to those in their other language – there is the possibility of spontaneous interference.

6.2   Intraference

In this section, I argue that essentially the same mechanism that causes interference also causes the innovation of certain types of internal language changes. Interference phenomena do not require the coexistence of two distinct codes in the mind of a single speaker. Different elements of the same language can interfere with each other if they share enough linguistic substance, in particular meaning. In this way, a word or construction from the same language can be used in a function normally expressed by a different word or construction in that language. To distinguish this identification process from the interlingual one, I will call it INTRAFERENCE.

Another way of describing intraference is to say that the notion of functional similarity of variants applies to overlapping meanings in a single code as well as overlapping meanings in distinct codes in an individual speaker's mind. In addition to interlingual identification in a (multilingual) speaker's mind, INTRALINGUAL IDENTIFICATION can take place in a speaker's mind. Intralingual identification is simply the recognition of the semantic relatedness of words, inflections and constructions. The following subsections will give lexical and morphological examples of intraference.

6.2.1   *The evolution of morphological paradigms*

Bybee (1985) develops a model of the mental representation and evolution of paradigmatic relations, at least for morphological paradigms, for which she has amassed substantial typological, diachronic, developmental and psycholinguistic evidence. In this model, the representation of morphological paradigms is governed mainly by two properties, semantic relevance and token frequency.

Semantic relevance is the degree of interaction of the meaning of the stem with the meaning of the inflection in semantic composition (Bybee 1985:13). An inflection that is more relevant affects the meaning of the stem to a greater extent than one that is less relevant. For instance, aspectual inflections significantly alter the semantic event type denoted by the verb stem (e.g. stative vs inchoative), but subject person agreement inflections do not; hence the former are more relevant than the latter. With respect to verbal inflections (the phenomenon investigated in Bybee 1985), Bybee argued for the ranking in (4) in terms of degree of relevance, a ranking generally confirmed by a cross-linguistic survey of the relative order of affixes relative to the stem (Bybee 1985:20–3, 33–5):

(4) aspect > tense > mood > person/number agreement

Bybee argues that, among other things, semantic relevance governs the mental representation of the organization of morphological paradigms (ibid. chapter 3). Forms whose meanings are semantically closer are more directly linked to each other than forms whose meanings are semantically more distant. Hence different person agreement forms of a single tense/spect/mood type are closely linked, but different tense/aspect/mood forms are more distantly linked.

Evidence for this hypothesis is the degree of phonological similarity of forms in a morphological paradigm. Forms that are more closely related semantically will also in general be more closely related phonologically. Closely related forms are built on the same stem. Token frequency, however, is a competing factor: forms with high token frequency may be independently represented units in the mind. Frequent forms thus develop and maintain irregularities, thereby increasing phonological differences between them and semantically closely related low frequency forms.

Bybee illustrates this generalization with Spanish and Latin paradigms (Bybee 1985:60–3); a small part of the Spanish first conjugation paradigm is given below, with person/number forms arranged in the usual way (singular. and plural in successive columns, 1st through 3rd person in successive rows):

(5) *Present indicative*   *Imperfect (past)*

canto	cantamos	cantaba	cantábamos
cantas	cantáis	cantabas	cantábais
canta	cantan	cantaba	cantaban

The person/number forms for each tense/aspect form are more closely related to each other than to other tense/aspect forms: they are built on the same stem (the *-a* stem in the present and the *-aba* stem in the imperfect). Moreover, one can interpret the forms in each tense/aspect as being built on the 3rd singular form, which is the most frequent person/number form (etymologically incorrect, but see below). The one exception is the 1st singular present indicative – but it is the next most frequent form after 3rd singular (see the token frequency counts in Bybee 1985:54, 71 and Greenberg 1966:45).

Bybee presents developmental, experimental psycholinguistic, and diachronic evidence for the formal relatedness of forms in a morphological paradigm in terms of semantic relatedness and token frequency. It is the diachronic evidence, of course, which interests us here. That evidence is the leveling and restructuring of morphological paradigms, resulting in a greater similarity of phonological forms of the same verb. An example from the evolution of the present tense paradigm of 'do' from Old to Middle English is given below (Bybee 1985:64, from Moore & Marckwardt 1968):

(6)			*Old English*	*Middle English*
Present indicative				
Singular	1st		dō	do
	2nd		dēst	dost
	3rd		dēth	doth
Plural			dōth	do

Morphological leveling alone is evidence of intraference. The meanings of the verb forms all overlap: they all denote the same type of event or state. Intraference is the consequence of identification of the meaning of one form with an overlapping meaning of another form, leading to the introduction of the other form with the first meaning.

For example, 2nd and 3rd person singular meanings are closely related to the 1st person singular meaning in the same tense and mood. The Old English root for 1st person replaces the Old English root for 2nd and 3rd person in Middle English, and so combines with the suffixes for 2nd and 3rd person. The resulting Middle English forms are fudged forms brought about by the 'contact' – intralingual identification – of the 1st and 2nd/3rd person singular present indicative forms.

The intraference account is compatible with Bybee's own analysis. It shares with Bybee's model the assumption of an activation network representation of linguistic knowledge (see §7.2), so that meanings are linked together to varying degrees of strength (closeness). It also shares with Bybee's model the notion that innovation results in the reorganization of linguistic knowledge, based on the relation between form and meaning.

Sometimes the fudged forms in analogical leveling are not etymologically 'correct'. Examples from the evolution of Provençal and Slavic verbal paradigms are given below:

(7) a. Old Provençal preterite paradigm (Bybee 1985:55):

    améi   amém
    amést   amétz
    amét   améren

   b. Preterite paradigms from Modern Provençal dialects (ibid. from Meyer-Lübke 1923:352 and Ronjat 1937:193 respectively):

	Charente		*Clermont-Ferrand*	
	cantí	cantétem	cantéte	cantétem
	cantétei	cantétei	cantétei	cantétetz
	cantét	cantéten	canté	cantéton

(8) a. Old Church Slavonic present tense of 'be' (Schmalstieg 1976:134):

jes-mĭ	jes-mŭ
jes-i	jes-te
jes-tŭ	sǫtŭ

   b. Polish present tense of 'be' (Teslar 1957:190):

jest-em	jest-eśmy
jest-eś	jest-eście
jest	są

These examples show that other members of the person/number paradigm take the 3rd singular stem as their base on which the new non-3rd person forms are derived, as can be seen by the intrusion of -*t* in most of the other forms in the descendant languages. In the Charente dialect of Provençal, the 1st person singular resists leveling, as does the 3rd plural in Polish; both forms are relatively high in token frequency. In the Clermont-Ferrand dialect of Provençal, the 1st singular form is based on the earlier 3rd singular, but the 3rd singular itself has eroded, again a result of its high token frequency.

6.2.2 Lexical semantic change

I begin with an anecdotal example of a lexical change that has diffused considerably in the speech communities I have lived in over the past two decades or so. The English word *homogeneous* 'of the same kind', once pronounced [homoˈdʒinijəs], is now pronounced [həˈmadʒɨnəs] by ever-increasing numbers of people. The novel pronunciation is identical to that of another English word, *homogenous* 'of the same origin'. I suggest that the shift in pronunciation of *homogeneous* is due to intraference from *homogenous*. Another way of putting it is that *homogenous* now also means 'of the same kind'. Indeed, one can find this in lightly edited prose such as an environmentalist newsletter, describing the road from Ubehebe Crater to Racetrack Valley in Death Valley National Park:

(9) This 'freeway' is essentially a broad trench scooped out of the desert's surface and lined throughout its length with an homogenous grey gravel. (*The Survivor*, Spring 1996, p. 16)

It is highly likely that the writer was referring to the uniform color or size of the gravel, not its origin.

The motivation for the change is the similarity in meaning of *homogeneous* and *homogenous*. The closeness of the meanings of the two words means there is a high degree of overlap in meaning, thus allowing for intralingual identification. Intralingual identification then gives rise to intraference: the form [həˈmadʒɨnəs] is employed for the meaning 'of the same kind'.

Lexical intraference is pervasive. Lexical roots are constantly sliding around among closely related meanings. Examples in language change can be found on almost every page of Buck's comparative synonyms of Indo-European languages (Buck 1949). I give one particularly clearcut example here: item §18.31, ASK (Buck 1949:1264). Buck distinguishes two closely related meanings, ASK[1] 'question, inquire' and ASK[2] 'request'. Example (10) illustrates the distribution of the two meanings for the Proto-Indo-European root *prek̂-, *pr̥(k̂)-sk̂-:

(10)	ASK[1] 'question, inquire'	ASK[2] 'request'
Latin		poscere
Irish (Old/Middle)	com-aircim	arcu
Welsh		arch
Gothic	fraihnan	
Dutch	vragen	
Old High German	frāgēn	
Lithuanian		prašyti
Latvian	prasīt *(rare)*	prasīt
Church Slavic	vŭ-prositi	prositi
Sanskrit	pracch-, praç-	
Avestan	fras-	
Armenian	harçanem	
Tocharian B	prek- *(middle)*	prek- *(active)*

Individual forms vacillate between these two meanings in various branches of Indo-European, and even in a single branch. This phenomenon gives rise to the legions of *faux amis* in closely related languages and dialects.

Lexical intraference is the use of a word form with one meaning for a closely related meaning. If another word form already exists for that meaning, lexical intraference leads to competition and possibly eventual replacement of the older word form with the newer one (see §7.3). Sometimes the replacement is incomplete because the new form enters only part of the morphological paradigm of the old form. The result of incomplete intraference is a suppletive morphological paradigm. For instance, the past tense form of Middle English *go*, *eode* (also suppletive), was replaced by the (irregular) past tense form of *wend* 'turn around/away':[1]

(11)		Middle English (S varieties)		Modern English	
	Infinitive	*go*	*wend* 'turn around/away'	*go*	*wend*
	Past	*eode*	*went(e)*	*went*	*wended*

By the Middle English period, *wenden* was 'almost synonymous with *go* already in Chaucer' (Brunner 1965:86). The semantic similarity of *eode* and *wenden* led to intraference in the past tense only.

Presumably, a similar development is found in Italian 'go' (Buck 1949:694, §10.47):

(12) **andare**

vado	andiamo
vai	andate
va	vanno

The root *and-* is said to derive from Vulgar Latin **ambitāre*, which in turn may come from Latin *ambīre* 'go around' and/or *ambulāre* 'walk' (ibid.). The root *va-* is said to derive from Latin *vādere* 'go rapidly, rush, advance' (ibid.).

6.2.3 *Mechanisms for intraference*

The analysis of the mechanism for intraference is identical to that for interference. The mechanism for innovation in intraference is intralingual identification. Once intralingual identification of related forms is made, then two variant forms for one meaning, i.e. two variant linguemes of a variable, exist, and choice of one form over another is selection.

The most often proposed explanation for intraference is an intentional one, namely the poetic function of expressiveness (§3.4.4). This explanation has been offered by a wide range of theoretical historical linguists (see §3.4.4 for references).

It is certainly the case that many adult innovations are of just this sort: intended, even conscious, novel forms. A typical example is this overheard innovation of a constructional idiom:

(13) C: [drinking tea] Boy that really hits the spot.
      (pause)
      How's your scone?
      J: (pause) It hits a lot of spots.
      C: (laugh)

J's novel combination of the quantified expression [*a lot of N-s*] with the idiom [*NP (really) hit-TNS the spot*] is a deliberately novel expression, recognized as such – C laughs – but also expresses a meaning similar to the more pedestrian expression *It hits the spot in a lot of different ways*.

Expressiveness is generally invoked as a mechanism for innovation, not selection. Yet it appears to be invoked here for selection (the result of intraference) rather than innovation (the cause). It is possible to interpret expressiveness as a mechanism for innovation in intraference, however. Expressiveness may be the mechanism employed, consciously or unconsciously, by the speaker to establish intralingual identification, that is, connect two meanings in such a way that the expression for one can be used for the other in the context. Expressiveness would then be interpreted as simply seeking a novel expression for a particular concept on a particular occasion of language use. In other words, it may be that intraference for the sake of expressiveness is an 'on line' phenomenon, as Romaine suggests for interference (see §6.1).

As with interference, however, we must not leave out the possibility of a spontaneous intraference explanation. In §6.1, I suggested that in interference, there might be 'leakage' via spreading activation through the cognitive links established in a bilingual speaker's mind between words or constructions with similar functions in her two language systems. In the same way, there might be 'leakage' via spreading activation through the cognitive links established between words/constructions with similar meanings/functions in a single language system. Alternative forms or constructions in different parts of the linguistic system can be linked by virtue of their external substance, that is, their closely related meanings and discourse functions in particular contexts. Once these links are made, it is possible for innovations to occur spontaneously via these links.

6.2.4   Constraints on intraference

Intraference is based on intralingual identification, which is interpreted here as the establishment of connections between semantically closely related forms. The network of connections between related concepts is a CONCEPTUAL SPACE (also called a mental map, semantic map/space, or cognitive map/space; see Croft to appear b). The chief constraint on intraference is that intraference is predicted to occur between closely related or neighboring functions in conceptual space. Examples of these are the gradual spread of relative clauses formed by WH words up the grammatical relations (accessibility) hierarchy (see Romaine 1982), or the gradual spread of (reanalyzed) Finnish participial subordinate clause subjects and the Russian genitive/accusative objects down the animacy hierarchy (see Timberlake 1977).

In the evolution of morphological paradigms, closeness in conceptual space is a function of semantic relevance. It is predicted that analogical leveling of paradigms will occur among closely related forms. The examples of analogical leveling given by Bybee (see §6.2.1) confirm this prediction. The examples all involve leveling of person/number forms within a particular tense/aspect/mood category, and person/number forms of a single tense/aspect/mood category are semantically closer to each other than they are to their counterparts in other tense/aspect/mood categories.

Intraference is similar to Harris & Campbell's mechanism of extension. Harris & Campbell define extension as generalizing an already existing rule of the grammar (Harris & Campbell 1995:97). Intraference is here defined in terms of extension of a form to a function not previously associated with that form. The formulation of intraference here conforms to the model of innovations arising from language use, which requires formulation in terms of the form–function mapping. Also, Harris & Campbell consider borrowing[2] to be a distinct mechanism for change, whereas I argue here that interference and intraference employ basically the same mechanism for innovation, inter-/intralingual identification.

Harris & Campbell argue that one can treat extension as generalization. That is, each extension is the removal of a condition on a rule. In their view, at each step in the process there are necessary and sufficient conditions for the application of the rule, and extension is the removal of one or more of such conditions at a time. Thus, at each step of the process the domain of application of the rule is a natural class (Harris & Campbell 1995:114).

Harris & Campbell's constraint is too strong, since many extensions lead to polysemy (that is, extension to related meanings without the resulting range of application being reducible to a general set of conditions). This is particularly true of lexical diffusion, where a rule is extended one lexical item at a time (see §7.4.3). Harris & Campbell argue that in lexical diffusion, the rule applies to a natural class larger than the domain of application, the exceptions to the rule are conditions on the rule, and diffusion of the rule to the exceptional lexical items constitutes removal of conditions on the rule (Harris & Campbell 1995:113–14). But this strategy for handling counterexamples to Harris & Campbell's constraint renders their constraint vacuous. Any change which leads to a domain of application that is not a natural class can be reformulated as applying to a natural class with exceptions.

The constraint on intraference of nearness in semantic space allows for lexical diffusion and polysemous extension. Figurative semantic extensions such as metaphor and metonymy appear to pose difficulties for the nearness constraint. On the other hand, semantic links can be made in a variety of ways. Metaphorical mappings are established between unrelated semantic domains, such as time and money in *I spent a lot of time on this*, based on more schematic semantic properties shared between the two domains (see Lakoff & Johnson 1980; Lakoff 1990; Clausner & Croft 1999). Speakers creating novel metaphors are establishing intralingual identification between the source and target domains of the metaphor. Likewise, metonymic mappings involve semantic links of association within a semantic frame (Fillmore 1982, 1985). The question then arises, what sort of semantic links are not possible? It is hoped that a model of semantic structure will emerge from cognitive semantics that will describe expected and unexpected sorts of semantic links (see Cruse & Croft to appear).

It is not clear how much directionality we can attribute to intraference. Nearness in semantic space is a symmetric relation; there is no inherent directionality in intraference as I have formulated it. In the case of analogical leveling in morphological paradigms, token frequency provides a constraint on directionality of intraference: the higher frequency forms intrafere with the lower frequency forms. In the examples of analogical leveling given in (7)–(8), the 3rd person singular form is the one that intraferes with the other person/number forms, and 3rd person singular generally has the highest token frequency. The 1st person singular has the highest token frequency after 3rd person singular; hence we sometimes encounter the 1st person singular form intrafering with the other singular person forms (as in example (6)).

Token frequency provides directionality for intraference, at least in morphological paradigms. Likewise, hierarchies such as the animacy and grammatical relations hierarchies mentioned above provide directionality for intraference. However, it appears that intraference does not implicitly define directionality in semantic change in the way that metanalysis does (see §5.5 and §6.3.2). Perhaps this is what should be expected, given the multidirectionality of semantic change. There is one domain of semantic change, however, where unidirectional changes predominate. This domain is grammaticalization, to which we now turn.

6.3   Grammaticalization

6.3.1   *Grammaticalization processes*

Grammaticalization, the last process of innovation in grammatical change to be discussed here, is in fact probably the source of the majority of grammatical changes that languages undergo (Haspelmath 1998a). GRAMMATICALIZATION is the process by which constructions with specific lexical items develop grammatical functions, leading to the reinterpretation of the lexical items as possessing grammatical functions. Grammaticalization is often described as a process by which individual lexical items evolve grammatical functions (e.g. Heine, Claudi & Hünnemeyer 1991:2), but it is more recently recognized that lexical items develop grammatical functions only in specific constructional contexts (see §3.3.3). That is to say, grammaticalization, like form–function reanalysis, is essentially syntagmatic (Hopper & Traugott 1993:156).

Grammaticalization can be divided into three types of largely unidirectional processes, phonological, morphosyntactic and functional (semantic/pragmatic; Heine & Reh 1984:16–46). These three processes tend to be diachronically synchronized, that is, elements in grammaticalizing constructions tend to undergo all three processes to a greater or lesser extent. The processes in each type can be further subdivided into 'paradigmatic' and 'syntagmatic' (Lehmann 1982:125–60, 1985). ('Paradigmatic' changes should be interpreted here as those 'affecting only one element in the grammaticalizing construction', and 'syntagmatic' as 'affecting more than one element'.) Table 6.1 is based on an integration of Heine & Reh's and Lehmann's classifications of grammaticalization processes (Croft 1990:230–9; italicized terms refer to the process as a whole).

An example can be given that illustrates most of the processes found in Table 6.1. One of the most often cited examples of grammaticalization is the evolution of the English construction with *go* and an infinitival purpose clause, as in *I'm going (downtown) to buy a CD player*, to a future, as in *I'm gonna buy a CD player*. The phonological processes affect the invariant parts of the construction (see §6.3.2). The form *going to* [gowɪŋ tə] evolves into *gonna* [gʌnə] via reduction of the first two syllables and of the resulting vowel, coalescence of the two morphemes, and adaptation of the velar nasal and the alveolar stop to an alveolar stop. Morphosyntactically, the former purpose clause is made obligatory, and there is loss of independent status of infinitival *to* (fused in *gonna*) and attachment of the contracted auxiliary to the subject phrase (virtually

TABLE 6.1   Grammaticalization processes

Phonological

Paradigmatic: *attrition*: reduction/erosion > phonological loss

Syntagmatic: *coalescence*: free morpheme > cliticization, compounding >
affixation > loss
adaptation (including assimilation)

Morphosyntactic

Paradigmatic: obligatorification > fossilization > morphological loss
paradigmaticization: open class > closed class > invariant
element

Syntagmatic: *rigidification* [word order]
loss of independent syntactic status > morphological fusion
> loss

Functional

Paradigmatic: extension of semantic range > loss of function

Syntagmatic: *idiomaticization*: compositional & analyzable >
noncompositional & analyzable > unanalyzable

---

obligatory with *gonna*). Functionally, the motion verb is extended to nonmotion contexts, and the meaning of the construction as a whole is extended from purposive to future.

Grammaticalization processes are the ultimate source of all constructions with so-called function words or grammatical inflections, including the following typologically common grammatical changes (see Haspelmath 1998b:137):

(14)   a.   full verb > auxiliary > tense/aspect/mood affix
b.   verb > adposition
c.   noun > adposition
d.   adposition > case affix
e.   adposition > subordinator
f.   emphatic personal pronoun > clitic pronoun > agreement affix
g.   cleft sentence marker > highlighter
h.   noun > classifier
i.   verb > classifier
j.   demonstrative > article > gender/class marker
k.   demonstrative or article > complementizer or relativizer
l.   collective noun > plural affix
m.   numeral 'one' > indefinite article
n.   numerals 'two' or 'three' > dual/paucal/plural number affix

I will not discuss the details of the various coordinated grammaticalization processes in Table 6.1, or the common grammaticalization paths given in (14).

These are all extensively discussed in the literature (see §3.3.3 for references). Instead I will focus on the mechanisms that have been proposed to underlie these processes.

Before examining the mechanisms underlying grammaticalization, we must first address some putative counterexamples to grammaticalization. These putative counterexamples are presented as problems for the general claim of unidirectionality of grammaticalization. In fact, they appear to involve one proposed grammaticalization process left out of Table 6.1, condensation of larger syntactic units (e.g. clauses) into smaller ones (e.g. phrases).

Some of the counterexamples involve the reversal of phonological coalescence, where an affix becomes a clitic. Examples include Estonian question and emphatic particles *es, ep* < *-es, -ep* (Campbell 1991), and the English possessive clitic *-'s*, from the genitive suffix *-s* (Janda 1980, 1981; Harris & Campbell 1995:337; Allen 1997[3]). These appear to be relatively sporadic compared with the large number of cases of coalescence in grammaticalization.

Another type of counterexample represents a commonly occurring phenomenon, however. Elements that combine with smaller syntactic constituents such as noun phrases are extended in use such that they combine with larger constituents such as clauses, violating the process of condensation (Tabor & Traugott 1998). The two most common examples are the grammaticalization of adpositions to subordinators ((14e); Genetti 1986; Heine, Claudi & Hünnemeyer 1991:153) and of demonstratives or articles to complementizers or relativizers ((14k); Heine, Claudi & Hünnemeyer 1991:179–86). Tabor & Traugott survey these and other counterexamples to condensation. Tabor & Traugott argue that condensation should not be considered a unidirectional grammaticalization process; the syntactic scope of a grammaticalizing element is determined instead by semantic and other factors. Tabor & Traugott's arguments can also be applied to the sporadic cases of violations of coalescence. The Estonian particles modify clauses and the English *-'s* genitive governs a noun phrase, so their phonological liberation is partly justified by their semantic scope.

Another grammaticalization process proposed in earlier studies is also problematic. Heine & Reh (1984:41–3) argue for a grammaticalization process they call simplification. They give examples of the loss of gender distinctions in various languages, where one gender form comes to be used for all noun/pronoun classes (e.g. Class 9 agreement in Kenya Pidgin Swahili). Lehmann refers to another sort of simplification, the loss of the ability to inflect, as a process of grammaticalization, which he subsumes under attrition (Lehmann 1985:307).

One apparent counterexample to simplification is the addition of distinctions through morphological fusion (cf. Heine & Reh 1984:40–1). For example, subject agreement inflections on verbs in many Melanesian languages display a realis/irrealis modal distinction. It is likely that at an earlier stage, there was a single subject pronominal form that fused with realis/irrealis modal markers in the process of becoming an agreement marker.

It appears that simplification in itself is not a unidirectional grammaticalization process; instead, what has been called simplification should be attributed to other grammaticalization processes. The replacement of distinct grammatical forms by one single form in a paradigmatic set, as in Heine & Reh's gender example, is an example of paradigmaticization. The loss of a morphosyntactically distinct inflectional category in a construction (the phenomenon described by Lehmann) is an example of morphological loss. Finally, morphological fusion and loss can be subsumed under coalescence.

In the next section, I will examine mechanisms for the phonological, morphosyntactic and functional processes of grammaticalization. Grammaticalization differs from other semantic changes in two respects. First, it involves semantic changes that converge on a particular set of semantic categories, so-called 'grammatical' semantic categories such as the endpoints of the processes listed in (14). Second, this process is accompanied by formal processes which essentially involve the syntactic 'freezing' of the construction expressing the meaning, and the phonological coalescence and erosion of particular elements in that construction.

6.3.2 *Mechanisms for grammaticalization*

Keller (1990/1994) offers an interpretation of a model of language change developed by Lüdtke (1980, 1985, 1986) which provides an account of the formal processes of grammaticalization (see also Haspelmath 1998a:52). I will describe this model as the PERIPHRASIS–FUSION–EROSION cycle. The result of each phase in the cycle creates the conditions for the next phase of the change.

6.3.2.1 Periphrasis and semantic extension

The first phase, PERIPHRASIS (Lüdtke's *amplification sémantactique*; Lüdtke 1986:23–7), is the recruitment of a new, periphrastic construction for a particular function. The new construction is usually more or less sanctioned by the existing rules of the grammar. The new construction is a more complex construction whose compositional meaning is closely related to the novel function for which it is used.

Some linguists have argued that expressiveness is the intentional mechanism to account for this first step in grammaticalization: a speaker creates a novel periphrastic expression for the function in question (e.g. Lehmann 1985:314–17; Heine, Claudi & Hünnemeyer 1991:78; Heine 1994:259). One failing of the expressiveness account, however, is that a new construction may arise for a grammatical function (e.g. plural marking) which did not previously have grammatical expression in the language. This problem is avoided by another intentional mechanism for periphrasis, avoiding misunderstanding (Keller 1990/1994:94; see §3.4.4 and also Langacker's 'perceptual optimality' [Langacker 1977:128]). Both Keller and Lüdtke argue that speakers introduce a certain degree of redundancy in communication in order to avoid misunderstanding.

But there is an upper limit as to how clear one can be with a given expression: 'to increase redundancy beyond the acoustically possible, one must use lexical means' (Keller 1990/1994:109), i.e. periphrasis.[4]

I have presented the first phase of grammaticalization in terms of the formal properties of the construction that is extended to the new function. Of much greater concern for grammaticalization theorists is the functional (semantic/ pragmatic) side of this process, namely how a construction gets extended to a new grammatical function. The main question is how to account for the essentially unidirectional semantic/pragmatic changes in grammaticalization.

There are two broad theories of the semantic processes underlying grammaticalization: metaphorical extension and pragmatic inference. Metaphorical extension is the transfer of a concept from one conceptual domain to another. One of the commonest types of metaphorical extension is that from space to time; compare *from New York to Chicago* and *from May to September*. Pragmatic inference (Traugott & König 1991; Hopper & Traugott 1993:75–77) is a type of metanalysis: a contextual ('pragmatic') property of the meaning is reanalyzed as an inherent ('semantic') property of the meaning, and a related inherent property is reanalyzed as a contextual one (see §5.4).

Both metaphor and metanalysis would provide unidirectionality. However, metaphor requires explicit ranking of conceptual domains from the 'less metaphorical' to the 'more metaphorical' (see (16) below). Metanalysis implicitly predicts unidirectionality whenever the inherent feature affected entails the presence of the contextual feature most of the time, but not vice versa.[5]

Traugott & König (1991) argue that both processes are required in order to account for grammaticalization, but that they operate in different grammatical domains: the development of 'tense, aspect, case and so forth' is metaphorical, but the development of connectives involves pragmatic inference (metanalysis; Traugott & König 1991:190). The implicit unidirectionality of metanalysis yields for example the changes temporal > causal and temporal > concessive in connectives (ibid. 193).

Heine, Claudi & Hünnemeyer (1991) argue that all grammaticalization processes involve pragmatic inference, which they called context-induced reinterpretation. They hypothesize that pragmatic inference represents the microstructure of the grammaticalization process, while metaphor represents the macrostructure. They convincingly demonstrate that the sort of changes that Traugott & König describe as being only metaphorical involve pragmatic inferencing. Their method is to show that for any apparent quantum leap between two meanings or situation types, there is a continuum of situation types that bridge the gap between the two such that pragmatic inference will allow a speaker to extend the meaning gradually from one situation type to the other. They give examples of intermediate situation types for allative > purposive > future (Heine, Claudi & Hünnemeyer 1991:70, given in (15) below); comitative > instrumental (ibid. 104, from Schlesinger 1979:310); Ewe *gbé* 'back' > 'back of [object]' > 'behind' (ibid. 65–8); Ewe *kpɔ́* 'see' > 'really' > counterexpectation (ibid. 194–7):

(15)   a.   Henry is going to town.
      b.   Are you going to the library?
      c.   No, I am going to eat.
      d.   I am going to do my very best to make you happy.
      e.   The rain is going to come.

Examples (15a–b) can be interpreted as a pure allative situation type, but with a human subject, it is plausible to infer an intention on the part of the subject. If intention is interpreted as an inherent part of the meaning of *to*, then the complement of *to* can be an intended action as well as a spatial destination, as in (15c). In (15c), the motion meaning for *go* remains if we assume that it is an answer to (15b). In (15c), future time reference is a contextual inference but in (15d), the motion meaning may be absent and the (intentional) future meaning is then metanalyzed as an inherent aspect of the construction. Finally, while prediction is a contextual inference in (15d), it is metanalyzed as inherent and applied to an inanimate subject in (15e).

Having given several such microstructural analyses, Heine *et al.* argue that one can still interpret grammaticalization as metaphorical because if one selects certain points along the continuum, the process then appears to make a quantum leap from one conceptual domain to another. But the metaphorical interpretation is superfluous and even misleading. It is superfluous because the microstructural analysis as metanalysis is sufficient to describe grammaticalization. Worse, the metaphorical intepretation of grammaticalization is misleading as an empirical description of the process and hence of the cognitive processes underlying grammaticalization. Metaphor involves a quantum leap from one conceptual domain to another (Lakoff & Johnson 1980), yet grammaticalization is a gradual process. There is good evidence for metaphor in lexical semantic change, but not so clearly in grammaticalization. Nevertheless, metaphor may constrain the types of metanalysis that constitute grammaticalization.

There is one reason why one might want to invoke metaphor in grammaticalization, and that is to motivate unidirectionality. Heine *et al.* propose the following ranking of domains for metaphorical transfer:

(16)   person < object < process < space < time < quality [state]

However, some of these categories are rather loosely defined, and not all lexical metaphors obey this hierarchy. Consider for example the metaphor TIME IS MONEY (Lakoff & Johnson 1980:7–9), as in *I have no time for this.* Here, possession is the source domain transferred to time. Possession is a quality in Heine *et al.*'s scheme, because it is a stative relation; but it is lower in the hierarchy than time. Thus, the hierarchy in (16) is specific to grammaticalization processes, and so requires explanation. (Besides, the hierarchy still does not account for the intermediate situation types in grammaticalization paths.)

Pragmatic inference or metanalysis, on the other hand, offers the possibility of a general explanation of unidirectionality: the contextual property is usually entailed by the inherent property but not vice versa. I believe this hypothesis has a chance of success for accounting for unidirectionality in grammaticalization, based on the examples given in Heine, Claudi & Hünnemeyer (1991). For example, allative motion with a human subject usually entails intention, but not vice versa (many intended actions do not imply directed motion on the part of the intender), and intention usually entails prediction, but not vice versa (predicted events without human subjects and sometimes even with them often are unintended).

Of course, this hypothesis cannot be entirely persuasive without a systematic survey of grammaticalization paths and their intermediate situation types, which is beyond the scope of this book. Likewise, there may be some grammaticalization processes in which a quantum-leap metaphorical change does take place, rather than a gradual shift driven by metanalysis.

The directionality of semantic change in grammaticalization may not always be predictable from the metanalysis of utterances in context. Whether it is or not, the fact of the continuous, gradual nature of the extension of function in many attested cases of grammaticalization demonstrates that the structure of conceptual space plays a significant role in defining grammaticalization paths (see e.g. Haspelmath 1997), as it does with intraference.

6.3.2.2 Fusion and morphosyntactic 'freezing' of a construction

Once a periphrastic expression has been chosen to express a novel meaning, it then undergoes FUSION, that is, it is perceived as a fixed unit (Lüdtke 1986:27–31; Keller 1990/1994:110). Lüdtke and Keller present this as a psychological phenomenon, that is, entrenchment (see §2.4.2). However, it is also a social phenomenon, namely the conventionalization of the periphrastic expression with a particular meaning. In other words, the fusion phase involves propagation of the construction as a variant lingueme for the new function.

As will be seen in chapter 7, conventionalization involves the reduction of variation in forms to express a particular function, that is, the reduction of variant linguemes. One way to reduce variation is, of course, to eliminate the older form. However, there often are variants of the new construction, such as the variety of postverbal negative emphatic markers in the history of French (*pas, point*, etc.; see §5.4.1), that compete to be the conventional expression of the function. Among the ways to reduce this sort of variation are to: (i) fix the word order of the construction – i.e. rigidification; (ii) eliminate optionality – i.e. obligatorification; (iii) reduce the range of elements that fit into a slot in a construction to a closed class or an invariant element – i.e. paradigmaticization. These strategies correspond to the morphosyntactic processes of grammaticalization in Table 6.1.

It may not be obvious that two alternative forms of a construction are actually in competition. Consider the following example of paradigmaticization eventually resulting in an invariant element. Many languages in the Austroasiatic family have numeral classifiers, used in combination with a numeral modifying a noun (Adams 1989). In some Austroasiatic languages such as Wa, the classifiers are specific to particular classes of nouns (Adams 1989:180). The classifiers appear not to be in competition with each other. But in other languages of the family such as Vietnamese, one classifier starts to be used with other noun classes, in which case it is competing with other classifiers (ibid.). The existence of intraference entails that a form can become a competitor for any neighboring form in conceptual space, especially if the intrafering form is more frequent (see §6.2). The same remarks apply to variants that differ in word order or in the presence/absence of an element of the construction (i.e. optionality).[6]

6.3.2.3   Erosion, (mostly) phonological

The last stage in the grammaticalization cycle is EROSION of the conventionalized expression (Lüdtke's *usure phonique*; Lüdtke 1986:15–23; Keller 1990/1994:108). Erosion is generally treated as phonological, that is, reduction, coalescence and adaptation. However, as noted in §6.3.1, coalescence and erosion may apply also to morphemes as well as phonemes. Hence the correlation between periphrasis, fusion, erosion and functional, morphosyntactic and phonological processes respectively is not quite perfect.

The principle of economy is invoked by Lüdtke and Keller to account for erosion. As was argued in §3.4.4, it is possible to interpret the essentially psychological principle of economy as a social-interactional phenomenon, by exploiting the principle of immediacy in coordination by interlocutors on a single meaning and the principle of joint salience in the interlocutors' common ground (§4.2.4). In fact, since the range of possible phonological reductions of a construction is quite wide (everything from full and distinct articulation of every phoneme to a minimally distinct mumble), it is clear that the speaker chooses degree of reduction of a constructional form with the hearer in mind.

Only certain elements in the construction will be phonologically eroded, namely the specific morphemes that are associated with the construction, the more invariant the better. To use the same example from §6.3.1: in the English *go*-future, [sBJ *be going to* VP$_{inf}$], *be* is always present but in its usual range of forms, while the string *going to* is always present in just that form. Thus, it is *going to* that reduces to [gʌnə]; next, certain forms of *be* reduce to enclitics on the subject in this construction as they do elsewhere, due to the high token frequency of those forms compared with the variable parts of the construction (subject, infinitival verb phrase).

Of course, it is precisely the specific, especially invariant, morphemes associated with the construction that are interpreted by the interlocutors as encoding the meaning characteristically associated with the construction as a whole (cf. §5.1). It is this fact that gives the impression that grammaticalization is a process affecting individual morphemes (and the lexemes they are derived from). However, phonological erosion occurs only when the individual morphemes have the meaning that is conferred on them by the construction. For this reason, grammaticalization theorists now recognize that grammaticalization applies to whole constructions, not just lexemes and morphemes.

As erosion proceeds, the need not to be misunderstood may assert itself, and the periphrasis–fusion–erosion cycle may repeat itself for the particular function in question. Also, the grammaticalized construction may itself be extended to a new function, that is, it may be drawn into a periphrasis–fusion–erosion cycle for a new function.

6.3.2.4 Grammaticalization and structural reanalysis

Structural reanalysis plays an important role in some theories of grammatical change (e.g. Harris & Campbell 1995), and is often implicated in grammaticalization. STRUCTURAL REANALYSIS is the reanalysis of the syntactic structure of a construction, and thus differs from form–function reanalysis as described in chapter 5. A typical example of genuine structural reanalysis is the reanalysis of an external possessor as an adnominal possessor in some varieties of German (Haspelmath 1998a:59):

(17)   [Da zerriss$_V$ [dem Jungen]$_{NP}$ [seine Hose]$_{NP}$]$_S$
       'Then the pants tore on the boy.'

(18)   [Da zerriss$_V$ [[dem Jungen]$_{NP}$ seine Hose]$_{NP}$]$_S$
       'Then the boy's pants tore.'

Haspelmath (1998a) argues that although a number of grammaticalization theorists assume that structural reanalysis plays a significant role in grammaticalization, it is a distinct process. According to Haspelmath, genuine structural reanalysis does not involve the loss of syntactic autonomy or phonological substance; the syntactic relations or dependencies change in an abrupt manner; and the process is 'potentially reversible' (ibid.). Grammaticalization, on the other hand, does involve loss of autonomy and substance; the process is gradual, and it is unidirectional.

The phenomena within grammaticalization which have sometimes been interpreted as structural reanalysis are word class changes, alleged restructuring of the syntactic tree, reversal of head-dependent relations, clause fusion, and changes in grammatical relations. Haspelmath argues that these processes have the three aforementioned properties of grammaticalization – this is not really in dispute – and that the reanalysis interpretation depends on certain assumptions about syntactic representation that need not be the case.

Haspelmath's arguments can be summarized as follows. Word class membership is a matter of degree, and the changes in word class are gradual. Using dependency relations instead of constituency for syntactic representation eliminates the alleged syntactic restructuring in grammaticalization. Some theories of heads would lead to absence of reversal of head-dependent relations in grammaticalization. Clause fusion is actually change in word class (syntactic category) membership (e.g. verb > auxiliary). Finally, grammatical relation changes can be interpreted as gradual extension (intraference) of the semantics of an argument structure construction (case frame) to a new event class.

Haspelmath's arguments suggest that structural reanalysis is not as common a syntactic change as has previously been believed.

This section concludes the survey of mechanisms for innovation. I have argued that a wide range of types of grammatical change involve changes in the form–function mapping, in syntagmatic processes (form–function reanalysis and grammaticalization) and in paradigmatic processes (interference and intraference). Change in the form–function mapping is not the sole mechanism for grammatical innovation. Processes such as phonological erosion and genuine structural reanalysis in grammatical constructions cannot be interpreted as involving the form–function mapping. Nevertheless, change in the form–function mapping of words and constructions plays a major role in innovation of grammatical changes in languages.

Notes

1   The past tense *went(e)* is actually a 13th-century innovation for the earlier past tense *wende* (David Denison, personal communication).

2   Harris & Campbell use the term 'borrowing' for all contact-induced change, in contrast to Thomason & Kaufman 1988; see §8.3.

3   Allen argues convincingly against Janda's hypothesis that the transition from affixal to clitic -*s* occurred because of the convergence of affixal -*s* with a pronominal *(h)is* possession construction. Allen's proposal, that the affixal -*s* became a clitic after spreading (at least optionally) to the entire nominal paradigm makes it even more clear that the change was from an affix to a clitic, rather than from a word (the pronoun *his*) to a clitic.

4   It might be suggested that avoiding misunderstanding is the mechanism underlying intraference as well. However, intraference does not generally involve the asymmetry between a longer (periphrastic) expression and a shorter one. One situation in which avoiding misunderstanding might motivate intraference is the replacement of a form with a wide range of functions by a form with a narrower range of functions, as suggested by Bybee (personal communication) for the extension of the progressive into the ongoing present function.

5   Traugott & König argue that metanalysis is actuated via an intentional mechanism, namely the Gricean principle of informativeness: be as informative as possible (Traugott & König 1991:191). However, given the framework of the indeterminacy of the form-function mapping defended in chapters 4–5, it is not necessary to appeal to an intentional mechanism here.

6   It would appear that it is at the fusion stage that idiomatization of the expression for the meaning in question takes place. In fact, idiomatization takes place at the periphrasis stage, that is, at the innovation, not propagation, of the construction with its new function. Any novel use of language is partly nonconventional (§4.3). The nonconventionality of the novel use is reflected in the (non)compositionality of the expression. Further steps in the idiomatization process (e.g. loss of analyzability) occur with further semantic extensions of the construction, i.e. new cycles of periphrasis–fusion–erosion.

Chapter 7

Selection (propagation) of innovations in language change

7.1 Introduction

Altered replication and selection, as defined in §2.3, are the two fundamental processes involved in the framework for analyzing evolutionary processes. Altered replication of the replicator is innovation in language change. Selection of interactors is the propagation of an innovation in language change. It has been argued in the preceding chapters that the mechanisms for innovation are functional: more precisely, the mechanisms involve remappings of the link between form and function in a conventional linguistic sign or lingueme – the replicator. Chapters 5 and 6 discussed a range of mechanisms for innovation, and the processes of language change that appear to be the result of those mechanisms.

In contrast, the mechanisms for propagation of innovations in language change are social, that is, they involve the relationship between the speaker – the interactor – and the society to which she belongs. Propagation is essentially the adoption of a convention. Thus, two fundamental prerequisites to an understanding of mechanisms of propagation are the structure of society (relevant to the language used in the society) and the nature of conventions. These two concepts were given an initial explication in §4.2.3 and §4.2.4. In §7.2 and §7.3, I will elaborate on these concepts in order to lay the groundwork for a theory of the mechanisms for propagation. In §7.4, I will interpret current sociolinguistic theories in the evolutionary framework. There I will argue that the basic mechanism for propagation is the speaker identifying with a social group, and that patterns of propagation in social populations that are parallel in significant respects to patterns of selection in biological populations.

7.2 Communities, societies and the internal/external distinction in language change

In §4.2.3, I argued against the naïve view of a speech community as a homogeneous, sharply bounded group of individual speakers. Instead, a speech community is a grouping of individuals by their participation in a social domain. The social domain can be defined by the shared expertise of the members of the community, by virtue of which the members of the community share common ground (mutual knowledge and beliefs). Shared expertise in a community is

166

not the only basis for common ground between individuals. Individuals can gain common ground through experience shared directly (perceptual basis) and indirectly, via conversation (discourse basis). Finally, different communities have distinct codes (in the sociolinguistic definition of a code).

The chief consequence of the sophisticated approach to speech communities is that all individuals belong to multiple communities, and hence all individuals are to some degree multilingual. This latter fact is obvious when there are two or more codes that are usually described as different languages. It is not so obvious when the various codes are usually described as parts of the same language. On the other hand, sociolinguistic analysis has made it amply clear that all speech communities (in the naïve sense of that word), including so-called monolingual communities, possess variation in linguistic form to some degree. Sociolinguists describe this variation as structured heterogeneity (see §3.2), ordered by social domain – that is, community in the sophisticated sense. In this section, I will develop a description of sociolinguistic heterogeneity in terms of the social structure and the linguistic behavior of communities in the sophisticated sense.

Clark (1996:103) gives the following examples of what he calls 'common' communities defined by shared expertise. I have reordered Clark's list, giving his examples of communities:

(1)	Nationality	American, Canadian, Dutch
	Residence	New Zealanders, Californians, Glaswegians
	Ethnicity	Blacks, Hispanics, Japanese-Americans
	Language	English speakers, Japanese speakers, German speakers
	Cohort [Age]	teenagers, senior citizens, thirty-year-olds
	Gender	men, women
	Education	university students, law students, high school graduates
	Occupation	ophthalmologists, plumbers, used-car dealers
	Employment [Place]	Ford auto workers, Stanford faculty, *Newsweek* reporters
	Subculture	rock musicians, drug addicts, teenage gangs
	Hobby	pianists, baseball fans, philatelists
	Religion	Protestants, Baptists, Muslims
	Politics	Democrats, libertarians, Fabians

The reader familiar with sociolinguistics will immediately recognize commonly used social variables in sociolinguistic research, in particular gender, age cohort, education and occupation (more broadly defined as social classes in class-based research; see Labov 1972b). Also, most sociolinguistic research fixes the value of certain other social variables which define other types of communities on the list in (1): the language of the speakers and a combination of nationality, residence and ethnicity (e.g. white Philadelphia English speakers). Hence, we may interpret correlations of linguistic variants with social variables as correlations of those variants with communities. We will return to this point below.

Clark also points out that communities are nested in degrees of greater or lesser inclusiveness, and gives these examples (among others; Clark 1996:104):

(2) Residence   North Americans ⊃ Americans ⊃ Westerners ⊃ Californians ⊃ Northern Californians ⊃ San Franciscans ⊃ Nob Hill residents

Occupation   middle class ⊃ professionals ⊃ physicians ⊃ ophthalmologists ⊃ ophthalmic surgeons

Language   English speakers ⊃ speakers of New Zealand English ⊃ speakers of Auckland English dialect

The nesting of communities can be compared with the nesting of populations of biological organisms referred to in §2.2 (see Grant 1981:81, Fig. 7.1, for a more fine-grained nesting of biological populations):

(3) Organisms   species ⊃ geographical race ⊃ deme

The nesting of biological organisms is defined in terms of degree of reproductive isolation: species are more or less completely isolated reproductively from other species, while geographical races and demes are relatively isolated reproductively from other races in the same species and other demes in the same race respectively.

The relevant nesting of individuals in communities for the evolutionary model of language, then, is in terms of their communicative isolation in that community. And the nesting of communities in (2) intuitively does provide an approximate guide of the degree of communicative isolation. Nob Hill residents, other things being equal, are more likely to talk with other Nob Hill residents than with other San Franciscans taken as a whole, and so on up the scale. Ophthalmic surgeons, other things being equal, are more likely to talk with other ophthalmic surgeons (on the job, at conferences, etc.) than with other physicians taken as a whole, and so on up the scale. Of course, if an ophthalmic surgeon is a neighbor with a lawyer on Nob Hill, she may talk more with the lawyer than with another ophthalmic surgeon living in Chicago. However, that is by virtue of the fact that they are neighbors, and so are in the same exclusive community based on residence, not (only) the fact that they are both in the more inclusive occupational community (professionals).

We may now relate community exclusivity and communicative isolation to other significant sociolinguistic concepts. Milroy & Milroy (1985) and Milroy (1992b) argue that the strength of an individual's tie to other individuals in the community is the most significant factor in the maintenance of linguistic conventions ('community norms' in their terminology) and the transmission of change. They adopt the following definition of TIE STRENGTH: 'The strength of a tie is a (probably linear) combination of the amount of time, the emotional intensity, the intimacy (mutual confiding) and the reciprocal services which characterize a tie' (Granovetter 1973:1361, cited in Milroy 1992b:178). I suggest that the strength of a tie is relevant to language evolution because it correlates with degree of communicative interaction: we talk more to those with whom we have strong ties, and in fact our strong ties are strong in significant part due to the degree that we talk with those people. The weaker the tie is to someone, the greater our communicative isolation from that person.

The deme is an important unit of organization in biology (Hull 1988:433): as noted in §2.2, it is the unit where individuals have equal likelihood of mating, and where one can say with confidence that the individuals share the same gene pool. In §2.2, I suggested that the equivalent unit of organization in society is the social NETWORK, the group of people which is most likely to talk with one another, and less likely (or less frequently) to talk to other people outside the group. I suggest that what distinguishes the social network from more inclusive communities as defined by Clark is a high degree of personal common ground shared by individuals in the network, in contrast to common ground derived from shared expertise in the community as a whole. Personal common ground is based on directly shared experiences and experiences shared through conversation. Personal common ground is closely related to the first criterion proposed by LePage & Tabouret-Keller (1985:187) for the focusing of a group of individuals, a concept closely related to tie strength, namely 'close daily interaction in the community'. Thus, personal common ground follows as a consequence of communicative interaction; the more communicative interaction, the more personal common ground.

Persons in more exclusive communities in the nested scales in (2) are more likely to share substantial personal common ground. To continue our example from above, two ophthalmic surgeons probably have attended the same conferences, heard the same papers, know the same fellow ophthalmic surgeons, and talked to each other about their own professional experiences; this is less likely if the two are physicians with different specialties. The more communities shared among individuals, and the more exclusive the shared communities are, the more personal common ground will be shared. If in addition our opthalmic surgeons are also neighbors on Nob Hill, they will have shared the same events (a heat wave, a crime wave) and talked to each other about their own experiences living on Nob Hill (e.g. remodeling their houses, traffic problems, a fire down the street).

Strong ties correlate with the two chief measurements of social networks, network DENSITY and network MULTIPLEXITY. Network density is the number of connections of any kind between individuals in a group (see e.g. Chambers 1995:71), that is, whether they know each other or not. Network multiplexity is the number of different ways in which individuals in a network know each other, e.g. family relations, workmates, classmates, shared activities. Multiplexity corresponds to the number of communities which are shared among individuals in the network, and density corresponds to the number of links among individuals in any community which they may share. As we noted above, the more communities shared among individuals in a network, and the more exclusive those communities are, the stronger the ties among the individuals in the network.

The preceding paragraphs illustrate the fact that groups of human beings in social terms differ from groups of organisms in biological terms in a significant respect. Human beings can and do belong to multiple communities, while organisms belong to just one deme. One consequence of this fact is that two people may belong to a very exclusive community and yet not be members of other communities at all. For example, a mother and her teenage son may belong to a very exclusive community in terms of residence (the same house) and family (nuclear family members), but are in different communities in other ways, e.g. gender (female vs male), age (teenage vs middle aged), hobby (gardening vs classical piano), etc. As a result, there may be a high degree of communicative interaction among individuals who belong to different communities. Of course, to some extent the communicative interaction is domain-specific: mother and son will talk a lot about household chores and family members, but not much about classical music. But there will nevertheless be significant transmission of language, that is, replication of linguemes, from one community code to another. And a large part of the reason for that is the relationship between community codes.

One of the most obvious ways to differentiate community codes is by comparing their communal lexicons. In the communal lexicons of two communities, one can find differences in form, meaning or both. Clark (1998) gives the following examples of differences between the community of Americans in general (defined in terms of nationality) and the community of American miners (defined in terms of occupation):

(4) *Specialized form, same meaning*
     [Miners: hoist, 'conveyance between levels of mine']
     [Americans: (mine) elevator, 'conveyance between levels of mine']

(5) *Specialized meaning, same form*
     [Miners: raise, 'shaft between 2 levels of a mine']
     [Americans: raise, 'increase in salary']

(6) *Specialized form–meaning pairing*
     [Miners: stope, 'type of mine cavity']

However, the fact of the matter is that there are an enormous number of lexical items, grammatical elements, and grammatical constructions whose form and meaning are identical across these communities:

(7) *Same form–meaning pairing*
     [Miners: walk, 'move on foot']
     [Americans: walk, 'move on foot']

(8) *Same form–meaning pairing*
     [Miners: be, 'predication of a nonverbal concept']
     [Americans: be, 'predication of a nonverbal concept']

(9)   *Same form–meaning pairing*
      [Miners: +PL, 'more than one object']
      [Americans: +PL, 'more than one object']

(10) *Same form–meaning pairing*
      [Miners: DEM *precedes* NOUN, 'deictic specification of location of object']
      [Americans: DEM *precedes* NOUN, 'deictic specification of location of object']

In other words, there is a large amount of shared expertise, namely core expertise about the world and about human beings' conceptualization of the world for communicative purposes, that is largely the same across domains (see §4.2.3). This core expertise is often expressed by the same form–meaning pairings across community codes. When it is, we generally speak of the different community codes as being part of the same language (in sense of language as a conventional signaling system). In doing so, we ignore differences in community lexicon – and in community grammar. The latter sort of variation is what sociolinguistic analysis typically focuses its attention on.

As mentioned above, variationist sociolinguistic analysis focuses on certain types of community. It generally holds invariant residence (defined quite exclusively), nationality, and language; and examines different communities within this group based on age cohort, gender and sometimes occupation (class), education and/or ethnicity. This sort of analysis implicitly assumes that communities based on residence in particular (nationality generally following from residence) have a different status from communities based on age cohort, gender, occupation, etc.

In fact, this is a reasonable assumption, at least for the geographically relatively nonmobile groups typically studied by modern variationist sociolinguists: inner-city communities, particularly lower-class communities including street gangs (Labov 1972a, Milroy 1987); adolescent students (Eckert 1989); geographically isolated groups such as in Martha's Vineyard (Labov 1963/1972); to name a few classic studies. That is, communities based on residence of these types are more communicatively isolated from other communities than communities based on age cohort, gender or occupation. People belonging to different age cohorts, genders and (to a lesser extent) occupation are more likely to talk with each other because they tend to live together, work together and engage in social transactions with each other. In other words, there is a higher degree of continuous contact among different age cohorts and gender than among different neighborhoods or larger geographical units.

Indeed, sociolinguists still use the word 'community' to describe a group of individuals largely based on residence, regardless of the heterogeneity of other communities (in the strict sense used in this book) to which these same individuals belong. As noted in §4.2.3, I will use the term SOCIETY to describe a set of individuals among whom there is a certain degree of communicative interaction, that is, relatively strong ties, and – more important – a certain degree of communicative isolation (weak ties or no ties) with respect to other societies. In that communicative isolation is more important than communicative interaction, a society is analogous to the species concept in biology (Grant 1981:91; see §2.2).

There is enough relative communicative isolation among communities based on age and gender within a society as defined in the preceding paragraph for differences to exist. But there is enough communicative interaction – contact – between these communities in a society that these differences will be manifested in proportions of variants of a linguistic variable, that is, variant linguemes. In other words, societies – groups of individuals held together by relatively strong network ties – typically based on geographical residence are linguistically variable because they are socially heterogeneous in terms of other community types. But the variation is probabilistic rather than categorical because these other community types are not communicatively isolated; they involve the same individual speakers. If we think of the variation as representing a lingueme pool in the population of utterances created by speakers in the society, then the heterogeneous character of a language – defined as a population of utterances – and the structured nature of that heterogeneity (in terms of correlations between variants and communities), is to be expected in the evolutionary framework adopted here.

One consequence of the evolutionary model of language, and of the sociolinguistic model of language that it accounts for, is that speakers must be able to represent knowledge of the structured heterogeneity of the makeup of the lingueme pool. This sort of speaker knowledge can be reasonably represented using SPREADING ACTIVATION MODELS of human cognition (Collins & Loftus 1975; Elman & McClelland 1984; Cruse & Croft to appear ch. 12). Spreading activation models allow for the representation of quantitative values associated with the relevant unit of knowledge (such as a lingueme) in terms of degree of activation. Degree of activation in turn is primarily determined by exposure to tokens of the unit in question in the environment (such as uses of a lingueme in utterances). Activation of one node or set of nodes in a network can activate (or inhibit) other nodes.

Degree of activation corresponds to knowledge of the proportions of the variants of a lingueme in the community. Activation of a lingueme involves activation of the nodes or sets of nodes corresponding to the lingueme's form, meaning, and the community in which the utterance occurs. (The latter is determined not only by the speakers but also the situation and topic of the utterance: a lingueme occurring in a conversation about classical music at a concert will activate a different community than the same lingueme occurring in a conversation about cooking dinner at home between the same two people.) Although I cannot develop this model further here, it should be clear that the spreading activation network model can in principle represent the sort of linguistic knowledge that the evolutionary and sociolinguistic theories require of speakers.

Of course, it need not be the case that the core expertise shared across communities is expressed by the same form–meaning pairings. Instead, a different set of form–meaning pairings may be used. In this case, we usually speak of a multilingual society. One might expect there to be competition or mixture between the two sets of form–meaning pairings, that is, the two lingueme pools, that are spoken in the same society, indeed by largely the same individuals. The evolutionary framework predicts that competition or mixture between two lingueme pools will be resisted to the extent that there is separation (communicative isolation) and equality of the communities, that is, the domains of shared expertise found in the society. This in fact appears to be the case (see §8.5).

We may summarize the model of communities as follows. Communities are defined by shared expertise. Communities exist in greater or lesser degrees of inclusiveness/exclusiveness. An important boundary in the degree of exclusivity of a community is the boundary inside which members share a significant degree of personal common ground, which can be obtained only through direct contact, in particular direct communicative interaction. A significant degree of personal common ground corresponds to a social network with reasonably strong ties in sociolinguistic theory, and a deme in evolutionary biology.

Unlike the organization of biological organisms in demes, however, all individuals in a society are members of multiple communities. Each community has its own code, hence all individuals in all societies are multilingual. However, much of the shared expertise in a community is common across communities, and the code is often common as well. Certain communities, particularly those based on residence (and ethnicity or nationality), tend to be relatively communicatively isolated. Other communities, such as those based on age, gender and occupation, tend not to be as communicatively isolated.

A society is defined as relatively communicatively isolated from neighboring societies, and typically is defined in terms of geographical region and (where relevant) ethnicity or nationality. With respect to other community types, such as age, gender and occupation, a society is heterogeneous. The language – the population of utterances and the lingueme pool it defines – of a society is structured in a corresponding fashion. Variant linguemes are correlated with different communities in the society, but the correlation is not categorical, because of lack of communicative isolation between different communities in the same society (multilingual societies will be discussed in chapter 8.)

In fact, much of the variation in sociolinguistic studies has been shown or is hypothesized to represent language change in progress. That is, the variation represents the propagation of a novel variant in the community, that is, the selection of a variant of a lingueme as the conventional sign for that concept in that community. In order to situate the results of sociolinguistic research on the propagation of variants in the evolutionary framework, it is necessary to return to another theoretical construct from chapter 4, convention, and link it to sociolinguistic research on the one hand and the evolutionary framework on the other.

7.3   Propagation and the adoption of conventions

The propagation of a novel linguistic variant is essentially the adoption of a new linguistic convention by the community. This process takes time, and in fact may never go to completion, that is, complete replacement of the old convention by the new one. Moreover, many innovations are not selected, or do not survive very long.

In describing a linguistic convention in §4.2.4, I assumed (as did Clark and to a lesser extent Lewis) that a single conventional signal would be used for speaker and hearer to coordinate on a particular recurrent situation type (ignoring for the time being the problems described in §4.3 in identifying a recurrent situation type). Lewis, however, did allow for degrees of conventionality in his definition (Lewis 1969:76–80). The various 'almost's in the Lewis & Clark definition of convention in §4.2.4 correspond to different ways in which a signal could be a convention of the community to varying degrees. The Lewis & Clark definition of convention is reproduced below, this time with the 'almost's indexed by the parameters by which convention can vary in degree:[1]

(11)   1   a regularity in behavior (producing a string of sounds)
      2   that is partly arbitrary
         a.   other regularities in behavior would be approximately equally preferable by $almost_3$ everyone in the community
      3   that is common ground in a community
      4   as a coordination device
         a. $almost_1$ everyone in the community conforms to it
         b. $almost_2$ everyone expects $almost_1$ everyone else to conform to it
         c. $almost_4$ everyone would prefer any additional member of the community to conform to it if $almost_1$ everyone in the community already conforms to it
         d. $almost_4$ everyone would prefer any new member of the community to conform to another regularity if $almost_1$ everyone in the community were already conforming to it
      5   for a recurrent coordination problem (communicating a meaning)

The different 'almost's in the definition can be defined as a proportion or percentage. In fact, the two significant 'almost's in the development of a convention are '$almost_1$', which defines the proportion of use of the signal as a linguistic convention in the community, and '$almost_4$', which defines the proportion of members of the community that prefer the use of one convention over another. I will use two simple examples, from the terminology of historical linguistics and 19th-century French aviation terminology, to illustrate this point.

The class of linguistic changes discussed in §6.3 is called *grammaticalization* by some historical linguists and *grammaticization* by others. It is clear from the literature that both terms are current and are used roughly for the same recurrent coordination problem. Let us assume for the sake of argument that in fact the two terms are used equally, that is, in about half of the cases when a historical linguist wants to refer to the phenomenon, *grammaticalization* is used, and in the other half, *grammaticization* is used.

It is reasonable to assume that clause 2 of the definition is largely invariant. It is approximately equally arbitrary to choose either *grammaticalization* or *grammaticization* as the convention of the historical linguistic community. That is, almost$_3$ all members of the community would a priori accept either word. To be sure, there might be some who find one somewhat preferable (e.g. *grammaticalization* because of Meillet's precedent, *grammaticalisation* in French); but there is no major difference between the two. In fact, it appears that a fair degree of difference in functional utility of alternative conventions must be allowed, in order to allow for the typological diversity of conventional linguistic structures used for a given function across the world's languages. This is to say that in general, differences in functional utility do not play a role in the propagation of a variant; only differences in social utility do (see §2.4.2, §7.4.3).

The crucial part of the definition is clause 4. 'Almost$_1$ everyone' is in fact only about half: about half$_1$ of the community uses *grammaticalization* and half$_1$ *grammaticization*. However, the two half-conventions are known to almost everyone in the community. For example, although I use the term *grammaticalization*, when I read an article on *grammaticization*, I recognize what the author is talking about, and I recognize that the author is using a partly conventional alternative to the half-convention that I follow. (If the author used *smurtification* instead, then he or she would not be conforming to any convention of the community.) So do most of my colleagues, that is, almost$_2$ everyone in the community expects about half$_1$ of the community to conform to *grammaticalization* (or *grammaticization*, mutatis mutandis). It is possible that some members of the community who read very selectively may not know of the existence of the other convention; but this is probably a small minority, and certainly would not include the central members of the community.

Likewise, the preference for using either *grammaticalization* or *grammaticization* is central to the propagation of a convention. How many members of the community would prefer that others use *grammaticalization* if only about half$_1$ of the community are using it? Presumably, 'almost$_4$' will include the half that uses *grammaticalization*. But the same group would also prefer an alternative regularity, e.g. *grammaticization*, if enough of the community, say half$_1$, were already conforming to it. In other words this part of the definition of convention implies that members of a community would prefer almost everyone in a community to conform to the same convention, whatever it is; that is, everyone would eventually conform to a single convention. (There would of course be a few stubborn diehards who insist on using an alternative form even when almost everyone else has abandoned it; but we must allow for the existence of such types in a realistic theory of convention.)

The preference for a unique convention does indeed appear to be a phenomenon of human language. All languages are heterogeneous, as noted in the preceding section. That is, a language's lingueme pool has multiple variant linguemes, that is, multiple partly conventional signals for a particular meaning.

The variants typically correlate with communities within a society, but most speakers use multiple variants, albeit in different proportions, in the utterances they produce. Nevertheless, there appears to be a natural human tendency for a community to select one alternative as the conventional signal for a recurrent coordination problem. That is, there seems to be a natural human tendency to increase the conventionality of one variant of a lingueme in a community at the expense of another, albeit over a long period of time in many cases. We may call this the FIRST LAW OF PROPAGATION.

A striking example of the First Law of Propagation is the development of technical terms for newly discovered or invented phenomena. At first, a wide range of terms is used, and this range is relatively quickly reduced, ultimately to one term. This pattern is observed in a number of cases in a study of 19th-century aviation terms in French (Guilbert 1965). The hot-air balloon (without a means to direct its motion) was invented by Montgolfier in 1783. He called it a *machine aérostatique*, but it was also called *aérostat* by the end of that year. Other terms used in 1783–1784 were *statique*, *globe aérostatique*, *ballon aérostatique*, and the truncations of the latter two, *globe* and *ballon* (Guilbert 1965:54). There was even the feminine form *aérostate* along with masculine *aérostat* (ibid.); the *Journal de Paris* assumed that the latter referred to the activity and the former to the machine itself (ibid.).[2] But the masculine *aérostat* was quickly established; by 1798 the Académie's dictionary included only *ballon aérostatique* and *aérostat*. The truncation *ballon* and *aérostat* were the only terms used in the 19th century and were essentially synonymous throughout this period (Guilbert 1965:57). Yet as early as 1787, it was noted that there was a difference between the two terms, which held through the 19th century: *aérostat* was more learned or scientific, *ballon* more popular (Guilbert 1965:54–5, 57). *Aérostat* was also used to describe any machine that hovers in the air, not just a balloon in the period 1861–1891 studied by Guilbert; *ballon* was never used in this context (ibid. 58). Later the terms were largely replaced by *montgolfière*, which was used sporadically in this period (ibid. 588).

It is not immediately obvious why the First Law of Propagation holds. After all, human beings have the memory capacity to handle multiple variants for many linguemes; bilingual individuals have two complete sets, for example. And members of a community can expect other members to know all of the variants, if they know them themselves. If there is more than one solution to a coordination problem, and speaker and hearer know all of the solutions, any solution can be used. Yet there is a strong tendency to avoid complete synonymy, that is, multiple forms with the same meaning and the same social (community) value. For bilinguals, the two languages will have different social values, and so the variants of a lingueme are not completely synonymous. However, there is a plausible social explanation of the First Law of Propagation, which will be presented in §7.4.2.

There are three ways in which increasing the conventionality of a variant of a lingueme can be done, corresponding to modifying one of the three clauses of the definition of convention that do not involve a qualifying 'almost'. The first two ways include what Trudgill calls reallocation of variants that arise in contact situations (Trudgill 1986:110); the third involves replacement of one variant by another (e.g. through processes of leveling and simplification; see Trudgill 1986 and §7.4.4).

The first way is to modify clause 5 of the definition of convention. That is, speakers will divide the coordination problem so that the alternative forms are used for distinct functions. This corresponds to elimination of synonymy and subsequent functional specialization or division of the meaning of the competing forms. For example, in my speech I distinguish the meanings of *grammaticalization* and *grammaticization*. Heine, Claudi & Hünnemeyer (1991:13, 20–1) note that the terms have been used for two relatively distinct stages of the diachronic process: the conventionalization or syntacticization of a discourse-pragmatic strategy, and the further reduction of the conventionalized strategy. I restrict *grammaticalization* for the latter stages and would define *grammaticization* as the first stage. If this functional division of labor were adopted, then each form would be much more conventional in its restricted function than it was in its broader function. (In fact, *grammaticization* would then compete with *conventionalization* and *syntacticization*.)

This particular innovation has not itself been propagated. But there are many cases of a functional division of labor for competing conventions, such as the split between the two plurals *brethren* and *brothers* mentioned in §2.4.3. A partial separation of meanings was described above for *aérostat* vs *ballon*, where the latter was not used for a hovering machine other than a balloon (e.g. a helicopter). The counterpart change in phonology would be reallocation of variants as allophones occurring in complementary phonological variants, as has happened with the variants [i] and [ə] of the variable /ɪ/ in South African English (Trudgill 1986:161, citing Lanham & Macdonald 1979).

The second way to increase the conventional status of alternative forms is to modify clause 3 of the definition of convention. That is, speakers will divide the community or set of communities and associate the distinct forms with distinct communities. For example, I heard a historical linguist suggest that *grammaticalization* tends to be used by European-trained historical linguists and their students, while *grammaticization* tends to be used by American-trained historical linguists and their students. Setting aside the validity of this observation (it is only partly true), it represents an attempt to divide the usage by community based on education. If it were true, or if speakers shifted to conform, then each form would be much more conventional in its restricted community than either was in the wider community.

This phenomenon is also familiar to historical linguists and sociolinguists. Otherwise synonymous forms come to be associated with different stylistic registers (corresponding to different situation types associated with different communities), or with different communities within a society, such as age cohort, gender, or class/occupation (see §7.4.1). An example is the social or stylistic difference between *aérostat* and *ballon*: the former was used in the scientific community, the latter in the wider French community. The phonological counterpart is the reallocation of phonological variants as stylistic and/or social variants (Trudgill 1986:108–26).

The third and last way to increase the conventional status of alternative forms is to modify clause 1 of the definition of convention. That is, speakers will increasingly select one form over the other. The end result of this process is of course the propagation and increased conventionality of the selected form, and ultimately the loss (extinction) of the alternative form. This is the type of change that is focused on by sociolinguistic analyses of language changes in progress.

In fact, combinations of the three ways to increase the conventional status of alternative forms can occur. For example, there was a partial functional split of *aérostat* and *ballon* as well as a split of the terms into two different communities (and their eventual replacement by *montgolfière*). And complete replacement may never occur due to a functional or social specialization of the losing variant. However, the first two processes do not involve differential perpetuation of replicators (the variants); each variant survives in its newly defined niche. For this reason, we will now focus on the third way, direct competition and eventual replacement. Competition leading to perpetuation/extinction is the one process of the three that corresponds directly to the propagation of a gene allele in biological populations.[3]

The propagation of a linguistic variant is a selection process: one variant is selected over another one. Selection is a process that takes place among interactors, however. A speaker does not produce one linguistic variant in preference to another in an utterance because of its linguistic properties. A speaker identifies herself with a community or a subset of a community and that causes her to produce one linguistic variant in preference to another. In order to understand this process, one must look at the social structure of communities, that is, populations of speakers.

7.4   Propagation and the structure of speaker populations

A number of proposals have been made by sociolinguists and dialectologists about the structure of speaker populations and the types and paths of changes that occur. These proposals are supported by a wide range of empirical evidence. There are certain striking parallels between certain of these proposals and the structure of biological populations with respect to selection.

As was discussed in §3.3.1, sociolinguists generally assume that the two competing variants already exist, and that one of them has entered into the society or network[4] via contact (cf. the Kerswill quotation in §3.3.1). We will begin with that assumption, and then examine the situation with innovation proper, that is, altered replication of a lingueme.

7.4.1   *The locus of channels of propagation in the population*

The first question to be dealt with is how a novel variant is introduced into a community and then spreads. Milroy & Milroy (1985) and Milroy (1992b) offer a theory based on the structure of the speaker population, the weak-tie theory, and argue for it in favor of an alternative theory proposed by Labov (1980). Labov argues that the channel for a novel variant to enter a community from outside is an individual with high prestige and extensive contacts in the community but who has many contacts outside that community (Labov 1980:261; cf. Milroy & Milroy 1985:343; Milroy 1992b:172). Milroy questions the existence of such an individual: 'it is doubtful whether an individual can be a central member of a close-tie community and at the same time have large numbers of close-tie outside contacts' (Milroy 1992b:174).

The Milroys argue instead that it is an individual with weak ties, to both the network in question and to outside networks, who introduces a novel variant to a network. This is the pattern that they find in their Belfast work: the highest users of novel variants are the individuals (males or females) for whom the variant is not correlated with strong network ties: 'in the case of both /ɛ/ and /a/ it is the persons for whom the vowel has less significance as a network marker who seem to be leading the linguistic change' (Milroy & Milroy 1985:361). This is true whether the variant has high prestige in the outside society (/ɛ/ raising) or low prestige (/a/ backing; ibid.). The same pattern is found according to the Milroys in a range of anthropological and sociological studies (Granovetter 1973, 1982; Rogers & Shoemaker 1971, cited in Milroy 1992b:177–8, 184). In contrast, individuals with strong ties to each other – the central members of the network – maintain the linguistic conventions of the network, and tend to resist changes from the outside. The weak-tie theory can also account for the fact that it is the social classes in the middle of the hierarchy that lead linguistic changes: the highest and lowest classes in a society tend to have the strongest ties in their network, whereas the intermediate classes (upper working class, middle class) are more mobile and have mostly weak ties to each other (Milroy 1992b:181).

The weak-tie theory for the introduction of novel variants into a network or community can be described in terms of the structure of a society in §7.2. Individuals with strong ties to each other form a network and generally are relatively communicatively isolated from other networks. Individuals with weak ties to other networks do not have as strong ties to their own network (since some of their links are to other networks). Moreover, they are therefore not as communicatively isolated as the members with strong ties to each other. Weak-tie individuals are significantly exposed to the external variant; they come to use it, and thus introduce it into their own network. The Milroys call such individuals 'innovators'. However, such individuals have not actually created the novel variant (via altered replication); they have replicated it from an outside network and thereby introduced it into their own network. Since I have used the term 'innovation' for altered replication, I will use the term INTRODUCER instead for the Milroys' 'innovator'.

The Milroys argue that a strong-tie network functions as a convention (norm) enforcer (Milroy & Milroy 1985:363): 'many studies, both urban and rural, have shown that a close-knit network structure functions as a conservative force, resisting pressure for change originating from outside the network' (Milroy 1992b:177). Why might this be so? It may be that being part of a strong-tie network gives an individual a sense of social identity. In contrast, weak ties to different networks do not give an individual a sense of social identity: he or she feels that he or she belongs only partly to any one group, and perhaps that he or she does not really belong to any group. Hence the weak-tie speaker will be more variable in her usage, in particular, using the outside variant in the network to which she nominally belongs and thus introducing it into the network.

I have suggested that a mechanism based on a desire for a social identity operates to select variants from the outside for weak-tie individuals and replicate them in the network to which they belong. Although the social mechanism of selection does not operate in biological evolution, of course, one can find a population structure in biological species that is equivalent to the structure that channels innovations from one linguistic network to another. The phenomenon of contact-induced change in language is equivalent to hybridization, rare in animals but commonly found in plants and other so-called lower organisms (see §8.1). A common pattern of successful hybridization is INTROGRESSION: 'introgressive hybridization . . . is the repeated backcrossing of a natural hybrid to one or both parental populations. It results in the transfer of genes from one species or semispecies to another across a breeding barrier' (Grant 1981:205). The individual with weak ties to two or more strong-tie networks is equivalent to the hybrid plant: repeated interaction with other members of one or both networks leads to the transfer of a lingueme from one social network to the other.

7.4.2 Direction of propagation in populations

The population structure described by the pattern of strong and weak ties in societies locates the channels for variants to pass from one group to another in weak-tie individuals. However, the weak-tie model does not account for the directionality of the transmission of variants, as the Milroys are aware (Milroy & Milroy 1985:368; Milroy 1992b:194, 207–20). A further factor must be introduced in order to describe the selective advantage of the variant. This factor is often analyzed as an asymmetric relationship between the two social networks, particularly in class-based approaches such as Labov's. This relationship is usually described as a POWER relationship (Brown & Gilman 1960/1972; Brown & Levinson 1978/1987). Brown & Gilman describe power as the ability of one person to control the behavior of the other (Brown & Gilman 1960/1972:255). The power asymmetry holds between different communities of the same type. For example, the social structure of Western societies generally ranks older over younger age cohorts, men over women, and upper class over middle class over working class in the power hierarchy.

Brown & Gilman contrast power with SOLIDARITY, a symmetric relation between individuals equal in the power ranking that ranges from intimate to formal (Brown & Gilman 1960/1972:257). Solidarity thus involves social

distance as well as equal status in the power hierarchy: highly solidary individuals are both intimate (distance) and equal (power). Brown & Levinson
separate the two variables of power and distance in their discussion of politeness phenomena in general (Brown & Levinson 1978/1987:74; Brown & Gilman
examined one sort of politeness phenomenon, the usage of 'formal' vs 'familiar'
pronouns of address in European languages). Brown & Levinson argue that
the degree of politeness in language is dependent on power, distance, and the
culturally defined degree of imposition of the illocutionary act carried out by
the speaker (Brown & Levinson 1978/1987:76). Power and distance can vary
independently: in addition to intimate and distant equals, there can be intimate
and distant unequals (an example of intimate unequals is parent and child).

Distance can be identified with tie strength in a social network. Power corresponds to PRESTIGE in a class-based model such as that used by Labov (§3.4.3).
The power/prestige asymmetry implies that the variant used by the more powerful community will be propagated into the less powerful community. In most
sociolinguistic studies, those of urban varieties in North American and Britain,
the variants that are associated with the powerful groups form the standard,
while the less powerful group's variants are called the vernacular. Hence, many
studies document the gradual intrusion of the standard into a local vernacular.
However, this pattern of propagation is not always the case: speakers sometimes propagate variants from groups that are lower in the power hierarchy.
This apparent inversion of the role of power in propagating language change
has been called 'negative prestige' (Labov 1966:499–501) and COVERT PRESTIGE
(Trudgill 1972; the latter term is now more commonly used).

The existence of covert prestige clearly indicates that power/prestige in itself
does not define the direction of propagation of variants in communities. Some
other factor sometimes correlated with power is the relevant factor. Many
sociolinguists analyze this other factor as an ACT OF IDENTITY (LePage &
Tabouret-Keller 1985; see §3.4.3), the desire of a speaker to identify with one
social group over another. Speakers wish to identify with a particular group
and in so doing replicate the linguistic variants associated with that group. In
many cases, speakers wish to identify with a more powerful group, particularly
speakers with weak ties to a local network who may have some doubt about
their social identity. In other cases, speakers may wish to identify with a less
powerful group, particularly speakers in a strong-tie network with a local group
speaking a vernacular (recall the observation that strong ties create a social
identity that individuals might want to associate themselves with). Hence, the
factor determining the direction of change is social identification, not power
per se.

The theory that choice of a variant is a result of an act of identity with a
social group, that is, social identification, can also subsume certain aspects of
the theory of ACCOMMODATION (Giles & Smith 1979; Trudgill 1986). The theory
of accommodation in sociolinguistics was developed by Giles and his colleagues,
based on theories in social psychology (see Giles & Smith 1979:47–53). The
theory of accommodation argues that a speaker alters her speech in order to

accommodate to the hearer, leading to the convergence in the form of the speech of the interlocutors.

There are in fact two types of accommodation phenomena examined by Giles & Smith (they do not note this distinction). The first type represents adjustments of speech in order to compensate for the fact that the hearer is from a different community (e.g. Canadian vs English in the experiment reported in Giles & Smith 1979). These adjustments include slower speech rate, elaboration of content (to adjust to absence of certain common ground with the outsider), and simplification of grammatical constructions (Giles & Smith 1979:45–6). These adjustments do not necessarily involve shifting to the conventions of the hearer's community; instead they represent a style of communication with individuals outside one's community. When the adjustments do represent convergence, for instance in the case of language directed towards children or foreigners, the speaker is in fact adjusting to the incomplete and/or hesitant acquisition of the speaker's language by the hearer.

The second type represents adjustments of speech that result in the speaker shifting towards the conventions of language of the community to which the hearer belongs. These adjustments include changes in pronunciation, pause and utterance lengths and vocal intensity (Giles & Smith 1979:46). Of these, the latter two do not represent conventions of the signal sytem, but rather conventions of conversational interaction, or perhaps even characteristics of just the individual hearer. However, shifting one's pronunciation is an instance of shifting the linguistic conventions adhered to by the speaker towards those of the hearer. In this case, the speaker is adjusting her conventions of speaking in order to identify with the community of the hearer.[5]

Another phenomenon that can be accounted for by the principle of social identification is the stylistic dimension in sociolinguistic research. Many sociolinguistic studies elicit linguistic behavior in a range of interactional settings that are ranked on a style hierarchy. The settings typically used are (from most to least formal style): reading minimal pairs in a word list; reading a word list; reading a passage; oral interview; and casual conversation (see e.g. Chambers 1995:6). Chambers states that 'the essential difference between speech styles is the amount of self-monitoring people do when they are speaking' (ibid.). The results of study after study demonstrate that there is a shift of proportion of variants in the same direction as is found in groups ranked by social class: the more formal styles elicit a greater proportion of the higher (standard) variants.

This shift can be analyzed in terms of social identification. A higher degree of self-monitoring brings greater attention to the language used by speakers. Linguistic awareness taps into attitudes about language, more precisely, attitudes about the social groups using language. In an interview context with a stranger who is studying language, speakers will most likely want to identify themselves with the 'correct', that is, standard, variety and shift their language production accordingly, to the extent that they are able to do so. The result is style-shifting parallel to shifting to the variants associated with the higher social group.

The existence of covert prestige and accommodation demonstrates that acts of identity do not always imply identification with a single social group in a society. The existence of style-shifting further demonstrates that acts of identity are not invariant for individual speakers. On particular occasions of use, a speaker will want to identify first with one group, then with another, depending on the conversational situation.

Finally, acts of identity may be able to account for the First Law of Propagation, that speakers in a particular community tend to converge on a single variant for a given coordination problem, that is, for conveying a particular meaning (see §7.3). A regularity in behavior, such as using a particular lingueme, does more than convey a particular meaning. It also serves as an act of identity with a community by the speaker. The best way that a lingueme can serve as an act of communal identity is if there is a single variant associated with the community. As noted in §7.3, multiple variants divide community identity, so to speak, and tend to be resolved by differentiation of the two conventions, or abandonment of one convention for the other.

Another way of putting it is that a linguistic convention simultaneously solves TWO coordination problems: establishing a mutual understanding of the meaning to be conveyed, and establishing or confirming a communal identity. Establishing a communal identity is also a coordination problem among the members of the community; it succeeds only if the members of the community all conform to it. When a speaker uses a lingueme associated with a particular community, she is defining her communal identity (at least for the particular conversational exchange), as well as bringing her communicative intentions into the interlocutors' common ground (compare the description of focusing in LePage 1992:78–9). The consequence of solving the coordination problem of establishing communal identity is convergence on a single convention, i.e. the First Law of Propagation.[6]

In sum, the factor in language use granting selective advantage to an individual speaker (and thus to the way she talks) is the desire of hearers who interact with her to identify with the community to which she belongs. This selective advantage ensures the differential perpetuation of the replicators she produces, that is, the propagation of the linguistic variants associated with the community to which she belongs. However, the fact that identification with a particular social group varies from situation to situation means that no variant will have an absolute selective advantage over all other variants. This fact ensures the perpetuation of variation in a language, even as the language changes in specific directions.

7.4.3 *The time course of propagation: the S-curve*

From detailed quantitative historical linguistic studies, it appears that the time course of the propagation of a language change typically follows an S-curve. The S-CURVE has been noted by many researchers (see Kroch 1989:203 and Chambers 1992:693–5 for references to earlier observations). However, the

S-curve pattern is not uniform across the grammatical contexts of a particular language change. An equally widely observed phenomenon is that language changes appear to have progressed farther in some grammatical contexts than others. These contexts presumably favor the change for functional reasons (e.g. phonetic reasons for phonological changes), that is, reasons of the sort proposed for innovation (altered replication; see §3.4.4). This has led to the suggestion that functional factors as well as social factors play a role in the propagation of change. That is, certain contexts which are functionally favorable are said to accelerate the time course of the change.

Kroch (1989) argues that changes that appear to have accelerated in certain contexts have not done so. A unitary language change follows the same S-curve in all contexts, that is, the S-curve has the same slope, which corresponds to a constant value in the logistic function that mathematically describes the S-curve (Kroch 1989:204). The difference in absolute frequency of the novel variant in different contexts is due to either a difference in the initial frequency of the novel variant in the different contexts, or a different starting time for the innovation in the different contexts. Kroch offers one piece of evidence, from the history of periphrastic *do* in English, that the former scenario is the correct one. Periphrastic *do* is used least frequently in affirmative declarative contexts, compared with negative and/or interrogative contexts. Yet since affirmative declarative contexts are the most common ones, occurrence of periphrastic *do* in its least-favored context is observable from the beginning of the change. In fact, periphrastic *do* occurs in affirmative declarative contexts from the beginning of the change (Kroch 1989:230).

Kroch's analysis has two important implications. First, it suggests that functional factors are involved at only the innovation of a change, determining the relative frequency of the novel variant in different contexts:

> the pattern of favoring and disfavoring contexts does not reflect the forces pushing the change forward. Rather, it reflects functional effects, discourse and processing, on the choices speakers make among the alternative available to them in the language as they know it; and the strength of these effects remains constant as the change proceeds. (Kroch 1989:238)

If the functional factors do indeed represent constant facts of human communicative interaction, then one would expect them to remain constant over time. These observations confirm the hypothesis in §2.4.2 that the propagation of a change is purely social, and its innovation is functionally motivated.

Second, the S-curve pattern must represent some fairly fixed and regular process, if a speaker is able to maintain the rate of propagation of a change in different contexts even when those contexts have different absolute frequencies of occurrence of the novel variant. We will return to this point below.

Kroch points out that the logistic is only an approximation of the time course of a language change. The logistic function has a zero value (the absolute beginning of a change) at $-\infty$, and the value of 1 (the completion of change) at $+\infty$. Kroch writes, 'Of course, actual linguistic changes have starting and ending points, so the model can only approximate real data, and this approximation falsifies the change process precisely at the beginnings and ends of changes' (Kroch 1989:204). Kroch is correct of course, but nevertheless it should be noted that the beginnings and endings of changes are farther away than one might think.

When does a language change begin? The basic premise of this book is that language change consists of two processes: altered replication of a replicator, i.e. innovation; and differential replication of replicators leading to survival/ extinction, i.e. propagation. That is, change = innovation + propagation. The terminology in sociolinguistics and historical linguistics is quite confusing on this, as noted in §1.2. For instance, Kroch appears to describe innovation as the beginning of the propagation phase, not the initial production of altered replicators: 'at the beginning of a change p [the frequency of occurrence of the change] jumps from zero to some small positive value in a temporal discontinuity, which Weinreich, Labov and Herzog (1968) dubbed the "actuation" of the change' (Kroch 1989:205). Milroy uses innovation in basically the same sense as I do in this book, but describes propagation as 'change' (Milroy 1992b:201–3), and uses the term 'innovator' to describe the person in a network who gives a change a social value (this is why I have chosen the term 'introducer' instead).

Milroy, however, recognizes that there are two distinct stages in the process. The first stage, innovation proper, is the isolated production of altered replicators by speakers, for the reasons described in chapter 5 and §§6.1–6.2, before they have acquired any social value. As noted in §3.3.2, close analysis of both historical corpora and sociolinguistic field recordings reveals that random occurrences of an altered replicator occur, sometimes for a very long period of time, before the altered replicator acquires a social value and thus takes off, that is, starts to be propagated. If we treat the period of random altered replication as the beginning of the S-curve, as Milroy does (Milroy 1992b:202), then the beginning may extend quite far back in time.

Conversely, one cannot assume that a change ever entirely ends, if there is a residue of relic forms or vestigial variants (Trudgill 1999). It may be that the relic forms will, over a long period of time, eventually be subjected to the change in process. The change cannot be said to have been completed until every last relic form is gone. One reason why a change appears to end abruptly is that other changes interrupt its progress. For example, Kroch notes that the process of change for periphrastic *do* undergoes an abrupt change of direction in the mid 16th century: what appeared to be a unitary change of *do* in various grammatical contexts breaks up, with *do* going in different directions at different rates in different contexts (e.g. affirmative declarative *do* declines at this point). Thus, the tail of the S-curve may be very long but never is achieved due to other interfering changes in the language. In other cases, the vestigial variants survive in surprising ways, as stereotypes of older or more traditional speakers, in remembered phrases, in passive community knowledge of the vestigial variant, and in the sporadic occurrence in one or two unusual speakers

(Trudgill 1999). In sum, the S-curve may fit historical linguistic facts more closely than Kroch suggests.

How does a random process acquire a social value? Innovations at their source do not conform to pre-existing conventions of speech and may also be nonintentional (see §3.4). One innovative utterance does not entrench the innovation, even for the producer of the innovation. One cannot assume that a speaker's grammar has changed just because the speaker has produced an innovation. The innovations must be reinforced by use in order to become part of the mental knowledge of a speaker.[7] If innovations are perceived as lacking social or stylistic value, then they are perceived as 'errors' (and often described as such).

A similar argument to that put forward in §5.1 can be used to describe the transition from innovation to propagation. In §5.1, I argued that the experience being communicated by the speaker is very complex, and so is the relationship between the experience and the grammatical structures used to convey it. But the complexity does not end there. Speakers are trying to achieve many other things besides communicating information. As Keller says:

> Under normal circumstances, we do not choose our linguistic means according to exactly one maxim. When we are talking, we try to kill several birds with one stone: we try to conform, attract attention, be understood, save energy. It is extremely rare that someone wants nothing but to be understood. (Keller 1990/ 1994:105)

Moreover, the goals that the speaker is trying to achieve differ from context to context (ibid. 106).

The hearer must disentangle the complex matrix of social intentions of the speaker from each other and from the intention of the speaker to be understood (that is, to be understood to convey the information she intended to communicate). It is thus quite possible that an innovation, which does not adhere to prior conventions of the community, is reanalyzed by the listener as a social indicator (in Labov's sense of that term). At that point, the innovation passes from an 'error' – that is, a form lacking any social value – to a socially defined variant in the mind of the hearer. The hearer later replicates the innovation in another context, intending it to be understood by his interlocutors as having a social value. If his interlocutors understand his intention in this context, then the propagation of the innovation has begun.

This description of the transition from innovation to propagation applies most clearly to genuinely novel variants produced by speakers. When an introducer produces a variant from one social group that is new to her own social group, often that social group is already aware of the existence of the variant in the other social group and thus the variant already has a social value (e.g. it is the standard form). Nevertheless, it is possible for the social identity of an introduced variant to be reanalyzed by the social group to which it is introduced. Two of the variables studied by Milroy and Milroy, /ɛ/ raising and /a/ backing, have their source in rural varieties of Ulster Scots (Milroy & Milroy

1985:354, 358). Yet 'a comparison of the diffusion mechanisms and distribution patterns of /a/ and /ɛ/ in Ulster shows that elements originating from the same (rural) dialect can take on, apparently arbitrarily, entirely different social values in their new urban context' (ibid. 381).[8]

Proceeding beyond the inception of propagation, at least the introduction of a variant by weak-tie individuals, Milroy and Milroy propose that the next stage of the propagation process is use of the novel variant by individuals who they call the EARLY ADOPTERS (Milroy & Milroy 1985:367, taken from Rogers & Shoemaker 1971). Early adopters are more central members of the social network, linked by strong ties to the other central members of the social group. Milroy & Milroy further propose that since early adopters are central members of a close-knit group, and thus are predisposed to maintain the network's conventions rather than shift, they must be exposed to many occurrences of the novel variant, presumably on the part of introducers, in order to adopt it (Milroy & Milroy 1985:368). Once early adopters adopt the novel variant, it can then spread rapidly through central members of the group, representing the middle, rapid increase, stage of the S-curve. Finally, the novel variant will diffuse to other peripheral members of the society (Milroy 1992b:184), representing the final stage of the S-curve.

There are two problems that the Milroys' analysis of the time course of a change must address, both based on the assumption that the S-curve pattern of the time course of a linguistic change is regular. The first problem is that there are also societies that are characterized by large numbers of weak ties and relatively few strong-tie networks. Typical examples are larger political-geographic units with a great deal of geographical and social mobility (see §7.4.4). The Milroys state a principle governing the differences in patterns of change in the two types of society: 'linguistic change is slow to the extent that the relevant populations are well established and bound by strong ties, whereas it is rapid to the extent that weak ties exist in populations' (Milroy & Milroy 1985:375). Yet presumably the S-curve pattern applies to both types of society. In fact, all of the examples of S-curve patterns described by Kroch are of long-term changes found in a wide range of written records, probably representing a relatively cosmopolitan, weak-tie society.

One possible solution to this problem has to do with the slope of the S-curve. Kroch's examples demonstrate that although all of the changes he describes follow the S-curve, the S-curve itself may be stretched over different lengths of time, represented by differences in the constant s, the slope of the logistic function (Kroch 1989:204). It could be the case that societies with a greater proportion of strong ties will have a low slope to the function, meaning that the change takes longer to be propagated, while societies with a greater proportion of weak ties will have a high slope to the function, meaning that the change takes less time to be propagated. Such a hypothesis can be empirically tested.

However, there is a second, more intractable, problem with the Milroys' analysis. Kroch presents evidence that different frequencies of a novel variant in different contexts represent the same change at different stages of the S-curve in the different contexts. If Kroch's analysis is correct, then the same language change is at different stages of the S-curve for the same speakers. Yet the Milroys' model suggests that different stages of the S-curve are associated with different speakers, defined by their position in the social network (introducers, early adopters, other central members, other peripheral members). These two models of the S-curve are inconsistent.

Labov has proposed a mechanism of change underlying the S-curve that is compatible with Kroch's model (Labov 1994:65–7; Labov does not mention Kroch's model in this context). Labov models the S-curve with a binomial distribution, which like other S-curve functions 'can be generated by a model in which the probability of contact between the two [variants] governs the rate of change' (Labov 1994:66). To put it in evolutionary terms, Labov argues that the rate of change is a function of the proportion of the lingueme variants available to each speaker, based on the history of her communicative interaction with other speakers. Labov also assumes a relatively low selection pressure and hence a small shift in variant frequencies in the lingueme pool at each stage of the process (ibid.).

Thus, if interlocutors in a speech situation use different variants of a lingueme, there is a small constant probability that there will be a shift towards the variant associated with the social group favored for an act of identity on the part of the interlocutors in future replications of the lingueme. Summing over the totality of such communication encounters yields the S-curve. At the beginning of the change, few speakers are exposed to both variants and in relatively few interactions; so the change in variant frequencies is slow. In the middle of the change, most speakers are exposed to most variants in many interactions, and the change in variant frequencies is therefore fastest. At the end of a change, again few speakers are exposed to both variants and in relatively few interactions; so the change in variant frequencies (in this case, eliminating the last occurrences of the losing variant) is again slow.

The last question to be addressed in this section is the nature of the change that proceeds by an S-curve. Kroch's examples are all cases of grammatical change occurring in a variety of grammatical contexts. As we have seen, Kroch's analysis allows for two possible scenarios: the grammatical change starts at different times in different grammatical contexts, but follows the same S-curve; or the grammatical change starts at the same time in all grammatical contexts, but at different initial frequencies, and each context follows the same S-curve from its initial frequency. The first scenario would correspond to grammatical spread of a change from one context to another; the second to simultaneous change (but with different favoring factors in different contexts).

Kroch argues for the second scenario for English periphrastic *do* up to the mid 16th century. On the other hand, grammaticalization is always characterized as a spread into new grammatical contexts, typically with a fairly abrupt semantic change (such as metanalysis) on the part of the construction undergoing grammaticalization. However, this description of grammaticalization is orthogonal to the sort of grammatical changes described by Kroch. The time course of a change is the selection process. In analyzing the time course of a grammaticalization process, one must compare the competing variants. For instance, in examining the time course of the grammaticalization of *since* to a causal connective, one must examine the selection of *since* over other causal connectives of English. The emergence of causal *since* from temporal *since* is an instance of a branching lineage via altered replication, not an instance of selection.

In phonology, however, there is a long-standing debate over two alternative implementations of the S-curve, neogrammarian change and lexical diffusion. NEOGRAMMARIAN CHANGE proceeds by incremental phonetic shifts in all words in which the phoneme occurs. Proponents of LEXICAL DIFFUSION argue that sound change proceeds by abrupt phonetic changes but gradually across the lexicon. There appears to be a consensus that both neogrammarian and lexical diffusionist changes occur, but some argue that lexical diffusion is extremely widespread (Wang 1969; Chen & Hsieh 1971; Chen & Wang 1975; Wang 1977; Chambers & Trudgill 1980:174–80; Chambers 1992:694–5; Milroy 1992b:161–2; and other references cited in Labov 1994:438), while others argue that neogrammarian changes are the more widespread (Labov 1981, 1994:419–543).

It is also possible for a change to be both lexically gradual and phonetically gradual. Chambers & Trudgill describe transitional areas between the northern English and southern English varieties, involving the variables (u) and (a) (Chambers & Trudgill 1980:132–42; Trudgill 1986:59–62). Some transitional areas are acquiring the southern variant of (u), [ʌ], in a lexically gradual but phonetically abrupt fashion, i.e. lexical diffusion. These are called MIXED LECTS. Other areas use a phonetically intermediate value, [ɤ], but also in a lexically gradual fashion; these are FUDGED LECTS (see §2.2, §6.1). Fudged lects are thus both lexically and phonetically gradual (Trudgill 1986:61). Bybee (2000) also argues that *t/d*-deletion in English is both phonetically gradual (duration of lingual gesture) and lexically gradual (dependent on the token frequency of individual words).

We can describe both types of sound changes in the evolutionary framework. Linguemes exist at several levels of inclusiveness; both phonemes and lexemes are linguemes. Phonetically gradual change is altered replication of a phoneme lineage, and lexically gradual change is altered replication of multiple lexeme lineages. Once again, however, we must identify the competing variants in order to characterize the selection process in neogrammarian and lexical diffusionist change. Both types of sound change are gradual in another sense. Whether the change is phonetically gradual or lexically gradual (or both), both the older and newer variants can occur in the speech of the same speakers (Trudgill & Foxcroft 1978/1983). Selection occurs in the choice of the older or newer form, whether that form is a phoneme or a lexical item.

It is more disputable whether the selection mechanism is social, of the sort described in §7.4.2, in both types of sound change. Labov argues that neogrammarian changes are correlated with social variables, but that there is no social conditioning of lexical diffusion (Labov 1994:527). Milroy on the other hand argues that the shifts in Belfast /a/ and other variables involve lexical diffusion (Milroy 1992b:161), but they are also associated with social network structure (ibid. 109–22). If so, then the same selection mechanism is involved in both types of change. The major difference is that the selection process operates one word at a time in the lexical diffusionist approach, selecting one variant over the other, and also word by word, such that some words complete the change before other words.

Lexical diffusionists have argued that token frequency of words plays a major role in diffusion of a change word by word, that is, across the lexicon (e.g. Phillips 1984; but see Labov 1994:483–5). If so, then word token frequency must be posited as a mechanism of selection. However, in tracking the course of the change, word token frequency may be analyzable in the same way as Kroch analyzes the differential grammatical conditioning in grammatical changes. (I assume that Kroch would analyze the differential phonetic conditioning of neogrammarian sound changes in the same way.) That is, one of the two scenarios applies. The first scenario is that word token frequency governs the initiation of the S-curve, but all words follow the same S-curve. The second scenario is that token frequency of a word may govern initial proportional frequencies of the novel variant, but when the change takes off, all words follow the same S-curve. However, the lexical diffusionist analyses cited above do not provide quantitative detail for individual word forms to test Kroch's hypothesis. It would however be a striking confirmation of Kroch's analysis if lexical diffusion of sound change followed a similar pattern to grammatical change.

7.4.4   *The macrostructure of speaker populations and propagation*

The preceding sections dealt with what could be called the microstructure of speaker populations: the relations holding between individuals in relatively small populations. Historical dialectologists have observed significant patterns at the macrostructure of speaker populations, representing large geographical regions with large populations. The main pattern observed resembles a widely observed pattern in evolutionary biology, and may have a similar explanation.

The main pattern observed by historical dialectologists was formulated by Matteo Bartoli in the following two principles (Bertoni & Bartoli 1925, cited in Mańczak 1988:349):[9]

(12)   I.   The more isolated area usually preserves the earlier stage.

     II.   If one of two linguistic stages is found in peripheral areas and the other in a central area, the stage occurring in the peripheral areas is usually the earlier one.

Mańczak argues that the second principle has been improperly formulated. Using lexical evidence from Italian, French (central areas), Spanish and Romanian (peripheral areas), he argues that innovations can occur in peripheral areas as much as in central areas (Mańczak 1988). This is because peripheral areas (unlike completely isolated areas) may innovate by virtue of contact with other languages (ibid.).

What appears to distinguish central from peripheral and isolated areas are the types of changes that occur, not whether language change occurs. In central areas, there is a tendency towards leveling of distinct forms used in the geographical communities making up the central area. Leveling may involve adoption of one geographical community's convention by the other communities in the central area, or it may involve convergence onto a new convention that is in some way a compromise, typically a simplification, of two or more communities' conventions. This process, now called KOINÉIZATION because it represents the creation of a koiné for communication in the central area, was proposed by Jakobson 1929/1962, and is documented by Andersen (1988) and Trudgill (1986, 1989, 1996a). In this respect, the retention of archaic features in isolated areas probably represents the nonparticipation of the isolated communities in the koinéization and diffusion of novel variants arising in the central area.

Andersen (1988) demonstrates that in contrast, in peripheral and isolated areas, certain changes occur which represent a distinctive, often more complex, grammatical structure. Andersen offers evidence of phonological elaboration, including the development of palatalization from a secondary articulation to separate glides and then independent fricatives in peripheral areas of Polish, and the occurrence of parasitic consonants in isolated and/or peripheral dialects of Romantsch, Provençal, French, the Dutch-German area and Denmark (Andersen 1988:56–66). These processes are all phonetically motivated, and so represent natural phonetic developments taken to a high degree of elaboration. Trudgill has documented further examples in papers leading to a forthcoming monograph on language in isolation (Trudgill 1989, 1992, 1996a).

The equivalent phenomenon in evolutionary biology is the founder population theory of speciation, originally proposed by Mayr in 1942 (Mayr 1982:600–6). Mayr argued that speciation, that is, the divergence of a population to the point that it is reproductively isolated from the rest of its species, occurs most frequently in an isolated population, the founder population. Later research suggests that in fact it is small populations, not simply isolation, that is the primary engine for speciation: 'There is little doubt observationally that rapid speciation is most easily accomplished in very small populations' (Mayr 1982:603). In contrast, large populations tend to be evolutionarily inert: 'new alleles, even favorable ones, require very long periods of time to spread through the entire species range. Genetic homeostasis . . . strongly resists any changes in a large, undivided gene pool' (Mayr 1982:602; see also Grant 1981:24–6).

The reason for this pattern appears to be that the isolated population 'contains only a small fraction of the total genetic variability of the parent species' (Mayr 1982:602). This fact allows for drastic changes at the genetic level (not fully understood; ibid. 605–6) which would not occur in the large parent population. The genetic changes in turn lead to significant changes in the phenotype of the offspring of the founder population, and eventually speciation in the successful cases.

The geographical patterns for language change and speciation are similar except in one apparent respect: changes occur in the central areas of a language, while change does not occur (or occurs only quite slowly) in the large central population of a species. The difference can be accounted for in looking at the explanation for the linguistic pattern. The linguistic pattern as described above represents existing smaller populations that are in relatively high contact with each other (Trudgill 1989, 1996a), not only through geographical contiguity but also by means of greater socioeconomic interaction in general (note that most of the studies of this phenomenon apply to European languages representing large-scale political and economic entities). It is the linguistic result of the high level of contact – the levelled or simplified variety – that should properly be compared to a large biological population. And the leveled or simplified variety is relatively more stable (other than further simplification or leveling).

Trudgill argues that the explanation for the linguistic pattern is not merely high contact but also loose-knit social networks, that is, weak-tie networks (Trudgill 1992, 1996a). These two social phenomena frequently coincide, as noted in §7.4.1 (see Trudgill 1996a:4). In fact, high contact on a large scale would be extremely difficult to maintain. The opposite combination, low contact and close-knit (strong-tie) networks, also frequently coincide; these are peripheral or isolated areas (Trudgill 1992:201; 1996a:4, 11). Moreover, a close-knit network is of necessity small in size: it is difficult for everyone to know and talk to everyone else in a large society. Large size societies tend to be loose-knit overall, although, of course, there may be close-knit networks within the society – and, as one might expect, the latter tend to be socially marginalized and hence peripheral groups (lower class, street gangs, etc.; see §7.2).

The significant factor with respect to high contact is the degree of adult second-language (or second-dialect) learning involved (Trudgill 1992:197–9; 1996a). In most high-contact situations, there is a high degree of adult second-language learning, which contributes to the leveling and simplification observed in those situations. Some close-knit societies may also have extensive contact – Trudgill gives the example of the native American languages of the Pacific Northwest and the Caucasus – but they also have bilingualism from childhood, and hence less adult second-language learning (Trudgill 1989:234).

The small, close-knit networks are those in which linguistic conventions can be maintained in resistance to outside contact, which is typically relatively minimal anyway. Trudgill also proposes that isolated close-knit networks are those that allow a grammatical change to follow through to completion, leading to the elaborated structures that seem to be characteristic of such groups (Andersen 1988; Trudgill 1996a:8), including phonological fortition processes and complex allophony and allomorphy.[10]

In sum, linguistic changes that are difficult for the nonnative speaker – assimilation, fast speech phenomena, longer words – and changes that are more likely to occur or survive in close-knit networks – elaborate changes, allophonic complexity, complex phoneme segment inventories – will be found in small isolated societies (Trudgill 1996a:12). Conversely, linguistic changes that are easy for the nonnative speaker – mergers, simplification, shorter words – and changes that are more likely to survive in looseknit networks – so-called 'unmarked' or 'natural' grammatical structures – are more likely to be found in large societies characterized by high contact.

The equivalence of the linguistic and biological patterns should now be clearer. Gene flow throughout the biological population ensures that the genetically prevalent alleles remain prevalent in the entire population, leading to relative homogeneity and stasis in a large population. Likewise, high contact leads to competition between lingueme variants, and the resulting leveled variant then predominates over the central area. Only a subset of alleles is found in a small, isolated founder population of biological organisms, and significant genetic changes can then occur. Likewise, linguistic isolation allows for processes of change to evolve to an elaborate degree that would otherwise be curtailed by leveling or simplification in a larger, more loose-knit society.

In addition to the geographical linguistic pattern which parallels the geographical biological pattern, there is a social pattern of the propagation of a language change that follows from the community structure of a society. This is the observation that diffusion (propagation) of novel variants jumps from population center to population center. Trudgill (1974/1983:52–87) gives evidence of this pattern with the diffusion of uvular /r/ across the languages of Western Europe, diffusion of changes to /æ/ on the Brunlanes peninsula in southern Norway, and the replacement of interdental fricatives by labiodental ones in Norwich; Chambers and Trudgill give a further example of /æ/ raising in northern Illinois (Chambers & Trudgill 1980:189–92).

Uvular /r/ appears to have originated in Paris, but it then jumped to other major Western European cities, as well as diffusing to the rest of France in the usual geographical pattern. The pattern is clear when one looks not simply at the presence of uvular /r/, but its presence in some educated speech, most educated speech, and uneducated speech (Trudgill 1974/1983:58, map 3.3). This division demonstrates that uvular /r/ is spreading from educated speech to uneducated speech partially independently of geography. Likewise, diffusion of changes to /æ/ jumps from city to city in Brunlanes; Norwich changes in fricatives originate in London and are transmitted to Norwich, and the percentage of /æ/ raising in northern Illinois is a function of the size of the town as well as distance from Chicago (the origin of the innovation).

Trudgill uses a formula from geography, the gravity model, which measures influence as a function of both population size and geographical distance of the influencing center(s) from the area potentially being influenced (Trudgill 1974/1983:73–4). It appears that the gravity model fits some data very well (Chambers & Trudgill 1980:200–2). Nevertheless, it cannot be simply the size of the center that determines linguistic influence. There has to be communicative interaction between speakers in the centers which jumps across intervening areas (or at least is less pronounced between the center and the intervening areas). For example, the influence patterns in Brunlanes have changed over time, apparently due to a shift in importance from sea to land transport links (Trudgill 1974/1983:80–2).

It seems clear from these examples that there is communicative interaction among members of the same community (the educated elite, or city dwellers in general) across geographically separated centers at least as much as there is communicative interaction between members of different communities (the elite vs other classes, the urban vs the rural) in the same geographical area. This pattern is a manifestation of one of the basic differences between linguistic communities and biological populations: an organism belongs to only one deme, defined largely geographically (within its ecological niche), whereas a speaker belongs simultaneously to multiple communities, defined geographically, socially and in other ways (§7.2). The analysis of the structure of a speaker population is in fact richer and more complex than that of a biological population. As will be seen in the next chapter, this is also true of the phylogenetic structures describing the descent of languages.

Notes

1 The numbers correspond to the numbers indexing the various degrees d_i in Lewis (1969:79). I have left out two further dimensions by which a signal could be a convention to some degree d: the degree of occurrence of the recurrent coordination problem for which the signal is used (Lewis' d_0), and the degree to which an individual cannot simultaneously conform to the regularity in question and an alternative regularity (Lewis' d_5).

2 The term *aéronef*, first mentioned in 1844 (Guilbert 1965:46), was also used as both masculine and feminine at first (ibid. 47).

3 The first two ways resemble one of the processes of selection between species competing for the same ecological niche (biotic sympatry): the two species may survive by ecological differentiation, that is, specializing into slightly different niches (Grant 1981:119–20). This is selection at the level of species in biology, whereas I am describing selection at the level of organisms (speakers). However, recall that Hull's generalized theory of selection is independent of levels at which selection occurs (§2.3). It so happens that a mechanism operating at the interspecific level in biological evolution is similar to two mechanisms operating at the speaker level in language evolution.

4 I am using 'society' as it is defined in §7.2; as noted there, the term 'community' is generally used for this construct by sociolinguists.

5 In fact, this may not always be welcomed by the hearer. In the experiment with English subjects evaluating a Canadian's speech reported in Giles & Smith 1979, for instance, shift in pronunciation (genuine convergence) was evaluated negatively by subjects, while shifts in speech rate and content (the first type of accommodating behavior) were evaluated positively (Giles & Smith 1979:60). In other words, social identification is not always identification with the hearer's community, at least with respect to conformity to linguistic norms.

6   There is one significant exception to the First Law of Propagation. In some aboriginal cultures in Australia (see for example Heath 1981) and New Guinea (Bernard Comrie, personal communication), words identical or similar to the names of recently deceased persons are tabooed for some period of time. One of the strategies for dealing with the death taboo on words is 'to maintain elaborate stocks of synonyms for common nominal concepts, so that one noun may be temporarily taboo without creating problematic lexical gaps' (Heath 1981:361). Clearly, this is a cultural context in which the existence of synonymy has a positive value. However, the existence of the death taboo in some cultures does not invalidate the First Law of Propagation in other social contexts and in other societies. (I thank Bernard Comrie for bringing this fact to my attention.)

7   It is possible that an innovation is particularly salient in some respects and may thus become part of the linguistic system quite rapidly. For example, when I innovate a word such as *intraference* for the first time, it can become a part of my linguistic system in a relatively small number of replications (uses).

8   There still remains the question of how a genuine innovation, not a variant from a neighboring social group, is taken up and propagated. One plausible hypothesis is that only the innovations of weak-tie members have a chance of being propagated; innovations by strong-tie members are not propagated because of the strength of the existing conventions of language in the strong-tie group. One might also argue that innovations by strong-tie members would be propagated precisely because they began in the center of the network. This may be true of explicitly legislated changes by the power elite; however, these changes are a tiny minority of the changes that occur.

9   Bartoli formulated five principles; he later withdrew the fourth and fifth principles. The third principle, that earlier forms are found in larger areas, does not seem to hold, based on the evidence discussed in this section.

10 The fact that certain social situations favor the opposite sort of linguistic changes that are considered to be 'optimal' or 'natural' on functional grounds is additional evidence that functional considerations do not play a role in selection (propagation). Instead, the more complex older forms, or elaborated 'dysfunctional' innovations, are propagated through the speech community.

Chapter 8

The descent of languages

8.1 Phylogeny in biology and language from a plantish point of view

In a number of places (e.g. Hull 1988:416), Hull complains of the zoöcentric orientation of much thinking about evolution (especially views of evolution outside biology). We have already encountered one context where looking beyond animals to plants has had a liberating effect: recognizing that levels of organization in biology are not well defined, and hence they should be separated from the generalized theory of selection (§2.3). This chapter will illustrate another aspect of the evolutionary framework where taking a plantish point of view offers some insights into the nature of language evolution, namely phylogeny or the historical descent of species.

The zoöcentric view of phylogeny is that all new species come into being by divergence. A species is a population of interbreeding individuals that is reproductively isolated from other species. The population itself usually is divided into races and demes, which are defined by partial reproductive isolation (i.e. a lower probability of interbreeding) from sibling races or demes. Over time, races can become more reproductively isolated. Once the former race is more or less fully reproductively isolated, it has diverged to the point of becoming a new species.

The zoöcentric view of phylogeny corresponds to the family tree model of language families in linguistics. A language (a population of utterances) is produced by a population of speakers who talk to each other but are communicatively isolated from other language speakers. The language, or more precisely the population of speakers, can be divided into geographical dialects, more precisely subpopulations of speakers, which are defined by partial communicative isolation from sibling dialects. Over time, dialect speaker populations can become more communicatively isolated. Once the former dialect subpopulation is more or less fully communicatively isolated, it has diverged to the point of becoming a new language.

Patterns of divergence lead to tree structures in phylogenies. Every species has a single (former) species as a parent. Every language has a single (former) language as a parent. But this model has often been challenged in linguistics. Some changes diffuse across language and dialect boundaries, ignoring boundaries of past divergence. This pattern inspired the wave model in 19th-century historical linguistics, where linguistic features move through a set of languages/

dialects to different degrees of extent and in different directions, leading to divergent linguistic varieties. Also, the results of language contact – borrowings and substratum structures – challenges the integrity of languages as historical entities originating from a single parent. Finally, pidgins, creoles and mixed languages challenge the family tree model of language birth by divergence in a number of ways.

The facts of language contact and its results appear to challenge any attempt to develop an evolutionary model for languages based on speciation via the divergence of populations in biology. One might be able to ignore borrowing and substratum structures if the bulk of the linguemes of the language have lineages traceable to a single parent. But this is much more difficult to do in the case of pidgins, creoles and mixed languages. The problems with the latter sorts of languages have led Thomason & Kaufman to argue that such languages simply do not have any ancestors, that is, they do not have a place in the phylogeny of languages:

> a claim of genetic relationship entails systematic correspondences in all parts of the language because that is what results from normal transmission: what is transmitted is an entire language – that is, a complex set of interrelated lexical, phonological, morphosyntactic, and semantic structures . . . *a language can not have multiple ancestors in the course of normal transmission.* To be sure, mixed languages in a nontrivial sense exist, but by definition they are unrelated genetically to the source(s) of any of their multiple components. (Thomason & Kaufman 1988:11, emphasis original)

Thomason & Kaufman make two assumptions, neither of which is valid in the evolutionary framework for language change proposed in this book.[1] First, Thomason & Kaufman's theory of phylogenetic relationship assumes an essentialist theory of a language, namely, that it has a coordinated set of structures, phonological, morphosyntactic and semantic, such that if its apparent descendants are lacking in enough of these structures, then it no longer can be considered a member of that language group. To be precise, Thomason & Kaufman do not argue that there is a specific linguistic trait that is essential; instead they argue probabilistically that enough linguistic traits in enough aspects of the language are replicated in normal transmission to classify that language in the genetic family in question. Still, this is a weaker variant of an essentialist model. In the population model adopted in this book, the lingueme pool can change radically without a language ceasing to be a genetic descendant of its parent.

Or parents. The second assumption made by Thomason & Kaufman is that the family tree model is the only correct one for describing (phylo-)genetic relations among languages; that is, a language can have only one phylogenetic parent.[2] This assumption leads them to describe mixed languages as having no linguistic genetic parents instead of having multiple linguistic genetic parents. Thomason & Kaufman describe the development of mixed languages as 'nongenetic' (Thomason & Kaufman 1988:108). This leads to the second point.

If we take 'genetic' as referring to the process of evolution described by the generalized theory of selection as proposed by Hull and as applied to language change in this book, then we can see the development of mixed languages as genetic in the sense used in this book, that is, mixed languages can be placed in a phylogeny. The difference is that they do have multiple parents, contrary to the family tree model (cf. Trudgill 1996b).

In fact, in biology there are very similar phenomena to language contact once one leaves the animal kingdom, moving no further than to the plant kingdom (Grant 1981; see also Hull 1988:450). Genes can be transferred from one plant species to another by the process of introgression, described briefly in §7.4.1 (Grant 1981, chapter 17). If the two species hybridize, then the hybrids can backcross repeatedly with the first species, thereby introducing genes of the second species into the gene pool of the first species.

The process of HYBRIDIZATION itself is extremely common in plants, occurring in a wide variety of ways in genetic terms (Grant 1981; more than half the book is devoted to the processes of hybridization). Sometimes hybrids lead to the partial or complete merging of the formerly independent divergent species into a new species subsuming both of the former species. The merging of formerly divergent phylogenetic lines is called RETICULATION. In other cases, the hybrids can themselves create a new, third species, if they become reproductively isolated and succeed in reproducing themselves (Grant 1981, chapters 19, 20 and 35).

Thus, even in the biological world it is not a necessary fact of evolution that new entities are created solely by divergence: 'The process of evolutionary divergence is not inexorable. Within wide limits it is subject to reversal' (Grant 1981:72). Thus even in biology the tree model is inadequate: 'If a phylogenetic tree is the extension of the normal pattern of animal speciation, plant speciation has often led to the formation of a phylogenetic web' (Grant 1981:76; see for example the phylogenetic diagram for species in the genus *Clarkia* in Grant 1981:332, Fig. 25.3). The following sections will survey the sources of linguistic diversity from a plantish point of view.

8.2 Primary language birth: societal divergence and normal transmission

Grant retains the term PRIMARY SPECIATION to describe speciation by divergence (Grant 1981:153). I will use the term PRIMARY LANGUAGE BIRTH to describe the evolution of new languages by divergence.

More accurately, primary language birth must be described as a consequence of societal divergence. The linguemes of a language are only the replicators. The interactors are the individual speakers of the language. The speakers form a population, that is the society, which is communicatively isolated from other languages. (Communicative isolation is never entirely complete; see §8.3.) The utterances they produce also form a population, that is, their language. The linguemes of the language form a lingueme pool. It is the behavior of the inter-actors, however, which leads to any changes in the constitution of the lingueme pool, that is, selection of variants and thus the propagation of a change.

As argued in §7.2, a society is heterogeneous in two ways: it is made up of multiple communities defined by domains of shared expertise, and individuals are linked to other individuals by ties of different strengths, with a limiting case of zero (no tie at all). The pattern of tie strengths defines subpopulations of the society, which are relatively communicatively isolated. To the extent that subpopulations of the society are communicatively isolated, the lingueme pools of each subpopulation are distinct. The structure of each lingueme pool will be slightly different, but the differences may increase over time through different social selection processes operating in each subpopulation.

Biologists describe a variety of ISOLATING MECHANISMS for organisms. The biological isolating mechanisms are divided into three types (Grant 1981:111–12): geographical, ecological and reproductive. Equivalents to all three types of isolating mechanisms are found in language as well.

The classic isolating mechanism in language as in biology is geographical separation. Geographical separation is the spatial separation of speakers in two populations to a distance beyond the normal geographical mobility of the speakers. Two populations of highly mobile speakers would have to be quite widely separated in order for geographical separation to lead to communic-ative isolation. Nevertheless, even in the contemporary highly mobile, long-distance communication world, a large enough proportion of the population is sufficiently isolated for differences between American and British English to survive and flourish (in particular, accent and vocabulary, but also some sig-nificant grammatical differences).

A second linguistic isolating mechanism is social separation and relative lack of social mobility. This isolating mechanism is equivalent to ecological separation, treating social differences as equivalent to ecological differences (see §2.4.2). Some individuals may not talk to each other even if they live in the same geographical area for social reasons, e.g. they belong to different ethnic groups or different castes. In fact, many cases of social separation in a single geographical area involve separation by communities of a single society. That is, the different communities play different but interconnected roles in the society, and hence there is still significant communicative interaction between the communities (see §8.3.2).

Reproductive isolation is the lack of gene exchange via reproduction due to differences in the reproductive organs or reproductive behavior. The equivalent of biological reproduction is conversational intercourse between individuals. There is at least one case of reproductive isolation in language. Deafness con-stitutes a barrier to using voice and ears for communicative interaction, thereby isolating deaf speakers from the speaking language community. Deaf commun-ities have developed sign languages using hands and eyes for communication, instead of voice and ears. Of course, hearing individuals who are sighted can acquire a sign language; and deaf individuals can use lip reading to understand spoken language, and learn to produce spoken language themselves. Neverthe-less, the isolation from spoken language caused by deafness, even if it is not complete, has been sufficient to spawn sign languages which are conventional signaling systems as much as spoken languages are.

The family tree model is based not only on divergence as the primary mech-anism of language birth, but also on the normal transmission of language. Thomason & Kaufman define normal transmission as follows: 'a language is passed on from parent generation to child generation and/or via peer group from immediately older to immediately younger, with relatively small degrees of change over the short run, given a reasonably stable sociolinguistic context' (Thomason & Kaufman 1988:9–10). Normal transmission is a description of a social structure. There are no significant communicative interactions with individuals outside the society, and the only significant changes in the mem-bership of the population are through biological reproduction and death, not through individuals from other societies entering the population. If these social conditions hold, then the lingueme lineages will be traced back in time through that society alone, and back through that society's unique parent society, and so on. Any new linguemes will arise only through altered replication of the existing linguemes, and hence will belong to lineages confined to that society of speakers.

Of course, no society is purely communicatively isolated in the way that the hypothetical society described in the last paragraph is. There is always some degree of communicative interaction as a result of social contact. The follow-ing sections describe the chief linguistic consequences of that contact. The sections are organized by social parameters, those being the matrix in which lingueme transfer occurs. There are a number of social parameters that appear to play a role in determining the linguistic consequences of social contact. These parameters include: whether or not the societies merge into one group, or a new group is created from parts of the old groups; the degree of multilingualism in the community; the number and type of communities in the society through which contact takes place; and the stability of the social structure.

8.3   From contact to merger

Any linguistic change that is due to contact requires some degree of social contact and bilingualism on the part of at least one speaker of the language in question. The contact and the bilingualism may be minimal: one speaker acquiring (even imperfectly) a word spoken by a speaker of the other language is sufficient to introduce that word in the first speaker's original language, from which point it may be propagated. Of course the degree of bilingualism could be much more substantial, involving most speakers of the original language and good acquisition of the other language; and there will be all sorts of intermediate possibilities. But the contact is the result of some degree of communicative interaction between speakers of the two languages, which requires some minimal knowledge of both languages on the part of the speaker of the original language.

If a linguistic change through contact is propagated, what has happened in effect is that a lingueme – anything from a word, an inflection, a phoneme, a grammatical distinction, or a syntactic schema – has been transferred (more accurately, replicated) from the lingueme pool of one language to the lingueme pool of the other language. As was mentioned above, the equivalent process in biology is introgression: a hybrid backcrosses with one of the parent species and thereby introduces the transferred gene into the gene pool of the parent species. In identifying the equivalent process in language change, one must clearly distinguish the interactor and the replicator. In biology, the hybrid plant is an organism, that is, the interactor; it possesses genes (replicators) from both parent species. The hybrid interactor in language contact is the speaker who possesses some knowledge of both languages that she speaks, that is, possesses linguemes (replicators) of both languages. In other words, the linguistic equivalent of a hybrid organism is a bilingual speaker, not a mixed language; this misunderstanding has plagued other evolutionary accounts of language contact (e.g. Whinnom 1971). Communicative interaction of the (possibly only partially) bilingual speaker with other members of her society is the equivalent of backcrossing: the interaction replicates the acquired lingueme in the language of the society, and further differential replication of that lingueme can propagate it in the language until it is established as a convention.

The nature of the contact between two societies can then be described in terms of the nature of the lingueme flow from one language to the other, via bilingual speakers.[3] Lingueme flow is a function of two factors, associated with innovation and propagation. The first factor is the degree of bilingualism of speakers in the two societies; this will determine the amount and direction of lingueme flow. The second factor is the degree of group identification of the speakers in the two societies. The second factor is particularly important when there is a high degree of bilingualism: will the speakers of the original language shift completely to the acquired language, or will they resist, and to what extent will they resist?

8.3.1 *Language shift: effects on the acquired language*

Thomason & Kaufman divide language contact phenomena into those that have linguistic effects on the original language of a society coming under the influence of another society, and those that have linguistic effects on the acquired language. Thomason & Kaufman describe the effects of language contact on the original language as BORROWING: 'Borrowing is the incorporation of foreign features into a group's native language by speakers of that language: the native language is maintained but is changed by the addition of the incorporated features' (Thomason & Kaufman 1988:37). Borrowing will be discussed in §8.3.2 and §8.4.3.

Thomason & Kaufman describe the effect of language contact on the acquired language as SUBSTRATUM INTERFERENCE, which is the effect of language contact on the acquired language (if there is any). Substratum interference occurs when a speaker population SHIFTS to the language of another speaker population with which they are in contact. More specifically, substratum interference 'results from imperfect group learning during a process of language shift' (Thomason & Kaufman 1988:38).

The chief social factor characterizing substratum interference is that the society speaking the original language does not resist merging with the society speaking the acquired language; in fact, the speakers often wish to merge with the acquired language society. This contrasts with borrowing, where the speakers of the original language wish to maintain their distinct social identity, including their language, albeit sometimes not too successfully and sometimes under great pressure from the influencing society.

The chief linguistic effect of substratum interference is alteration of phonological and syntactic patterns (Thomason & Kaufman 1988:118–19). In particular, the alterations do not involve the actual morphemes, that is, form–meaning pairings or signs, but instead abstract or schematic patterns. For example, many members of the Austronesian language family spoken in or near Papua New Guinea have undergone a number of syntactic changes, including changes in basic word order and types of morphology, which make them resemble the non-Austronesian languages of Papua New Guinea. It is likely that these changes are due to shift. The case for shift is supported by the physical appearance of Melanesians (closer to Papuans) and by mitochondrial DNA studies of the Melanesian, Papuan and other Austronesian-speaking peoples (Melton *et al.* 1995; Redd *et al.* 1995). Compare for example the following sentences from Yimas, a Papuan language spoken in Papua New Guinea; Manam, a Melanesian language spoken on an island just off New Guinea (about 200 km from the Yimas territory), and Tongan, a Polynesian (Austronesian) language spoken well away from Papua New Guinea:

(1)   *Yimas* (Foley 1991:309):
      yara ya-   ka- kra -ŋa -t   -akn
      tree them- I- cut -BEN -PAST -him
      'I cut trees for him.'

(2)   *Manam* (Lichtenberk 1983:165):
      tamóata n-   taga -i   -áŋ -ʔo
      man   I.will- follow -him -BEN -you
      'I will follow the man for you.'

(3)   *Tongan* (Churchward 1953:112):
      na'a nau langa 'a e   fale mo'o Siale
      PST 3PL build ABS ART house for Charlie
      'They built a house for Charlie.'

Manam and Yimas have SOV word order, whereas Tongan has SVO order. Manam and Yimas have bound person markers and applicative suffixes such as the benefactive to encode oblique arguments, whereas Tongan has independent pronouns and prepositions. But Manam and Tongan are Austronesian languages, while Yimas is a Papuan language.

This pattern is in contrast to borrowing: 'while borrowed morphosyntactic structures are more often expressed by actual borrowed morphemes, morphosyntactic interference through shift more often makes use of reinterpreted and/or restructured [original language] morphemes' (Thomason & Kaufman 1988:114–15). Likewise, the phonological effects of shift may affect the phonetic realization of acquired language phonemes or phonotactic and metrical patterns, but they do not alter the basic phonemic content of morphemes. Of course, these patterns are linguemes just as much as actual words and morphemes are (see §2.4.3). SOV word order is a schematic syntactic lingueme, and a CVCV syllable structure is a phonotactic lingueme. I will call these SCHEMATIC LINGUEMES, contrasting with SUBSTANCE LINGUEMES, which are words and morphemes with actual phonemic substance.

Thomason & Kaufman state that the correlations substratum interference / schematic linguemes and borrowing / substance linguemes 'are too weak to have predictive value' (Thomason & Kaufman 1988:115). However, in §8.3.2 I will argue that structural borrowing of schematic linguemes, as opposed to the borrowing of grammatical substance linguemes, is more like substratum interference than borrowing proper. Thomason & Kaufman also note that borrowing of lexical substance linguemes often occurs if the shifting population is socially superordinate (Thomason & Kaufman 1988:116), giving the example of Norman French and English. However, it is quite possible that this is a case of borrowing by the subordinate population, especially if the loanwords are in domains of expertise dominated by the superordinate shifting population (as they generally are in the Norman French / English case[4]). After all, as Thomason & Kaufman repeatedly point out, it is easy to oversimplify the social patterns of each contact situation. Thus, the correlations may be stronger than Thomason & Kaufman imply.

We may now describe the process of substratum interference at the level of a single utterance. For example, a speaker may produce an utterance with a different word order (say, SOV instead of SVO) but the same native language words. The speaker's utterance is based on a combination of knowledge of the original language (with SOV order) and knowledge of the acquired language (its words). The speaker is combining a schematic lingueme from the original language and substance linguemes from the acquired language. The utterance is an innovation from the perspective of the lingueme pool of the acquired language: a new schematic lingueme has been introduced into the lingueme pool. But this innovation occurs through a lineage crossing from one language (the original language) to the other language (the acquired language).[5]

According to Thomason & Kaufman, the primary factor in substratum interference is the degree to which shifting language speakers do not perfectly acquire their second language. As we have seen, Thomason & Kaufman incorporate this factor as part of their definition of substratum interference. However, this is only half the story: innovation. There must be an explanation for how the innovation is successfully propagated in the language, that is, how it becomes a convention of the language.

Thomason & Kaufman identify several social factors that affect the degree of (successful) substratum interference: the relative size of the shifting population, its social status, and the length of time for the shift (Thomason & Kaufman 1988:119–20). A large shifting population relative to the native population of the acquired language, a socially superordinate shifting population, and a rapid shift all favor substratum interference. However, it is rare that a large socially superordinate population would shift (instead the subordinate population typically shifts); and if the superordinate shifting group is small, few interference effects are found. Thomason & Kaufman argue persuasively that the influence of Norman French on English and Frankish on French is smaller than is usually supposed (Thomason & Kaufman 1988:122–9).

Thus the most likely scenario for significant substratum interference is when the shifting population is larger than the native population, and the shift is relatively rapid. Another important feature of this scenario is that most of the population speaking the acquired language – namely the shifting speakers – is bilingual. The native speakers may be mostly monolingual, but in this scenario they form a small minority of the total population of the speakers of the language. The larger the number of bilingual speakers, the greater proportion of innovations will occur in the acquired language due to interference from the shifting speakers' native language.

The underlying mechanism in the successful establishment of substratum interference is the degree to which native speakers of the acquired language accept the shifting speakers' 'errors' as new conventions of the acquired language. That is, native speakers are willing to accommodate to the shifting speakers, even though the shifting speakers are not native speakers. Two of the three social factors described by Thomason & Kaufman provide motivation for native speakers to accommodate to nonnative speakers. (The third factor, rapidity of shift, is a rough index of the likelihood that shifting speakers acquiring the language will succeed in doing so perfectly, and thus pertains to innovation rather than propagation.) In the most common scenario, the native speakers are outnumbered, and the innovation is propagated through accommodation by the native speakers, or by a lack of access to enough native speakers on enough occasions of use. Or the shifting speakers have a social status which the native speakers wish to identify with, making them willing to accommodate to the nonnative speakers.

The above scenario shows how (typically schematic) linguemes from one language enter another language. Another, milder, consequence of shift is the simplification of the acquired language in certain respects (see, e.g. Trudgill 1979/1983; Trudgill 1989:232–3; Holm 1988:10). In the evolutionary framework, simplification is altered replication of the existing linguemes of the acquired language, not lingueme transfer. Although the society has undergone a change in membership through shift, the lingueme lineages can still be traced back into the ancestral population of the original members of the society.

8.3.2 Language maintenance / resistance: effects on the original language

The chief social difference between borrowing and substratum interference is that the society speaking the borrowing language maintains or even resists merging with the society speaking the source language of the borrowed linguemes.

Much of the interest in borrowing has centered around the sorts of linguistic features – in our terms, linguemes – that are borrowed, and any ranking of those features in terms of relative ease or difficulty of borrowing. Thomason & Kaufman argue that at least some earlier proposals for ranking of likelihood of borrowing suffer from the failure to distinguish between borrowing and substratum interference. They also argue that descriptions of borrowing patterns should be constructed with respect to degree of social contact, and propose a borrowing scale based on five degrees of contact.

The first degree of contact is called casual contact, defined as 'little bilingualism among borrowing-language speakers' (Thomason & Kaufman 1988:50, Table 3). At this stage, only content words are borrowed. Specifically, nonbasic vocabulary is borrowed, for 'cultural and functional . . . reasons' (ibid., 74). The fact that nonbasic vocabulary are the first linguemes to be transferred has long been observed. They are typically associated with domains of expertise found in the society speaking the source language but not in the society speaking the borrowing language.

This process can be described in terms of the model of speech communities developed in §4.2.3 and §7.2. The domain of expertise of the source society defines a community. Members of the borrowing society share in the domain of expertise, and use the code of the loaning society in that domain. Those linguemes in the code that are not already present in the borrowing society's language are the more likely to be transferred to the borrowing language, and those are more likely to be nonbasic vocabulary. Basic vocabulary, on the other hand, generally denotes the core expertise that is common across many communities in a society. Since that core expertise is present in any society, vocabulary for the core expertise is fairly strongly entrenched and is more likely to prevail over foreign basic vocabulary. (These are all probabilistic statements, of course.)

Higher degrees of contact involve 'much bilingualism among borrowing-language speakers over a long period of time' (Thomason & Kaufman 1988:50, Table 3). In the lexicon, function words begin to be borrowed, starting with conjunctions and various adverbial particles (stage 2 borrowing), and then other function words such as adpositions and then some basic vocabulary (e.g. some pronouns and numerals; stage 3 borrowing). The structural modifications described by Thomason & Kaufman for stages 2–3 borrowing are to a great extent grammatical patterns abstracted from the increasing amount of foreign vocabulary, such as new phonemes, new phonemic distinctions, metrical and phonotactic patterns (Thomason & Kaufman 1988:74–5).

Matras (1998) proposes an explanation for the category of the first function words that are borrowed. He argues that the conjunctions and adverbial particles that are borrowed perform discourse-regulating functions, that is, they are used by interlocutors to structure the flow of discourse in communicative interaction. Matras analyzes the borrowing of discourse-regulating function words as 'fusion' (Matras 1998:291). Fusion represents the employment of a single discourse-regulating grammatical subsystem, namely the one found in the loaning language.

Matras argues that 'fusion . . . is motivated by the need to reduce overload in the mental monitoring of hearer-sided language-processing activities in bilingual communicative interaction' (ibid.). This processing explanation motivates the reduction to a single discourse-regulating system, but it does not explain which system is chosen. There are social reasons motivating the choice of the source language, involving the relationship between the source and the borrowing society. Thomason & Kaufman observe that two-language contact situations commonly involve only one-way bilingualism: only the borrowing society is bilingual (Thomason & Kaufman 1988:95). In one-way language contact situations, one society presumes that it does not need to learn the other society's language; and so it is in that society's language that intersocietal communicative interaction takes place. That communicative interaction is structured by the discourse-regulating grammatical subsystem, which then becomes the conventional discourse regulating subsystem for all of the bilingual borrowing-language speaker's conversations. This represents a first step in the process of the absorption of the borrowing-language society by the source language society: the latter now defines the regulation of discourse for speakers in both societies.

The next stages in Thomason & Kaufman's borrowing hierarchy (stages 4 and 5) involve 'moderate to heavy structural borrowing' (Thomason & Kaufman 1988:83). There is an even higher degree of multilingualism and/or a longer period of contact with the source-language society than with slight structural borrowing. Structural borrowing comes in two types, however, which are not clearly distinguished by Thomason & Kaufman. One type is the transfer of substance linguemes, that is, actual inflectional morphemes and grammatical particles such as classifiers. The other type is the transfer of schematic linguemes, that is, grammatical (syntactic or phonological) patterns. As was pointed out in §8.3.1, transfer of schematic linguemes does not involve the borrowing of any actual forms, but just transfer of a word order pattern, or a calque of foreign construction using native morphemes, or a foreign allophone or metrical pattern onto native words. All of the examples that Thomason & Kaufman give of moderate to heavy structural borrowing involve mostly transfer of schematic linguemes and only a few cases of grammatical substance linguemes.

In fact, Thomason & Kaufman reserve the substantial transfer of grammatical substance linguemes to the case of extreme borrowing (see §8.4.3).

This difference in types of structural borrowing is significant because the transfer of schemas is generally found with substratum interference, but the transfer of grammatical forms generally is not (see §8.3.1). I suggest that it is not (just) intense contact between the two societies that leads to the transfer of schematic linguemes. Intense contact involves a high degree of multilingualism, just as is found in the cases of successful substratum interference. As we have seen, substratum interference generally requires a substantial group of second-language speakers merging with the acquired-language society, in other words, a large proportion of the population is bilingual. In the case of structural borrowing, a large proportion of the borrowing language population is bilingual.

But there must also be a significant degree of openness to nonnative patterns of speech by native speakers of the borrowing language. In the case of structural borrowing, however, the source language speakers are not bilingual in the borrowing language. Hence it must be the nonnative speech patterns of the native speakers themselves that are transferred, namely the speech patterns of their knowledge of the source language. Of course, the social reasons for the one-way bilingualism indicate the socially dominant status of the source language society, and (as in the case of substratum influence) the socially dominant status can be a mechanism for the adoption of their speech patterns. It is these two social features – extensive multilingualism and openness to accepting nonnative speech patterns – that the moderate to heavy structural borrowing languages have in common with substratum interference.

Multilingualism and openness to innovations may also underlie the CONVERGENCE in phonological and syntactic structure of the local varieties of Urdu, Marathi and Kannada in the Indian village of Kupwar (Gumperz & Wilson 1971), and the lesser degree of convergence found in the larger linguistic areas such as the Balkans, the Pacific Northwest and Mesoamerica. Thomason & Kaufman place the Kupwar varieties in the category of moderate structural borrowing. But unlike the other cases of moderate structural borrowing, there has apparently been relatively little lexical borrowing in Kupwar. Thomason & Kaufman state 'structural borrowing is invariably preceded by lexical borrowing' (Thomason & Kaufman 1988:113). Yet Gumperz & Wilson write that 'only morphophonemic differences (differences of lexical shape) remain' (Gumperz & Wilson 1971:155) – i.e. the actual words and grammatical morphemes are native to each language (see also ibid. 161–2). The following examples illustrate the parallel schematic linguemes and different substance linguemes (ibid. 157, 158):

(4) Kupwar Urdu: khã   gǝe   te   tu
     Kupwar Marathi: kǝṭṭǝ gel   hotas   twa
     Kupwar Kannada: yǝlli hog   idi   ni
                       where gone were (2sg) you
                       'Where did you go?'

(5) Kupwar Urdu: ye tumhar-ə ghər həy
     Kupwar Marathi: he tumc-ə   ghər hay
     Kupwar Kannada: id nim-d   məni eti
     this your-SUFF house is
     'This is your house.'

These three languages have coexisted in the village for centuries, but the speakers have not abandoned their traditional languages during that time (in fact, they live in separate neighborhoods; ibid. 153). There is also extensive symmetrical multilingualism (ibid.), not one-way bilingualism, in Kupwar. The languages have converged on a single set of schematic linguemes which are drawn from all three languages. In other words, there is no clear favored directionality for the flow of schematic linguemes from one society to another. The extensive multilingualism may have led to the presence of many utterances by second-language speakers in the population of utterances constituting each language. But there must also have been a moderately high degree of accommodation so that native speakers of each language propagated schematic linguemes from the other languages.[6]

LINGUISTIC AREAS probably represent a less dramatic example of the same phenomenon, partly due to the diffuseness of the broad geographical areas they represent. There was a great deal of movement and largely symmetrical multilingualism in the Balkans over a long period of time, for example (Thomason & Kaufman 1988:95). The various ethnic groups maintained their languages, but accepted a number of schematic linguemes from other languages, to the extent that linguists have observed the areal patterning of linguistic features.

Substratum interference through shift, convergence / linguistic areas, and structural borrowing all result in the transfer of schematic linguemes to another language. What all three have in common is a high degree of multilingualism and an openness on the part of native speakers to accepting nonnative schematic linguemes. In the case of substratum interference through shift, the native speakers may be outnumbered or outclassed by the nonnative speakers, and accommodate to them out of necessity. In the case of convergence and linguistic areas, the native speakers do not have to accommodate to the nonnative speakers but do so anyway, for reasons not entirely clear (beyond the extensive multilingualism). In the case of structural borrowing, the native speakers adopt the schematic linguemes of their own second language, probably due to the increasingly overwhelming dominance of that language's society.

We may now consider the relationship between social structures and the types of linguemes transferred in borrowing vs substratum influence. Borrowing appears to be a result of the partial, gradual adoption of the source-language social structures by the borrowing language, including the substance linguemes that go with them. It begins with adoption of expertise unique to the source-language society (nonbasic vocabulary), then, as multilingualism increases, the adoption (Matras' fusion) of the conversational structuring of the source-language society (discourse-regulating function morphemes), and then the adoption of some of the core expertise of the source-language society (some basic vocabulary and other function words). The adoption of the source-language spheres of action is gradual: despite the increasing extensiveness of the borrowing, the borrowing society still attempts to maintain some degree of independent identity. This appears to be the case with what Thomason & Kaufman call extreme borrowing, the results of which are more generally called mixed languages; these will be discussed in §8.4.3.

Substratum interference on the other hand is a result of a wholesale (even if drawn-out) shift on the part of the speakers. In other words, as many substance linguemes as possible are adopted from the acquired language (in the case of shift) or retained from the original language (in the case of convergence, linguistic areas and structural borrowing). In addition, the native speakers of the acquired language are open to accepting nonnative schematic linguemes. A possible explanation for this latter fact is that the social identity of the native speakers is being eroded by the influence of the society with which they are in contact, whether it is nonnative speakers surrounding them (shift, convergence, linguistic areas) or speakers of the source language whose society is gradually imposing itself on them (structural borrowing).

8.4 Hybridization in language

In the biological world, hybridization only occurs between relatively closely related populations. In §8.3, I argued that the linguistic equivalent of a hybrid organism is a bi- or multilingual individual. But an individual may be bilingual in distantly related languages. This suggests that either distantly related languages are much more similar to each other than distantly related organisms are, or that the restriction on linguistic hybridization is much looser than that for organisms. The answer is probably a little bit of both. All languages perform roughly the same functions, that is, express the same range of concepts, and utilize remarkably similar conceptualization processes for construing the world (although they may vary in which construal is applied to which real-world phenomenon). Biological organisms, in contrast, occupy a wide and varying range of ecological niches, and thus vary structurally much more than languages do. On the other hand, there is no restriction on the combination of languages that a multilingual can master, whereas there are sometimes rather surprising restrictions on the natural hybridization of ecologically and morphologically similar species (Grant 1981:197–8).

Hybridization of organisms requires a merger of the genotypes of the two parent species in the hybrid, since the phenotype – the hybrid individual – is an expression of the genotype (as a function of the organism's environment). As was noted in §2.5, the relationship between speaker and utterance is not the same as the relationship between the genotype and the phenotype. Nevertheless, multilingual speakers can in principle produce hybrid utterances and even hybrid languages. In this section, we will discuss some of the circumstances under which linguistic hybridization occurs.

8.4.1   Hybrid utterances in code-switching and code-mixing

A bilingual speaker in a bilingual society employs two distinct languages in her linguistic repertoire. But if the hearer is also bilingual, utterances from either language can be produced, if socially appropriate. Moreover, utterances made up of linguemes from both languages can be produced, again if socially appopriate. All degrees of hybridization of utterances are found, without sharp distinctions. However, it is not clear what status the population of hybrid utterances has in terms of a language.

The various degrees of hybridization of utterances are called CODE-SWITCHING and (in more extreme cases) CODE-MIXING (Romaine 1995). The strictest degree of separation of codes in a multilingual society is the use of only one code in each social domain. This obtains in the case of diglossia (Ferguson 1959/1972), in which a literary standard (called H for 'high') and a mutually unintelligible vernacular (called L for 'low') are used in discrete domains. Ferguson lists typical H domains as a religious sermon, political speech, news broadcast or personal letter, and typical L domains as instructions to servants or waiters, conversations with family, a radio soap opera and folk literature (Ferguson 1959/1972:236). In this case there is no merging of the lingueme pools of the two languages.

In bilingual communities, however, one also often finds what Gumperz (1982) calls conversational code-switching, where both codes are used in the same conversational encounter, to varying degrees of integration of the codes in single utterances. Gumperz describes code-switching as 'meaningful juxtaposition of . . . strings formed according to the internal rules of *two distinct grammatical systems*' (Gumperz 1982:66, emphasis original). In other words, the interlocutors construe the codes as distinct, and exploit the social value of the two codes in a single conversational encounter. When larger segments of discourse, such as whole utterances or whole sentences, occur in a single code, it is generally clear that the two languages (utterance populations) are still separate. In particular, the two codes represent alternative ways of saying the same thing: 'it is the juxtaposition of two alternative linguistic realizations of the same message that signals information, not the propositional content of any one conversational passage' (Gumperz 1982:84).

For there to be true hybridization of a language, there would have to be a single population of utterances defined by some social domain, with a random mixture of linguemes from both parent languages. Individual sentences or clauses would involve a mixture of linguemes. Each lingueme in the lingueme pool would be accepted by the speech community as the conventional signal for the relevant function in the code. There are a number of situations in which various subsets of these criteria appear to hold.

In most conversational code-switching, there are also utterances that involve code-mixing at all grammatical levels. Romaine discusses a passage produced by a Panjabi-English speaker, part of which is given below (Romaine 1995:122):

(6) *I mean*, mə khəd čana mə ke, na, jədo *Panjabi* bolda ɛ̃, *pure Panjabi* bola ωsi *mix* kərde rẽne ã. *I mean, unconsciously, subconsciously*, kəri janeɛ̃, pər *I wish, you know* ke mə *pure Panjabi* bol səka.
'I mean, I myself would like to speak pure Panjabi whenever I speak Panjabi. We keep mixing. I mean unconsciously, subconsciously, we keep doing it, you know, but I wish, you know, that I could speak pure Panjabi.'

Romaine suggests that no linguist believes that there are no syntactic constraints on code-switching (Romaine 1995:125). But in a critical review of the proposals for syntactic constraints, it appears that there are no constraints that cannot be violated. Even the tightest combination, a stem from one language with an affix from another, occurs, as in German/English *That's what* Papschi *mein-s to say* (cf. German *mein-t* 'means'; Romaine 1995:148–9, from Clyne 1987:756; Romaine also cites examples from Dutch/Turkish, Maori/English, Japanese/English and Finnish/English).

A number of sociolinguists argue that utterances which appear to violate proposed grammatical constraints on code-switching are cases of 'nonce borrowing', that is, they represent utterances of the borrowing language and not code-switches (see Romaine 1995:139–40, 145, 156). But if a borrowing is a nonce form, that means it is not incorporated as a conventional lingueme of the language. To be sure, borrowing begins with some bilingual speaker using a foreign word, which then is propagated through the speaker's community, including to other monolingual speakers. This is also a gradual process, with variation in the degrees of integration of the foreign word into the system of the language until it is fully conventionalized (see Romaine 1995:56, 59–62; Pfaff 1979; see also the conventionalization of innovations described in §7.3). But when the so-called nonce borrowing occurs in the middle of a highly code-mixed utterance, it hardly differs in status from code-mixing itself. Instead, positing a category of nonce borrowing appears to be used only to save the constraint in question: 'there are no unambiguous criteria which will decide in all cases what type of language contact phenomena we are dealing with' (Romaine 1995:157).

In fact, some utterances are so mixed that one cannot clearly decide whether the utterance is basically in one language (the so-called base language) with elements of the other language added, or vice versa (Romaine 1995; LePage 1992:76–7). Again, grammatical criteria proposed to determine the 'base language' give ambiguous or unintuitive results (Romaine 1995:44–9). In these cases, if not in code-mixing more generally, utterances appear to be a genuine mixture of linguemes from the two source codes, to almost any degree of grammatical intimacy.

Romaine suggests that the mixed utterances may form their own code (see Romaine 1995:160 and references cited there). That is, the mixed utterances may form a population of utterances distinct from both parent codes/languages. If this is true, these codes would satisfy the first criterion for hybridization. One question that arises is how stable this code is. Is there an independent lingueme pool of linguemes that conventionally designate various concepts? Or is the mixed code simply an unconventionalized mixture of linguemes from the two parent languages, used to perform certain social and pragmatic functions?

The degree of stabilization around a set of conventions has been described as the degree of focusing in a continuum from FOCUSED to DIFFUSE (LePage & Tabouret-Keller 1985; see also Milroy 1992b:61; Trudgill 1986:85–6). As Trudgill notes, LePage & Tabouret-Keller describe societies as varying in focusing depending on how close-knit the network is (LePage & Tabouret-Keller 1985:5), but then shift to describing the code itself as varying in focusing depending on how much variation is found (LePage & Tabouret-Keller 1985:181). The assumption is that the number and frequency of variants of a single lingueme in a language is dependent on the social structure. A more focused community or society defines a more sharply bounded population of utterances and a more uniform set of conventions.

Complete uniformity of conventions is an impossibility because of the heterogeneous structure of societies (§7.2). Complete diffuseness would be a totally ad hoc means of communication. But the degree of focusing of societies, and of their linguistic conventions, varies significantly within the bounds of those extremes. When examining hybrid languages, we must assess the degree of focusing of the society using the hybrid language as well as the contributions to the mixed lingueme pool from the parent languages.

8.4.2   *True hybrid languages*

There are some clear examples of true HYBRID LANGUAGES fitting the criteria given in §8.4.1. Like biological hybrids, they occur when the parent languages are closely related varieties. These are the cases of dialect mixing and koinéization discussed in §7.4.4 (Trudgill 1986, chapters 3–4).

For example, the urban varieties in Western European countries such as Britain developed in the past two centuries as a result of immigration from the rural areas to the cities in the Industrial Revolution. The population of utterances produced by the new urban speakers represented a mixture of the linguemes in the rural dialects spoken by the immigrants. Presumably the contact gave rise to a state of affairs in which linguemes from different rural dialects were used in individual utterances, or intermediate variants were created (see §7.4.4). Finally, the urban dialects have become relatively focused, that is, new conventions were established. These new conventions result in the loss of variants or their reallocation to social/stylistic functions in the urban society (Trudgill 1986:110–26).[7] The urban society is separated and delineated from the rural societies which the urban speakers came from. Of course, the focusing process is a gradual one, which can be measured by quantitative techniques applied to utterances produced by the community (see for instance Thelander 1979, described in Trudgill 1986:91–4).

Another example of hybridization between dialects is the development of standard varieties in many societies. Standardization can develop naturally (see Haugen 1966/1972 for a description of the process), when a particular city or region becomes politically, economically and/or socially dominant. This occurred in the case of English, French, German, Spanish and Italian in the period 1200–1500, and in Persian in the mid first millennium AD (Thomason & Kaufman 1988:209–10; see also Scatton 1983:9–10 on the recent development of the standard Bulgarian language). In all of these cases, there was also influence from speakers of other varieties, not to mention the mixture of dialects in the leading cities, resulting in a standard variety that contained elements from a range of dialects (and forms intermediate to those found in the source dialects; see §7.4.4).

Hybrid languages may occur where there is contact between two closely related languages as well, such as Spanish and Portuguese in Latin America. Uruguayan Spanish speakers are in contact with Brazilian Portuguese speakers on the Uruguayan-Brazilian border. The mixed utterances produced in contact have focused in some isolated communities in Northern Uruguay; the mixed variety is the only language spoken in those communities (Trudgill 1986:83–5).

There are other instances in which two relatively closely related varieties come into contact and produce hybrid utterances, but which do not appear to focus on a third variety which is distinct from the parent variety. These are the creation of socially defined continua, as in decreolization (see the description in Trudgill 1986:86–91), the spread of a standard, and of some diglossic situations.

Decreolization occurs when a creole (see §8.5.2) comes into contact with the language from which the bulk of the creole's vocabulary is drawn (the lexical source language), as in Guyana. Speakers of the creole who have access to the lexical source language to some degree produce utterances that represent a mixture of linguemes from the creole and the lexical source language; the range of immediate utterances is called a POSTCREOLE CONTINUUM. These utterances occur in social situations in which an intermediate identity between the creole society and the lexical source-language society is desired. These intermediate varieties are also hybrids. However, in diffuse societies the hybrid varieties have not stabilized as a distinct code. Instead, variants are chosen (or blended) from the creole and the lexical source language to express different degrees of social distance from the two extreme points in the social structure. Similar phenomena are sometimes found when a vernacular variety comes into contact with a standard variety, and in diglossic societies where a continuum of utterances is produced between the H and L varieties (see Heath 1989:10, 30–32 for discussion of code-mixing between Moroccan colloquial Arabic [L] and Classical Arabic [H]).

8.4.3 Mixed languages

The question remains, can a hybrid language arise whose parent languages are not closely related? That is, can a code that is mixed between distantly related languages become focused as a third code distinct from the two parent languages?

There are a number of cases of MIXED LANGUAGES reported in the literature. However, there is relatively little information on many of them, of either a social or linguistic nature. Nevertheless, it appears that there is a range of social situations and a range of linguistic mixtures. However, the mixing is always linguistically asymmetrical, albeit in different ways. There is a wide range of theories about the origins of mixed languages, but it appears that different mixed languages arose in fundamentally different ways (Matras 2000).

One question that often is raised about all mixed languages is the phylogenetic question: given a language A that appears to be a mixture of languages B and C, can we conclude that language A is 'really' a descendant (albeit dramatically altered) of language B or language C? In the evolutionary framework, we may break this down into two questions, based on the two populations involved in language evolution, the speakers (interactors) and the linguemes (replicators). We may compare the social contexts in which mixed languages arose, and then examine the lingueme pool defined by the mixed language in relation to the two parent languages.

The following discussion is very cursory, and does not do justice to the complexity of the social and linguistic facts of the situations described. Nevertheless, it attempts to divide mixed languages by the presumed historical social context of the speakers, and examines the nature of the lingueme pool of the mixed language spoken by the society in question. I suggest that there are at least three distinct social contexts with three different types of mixed languages: mixed marriage languages, death by borrowing, and semi-shift.

8.4.3.1 Mixed marriage languages

There are two mixed languages which appear to have arisen through marriages where the father came from one society and the mother from another, Mednyj Aleut (also called Copper Island Aleut) and Michif. These MIXED MARRIAGE LANGUAGES are precisely the two cases known by Thomason & Kaufman in which the grammatical system of one part (nominal) is from one parent language and of another part (verbal) from the other parent language (Thomason & Kaufman 1988:233). However, the make-up of the lexicon is different in the two cases.

Mednyj Aleut is spoken on Mednyj or Copper Island.[8] The Aleuts moved to Copper Island in the early 19th century (possibly moved there by the Russians), and Russian seal hunters moved there soon after. The Russian population was approximately 10% of Copper Island, and they married Aleut women. (This contrasts with neighboring Bering Island, where there was a much lower proportion of Russians, and the language remained basically Aleut.) The original populations were probably mutually bilingual (Thomason & Kaufman 1988:234). There was a period of Russian withdrawal, but now Russian is rapidly taking over on the island (ibid.).

The Mednyj Aleut language has Aleut noun stems, nominal derivations and nominal inflections, and Aleut verb stems and derivational morphology, but Russian verb inflections and associated forms, such as the imperfective future auxiliary (Golovko 1996). Some of the Aleut verbal affixes in Mednyj Aleut include subordinate verb forms and aspectual-modal concepts (Golovko 1996:66), though sometimes both Aleut and Russian constructions are used (ibid. 72–3). The contributions from both parent languages are largely preserved intact; in particular the Russian verbal constructions 'are perfectly ordinary morphologically complete Russian patterns' (Thomason & Kaufman 1988:237). A more subtle mixture of Russian and Aleut linguemes is found with verbal agreement, in which Russian number/gender forms agree with the subject possessors as in Aleut (Golovko 1996:68–70), and word order, in which largely Aleut nominal and verbal forms follow Russian word order (ibid., 72).

Michif is spoken in a number of Métis communities in Canada and the US, particularly in the Turtle Mountain area in North Dakota (Bakker & Papen 1997). The ancestors of present-day Michif speakers are believed to be the descendants of French trappers and (mostly) Cree women in Canada (Bakker & Papen 1997:296–7). The Métis have been multilingual during most of their history (ibid. 301, 352), but more recent generations include native speakers of Michif, and French and Cree are being lost in favor of English (ibid. 303). Michif is essentially restricted to the domain of the home (ibid.). Bakker & Papen hypothesize that the Michif language must have developed in the early 19th century, although it is first reported in the 1930s (ibid. 352–3).

The Michif language has largely Cree verbs including essentially their full complement of (complex) verbal inflections (ibid. 351). The noun phrase is largely French, albeit with some simplification (e.g. no count/mass distinction), and with Cree demonstratives, postpositions (in addition to mostly French prepositions) and even Cree obviative markers (ibid. 348, 351–2). There are some French verbs which take French inflections, though again reduced. The French and Cree items retain their independent phonologies (ibid. 349–50).

As Thomason & Kaufman have noted, Mednyj Aleut and Michif have in common the fact that nominal and verbal morphosyntax come from different parent languages. However, in Mednyj Aleut, the verb stems remain Aleut, while in Michif the lexical items in each category come from the corresponding parent languages. In both cases, the language of the presumed ancestral mothers is dominant: the lexicon of Mednyj Aleut is almost entirely Aleut, while the French noun phrase grammar is reduced compared with the Cree verbal grammar. Interestingly, in both cases the two components are close to the parent languages and not well integrated with each other (in the case of Michif's phonology). This is probably due to the persistence of bilingualism in both parent languages during most of the mixed marriage languages' history.[9]

The mixed marriage languages presented in this section appear to be extreme cases of the merging of substance as well as schematic linguemes between the distinct languages of the parent speakers. A more common situation in traditional societies was exogamous marriage patterns, where a marriage partner was required to come from a different society, which may speak a different language. Exogamy is one of the important sources of multilingualism in traditional societies. However, it normally does not lead to as extensive mixing as in Mednyj Aleut and Michif. Exogamy may involve speakers of more than one other language, unlike Mednyj Aleut and Michif, where only one additional language was involved (Russian and French respectively). This lessens the influence of any one external language. Also, the language of the society which the new spouse joined tends to be the dominant language; this was also true of Mednyj Aleut and Michif, where the mothers' language is dominant in the mixture.

One case of exogamy and language mixture has been examined in some detail, that which formerly held in eastern Arnhem Land in Australia (Heath 1978, 1981). In this area, languages that are quite distant genetically have been in contact through exogamous marriage patterns and through seasonal gathering for ritual purposes (Heath 1978:14–16). The social links between two pairs of societies, Ritharngu and Ngandi, and Nunggubuyu and Warndarag, were particularly strong (ibid.). The societies thus became bilingual, and the bilingualism was relatively stable.

From this sociolinguistic description, one might expect the mixing in Arnhem Land to exhibit properties of convergence and mixed marriage languages. This appears to be the case. There has been convergence of schematic linguemes, as one might expect in stable multilingual societies. In particular, there has been a convergence of phoneme segment inventories and surface phonotactic patterns across the languages (Heath 1978:66), independent of lexical borrowings (see below). Morphosyntactic sharing of schematic linguemes is also found, such as enclitic pronominals and the retreat of the infinitive in subordinate clauses in Ritharngu under Ngandi influence, and the restructuring of the usage of the Nunggubuyu case affixes under Warndarag influence (Heath 1978, ch. 4).

In addition, however, there has been substantial diffusion of substance linguemes, including grammatical substance linguemes, as one might expect in a mixed marriage language situation. Both pairs of language exhibit a substantial influx of lexical items from the other language in a wide range of categories, the number of borrowed words in Ngandi approaching 50% (Heath 1981:356). There has also been borrowing of substance linguemes for inflectional and derivational morphology, including many case affixes, noun class prefixes and a negative suffix (Heath 1978, ch. 3). As with the lexicon, more diffusion has occurred between Ritharngu and Ngandi than between Nunggubuyu and Warndarag. Ngandi has been more receptive of grammatical substance linguemes than Ritharngu (Heath 1978:143; he does not indicate overall directionality of lexical borrowings).

Heath compares the Arnhem Land situation to the stable multilingualism that led to convergence in Kupwar (see §8.3.2). On the one hand, the Arnhem Land language speakers were not as bilingual as those in Kupwar (Heath 1978:142). On the other hand, bilingualism in Arnhem Land is intrafamilial, and the distinct languages were not as sharply focused as those in Kupwar (Heath

1978:142–3; Heath 1981:361 indicates that the languages are still quite focused). I suggested in §8.3.2 that a covergence situation requires some degree of openness to the introduction of schematic linguemes as well as a high degree of bilingualism. It may be that the more intimate relationship of marriage between speakers of different languages in Arnhem Land led to a high rate of diffusion of substance linguemes as well. Unlike Mednyj Aleut and Michif however, there is not the massive introduction of whole integrated grammatical subsystems (such as the Russian verbal inflections in Mednyj Aleut). The difference in degrees of mixing of substance linguemes may be due to the fact that the entry of the Russians and the French resulted in a more substantial disruption of traditional social patterns compared with the exogamous marriage patterns in Arnhem Land (and possibly elsewhere).

8.4.3.2   Death by borrowing

Societies undergoing DEATH BY BORROWING are those which are defying cultural assimilation but gradually adopt more and more of the substance linguemes from the surrounding language, in which they are bilingual. The last phase in this process is what Matras calls FUNCTIONAL TURNOVER (Matras 2000:17–23): the basic vocabulary and sometimes some grammatical affixes of the original language are restricted to a secret or in-group register of the now-acquired language of the external group.

One well-documented example of extensive borrowing not yet approaching language death is the Asia Minor Greek dialects from before World War I (Dawkins 1916; see Thomason & Kaufman 1988:215–22). These dialects were spoken by Greek communities surrounded by Turkish communities. The Greek speakers were commonly bilingual, and some Greek speakers shifted to Turkish (and also to Islam; Thomason & Kaufman 1988:215). The Asia Minor Greek dialects exhibit extensive borrowing from Turkish of both non-basic and basic vocabulary (Dawkins 1916:197–8), function words including discourse-regulating function words, some derivational morphology and in some Cappadocian villages even nominal and verbal inflection morphology (see Dawkins 1916:203 for a summary). There has been some adoption of schematic linguemes from Turkish, including genitive and relative word order, but not extensively (Dawkins 1916:201–3; Thomason & Kaufman 1988:220–22; we would predict this from the lack of universal bilingualism; see §8.3.2).

Another example of extensive borrowing is the Arabic of Kormakiti in Cyprus. The speakers are universally bilingual in Greek: massive borrowing of Greek vocabulary has brought in Greek morphosyntax as well, while the Arabic words largely retain their Arabic morphosyntax (Newton 1964; see also Thomason & Kaufman 1988:105–7). The speakers are Maronites who left Lebanon some time after 1191, thus originally speakers of Arabic (Newton 1964:43). A third example of extensive borrowing, albeit not as focused, is Polish Romani (Matras 2000): much nonbasic vocabulary and some basic vocabulary, as well as discourse-regulating grammar and Slavic aspectual affixes, are borrowed from Polish. Again, the speakers are Roma who migrated to Poland.

If more and more of the source language were borrowed, there would remain little more of the original language than a core of basic vocabulary and some grammatical inflections and constructions. Yet the borrowing society may still resist assimilation into the surrounding society. Matras argues that for such societies, at some point 'the need to retain a special variety is stronger than the ability to transmit a coherent linguistic-grammatical system' (Matras 2000). At this point, there is a functional turnover: the original language is abandoned as a potentially general-purpose communication system.[10] The remaining elements of the original language – mainly its basic vocabulary – are then available as a register to employ in order to exclude outsiders from the communicative act. Since the remaining elements include basic vocabulary, they prove useful for this purpose.

Matras argues that functional turnover occurred in the Romani varieties of Western Europe (including Britain and Scandinavia), called Para-Romani. There is no currently existing Para-Romani language (Matras 2000), but instead an ability to insert Romani vocabulary into utterances in the local language (e.g. English or Spanish). Matras describes the process of employing Romani lexical items as lexical reorientation, and the retention of some (often fossilized) grammatical inflections as selective replication.[11]

Matras also suggests that the current status of Ma'a (Mbugu) is a result of functional turnover (Matras 2000). Ma'a is a language possessing a basic vocabulary, including personal, possessive and demonstrative pronouns, that is largely Southern Cushitic (Thomason & Kaufman 1988:225), though not from any one existing Southern Cushitic language (Greenberg 1999:627). But Ma'a also possesses much nonbasic vocabulary and almost all grammatical inflections that agree closely with its neighboring Bantu languages, Pare and Shambaa (Thomason & Kaufman 1988:223). Thomason & Kaufman note that 'different (and independent) sources present a picture of the Ma'a people as resisters of total cultural assimilation' (Thomason & Kaufman 1988:225; see also references in Thomason 1997:472).

Historically, Ma'a represents a case of extensive borrowing of Pare/Shambaa grammatical substance linguemes by a Southern-Cushitic-speaking society (Thomason 1997:478–82); for example, early 20th-century sources indicate that the Bantu inflections were not obligatory at that time, especially in ingroup communication (Greenberg 1999:629). However, the contemporary Ma'a speakers are all bilingual in a Bantu language which they call Mbugu which is very similar to Pare (Thomason 1997:469). The Ma'a language appears to be an in-group register (Thomason 1997:473, citing Mous 1994), though Thomason notes it is still learned as a first language (Thomason 1997:476). Hence it is possible that Ma'a has undergone functional turnover with lexical (re)orientation – more accurately, retention – of mostly Cushitic vocabulary and selective replication of a limited amount of Cushitic grammatical structure.

The result of death by borrowing is quite different from that of mixed marriage languages. In death by borrowing and ultimately functional turnover, much of the basic vocabulary is retained, with perhaps some grammatical inflections, while the rest of the grammatical structures are of the external society's language. After functional turnover, the original language linguemes represent a secret or in-group register, only one code of the society.[12]

8.4.3.3 Semi-shift

The third social situation breeding mixed languages is semi-shift. In SEMI-SHIFT, the speakers in a society appear to shift only part way to the external society's language. The semi-shift may be due to lack of full access to the external society's language, or may be a marker of a distinct social identity. The linguistic result of semi-shift is the mirror image of functional turnover: the vocabulary is that of the external society's language, while many grammatical inflections (substance linguemes) and most grammatical constructions (schematic linguemes) are at least in part those of the native-language society. Semi-shift is thus a sort of extreme case of substratum interference, which is the result of a more complete shift to the external society's language (see §8.3.1).

An example of semi-shift is Media Lengua, a mixed language in Ecuador (Muysken 1997). The Media Lengua communities were probably monolingual Quechua around 1900 (Muysken 1997:374). Then men began to work in the Spanish-speaking cities and became fluent in Spanish. Media Lengua arose as a home language in these communities. Media Lengua is clearly a stable code (ibid. 407–8). These communities are now mostly trilingual, although the oldest people may be native Quechua speakers and the youngest, native Spanish speakers (ibid. 374). Media Lengua employs almost entirely Spanish vocabulary (89%; ibid. 378) but almost entirely Quechua grammatical inflections (substance linguemes) and constructions (schematic linguemes).

Media Lengua does not look like an interlanguage: interlanguage does not usually contain native language grammatical inflections (Muysken 1997:405–7). The Spanish words are regularized and adapted to Quechua phonology for use with Quechua inflections, not unlike Spanish borrowings into Quechua. In other words, semi-shift differs from shift proper: semi-shift is more like a deliberate halfway shift, in this case by using Spanish vocabulary in a Quechua framework, rather than the stabilization of an interlanguage form.

Another possible example of semi-shift is Petjo, formerly spoken in Indonesia (van Rheeden 1994). Petjo is spoken by the descendants of Dutch fathers and Malay mothers, a group called Indos (van Rheeden 1994:224). Thus, Petjo has a social origin not unlike a mixed marriage language. However, it appears that Malay was always spoken alongside Petjo, and Dutch was only acquired at a later age, and often not completely (ibid.). Petjo is an in-group language; Malay is used for outside communication (ibid., 225).

Petjo has approximately 83% Dutch lexical items, including prepositions, conjunctions, numerals, articles and personal pronouns (ibid., 226–27). There are a significant number of Malay nouns and adjectives, mostly related to local natural and cultural objects, and some possessives, demonstratives, and the relative clause marker. There is also occasional mixing of verbal prefixes, e.g. *ge-goejoer* 'be poured over' and *di-scheiden* 'be separated' (ibid., 232; Malay in bold). However, most of the syntactic constructions and word order is calqued on Malay, as is the phonology.

Thus, Petjo seems to be almost entirely Dutch in substance linguemes, except for the usual sorts of lexical borrowings and a small number of function words, but almost entirely Malay in schematic linguemes. In fact, Petjo looks like an arrested example of a fairly advanced state of second language acquisition of Dutch (van Rheeden 1994:235), unlike Media Lengua. Given its social origin, Petjo is perhaps more like Mednyj Aleut, with most of its lexicon from one language and a few grammatical substance linguemes from the other language. On the other hand, the minimal presence of Malay grammatical substance linguemes in Petjo may be due to the minimal presence of grammatical substance linguemes in (Low or Bazaar) Malay (ibid., 229, 233). Unlike Mednyj Aleut and Michif, the second parent language, Dutch, was only rarely a home language. Thus, Petjo may be better described as a case of semi-shift towards Dutch, with a deliberate use of what little grammatical morphology Malay makes available.

In mixed marriage languages, death by borrowing (and functional turn-over), and semi-shift, the lingueme pool contains substantial numbers of linguemes from two parent languages. Nevertheless, in each case, the contribution is asymmetrical, and can be motivated by social factors. Semi-shift represents a shift of a society partway but not completely towards another social group and its language, acquiring its vocabulary but not its grammar (neither schematic linguemes nor substance linguemes). Death by borrowing and functional turn-over represent the cultural defiance of a society being overwhelmed by the surrounding society, retaining its basic vocabulary till the last. Mixed marriage languages are the closest to true hybrid languages, with grammatical substance linguemes functionally split between the two parent languages; but in the two well-documented cases, there is a predominance of the ancestral mothers' original language.

These three types of social mixing probably do not exhaust the possibilities, but they appear to account for the best-known examples of mixed languages. A model of language phylogeny must allow for reticulation of phylogenetic lines of descent for whole languages. But the phylogenetic model must also represent the different ways in which the two parent languages contribute to the lingueme pool of the daughter language, and the asymmetry of the contribution of each parent. It is also important to note that for all of the mixed languages discussed above, many if not all speakers were multilingual with one or both of the parent languages during much of the history of the mixed language. This prolonged multilingualism without (complete) shift, combined with the development of a social identity for a group distinct from the parent-language societies, appears to have played the major role in the stabilization of the mixed code in all three types.

Is there a way to describe the asymmetry of the lingueme contributions of the two parents across all mixed language types, such that one parent is primary? If the social classification of mixed languages proposed here is valid, then death by borrowing and semi-shift can be considered as special cases of extreme borrowing and incomplete shift respectively. If so, then the PRIMARY PARENT LANGUAGE is the one contributing the majority of the basic vocabulary linguemes. In death by borrowing, the original language would be primary, as in cases of less extreme borrowing. Even for functional turnover, one can describe the secret or in-group register as a code where the original language would be primary. In semi-shift, the acquired language would be primary, as it is in cases of a more complete shift.

This leaves the mixed marriage languages. Mednyj Aleut has a basic vocabulary that is largely Aleut, hence Aleut would be primary (in fact, Thomason & Kaufman consider Mednyj Aleut to be an example of extreme borrowing; Thomason & Kaufman 1988:237). Michif has a split in basic vocabulary between French nouns, adjectives, numerals and prepositions and Cree verbs, demonstratives and postpositions. Cree appears to be dominant, based largely on grammatical evidence.

But the social evidence of the make-up of the speaker population also points to primacy of Aleut and Cree: 90% of the population of Copper Island were Aleut at the time when Mednyj Aleut was formed, and 'the ethnic heritage of most Michif speakers is Cree' (Thomason & Kaufman 1988:231).[13] Thus, the social and linguistic patterns point towards Aleut and Cree as primary parents. The mixed marriage languages are therefore more like borrowing than shift (cf. Thomason & Kaufman 1988:237).

8.5 Creation of a new community or society

The languages and language types described in §8.4 all represent the creation of a new society of one sort of another; so the heading of this section would subsume those languages as well. The examples in this section are different from the preceding examples in that the social situation is generally much more complex. The languages described in this section are those known as lingua francas, pidgins and creoles. Despite the extreme variation of the social contexts in which they arise, the linguistic result is remarkably similar, hence the justification for discussing these languages together. Essentially, the linguistic result is the same as in shift and semi-shift: most of the vocabulary is drawn from a single parent language. But unlike shift or even semi-shift, the grammatical elements – substance linguemes and schematic linguemes – are not drawn from the same parent language, and in fact have disputed lineages.

Societies of individuals are never completely communicatively isolated (§8.2). Some individuals from one society will interact with other individuals in other societies for a variety of reasons, one of the most common reasons being trade (Mühlhäusler 1986:75). Such contacts may be relatively brief or random, but if they are reasonably stable, then an intersocietal community will develop, in the sense of community defined in §4.2.3 and §7.2.

The community's code will develop at the same time, of course. In some cases, the intersocietal code will simply be the language of one of the societies. That is, one society's language will function as a LINGUA FRANCA (Samarin 1962/1968), and the language is thus extended for use in a new domain. For example, English is a global lingua franca in a wide range of intersocietal communities; individuals from non-English-speaking societies learn English in order to communicate with other individuals.

The use of a lingua franca presupposes that members of the other society or societies have mastered the lingua franca at least to some degree. This fact in turn presupposes that the members of the other society or societies have sufficient access to the language of the society contributing the lingua franca, that is, there exists the opportunity to master the lingua franca on the part of the former. If this presupposition fails, then PIDGINIZATION is likely to occur.

One reason for insufficient access on the part of the other societies using the lingua franca is that the lingua franca is in fact the language of a third society, not.the language of the interacting societies. For example, Swahili is spoken natively on the coast of Kenya and Tanzania, but is used as a lingua franca much farther inland. Some of these inland areas use Swahili because Swahili traders settled there but others use Swahili as a second language lingua franca among other Bantu peoples (Holm 1989:564–6). The form of Swahili used is considerably simplified from the native language on the coast, a characteristic of pidgins (see below).

Another reason for insufficient access to the language drawn on for the intersocietal code is unwillingness on the part of the society speaking that language to give the other societies access to it. Thomason & Kaufman give a number of examples of withheld languages (Thomason & Kaufman 1988:175–7; see also Holm 1989:514). The members of the withholding society sometimes give the impression that the language they are using with outsiders is their own language, or they deliberately avoid using their full language with the other group(s).

These social factors create and maintain social distance between the two societies in question. Social distance between two groups who otherwise interact is the underlying motivation for pidginization: 'what is common to [social contexts of pidginization] is the original geographic, social and linguistic distance of the parties involved. In most cases, there remains a desire to maintain the social distance, and it is this desire that keeps jargons and pidgins alive' (Mühlhäusler 1986:81; JARGONS are not yet stabilized pidgins).

Jargons and the PIDGINS that develop from them are characterized by their simplified form. There are two reasons for simplification of a pidgin. The first is that the pidgin is used for only a single domain, such as trade or tourism (see Mühlhäusler 1986:75–84 for typical domains of pidgin use), and hence only a fraction of the entire communicative resources of the language from which its lexicon is drawn (the so-called lexifier language) are necessary for successful communication.

The second reason is that since one or both of the interlocutors do not know the full language, nonconventional coordination devices (see §4.3.1) are favored over conventional coordination. Shared expertise in the domain of trade, etc., joint attention including gestures, joint salience of common ground in the context, and other nonconventional devices are used to establish joint meaning (cf. Mühlhäusler 1986:137–8; Holm 1988:73). The conventional grammatical inflections and grammatical constructions of the lexifier language are largely dispensed with – up to a point.

The conventions of the lexical source language are preserved in the pidgin if they more or less coincide with the counterpart conventions in the language(s) of the other interlocutors. That is, interlocutors will use conventional coordination devices if they coincide. Thomason & Kaufman give a number of examples of pidgins, including many pidgins from non-European lexical source languages, containing rather complex or 'marked' linguemes. One of their examples is Chinook Jargon, used in the Pacific Northwest coast (see also Thomason 1983). In addition to a range of unusual phonemes, Chinook Jargon also possesses pleonastic pronouns, a variant VS order, a NEG V S order, and a question particle. All of these features are unusual in pidgins, but common to all of the Native American languages of the area. And, of course, it should not be forgotten that the languages underlying most European-based pidgins (Western European languages, West African languages, and Austronesian languages) share significant schematic linguemes, including SVO word order, prepositions, and preverbal auxiliaries derived from verbs, all of which are used in the pidgins based on these languages.

Thomason & Kaufman's arguments fit in with the analysis of coordination in communication in §4.2.4: converge on the most salient coordination device, conventional or nonconventional. In fact, Thomason & Kaufman's description of the mutual accommodation underlying pidginization is essentially a description of a first-party Schelling game: 'members of the new contact community make guesses about what their interlocutors will understand, and 'right' guesses are incorporated into the grammar of the developing contact language' (Thomason & Kaufman 1988:174).

The remaining conventional coordination devices in a jargon and a pidgin are its vocabulary. The striking fact about almost all pidgins is that the majority of the vocabulary of each pidgin is taken from one language. Mühlhäusler argues that this is a result of stabilization of a jargon into a pidgin (Mühlhäusler 1986:143). Although jargons may consist of a mélange of vocabulary, a pidgin will have most of its lexicon from one language for two reasons. If one of the groups of interlocutors is highly mobile, such as European sailors, then the only contact language in common with all of the groups in the community is that of the mobile population. If the two (or more) groups of interlocutors are not mobile, then other factors intervene: the socially dominant group may impose its vocabulary (as in the European slave plantations in the Caribbean), or the group in whose territory the contacts are made will impose its vocabulary (as in the jargons of medieval pilgrims and modern tourists; Mühlhäusler 1986:143–5). One of the very few exceptions to this principle is Russenorsk, a pidgin used between Norwegian and Russian traders of the 19th century (Broch & Jahr 1981; Holm 1989:621–4; Jahr 1996; Trudgill 1996b:9–10). Its vocabulary is approximately half from each language, reflecting the fact that the two social groups were essentially equal in power.[14]

The settling on vocabulary largely from a single source language makes the pidginization process look like shift. Thomason & Kaufman argue that the language that is being learned is not the lexical source language, but a simplified version of it (Thomason & Kaufman 1988:178). Moreover, the simplification is not due to imperfect learning but is a product of the lexifier language's native speakers (ibid.).[15] Nevertheless, it is still the result of shift to the simplified code by nonspeakers, and has similar linguistic effects: the nonspeakers acquire the vocabulary and some schematic linguemes (grammatical structures) of the simplified code, and import some of their own schematic linguemes (Thomason & Kaufman 1988:193; cf. also the widespread occurrence of European words in Atlantic creoles with African semantic range, polysemy, syntactic behavior or calques; Holm 1988:82–9).

The origin of the linguemes in European language-based pidgins is highly varied. In addition to vocabulary from the lexical source language, there is vocabulary from substratum languages, and schematic linguemes (grammatical patterns) from a variety of sources. Even in an apparently straightforward bilateral trade situation, such as that which gave rise to pidgins such as Russenorsk, the linguemes come from a variety of sources: 'besides a few words from Lappish, Finnish, Swedish, and French, there are a number of words from Dutch or Low German (e.g. *grot* 'big', *junka* 'boy') and English (e.g. *jes* 'yes', *ju* 'you', *verrigod* 'very good') and international nautical jargon (e.g. *skaffom* 'to eat')' (Holm 1989:621, citing an unpublished MS by J. A. Fox).

From a sociolinguistic point of view, this is not surprising. The trading and colonial communities which used these pidgins, and pidgin communities in general, were and are perhaps the most loose-knit social networks in existence. Speakers are often very mobile, with contacts with many societies; new slaves and laborers were constantly and rapidly being added to (and dying off in) the colonial plantations. The pidgin speakers are also socially quite distant from each other, as noted above, typically with uniplex links to other speakers (e.g. only trade). In accordance with the Milroys' theory of introducers being weak-tie individuals (§7.4.1), virtually all pidgin speakers are in a position to introduce and propagate linguemes from almost every code with which they come into contact.

Thus, there is probably some truth to all of the theories proposed for the origins of European-based pidgins – monogenesis from an Atlantic nautical jargon, substratum influences from Africa and Oceania, 'relexification' (shift) from one European lexical pidgin to another, not to mention motivated universal developments (see Holm 1988:27–70 for an overview). Nevertheless, for all pidgins, one can identify the lexical source language as the primary parent in the same way as for the mixed languages in §8.3.3: it is the parent providing most of the basic vocabulary linguemes.

In some cases, the extraordinarily loose-knit network (or part of it) may coalesce into a new society, with a full array of domains. In this case, the pidgin expands, becoming the code for more and more social domains, and undergoes CREOLIZATION, that is, the language becomes a native language for the younger generation of users – the most intimate social domain.

A sharp line is generally drawn between an EXPANDED PIDGIN (still a second language for its users) and a CREOLE (a first language for its users). However, a sharp line cannot be drawn in reality. No clear cases of ABRUPT CREOLIZATION – nativization of a jargon – have been attested (Holm 1989:631, Mühlhäusler 1986:8), and rather few examples of nativization from an unexpanded pidgin (Mühlhäusler 1986:8). In the most commonly attested case, nativization of an expanded pidgin, 'competent adult non-native speakers always coexist with the children growing up as native speakers, making it impossible to determine with any certainty which group is contributing what to the structure of the emerging creole' (Holm 1989:631). Also, creolizing societies are multilingual societies (after all, the parents' generation are not native speakers), and the children may grow up multilingual in the pidgin/creole and other languages of the society, thereby eroding the distinction between native language and second language.

The evolutionary status of a creole developing from an expanded pidgin is fairly straightforward. Its linguemes generally come from the pidgin (although some may be borrowed from other languages spoken in the society), or are created from the pidgin's linguemes via altered replication, particularly grammaticalization (Mufwene 1996b). The problems in the phylogeny of a creole are essentially inherited from its pidgin parent.[16]

8.6   Language death: selection at the societal level?

Language death is a result of the differential survival of whole languages. It is possible to analyze language death as selection at a higher level of organization. In order to do so, one must identify the replicator, the interactor, the environment and the relevant causal mechanisms for differential replication and selection at the level of a whole language.

In this analysis, the interactor is the society as a whole. The relevant organic structure that the society possesses is the social domains of language use and their interrelationships (Fishman 1965/1972; see §4.2.3). Fishman (1972) suggests a concrete mechanism for selection. He proposes that language maintenance in multilingual communities is supported by a sharp differentiation of social domains (and presumably, their stability over time; Fishman 1972:51). If there is no sharp differentiation, or if the structure of social domains is disrupted (e.g. by the impact of European invaders and colonizers), then one language may invade the social domain of the other and ultimately replace it.

The interaction of the society with its environment – other societies with which it comes into contact mostly, but possibly also its physical environment – thus leads to the survival/extinction of the replicator, which is the language's lingueme pool taken as a whole (cf. Mufwene to appear). The interactor – the society – can also cause altered replication. For instance, a society can alter its language through borrowing, coinage, calquing and creation of new constructions, and development of a written style in order to extend the language to new domains or stylistic registers – or by not doing so, thereby allowing another language to occupy that social niche instead.

This is a process of social evolution. The processes described by Fishman are essentially social: contact between societies (including immigration and conquest), and changes in the organization of domains of social interaction. These social processes happen to have linguistic consequences because of how languages are identified with the societies that speak them, or are identified with particular social domains in a multilingual society.

This may not be the correct analysis. After all, in the standard neo-Darwinian model, competition between species is usually reduced to competition between organisms belonging to those species, and selection is said to operate at that level only: '[Species] compete, but probably competition between organisms of the same and different species is more important than competition between one species and another species' (Ghiselin 1987:141, cited in Hull 1988:219). It may be that the social processes in choosing which language to use in a society should be analyzed as choices made by speakers: they do not replicate the linguemes of their traditional language in utterances in a community, or they even abandon the community altogether (e.g. abandoning a traditional religion). Both of these choices would result in the extinction of the language of the community.[17]

Nevertheless, some biologists argue for selection at the species level, arguing that species have a population structure that can be replicated. Likewise, the proliferation of European standard languages at the expense of indigenous languages may be due in part to their social structure. That is, European standard languages are already fully developed for use in the full array of domains of expertise of the modern world, with vocabulary and writing systems and the technology to support them (cf. §3.5). The sociolinguistic structure of the European standard languages is replicated when indigenous groups join the modern world (so to speak). That is, the European standard languages proliferate in the indigenous groups' society and the indigenous languages go extinct.

It should go without saying that the analysis of the facts of language death and language shift in terms of selection at the language level should NOT be given an evaluative interpretation such that the indigenous languages are 'inferior'. That would be social Darwinism. Consider again the biological parallel. European species such as starlings and Mediterranean annual grasses have invaded and eliminated North American songbird species and perennial bunchgrasses respectively. Biologists do not assume that this fact demonstrates that the native American species are 'inferior'. On the contrary, biologists are in the vanguard of the movement to save endangered species, and linguists should be in the vanguard of the movement to save endangered languages.

Notes

1   However, as will be seen below, I will adopt much of Thomason & Kaufman's model of the relationship between society and language in contact situations; their assumptions about genetic descent do not invalidate their social and linguistic analyses of contact situations.

2   Thomason & Kaufman actually split this assumption into two: genetic relationships can be defined only in cases of normal transmission, and languages transmitted by normal transmission cannot have multiple parents (Thomason & Kaufman 1988:100–11).

3   Bilingual speakers are typically weak-tie members of the society (§7.4.1): their bilingualism reflects their position between two societies. In the case of multilingual societies, however, speakers of the society's languages are not necessarily weak-tie members.

4   See also Thomason & Kaufman 1988:129, where they suggest that Gaelic loanwords into Irish English were introduced by English speakers.

5   Matras calls this combination 'convergence' (Matras 2000).

6   Thomason & Kaufman argue that there was already a fair degree of structural similarity between the three languages in Kupwar, due in fact to the ancient shift of Dravidian speakers to Indic languages (Thomason & Kaufman 1988:86).

7   Trudgill considers reallocation a problem for the theory of accommodation (Trudgill 1986:125). As noted above, no society is completely homogeneous, and thus no society will be completely focused, so variants may remain to signal the heterogeneity of the society.

8   The sociohistorical information in this paragraph is drawn from Thomason & Kaufman 1988:233–8, in turn taken largely from Menovščikov 1969; see Thomason & Kaufman for further references.

9   Trudgill 1996b describes these languages as 'dual-source creoloids', that is, languages which underwent significant changes due to shift ('creoloid') but have two parent languages.

10 Matras argues that functional turnover is a relatively abrupt process, not the end result of gradual borrowing (Matras 2000); there is no assumption in the passage above that functional turnover is the endpoint of a gradual borrowing process, despite my name for the general case.

11 Matras also cites some examples of secret-language registers in Germany such as Lekoudesch, used by Jewish cattle traders until 1933 and drawing on Ashkenazic Hebrew; and Jenisch, a generic term for secret lexicons including items from Romance, Ashkenazic Hebrew and Romani used by commercial nomads (Matras 2000). It appears that these registers originated at least partly through contact with Romani speakers and may represent a sort of adoption or borrowing of Romani, etc. vocabulary for a secret register (ibid.).

12 Trudgill 1996b describes a similar case as a 'reverse creoloid', giving the example of Shetland Island Scots, which retains 'considerable amounts of Scandinavian (Norn) influence, particularly in lexis' (ibid. 12).

13 Bakker & Papen state that the Métis formed their own distinct cultural identity (Bakker & Papen 1997:296). However, they note that in one the earliest phases of the formation of the Métis culture, during the late 18th century, the children of French-Indian unions 'generally continued to live with their Indian mothers' (ibid. 297), and that in the early 20th century, 'Cree monolingualism was not at all

uncommon among uneducated Métis' (ibid. 301). Both of these observations suggest a cultural orientation of the Métis more towards the Indians than towards the French.

14 Mühlhäusler suggests that Russenorsk remained a jargon, since some lexical items varied between Russian and Norwegian sources (Mühlhäusler 1986:143). However, Jahr (1996) argues convincingly that Russenorsk is a stabilized pidgin.

15 In fact, this is not always true: in the example of Swahili given above, simplification is partly due to the behavior of nonnative speakers in using it as a lingua franca. However, this may be more like the simplification process that sometimes occurs in shift (see §8.4.1) than pidginization.

16 Thomason & Kaufman propose that mutual accommodation, the same mechanism as they propose for pidginization, is involved (Thomason & Kaufman 1988:153). In other words, the process for abrupt creolization (and its problems for phylogeny) is essentially the same as those for pidginization discussed above.

17 In fact, selection at the societal level requires that the replicator be the lingueme pool taken as a whole: one language simply replaces another in the social domain. The cases of mixing described in §§8.3–8.4 would not count as differential replication at the societal level.

Chapter 9

Towards an evolutionary linguistics

This book has presented a program for rethinking language change in evolutionary terms. Two fundamental theses underlie this framework. First, there is a general theory of selection, most fully developed in evolutionary biology, which shows that evolutionary processes operate at two levels, replication and selection (Hull 1988). Second, this model can be applied to language by taking the speaker as the unit of selection and the lingueme as the unit of replication; this is the Theory of Utterance Selection (§2.4.1). The result is a framework for language change encompassing both innovation and propagation in language change. The framework firmly situates both innovation and propagation in a uniform model of language change through language use (§2.5; chapter 3).

But much of the presentation has implications for language taken as a whole. In fact, any theory of language change gives one the opportunity to look at language as a whole. Language change cannot be separated from language structure (phonology, morphology, syntax), language function (semantics, pragmatics, discourse analysis, and phonetics with respect to phonology), language in the mind (psycholinguistics, first and second language acquisition), language in society (sociolinguistics), language variation (sociolinguistics again), or language diversity (typology, genetic linguistics, language contact studies, pidgin and creole linguistics). This has been demonstrated by the fact that all of these areas of linguistics had to be drawn on in some way or another in the course of arguing for the evolutionary framework for language change in this book.

In fact, language change is the glue that holds all of these facets of language together. The study of language change can easily be transmuted into the study of language itself, because language is fundamentally a variable, dynamic phenomenon. The focus on a linguistic system described and criticized in §1.1 has obscured this fact for the last century. But, as argued there, a linguistic system taken in isolation is a mythical object, neither a type nor a token, and hence not a proper object of scientific study. The proper objects of the study of language are actually occurring utterances and an actual speaker's knowledge about her language.

An evolutionary analysis of actual language (utterances and speaker knowledge) posits the existence of further entities: linguemes and their interrelationships in utterances and in the speaker's mind (§2.4; chapter 6); the delimitation of populations of speakers and utterances into communities and societies and the languages/codes associated with them respectively (§4.2.3); and conventions of language as a speaker's knowledge of the common ground between her and her interlocutors (§4.2.4). These concepts reintroduce the notion of a linguistic system, now empirically firmly grounded in existing speakers and utterances. But the linguistic system that the evolutionary framework reveals is quite different from that posited in the structuralist and generative traditions.

What does the linguistic system look like from an evolutionary perspective? The fact that language is so prone to hybridization (mixing) in utterances, dialects and languages offers a hint as to the true nature of the linguistic system. Grant makes an interesting and important observation as to why plants are more prone to hybridization and hybrid speciation than animals are. It is worth quoting him at length:

> An obvious and basic difference between plants and animals lies in the degree of complexity of the individual organism. The development of the relatively simple plant body is commensurate with an open system of growth by which new parts are built up in series. The animal body is a vastly more complex and delicately balanced organization and, furthermore, is one which must develop as a whole and by a closed system of growth. It is logical to suppose that the gene systems controlling growth and development differ correspondingly in complexity and integration in the two types of organisms.
>
> This single premise will account for the two main factors contributing to the partial or complete breakdown of species organization in many plant groups . . .
>
> A species possessing a highly integrated and finely balanced genotype will suffer relatively worse effects from interspecific hybridization than will a species with a simpler and more loosely coordinated set of genes. The relatively simple physiological-morphological organization of the plant body, reflecting a correspondingly relatively simple genotype, probably gives plants a greater tolerance for interspecific gene exchange than is present in most animal groups. (Grant 1981:75–6)

Grant's description of the organization of the animal genotype and phenotype is reminiscent of the structuralist description of a language system: a complex and finely balanced system, 'où tout se tient' in the famous phrase. This model of a language system may be derived in turn from the 19th-century model of a language as an organism – as an animal in particular, due to zoöcentrism.

I suggest instead that a language system is more like a plant than an animal. This suggestion is based on the high receptivity of languages to change by contact with other languages, often very different in grammatical structure (Thomason & Kaufman 1988:14–20), not to mention their high degree of communicative flexibility as described in §4.3. In essence, any lingueme can be borrowed without destroying the communicative power of a language: 'as far as the linguistic possibilities go, any linguistic feature can be transferred from any language to any other language' (Thomason & Kaufman 1988:14); 'given enough time and intensity of contact, virtually anything can (ultimately) be borrowed' (Harris & Campbell 1995:149).

A language is a loosely coordinated set of linguemes that is relatively simple compared with a truly finely balanced and complex system. Likewise, a speaker's knowledge about her language is not as finely balanced and complex a mental structure as some contemporary grammatical theories make it out to be. As Bolinger writes,

> Language may be an edifice where everything hangs together, but it has more patching and gluing about it than it has architectonics . . . a brick can crumble here and a termite can nibble there without setting off tremors from cellar to attic. I want to suggest that language is a structure, but in some ways a jerry-built structure. (Bolinger 1976:1)

Of course, the emphasis should be on the qualifier 'relatively'. Plants are extremely complex organisms compared with so-called lower forms of life, such as single-celled organisms. Plants are relatively simple only in comparison with animals. Likewise, human language systems are extremely complex compared with animal communication systems and various other sign systems, such as musical notation or the iconography of road signs. Nevertheless, the remarkable similarity of the phylogenetic patterns in languages and plants suggests that the structuralist model of a language is too rigid. Instead, as implied in this book, the linguistic system is not rigid, homogeneous, self-contained, or 'finely balanced'.

Although linguemes are organized in relationships of inclusiveness, higher-order linguemes often specify their lower-order parts independent of the autonomous organization of the lower-order structures (§2.4.3). Linguemes make up a lingueme pool replete with alleles (variants) which occur in various frequencies in a language (population of utterances), and in a speaker's mind relative to her exposure to the language (§3.3.1; chapter 7). These frequencies are dynamic, changing incrementally with every utterance spoken and heard. Linguemes are sufficiently loosely integrated that they can change relatively independently, and even be transferred from one phylogenetic line to another (chapter 8).

Communities and societies are not sharply delineated. Members of a society are simultaneously members of multiple communities (§4.2.3; §7.2), and no society is totally communicatively isolated from other societies (chapter 8). Nor are communities and societies homogeneous. Within a society and/or community, members themselves are differentiated by network tie strength (§7.4) and by the amount and type of common ground they share with other members of the community (§7.2). The heterogeneity and interpenetration of societies and communities is of course directly reflected in the heterogeneity of the languages delimited by them.

Conventions are conventions for communication – communication of social identification as well as semantic content (chapter 4; §7.4.2). But convention must always be supplemented by nonconventional devices for communication (§4.3.1). And the line between conventional and nonconventional communication is not sharp (§4.3). This fact allows the interlocutors to reanalyze the relationship between form and meaning, thereby allowing internal innovations to be spawned (chapters 5–6). Finally, conventions themselves are never 100%

invariant; conventions are always in the process of being acquired, replaced or lost (§7.3).

The evolutionary framework for language – EVOLUTIONARY LINGUISTICS – will require a rethinking of the model of grammatical knowledge developed by grammatical theory. The result of that rethinking will look quite different from most contemporary grammatical theories (see Croft to appear b). But evolutionary linguistics also offers hope for a reintegration of the now fragmented field of linguistics, with the aim of producing a coherent theory of language taken as a whole.

Glossary of terms

This glossary includes terms from evolutionary biology, philosophy, psychology, historical linguistics and sociolinguistics that have been used in the text. Each entry contains the term, the section(s) where it is introduced and first discussed, a brief definition, and a reference, usually to a general book which defines the term or (for less widely accepted terms) to the introducer of the term. Absence of a reference indicates terms with specialized meanings introduced in this book.

abrupt creolization *see* creole

accommodation §7.4.2 a mechanism for selection, by which a speaker alters her utterance to resemble more closely the conventions of her interlocutors (Giles & Smith 1979)

actuation *see* innovation

act of identity §7.4.2 a mechanism for selection, by which a speaker alters her utterance to resemble more closely the conventions of a community with which she wants to identify herself (LePage & Tabouret-Keller 1985)

age-graded variation §3.2 variation in a speech community that does not represent change in progress, but instead patterns of speech adopted by each cohort as they age (Chambers 1995)

allele §2.4.1 one of a set of genes that occurs at the same locus in a chromosome (Dawkins 1982b)

altered replication *see* replication

analogy §3.4.1 an innovation in a lingueme (typically, a member of a morphological paradigm) that is based on the form of a closely related lingueme (McMahon 1994)

artifactual phenomenon §3.3.2 a phenomenon that is created by human design, such as a tool

autonomous variety §2.2 a variety whose speakers perceive themselves as being linguistically distinct from any other speech community (Chambers & Trudgill 1980)

borrowing §8.3.1, §8.3.2 the result of language contact on a society attempting to maintain its language; a lingueme contributed by the encroaching language (Thomason & Kaufman 1988)

child-based theory §3.2 a theory of language change that treats a speaker's grammar as the replicator; altered replication occurs through a child learning a language, and selection occurs through the mortality of the older generation of speakers

code   §4.2.3   a language specific to a single community or domain (Wardhaugh 1992)

code-mixing   §8.4.1   the production of utterances in which linguemes from two different languages are mixed (usually, within a clause) to the point that it is difficult to specify which language is being spoken (Romaine 1995)

code-switching   §8.4.1   the process of using two languages in a single conversation in a single social setting, switching from one to the other typically above the clause level (Romaine 1995)

common ground   §4.2.3   mutual knowledge shared by a set of people. Communal common ground is shared by a community by virtue of shared expertise; personal common ground is shared by individuals by virtue of shared experience, direct (perceptual basis) or indirect (discourse basis) (Clark 1996).

communal common ground   *see* common ground

communal lexicon   §4.2.3   the lexical items specific to a particular community (Clark 1996)

communicative isolation   §2.2   the absence of significant communicative interaction between populations of speakers

community   §4.2.3   a population of speakers defined by some sort of shared expertise (Clark 1996)

community's meaning   §4.3.2   a lineage of the meanings (including full contextual meaning) for a particular word or construction produced on occasions of use in a community

competence   §3.4.2   a particular speaker's knowledge about the linguistic conventions of the communities to which she belongs

conceptual space   §6.2.3   the organization in the mind of concepts with links of varying kinds and varying degrees of closeness; the space over which intraference takes place (Croft to appear b)

convention   §4.2.4   an arbitrary regularity of behavior (a coordination device) which is common ground in a community, used for a recurrent coordination problem (Lewis 1969). A linguistic expression is a linguistic convention. A commonly used term for 'convention' in sociolinguistics is 'norm' (e.g. Milroy 1992b).

convergence   §8.3.2   a linguistic situation arising when two or more groups speaking different languages cohabit, becoming multilingual but retaining their languages (Gumperz & Wilson 1971)

coordination device   §4.2.4   a behavior that is employed by individuals to solve a coordination problem (Lewis 1969). Coordination devices include convention, joint salience, explicit agreement and precedent.

coordination problem   §4.2.4   a situation where two people attempt to converge on the same solution to a problem, overcoming the fact that each cannot read the other's mind (Lewis 1969)

core expertise   §4.2.3   that shared expertise which is found in a large number of communities

covert prestige   §7.4.2   the type of prestige gained by a speech community in a subordinate position in society with which speakers want to identify by using lingueme variants of that speech community (Wardhaugh 1992)

creole, creolization §8.6 a pidgin that has become the first language of a group of speakers, and the process by which children acquire a pidgin and expand it (Mühlhäusler 1986). If the creole arises through children acquiring a jargon rather than a pidgin, the process is called abrupt creolization.

cryptanalysis §5.5 a type of form–function reanalysis where the speaker inserts an element overtly expressing a meaning that is covertly entailed by another element in the construction

death by borrowing §8.4.3 a process, resulting in a type of mixed language where the speakers are resisting an encroaching society but borrowing more and more linguemes from the encroaching society's language

deme §2.2 a population in a species which has a high likelihood of inter-breeding; less inclusive than a geographical race (Hull 1988)

density §7.2 *see* network

dictionary §4.3.2 the description of word meanings in the lexicon according to a view that the meaning of a word or construction can be reduced to a small finite set of semantic features (Haiman 1980a)

differential replication *see* replication

diffuse §8.4.1 the description of a society characterized by weak ties; its language is expected to have more variants and fewer fixed conventions (LePage & Tabouret-Keller 1985)

diffusion *see* propagation

diglossia §2.2, §4.2.3 the state of affairs in a society in which two languages exist but each language is used in different domains. The H variety is typically a second language and the L variety is a first language (Ferguson 1959/ 1972).

discourse basis §4.2.3 the experience shared by individuals by virtue of being reported by one individual to the other, which is one of the shared bases for personal common ground (Clark 1996; Clark calls this 'actional basis')

DNA §1.1 the molecule that contains the genes of an organism (Hull 1988).

domain §4.2.3 an area of human experience, which can be characterized by shared expertise, and gives rise to a community and a code for that community (Wardhaugh 1992)

downward specification §2.4.3 the view that information combining features of two different linguistic levels in the hierarchy of inclusiveness of linguemes should be represented at the more inclusive level

drag-chain §3.4.1 a change which is explained as arising in order to fill a gap in a language system (McMahon 1994)

drift §2.3 a shift in gene (lingueme) frequencies that occurs through altered replication but without selection (Hull 1988)

early adopters §7.4.3 central members of a social network who are hypothesized to transmit innovations from innovators to the rest of the network (Milroy & Milroy 1985)

economy principle §3.4.4 the principle that speakers minimize the effort involved in their linguistic expressions (Keller 1990/1994); motivated by the immediacy premise and constrained by the extent of the interlocutor's common ground

encyclopedia §4.3.2   the description of word meanings in the lexicon according to a view that the meaning of a word or construction must access all of the knowledge associated with the concept in question (Haiman 1980a)

entrenchment §2.4.2   the psychological routinization of a behavior, such as the behavior of recognizing a linguistic expression and producing it (Langacker 1987)

environment §2.3   the complex system with an interactor interacts as a cohesive whole, thereby causing differential replication of the relevant replicators (Hull 1988)

erosion §6.3.2   the stage in the grammaticalization cycle at which a grammaticalizing expression is phonologically and morphologically reduced (Lüdtke 1986; Keller 1990/1994)

essentialism §2.2   the view that a species is defined by a set of necessary properties of the organisms making up that species (Mayr 1982), or that a language is defined by a set of structural properties of that language (Chambers & Trudgill 1980)

etymology §2.4.3   a lineage for a word

exaptation *see* hypoanalysis

expanded pidgin §8.5   a pidgin that is used in a wide range of domains (communities) in a society (Mühlhäusler 1986)

explicit agreement §4.3.1   a nonconventional coordination device which solves a coordination problem by a preset, explicit agreement between the individuals (Lewis 1969)

extension *see* intraference

external change §1.2   a language change that arises as a result of contact between two societies speaking different languages (Hock 1986)

First Law of Propagation §7.3   the observation that competition between variants in a community always proceeds in the direction of establishing one conventional variant for a specific meaning in a particular community

focused §8.4.1   the description of a society characterized by strong ties; its language is expected to have fewer variants and more fixed conventions (LePage & Tabouret-Keller 1985)

form–function reanalysis §5.1   a mechanism for innovation in language change by which a speaker alters the mapping between formal component elements of an utterance and the elements of the semantic structure conveyed by the utterance

fudged form §6.1   an intermediate variant of a lingueme arising through contact between two existing varieties (Chambers & Trudgill 1980)

fudged lect §2.2, §7.4.3   a language variety possessing an intermediate variant arising through contact between two existing varieties (Chambers & Trudgill 1980)

functional explanation §3.4   an explanation of a language change by appeal to an intentional mechanism

functional turnover §8.4.3   the process by which a speech community encroached upon by another speech community gives up their language as a general purpose communication system, but retains its lexicon and possibly some constructions as a specialized register (code) (Matras 2000)

fusion §6.3.2 the stage in the grammaticalization cycle at which a grammaticalizing expression is established as a fixed conventional unit of the language (Lüdtke 1986, Keller 1990/1994)

gene §2.4 the basic unit of heredity in an organism, constituted in the DNA; also the replicator in the basic selection process in biological evolution (Dawkins 1982b)

gene pool §2.4.1 all of the genes found in a population of organisms (Dawkins 1982b)

genotype §2.5 the set of genes that define the phenotype of a particular organism (Dawkins 1982b)

geographical race §2.2 a population that is less inclusive than a species but is defined by a geographical sub-area occupied by the species; more inclusive than a deme (Hull 1988)

grammar §2.4.1 an actual speaker's knowledge about her language; the replicator in child-based theories of language change

grammaticalization §3.3.3, §6.3 the process by which a construction with full lexical items acquires grammatical functions thereby turning the lexical item(s) into grammatical morphemes (Hopper & Traugott 1993). The various grammaticalization processes are given in §6.3.1, Table 6.1. Grammaticalization processes can be arranged in a grammaticalization cycle of periphrasis-fusion-erosion.

grammaticalization chain §2.4.3 a lineage of a construction and its grammatical morphemes (Heine, Claudi & Hünnemeyer 1991)

heteronomous variety §2.2 a variety whose speakers perceive themselves as being linguistically a part of another speech community (Chambers & Trudgill 1980)

hybrid language §8.4.2 a language created by the merging of the lingueme pools of two other languages. Occurs only between closely related languages or dialects (cf. mixed languages).

hybridization §8.1 the process by which a new organism is created by the interbreeding of two organisms from different species (Grant 1981)

hyperanalysis §5.2 a type of form–function reanalysis where the speaker removes a semantic feature that has been inherent in an element of the construction and maps it onto the context (including linguistic context) instead

hypercorrection §3.4.4 a mechanism of innovation in sound change where the hearer factors out a phonetic feature in the signal that is part of the inherent specification of a phoneme (Ohala 1981)

hypoanalysis §5.3 a type of form–function reanalysis where the speaker takes a semantic feature of the context and maps it onto an inherent feature of an element of the construction. Same as exaptation (Lass 1990), regrammaticalization (Greenberg 1991).

hypocorrection §3.4.4 a mechanism of innovation in sound change where the hearer interprets a contextually determined phonetic feature in the signal as part of the inherent specification of a phoneme (Ohala 1981)

immediacy premise   §4.2.4   the assumption by interlocutors that the speaker will make the coordination problem posed by communication as quick to solve as possible (Clark 1996)

individual's meaning   §4.3.2   an individual speaker's actual knowledge about the lineage of the meanings (including full contextual meaning) for a particular word or construction produced on occasions of use to which she has been exposed (including her own uses)

inherent change   §1.2   changes to a single enduring entity over time (Hull 1988)

innovation   §1.2   the creation of a novel variant by altered replication of a lingueme in an utterance

innovator   *see* introducer

intentional mechanism   §3.4   a mechanism of altered replication or selection of linguemes by which a speaker produces a variant in order to achieve some other goal in the communicative interaction

interactor   §2.3   the entity that interacts with its environment in such a way as to cause replication to be differential (Hull 1988)

interbreeding   *see* reproductive isolation, population

interference   §6.1   the process by which a foreign language lingueme is produced in a language by interlingual identification (Weinreich 1968)

interlingual identification   §6.1   the mechanism by which linguemes from two different languages in a bilingual individual are identified as the same in some respect, allowing for interference (Weinreich 1968)

internal change   §1.2   an innovation that is produced by a mechanism other than interference by contact with another language (Hock 1986)

intraference   §6.2   the process by which a novel variant of a form with a new meaning is produced by intralingual identification. Basically equivalent to extension (Harris & Campbell 1995)

intralingual identification   §6.2   the mechanism by which a form is associated with a closely related meaning in the conceptual space of an individual language

introducer   §7.4.1   a speaker who introduces a variant of a lingueme from another community into the introducer's community. Same as innovator (Milroy & Milroy 1985).

introgression   §7.4.1, §8.1   the process by which a hybrid organism backcrosses with one of its parent species, thereby introducing genes from the other species into the gene pool of the first species (Grant 1981)

isolating mechanism   §8.2   a mechanism that brings about the reproductive isolation (or, in the case of speakers, communicative isolation) of a population of organisms (speakers) (Grant 1981)

jargon   §8.5   a simplified code of a language, used for communication in a restricted domain between two societies that do not have a language in common, that is not yet conventionalized (Mühlhäusler 1986)

joint attention   §4.2.3   the ability of two human beings to focus their shared attention on some entity (Clark 1996)

joint construal §4.3.3   the joint understanding by speaker and hearer of the meaning of the speaker's utterance (Clark 1996)

joint salience §4.3.1   a nonconventional coordination device exploiting the perceptual or cognitive salience of some entity or concept that is shared by two or more individuals (Clark 1996)

koinéization §7.4.4   the process by which a group of speakers of different dialects creates a new unified society with a new language that is based on the former dialects (Trudgill 1986)

language §2.4.1   a population of utterances. The term 'language system' is used where necessary to distinguish the population definition of a language from the view that a language is a system of conventions.

lexical diffusion §7.4.3   propagation of a sound change gradually through the lexicon, but involving phonetically abrupt altered replication of the lexical item with the new phonetic value (McMahon 1994)

lineage §2.3   the chain of replications of a gene (or lingueme) (Hull 1988)

lingua franca §8.5   a language used for communication among societies that do not have a language in common; specifically, the language of one of the societies in a relatively unsimplified form, in contrast to a pidgin (Wardhaugh 1992)

lingueme §2.4.1   a unit of linguistic structure, as embodied in particular utterances, that can be inherited in replication; the replicator in the basic linguistic selection process; the linguistic equivalent of a gene. The term 'lingueme' will refer to a lingueme token; otherwise the term 'lingueme type' is used.

lingueme pool §2.4.1   the total number of linguemes (including all variants) found in a population of utterances; the linguistic equivalent to a gene pool

linguistic area §8.3.2   a geographical area occupied by societies speaking different languages, but possessing some degree of multilingualism such that linguemes are diffused through the languages in the area (Chambers & Trudgill 1980)

locus §2.4.1   a specific location on a chromosome (or in an utterance) where a single gene occurs. Only one of a set of gene alleles (lingueme variants) can occur at a single locus (Dawkins 1982b). A linguistic locus corresponds to a linguistic variable in sociolinguistic theory.

meiosis §1.1   the process of cell division where a cell gives rise to two cells each with half as many chromosomes as the parent; essential to sexual reproduction (Hull 1988)

meme §2.1   a unit of cultural inheritance, analogous to a gene (or lingueme) (Dawkins 1976)

metanalysis §5.4   a type of form–function reanalysis where the speaker simultaneously interprets a semantic feature of the context as an inherent feature of an element of the construction, and interprets a correlated inherent semantic feature of the construction as a feature of the context. Same as pragmatic inference; the chief mechanism for semantic change in grammaticalization.

metaphor §6.3.2   a process of semantic change that is semantically abrupt, applying a word from one semantic domain (the source domain) to another domain (the target domain) by virtue of certain abstract schematic similarities between the domains (Lakoff & Johnson 1980)

mixed language §8.4.3   a language in which there are major portions of the linguemes in its lingueme pool from two (or more) parent languages (Thomason & Kaufman 1988)

mixed marriage language §8.4.3   a mixed language resulting from a high degree of mixed marriages between speakers of two languages; the two best-known cases (Mednyj Aleut and Michif) involve marriages between exogenous fathers and indigenous mothers

mixed lect §2.2   a language variety possessing lexical items with different variants of a phoneme arising through contact between two existing varieties (Chambers & Trudgill 1980)

multiplexity §7.2   *see* network

natural phenomenon §3.3.2   a phenomenon that occurs as a result of natural physical processes, without human intention involved (Keller 1990/1994)

neogrammarian change §7.4.3   a sound change that is phonetically gradual but occurs simultaneously in all lexical items containing the phoneme (McMahon 1994)

network §2.2, §7.2   a group of speakers defined by their social links with each other (Wardhaugh 1992). Networks vary in density (how many individuals know each other) and multiplexity (in how many different domains the individuals know each other). Individuals have relatively strong or weak ties, defined in terms of density, multiplexity, and intimacy of links with other individuals in the network.

nonconventional coordination device §4.3.1   a behavior other than convention that is employed by individuals to solve a coordination problem (Clark 1996)

nonintentional mechanism §3.4   a mechanism for altered replication or selection of linguemes that is an unintended side-effect of intentionally conforming to convention (i.e. normal replication)

norm *see* convention

normal replication *see* replication

perceptual basis §4.2.3   the experience shared by individuals by virtue of their directing joint attention to the experience, which is one of the shared bases for personal common ground (Clark 1996)

periphrasis §6.3.2   the stage in the grammaticalization cycle at which a construction is used for a novel function that is 'grammatical' (that is, falls into the regions of conceptual space that are typically expressed by grammatical morphemes in languages)

personal common ground *see* common ground

personal lexicon §4.2.3   the lexical items specific to a particular group or pair of individuals (Clark 1996)

phenotype §2.5   the manifested physical and behavioral features of an organism (Dawkins 1982b)

phylogeny §2.2 the historical patterns of descent for organisms (or languages) (Dawkins 1982b). In linguistics, the term 'genetic' rather than 'phylogenetic' is used.

pidgin, pidginization §8.5 a simplified code of a language, used for communication in a restricted domain between two societies that do not have a language in common, that has become conventionalized. The process of developing such a code is pidginization (Mühlhäusler 1986).

polytypic species, language §2.2 a species (or language) whose organisms (dialects) are so different structurally that they would be divided into multiple species in an essentialist view (Mayr 1982)

population §2.2 a group of organisms united by the possibility of interbreeding and defined by their reproductive isolation from other organisms (Mayr 1982). Reproductive isolation is relative for populations smaller than a species. A gene pool is a population defined by the population of organisms that contains them. The population approach to defining species contrasts with the essentialist approach. In language, a population is a group of speakers united by the possibility of communicative interaction and defined by their communicative isolation from other speakers. Communicative isolation is relative for populations smaller than a language. The utterances produced by speakers form a population, as does the lingueme pool contained in the population of utterances.

postcreole continuum §3.2, §8.4.2 a range of intermediate utterance forms that arise when a creole comes into contact with its primary parent language, and no focused intermediate variety develops (Wardhaugh 1992)

power §7.4.2 an asymmetrical relationship between members of two different communities such that one member (community) is dominant and the other subordinate in the relevant social context (Wardhaugh 1992). The dominant power group has greater (overt) prestige.

pragmatic inference §6.3.2 *see* metanalysis

precedent §4.3.1 a nonconventional coordination device by which speakers solve a coordination problem using an already established precedent (Lewis 1969)

prestige *see* power

primary language birth §8.2 the evolution of a new language by divergence of a dialect subpopulation from the parent language population

primary parent language §8.4.3 the language that contributes the majority of the basic vocabulary linguemes of a mixed language

primary speciation §8.1 the evolution of a new species by divergence of a subpopulation from the parent species population (Grant 1981)

propagation §1.2 the increase in frequency of a lingueme in a language by selection

push-chain §3.4.1 a change which is explained as arising in order to avoid two forms occupying the same position in a language system (McMahon 1994)

regrammaticalization *see* hypoanalysis

reinforcement §3.4.1 an innovation by which a new variant of a lingueme is concatenated with the older variant

repertoire §4.2.3 the set of linguistic codes that a speaker knows (Wardhaugh 1992)

replacement §3.4.1 an innovation by which a new variant of a lingueme is substituted for the older variant

replication §§1.1–1.2, §2.3 the process by which an entity (the replicator) produces a copy that possesses a version of inherent structure of the original entity (Hull 1988; Dawkins 1976). Replication can be normal (identical with the structure of the parent) or altered (not completely identical with the structure of the parent). Differential replication is the replication of a replicator at an increasing (or decreasing) relative frequency compared with other replicators.

replicator §2.3 an entity that replicates its structure (Dawkins 1982b, Hull 1988)

reproductive isolation §2.2 the (relative) absence of interbreeding between members of distinct populations of organisms (Hull 1988)

reticulation §8.1 the merging of two independent phylogenetic lines; common in plant species (Grant 1981)

S-curve §7.4.3 the typical pattern by which a novel variant is propagated through a population of utterances (Kroch 1989)

Schelling game §4.2.4 a type of cooperative game in game theory in which two players attempt to converge on the same solution to a coordination problem. In third-party Schelling games, the game is designed by a third person. In first-party Schelling games, including communication, the game is designed by one of the players, e.g. the speaker (Lewis 1969; Clark 1996).

schematic lingueme §8.3.1 a lingueme that is only a schema or template for a construction, word order, word structure, phonotactic structure, etc. A schematic lingueme does not contain any actual morphemes or phonemes.

selection §2.3 the process by which an interactor interacting with its environment causes differential replication of its replicators; also the evolutionary model of processes that requires the generation of variation by (altered) replication and the selection of variants (Hull 1988)

semi-shift §8.4.3 a process by which a group of speakers adopts most of the vocabulary of the language of another group of speakers, but retains the grammatical constructions and inflections or function words of its ancestral language

shared expertise §4.2.3 the shared knowledge, skills and practices in a domain of human activity. Shared expertise forms the basis for defining a community (Clark 1996).

shift §8.3.1 the process by which a society gives up its ancestral language for the language of another society (Thomason & Kaufman 1988)

sibling species, language §2.2 two species (languages) that are reproductively (communicatively) isolated but are so similar structurally that they would be considered a single species (language) in the essentialist approach (Grant 1981)

signal meaning   §4.3.2   the conventional meaning of a linguistic expression (Clark 1996)

signaling system   §4.2.4   a system of conventions for evoking a meaning in the hearer's mind that is in some sense equivalent to the meaning in the speaker's mind (Lewis 1969)

social network   see **network**

society   §4.2.3, §7.2   a group of individuals that are (relatively) communicatively isolated. A society includes all the communities which its members belong to.

solidarity   §7.4.2   a symmetrical relationship between two members of a community such that neither is in a power relation over the other, and the two are socially relatively intimate (Wardhaugh 1992)

speaker's meaning   §4.3.2   the meaning conveyed by a linguistic expression on a particular occasion of use, including all of its contextual richness (Clark 1996)

species   §2.2   a reproductively isolated population of organisms that interbreeds (Hull 1988)

speech community   *see* **community**

spreading activation model   §7.2   a model of the mental representation and thought where all knowledge is organized into a network of neural connections, and thought processes are modeled in terms of the activation of relevant nodes. Activation spreads from one node to other linked nodes (Collins & Loftus 1975).

strong tie   *see* network

structural (definition of a language)   *see* **essentialism**

structural reanalysis   §6.3.2   the assignment of a new syntactic structure to an existing construction (contrast with form–function reanalysis)

substance lingueme   §8.3.1   a lingueme containing specific phonological substance, i.e. one or more specific phonemes, morphemes or words

substratum interference   §8.3.1   the result of language contact when a society shifts to the language of another society; the linguemes contributed by the ancestral language of the shifting population to the acquired language (Thomason & Kaufman 1988)

sufficiency premise   §4.2.4   the assumption by interlocutors that the speaker will provide enough information in the coordination problem posed by communication to allow the hearer to solve it (Clark 1996)

symplesiomorphy   §2.2   a shared trait between two species or languages that is retained from the parent species (Lass 1997)

synapomorphy   §2.2   a shared trait between two species or languages that is an innovation of the two species (Lass 1997)

systemic functional explanation   §3.4   an explanation of a language change in terms of the speaker intentionally making the language system simpler, more symmetrical, etc.

teleological mechanism   §3.4.1   a mechanism of altered replication or selection of linguemes in which changing (or preserving) the language system in some way is the intentional goal of the speaker

tie strength *see* network

upward specification §2.4.3 the view that information combining features of two different linguistic levels in the hierarchy of inclusiveness of linguemes should be represented at the less inclusive level

utterance §2.4.1 an actually occurring piece of language, completely specified at all levels of structure, including its full contextual meaning on the particular occasion of use (i.e. speaker's meaning). The utterance is made up of linguemes, which are the replicators in utterance-based theories of language change.

utterance-based theory §3.1 a theory of language change that treats the linguistic features (linguemes) of an utterance as the replicator; altered replication and selection both occur through production of utterances in language use

Utterance Selection, Theory of §2.4.1 the theory that the utterance contains the paradigm replicators (the linguemes) in language change, altered replication of grammar largely occurs through form–function reanalysis, and selection occurs through social mechanisms

variable §2.4.1, §3.3.1 a locus for a set of variants of a lingueme

variant §2.4.1 one of a set of linguemes that can occur in one locus in a given utterance; equivalent to allele in biological evolution

variety §2.2 a population of organisms smaller than a species (Hull 1988); also a neutral term to describe a language, dialect or code (Chambers & Trudgill 1980)

weak tie §7.4.1 *see* network

References

ADAMS, KAREN LEE. 1989. *Systems of numeral classification in the Mon-Khmer, Nicobarese and Aslian subfamilies of Austroasiatic.* (Pacific Linguistics, Series B, No. 101.) Canberra: Australian National University.

AITCHISON, JEAN. 1989. *The articulate mammal: an introduction to psycholinguistics* (3rd edn). London: Routledge.

AITCHISON, JEAN. 1991. *Language change: progress or decay?* (2nd edn). Cambridge: Cambridge University Press.

AITCHISON, JEAN. 2000. Psycholinguistic perspectives on language change. *Handbook of historical linguistics,* ed. Richard D. Janda & Brian D. Joseph. Oxford: Blackwell.

ALLEN, CYNTHIA L. 1995. *Case marking and reanalysis: grammatical relations from Old to Early Modern English.* Oxford: Clarendon Press.

ALLEN, CYNTHIA L. 1997. Investigating the origins of the 'group genitive' in English. *Transactions of the Philological Society* 95.111–31.

ALLEN, CYNTHIA L. 2000. Obsolescence and sudden death in syntax: the decline of verb-final order in early Middle English. *Generative theory and corpus studies: a dialogue from 10ICEHL,* ed. Ricardo Bermúdez-Otero, David Denison, Richard M. Hogg & C. B. McCully, 3–25. Berlin: Mouton de Gruyter.

ANDERSEN, HENNING. 1973. Abductive and deductive change. *Language* 49.765–93.

ANDERSEN, HENNING. 1988. Center and periphery: adoption, diffusion, and spread. *Historical dialectology: regional and social,* ed. Jacek Fisiak, 39–83. Berlin: Mouton de Gruyter.

ANTTILA, RAIMO. 1989. *Historical and comparative linguistics* (2nd edn). Amsterdam: John Benjamins.

ARIEL, MIRA. 1990. *Accessing noun phrase antecedents.* New York: Routledge.

BAKKER, PETER & ROBERT A. PAPEN. 1997. Michif: a mixed language based on Cree and French. *Contact languages: a wider perspective,* ed. Sarah G. Thomason, 295–363. Amsterdam: John Benjamins.

BARSALOU, LAWRENCE W. 1987. The instability of graded structure: implications for the nature of concepts. *Concepts and conceptual development: ecological and intellectual factors in categorization,* ed. Ulric Neisser, 101–40. Cambridge: Cambridge University Press.

BARSALOU, LAWRENCE W. 1993. Flexibility, structure and linguistic vagary in concepts: manifestations of a compositional system of perceptual symbols. *Theories of memory,* ed. Alan F. Collins, Susan E. Gathercole, Martin A. Conway & Peter E. Morris, 29–101. Hillsdale, NJ: Lawrence Erlbaum Associates.

BAVIN, EDITH. 1992. The acquisition of Warlpiri. Slobin 1992, 309–71.

BELL, R. T. 1976. *Sociolinguistics: goals, approaches and problems.* London: Batsford.

BELLWOOD, PETER. 1991. The Austronesian dispersal and the origin of languages. *Scientific American* July 1991, 88–93.

245

BENGTSON, JOHN T. & MERRITT RUHLEN. 1994. Global etymologies. *On the origin of language*, ed. Merritt Ruhlen, 277–336. Stanford: Stanford University Press.

BERTONI, G. & M. G. BARTOLI. 1925. *Breviario de neolinguistica*. Modena: Società Tipografica Modenese.

BIBER, DOUGLAS. 1986. Spoken and written textual dimensions in English. *Language* 62.384–414.

BOLINGER, DWIGHT. 1975. *Aspects of language* (2nd edn). New York: Harcourt Brace Jovanovich.

BOLINGER, DWIGHT. 1976. Meaning and memory. *Forum Linguisticum* 1.1–14.

BOLINGER, DWIGHT. 1980. *Language, the loaded weapon*. London: Longmans.

BOWERMAN, MELISSA. 1982. Evaluating competing linguistic models with language acquisition data: implications of developmental errors with causative verbs. *Quaderni di semantica* 3.5–66.

BOWERMAN, MELISSA. 1988. The 'no negative evidence' problem: How do children avoid constructing an overly general grammar? *Explaining language universals*, ed. John A. Hawkins, 73–101. Oxford: Blackwell.

BRESNAN, JOAN & JONNI KANERVA. 1989. Locative inversion in Chichewa: a case study of factorization in grammar. *Linguistic Inquiry* 20.1–50.

BRIGHT, WILLIAM & A. K. RAMANUJAN. 1964. Sociolinguistic variation and language change. *Proceedings of the Ninth International Congress of Linguists*, ed. Horace Lunt, 1107–12. The Hague: Mouton.

BROCH, INGVILD & ERNST HÅKON JAHR. 1981. *Russenorsk: et pidginspråk i Norge*. Tromsøstudier i språkvitenskap 3. Oslo.

BROWN, PENELOPE & STEPHEN C. LEVINSON. 1978/1987. *Politeness*. Cambridge: Cambridge University Press. (Originally published as 'Universals of language usage: politeness phenomena', in Esther N. Goody (ed.), *Questions and politeness: strategies in social interaction*, 56–311. Cambridge: Cambridge University Press, 1978.)

BROWN, R. & A. GILMAN. 1960/1972. The pronouns of power and solidarity. *Language and social context*, ed. Pier Paolo Giglioli, 252–82. Harmondsworth: Penguin. (Originally appeared in *Style in language*, ed. Thomas A. Sebeok, 253–75. Cambridge, MA: MIT Press, 1960.)

BRUNNER, KARL. 1965. *An outline of Middle English grammar* (transl. G. K. W. Johnston). Oxford: Blackwell.

BUCK, CARL DARLING. 1949. *A dictionary of selected synonyms in the principal Indo-European languages*. Chicago: University of Chicago Press.

BYBEE, JOAN L. 1985. *Morphology: a study into the relation between meaning and form*. Amsterdam: John Benjamins.

BYBEE, JOAN L. 1994. The grammaticization of zero: asymmetries in tense and aspect systems. *Perspectives on grammaticalization*, ed. William Pagliuca, 235–54. Amsterdam: John Benjamins.

BYBEE, JOAN L. 2000. The phonology of the lexicon: evidence from lexical diffusion. *Usage-based models of language*, ed. Michael Barlow & Suzanne Kemmer, 65–85. Stanford: Center for the Study of Language and Information.

BYBEE, JOAN L. & ÖSTEN DAHL. 1989. The creation of tense and aspect systems in the languages of the world. *Studies in Language* 13.51–103.

BYBEE, JOAN L., REVERE D. PERKINS & WILLIAM PAGLIUCA. 1994. *The evolution of grammar: tense, aspect and modality in the languages of the world*. Chicago: University of Chicago Press.

BYBEE, JOAN L. & DAN I. SLOBIN. 1982a. Why small children cannot change language on their own: suggestions from the English past tense. *Papers from the 5th Interna-*

tional Conference on Historical Linguistics, ed. Anders Ahlqvist, 29–37. Amsterdam: John Benjamins.

BYBEE, JOAN L. & DAN I. SLOBIN. 1982b. Rules and schemas in the development and use of the English past tense. *Language* 58.265–89.

CAMPBELL, LYLE. 1991. Some grammaticalization changes in Estonian and their implications. *Approaches to grammaticalization, vol. I*, ed. Elizabeth Closs Traugott & Bernd Heine, 285–99. Amsterdam: John Benjamins.

CAVALLI-SFORZA, L. L., A. PIAZZA, P. MENOZZI, & J. MOUNTAIN. 1988. Reconstruction of human evolution: bringing together genetic, archaeological, and linguistic data. *Proceedings of the National Academy of Sciences of the USA* 85.6002–6.

CHAFE, WALLACE. 1982. Integration and involvement in speaking, writing and oral literature. *Spoken and written language*, ed. Deborah Tannen, 35–53. Norwood, NJ: Ablex.

CHAMBERS, J. K. 1992. Dialect acquisition. *Language* 68.673–705.

CHAMBERS, J. K. 1995. *Sociolinguistic theory*. Oxford: Blackwell.

CHAMBERS, J. K. & PETER TRUDGILL. 1980. *Dialectology*. Cambridge: Cambridge University Press.

CHEEPEN, CHRISTINE & JAMES MONAGHAN. 1990. *Spoken English: a practical guide*. London: Pinter Publishers.

CHEN, MATTHEW & HSIN-I HSIEH. 1971. The time variable in phonological change. *Journal of Linguistics* 7.1–13.

CHEN, MATTHEW & WILLIAM S.-Y. WANG. 1975. Sound change: actuation and implementation. *Language* 51.255–81.

CHOMSKY, NOAM. 1965. *Aspects of the theory of syntax*. Cambridge, MA: MIT Press.

CHOMSKY, NOAM. 1981. *Lectures on government and binding*. Dordrecht: Foris.

CHOMSKY, NOAM. 1986. *Knowledge of language*. New York: Praeger.

CHURCHWARD, C. MAXWELL. 1953. *Tongan grammar*. Nuku'alofa, Tonga: Taulua Press.

CLANCY, PATRICIA M. 1985. The acquisition of Japanese. Slobin 1985, 373–524.

CLARK, EVE V. & HERBERT H. CLARK. 1979. When nouns surface as verbs. *Language* 55.767–811.

CLARK, HERBERT H. 1992. *Arenas of language use*. Chicago & Stanford: University of Chicago Press and the Center for the Study of Language and Information.

CLARK, HERBERT H. 1996. *Using language*. Cambridge: Cambridge University Press.

CLARK, HERBERT H. 1998. Communal lexicons. *Context in language learning and language understanding*, ed. Kirsten Malmkjær & John Williams, 63–87. Cambridge: Cambridge University Press.

CLARK, ROBIN & IAN ROBERTS. 1993. A computational model of language learnability and language change. *Linguistic Inquiry* 24.299–345.

CLAUSNER, TIMOTHY C. & WILLIAM CROFT. 1999. Domains and image schemas. *Cognitive Linguistics* 10.1–31.

CLYNE, M. 1987. Constraints on code-switching: how universal are they? *Linguistics* 25.739–64.

COATES, JENNIFER. 1983. *The semantics of the modal auxiliaries*. London: Croom Helm.

COLE, PETER, WAYNE HARBERT, GABRIELLA HERMON, & S. N. SRIDHAR. 1980. The acquisition of subjecthood. *Language* 56.719–43.

COLLINS, ALLAN M. & ELIZABETH F. LOFTUS. 1975. A spreading-activation theory of semantic processing. *Psychological Review* 82:407–28.

CROFT, WILLIAM. 1990. *Typology and universals*. Cambridge: Cambridge University Press.

CROFT, WILLIAM. 1991. *Syntactic categories and grammatical relations: the cognitive organization of information*. Chicago: University of Chicago Press.

CROFT, WILLIAM. 1993. The role of domains in the interpretation of metaphors and metonymies. *Cognitive Linguistics* 4.335–70.

CROFT, WILLIAM. 1995a. Autonomy and functionalist linguistics. *Language* 71.490–532.

CROFT, WILLIAM. 1995b. Locative subjects and argument linking. Paper presented at the Workshop on Argument Structure, 17. Jahrestagung der Deutschen Gesellschaft für Sprachwissenschaft, Göttingen, Germany.

CROFT, WILLIAM. 1995c. Intonation units and grammatical structure. *Linguistics* 33.839–82.

CROFT, WILLIAM. 1996a. Linguistic selection: an utterance-based evolutionary theory of language change. *Nordic Journal of Linguistics* 19.99–139.

CROFT, WILLIAM. 1996b. 'Markedness' and 'universals': from the Prague school to typology. *Multiple perspectives on the historical dimensions of language*, ed. Kurt R. Jankowsky, 15–21. Münster: Nodus.

CROFT, WILLIAM. 1997. Review of Rudi Keller, *On language change: the invisible hand in language. Journal of Pragmatics* 27.393–402.

CROFT, WILLIAM. To appear a. Intonation units and grammatical structure in Wardaman and English.

CROFT, WILLIAM. To appear b. *Radical construction grammar: syntactic theory in typological perspective.* Oxford: Oxford University Press.

CROFT, WILLIAM, HAVA BAT-ZEEV SHYLDKROT & SUZANNE KEMMER. 1987. Diachronic semantic processes in the middle voice. *Papers from the 7th International Conference on Historical Linguistics*, ed. Anna Giacolone Ramat, Onofrio Carruba & Giuliano Bernini, 179–92. Amsterdam: John Benjamins.

CRUSE, D. ALAN & WILLIAM CROFT. To appear. *Cognitive linguistics.* Cambridge: Cambridge University Press.

DAVIES, WILLIAM D. & LUIS ENRIQUE SAM-COLOP. 1990. K'iche' and the structure of antipassive. *Language* 66.522–49.

DAWKINS, RICHARD. 1976. *The selfish gene.* New York: Oxford University Press.

DAWKINS, RICHARD. 1982a. Replicators and vehicles. *Current problems in sociobiology*, ed. King's College Sociobiology Group, 45–64. Cambridge: Cambridge University Press.

DAWKINS, RICHARD. 1982b. *The extended phenotype.* San Francisco: Freeman.

DAWKINS, R. M. 1916. *Modern Greek in Asia Minor: a study of the dialects of Silli, Cappadocia and Pháras with grammars, texts, translations, and glossary.* Cambridge: Cambridge University Press.

DE BOT, KEES, PAUL GOMMANS & CAROLA ROSSING. 1991. L1 loss in an L2 environment: Dutch immigrants in France. *First language attrition*, ed. Herbert W. Seliger & Robert M. Vago, 87–98. Cambridge: Cambridge University Press.

DECAMP, DAVID. 1971. Toward a generative analysis of a post-creole continuum. *Pidginization and creolization of languages*, ed. Dell Hymes, 349–70. Cambridge: Cambridge University Press.

DENISON, DAVID. 1990. The Old English impersonals revisited. *Papers from the 5th International Conference on English Historical Linguistics*, ed. Sylvia Adamson, Vivien Law, Nigel Vincent & Susan Wright, 111–40. Amsterdam: John Benjamins.

DIXON, R. M. W. 1980. *The languages of Australia.* Cambridge: Cambridge University Press.

DOBZHANSKY, THEODOSIUS. 1937. *Genetics and the origin of species.* New York: Columbia University Press.

DOKE, CLEMENT M. 1930. *Textbook of Zulu grammar* (2nd edn). Cape Town: Maskew Miller Longman.

DOWNING, PAMELA. 1977. On the creation and use of English compound nouns. *Language* 53.810–42.

DRACHMAN, GEBERELL. 1978. Child language and language change: a conjecture and some refutations. *Recent developments in historical phonology*, ed. Jacek Fisiak, 123–44. Berlin: Mouton.

DRESSLER, WOLFGANG. 1974. Diachronic puzzles for natural phonology. *Papers from the Parasession on Natural Phonology*, ed. Anthony Bruck, Robert A. Fox & Michael W. LaGaly, 95–102. Chicago: Chicago Linguistic Society.

DuBois, JOHN A. 1985. Competing motivations. *Iconicity in syntax*, ed. John Haiman, 343–66. Amsterdam: John Benjamins.

ECKERT, PENELOPE. 1989. *Jocks and burnouts: social categories and identity in the high school.* New York: Teachers College Press.

ECKMANN, JÁNOS. 1966. *Chagatay manual.* (Uralic and Altaic Series, 60.) Bloomington: Indiana University.

ELIADE, MIRCEA. 1952/1991. *Images and symbols: studies in religious symbolism* (transl. Philip Mairet). Princeton: Princeton University Press. (*Images et symboles: essais sur le symbolisme magico-religieux.* Paris: Gallimard, 1952).

ELMAN, JEFFREY L. & JAMES L. McCLELLAND. 1984. Speech perception as a cognitive process: the interactive activation model. *Speech and Language, Vol. 10*, ed. Norman Lass, 337–74. New York: Academic Press.

ESPINAL, M. T. 1992. Expletive negation and logical absorption. *The Linguistic Review* 9.333–58.

FAIRBANKS, G. H. & E. W. STEVICK. 1958. *Spoken East Armenian.* New York: American Council of Learned Societies.

FERGUSON, CHARLES. 1959/1972. Diglossia. *Language and social context: selected readings*, ed. Pier Paolo Giglioli, 232–51. Harmondsworth: Penguin Books. (Originally appeared in *Word* 15.325–40, 1959.)

FILLMORE, CHARLES J. 1982. Frame semantics. *Linguistics in the morning calm*, ed. The Linguistic Society of Korea, 111–37. Seoul: Hanshin.

FILLMORE, CHARLES J. 1985. Frames and the semantics of understanding. *Quaderni di semantica* 6.222–54.

FILLMORE, CHARLES J. & PAUL KAY. 1993. Construction Grammar Coursebook, Chapters 1–11 (Reading Materials for Ling. X20). University of California, Berkeley.

FISHMAN, JOSHUA. 1965/1972. The relationship between micro- and macro-sociolinguistics and the study of who speaks what language to whom and when. *Sociolinguistics: selected readings*, ed. J. B. Pride & J. Holmes, 15–32. Harmondsworth: Penguin Books. (Revised version of 'Who speaks what language to whom and when', *La linguistique* 2.67–88, 1965.)

FISHMAN, JOSHUA. 1972. The sociology of language. *Language and social context: selected readings*, ed. Pier Paolo Giglioli, 45–60. Harmondsworth: Penguin Books.

FOLEY, WILLIAM. 1991. *The Yimas language of New Guinea.* Stanford: Stanford University Press.

FORCHHEIMER, PAUL. 1953. *The category of person in language.* Berlin: Walter de Gruyter.

GABELENTZ, GEORG VON DER. 1901/1969. *Die Sprachwissenschaft: Ihre Aufgaben, Methoden und bisherigen Ergebnisse* (2nd edn). Leipzig/Tübingen: Gunter Narr. (Originally published 1901. Leipzig: T. O. Weigel Nachfolger.)

GADAMER, HANS-GEORG. 1972/1976. Semantics and hermeneutics. *Philosophical hermeneutics* (transl. David E. Linge), 82–94. Berkeley: University of California Press.

GELMAN, SUSAN A. & JOHN D. COLEY. 1991. Language and categorization: the acquisition of natural kind terms. *Perspectives on language and thought: interrelations and development*, ed. Susan A. Gelman & James P. Byrnes, 146–96. Cambridge: Cambridge University Press.

GENETTI, CAROL. 1986. The development of subordinators from postpositions in Bodic languages. *Proceedings of the Twelfth Annual Meeting of the Berkeley Linguistics Society*, ed. Vassiliki Nikiforidou *et al.*, 387–400.

GHISELIN, M. T. 1987. Species concepts, individuality, and objectivity. *Biology and Philosophy* 2.127–45.

GIBBS, RAYMOND W. JR. 1994. *The poetics of mind: figurative thought, language and understanding*. Cambridge: Cambridge University Press.

GILES, HOWARD & PHILIP M. SMITH. 1979. Accommodation theory: optimal levels of convergence. *Language and social psychology*, ed. Howard Giles & Robert N. St Clair. Oxford: Basil Blackwell.

GIVÓN, TALMY. 1979. *On understanding grammar*. New York: Academic Press.

GIVÓN, TALMY. 1981. Typology and functional domains. *Studies in Language* 5.163–93.

GLINERT, LEWIS. 1989. *The grammar of Modern Hebrew*. Cambridge: Cambridge University Press.

GOLDBERG, ADELE E. 1995. *Constructions: a construction grammar approach to argument structure*. Chicago: University of Chicago Press.

GOLOVKO, EVGENIJ V. 1996. A case of nongenetic development in the Arctic area: the contribution of Aleut and Russian to the formation of Copper Island Aleut. *Language contact in the Arctic: northern pidgins and contact languages*, ed. Ernst Håkon Jahr & Ingvild Broch, 63–77. Berlin: Mouton de Gruyter.

GOULD, STEVEN JAY. 1977. Eternal metaphors of palaeontology. *Patterns of evolution as illustrated by the fossil record*, ed. A. Hallan, 1–26. New York: Elsevier.

GRANOVETTER, MARK. 1973. The strength of weak ties. *American Journal of Sociology* 78.1360–80.

GRANOVETTER, MARK. 1982. The strength of weak ties: a network theory revisited. *Social structure and network analysis*, ed. P. V. Marsden & N. Lin, 105–30. London: Sage.

GRANT, VERNE. 1981. *Plant speciation* (2nd edn). New York: Columbia University Press.

GREENBERG, JOSEPH H. 1959/1990. The origin of the Masai passive. *Africa* 29.171–6. (Reprinted in Greenberg 1990, 412–18.)

GREENBERG, JOSEPH H. 1966. *Language universals, with special reference to feature hierarchies*. (Janua Linguarum, Series Minor 59.) The Hague: Mouton.

GREENBERG, JOSEPH H. 1966/1990. Some universals of grammar with particular reference to the order of meaningful elements. *Universals of grammar*, ed. Joseph H. Greenberg (2nd edn), 73–113. Cambridge, MA: MIT Press. (Reprinted in Greenberg 1990, 40–70.)

GREENBERG, JOSEPH H. 1978/1990. How does a language acquire gender markers? *Universals of human language, Vol. 3: word structure*, ed. Joseph H. Greenberg, Charles A. Ferguson & Edith A. Moravcsik, 47–82. Stanford: Stanford University Press. (Reprinted in Greenberg 1990, 241–70.)

GREENBERG, JOSEPH H. 1980. Circumfixes and typological change. *Papers from the 4th International Conference on Historical Linguistics*, ed. Elizabeth Traugott, Rebecca Labrum & Susan Shepherd, 233–41. Amsterdam: John Benjamins.

GREENBERG, JOSEPH H. 1981/1990. Nilo-Saharan movable k- as a Stage III article (with a Penutian typological parallel). *Journal of African Languages and Literature* 3.105–12. (Reprinted in Greenberg 1990, 476–83.)

GREENBERG, JOSEPH H. 1987. *Language in the Americas*. Stanford: Stanford University Press.

GREENBERG, JOSEPH H. 1990. *On language: selected writings of Joseph H. Greenberg*, ed. Keith Denning & Suzanne Kemmer. Stanford: Stanford University Press.

GREENBERG, JOSEPH H. 1991. The last stages of grammatical elements: contractive and expansive desemanticization. *Approaches to grammaticalization*, ed. Elizabeth Traugott & Bernd Heine, 301–14. Amsterdam: John Benjamins.

GREENBERG, JOSEPH H. 1999. Are there mixed languages? *Essays in poetics, literary history and linguistics*, ed. L. Fleishman, M. Gasparov, T. Nikolaeva, A. Ospovat, V. Toporov, A. Vigasin, R. Vroon & A. Zalizniak. 626–33. Moscow: OGI.

GREENBERG, JOSEPH H., CHRISTY G. TURNER II & STEPHEN L. ZEGURA. 1986. The settlement of the Americas: a comparison of the linguistic, dental and genetic evidence (with commentaries). *Current Anthropology* 27.477–97.

GRICE, H. PAUL. 1948/1989. Meaning. *Studies in the way of words*, 213–23. Cambridge, MA: Harvard University Press.

GRICE, H. PAUL. 1967/1989. Logic and conversation. *Studies in the Way of Words*, 1–143. Cambridge, MA: Harvard University Press.

GUILBERT, LOUIS. 1965. *La formation du vocabulaire de l'aviation* (2 vols.). Paris: Larousse.

GUMPERZ, JOHN J. 1968/1972. The speech community. *Language and social context*, ed. Pier Paolo Giglioli, 219–31. Harmondsworth: Penguin. (Originally published in *International Encyclopedia of the Social Sciences*, 381–6. New York: Macmillan.)

GUMPERZ, JOHN J. 1982. *Discourse strategies*. Cambridge: Cambridge University Press.

GUMPERZ, JOHN J. & ROBERT WILSON. 1971. Convergence and creolization: a case from the Indo-Aryan/Dravidian border. *Pidginization and creolization of languages*, ed. Dell Hymes, 151–67. Cambridge: Cambridge University Press.

HAEGEMAN, LILIANE. 1995. *The syntax of negation*. Cambridge: Cambridge University Press.

HAIMAN, JOHN. 1980a. Dictionaries and encyclopedias. *Lingua* 50.329–57.

HAIMAN, JOHN. 1980b. The iconicity of grammar: isomorphism and motivation. *Language* 54.565–89.

HAIMAN, JOHN. 1983. Iconic and economic motivation. *Language* 59.781–819.

HAIMAN, JOHN. 1985. *Natural syntax*. Cambridge: Cambridge University Press.

HAIMAN, JOHN. 1994. Ritualization and the development of language. *Perspectives on grammaticalization*, ed. William Pagliuca, 3–28. Amsterdam: John Benjamins.

HALLE, MORRIS. 1962. Phonology in generative grammar. *Word* 18.54–72.

HANKAMER, JORGE. 1977. Multiple analyses. Li 1977, 583–607.

HARE, MARY & JEFFREY L. ELMAN. 1995. Learning and morphological change. *Cognition* 56.61–98.

HARRIS, ALICE C. & LYLE CAMPBELL. 1995. *Historical syntax in cross-linguistic perspective*. Cambridge: Cambridge University Press.

HARRIS, KATERINA. 1976. *Colloquial Greek*. London: Routledge & Kegan Paul.

HASPELMATH, MARTIN. 1990. The grammaticization of passive morphology. *Studies in Language* 14.25–72.

HASPELMATH, MARTIN. 1997. *Indefinite pronouns*. Oxford: Oxford University Press.

HASPELMATH, MARTIN. 1998a. Does grammaticalization need reanalysis? *Studies in Language* 22.49–85.

HASPELMATH, MARTIN. 1998b. Review of Harris & Campbell 1995. *Linguistic Typology* 2.131–9.

HASPELMATH, MARTIN. 1998c. The semantic development of old presents: new futures and subjunctives without grammaticalization. *Diachronica* 15.29–62.

HASPELMATH, MARTIN. 1999. Optimality and diachronic adaptation. *Zeitschrift für Sprachwissenschaft* 18.180–205.

HAUGEN, EINAR. 1966/1972. Dialect, language, nation. *The ecology of language: essays by Einar Haugen*, ed. Anwar S. Dil, 237–54. Stanford: Stanford University Press. (Originally appeared in *American Anthropologist* 68.922–35.)

HAUGEN, EINAR. 1968/1972. The Scandinavian languages as cultural artifacts. *The ecology of language: essays by Einar Haugen*, ed. Anwar S. Dil, 265–86. Stanford: Stanford University Press. (Originally appeared in *Language problems of developing nations*, ed. Joshua A. Fishman, Charles A. Ferguson & Jyotirindra Das Gupta, 267–84. New York: Wiley.)

HEATH, JEFFREY. 1978. *Linguistic diffusion in Arnhem Land.* Canberra: Australian Institute of Aboriginal Studies.

HEATH, JEFFREY. 1981. A case of intensive lexical diffusion: Arnhem Land, Australia. *Language* 57.335–67.

HEATH, JEFFREY. 1989. *From code-switching to borrowing: a case study of Moroccan Arabic.* London: Kegan Paul International.

HEINE, BERND. 1994. Grammaticalization as an explanatory parameter. *Perspectives on grammaticalization*, ed. William Pagliuca, 255–87. Amsterdam: John Benjamins.

HEINE, BERND & MECHTHILD REH. 1984. *Grammaticalization and reanalysis in African languages.* Hamburg: Helmut Buske Verlag.

HEINE, BERND, ULRIKE CLAUDI & FRIEDERIEKE HÜNNEMEYER. 1991. *Grammaticalization: a conceptual framework.* Chicago: University of Chicago Press.

HERINGER, HANS J. 1988. An axiomatics of language evolution. Mimeo, Augsburg.

HOCK, HANS HEINRICH. 1986. *Principles of historical linguistics.* Berlin: Mouton de Gruyter.

HOGG, RICHARD M. 1992. Phonology and morphology. *The Cambridge history of the English language, Vol. I: The beginnings to 1066*, ed. Richard M. Hogg, 67–167. Cambridge: Cambridge University Press.

HOLM, JOHN. 1988. *Pidgins and creoles, Vol. 1.* Cambridge: Cambridge University Press.

HOLM, JOHN. 1989. *Pidgins and creoles, Vol. 2.* Cambridge: Cambridge University Press.

HOOPER, JOAN BYBEE. 1980. Child morphology and morphophonemic change. *Historical morphology*, ed. Jacek Fisiak, 157–87. Berlin: Mouton.

HOPPER, PAUL & ELIZABETH TRAUGOTT. 1993. *Grammaticalization.* Cambridge: Cambridge University Press.

HORN, LAURENCE R. 1978. Some aspects of negation. *Universals of human language, Volume 4: Syntax*, ed. Joseph H. Greenberg, Charles A. Ferguson & Edith A. Moravscik, 127–210. Stanford: Stanford University Press.

HORN, LAURENCE R. 1991. Duplex negatio affirmat . . . : the economy of double negation. *Parasession on negation, 27th Regional Meeting of the Chicago Linguistic Society*, ed. Lise M. Dobson, Lynn Nichols & Rosa M. Rodriguez, 80–106. Chicago: Chicago Linguistic Society.

HULL, DAVID L. 1988. *Science as a process: an evolutionary account of the social and conceptual development of science.* Chicago: University of Chicago Press.

HURFORD, JAMES R., MICHAEL STUDDERT-KENNEDY & CHRIS KNIGHT (eds.). 1998. *Approaches to the evolution of language: social and cognitive bases.* Cambridge: Cambridge University Press.

HYMES, DELL. 1972. On communicative competence. *Sociolinguistics: selected readings*, ed. J. B. Pride & J. Holmes, 269–93. Harmondsworth: Penguin Books.

IHALAINEN, OSSI. 1991. Periphrastic *do* in affirmative sentences in the dialect of East Somerset. *Dialects of English: studies in grammatical variation*, ed. Peter Trudgill & J. K. Chambers, 148–160. London: Longman.

INGRAM, DAVID. 1978. Typology and universals of personal pronouns. *Universals of human Language, Vol. 3: Word structure*, ed. Joseph H. Greenberg, Charles A. Ferguson & Edith A. Moravcsik, 213–48. Stanford: Stanford University Press.

JABLONSKI, D. 1986. Background and mass extinctions: the alternative of macroevolutionary regimes. *Science* 231.129.

JABLONSKI, D. 1987. Heritability at the species level: an analysis of geographic ranges of cretaceous mollusks. *Science* 238.360–3.

JACKENDOFF, RAY. 1990. *Semantic structures*. Cambridge, MA: MIT Press.

JAHR, ERNST HÅKON. 1996. On the pidgin status of Russenorsk. *Language contact in the Arctic: northern pidgins and contact languages*, ed. Ernst Håkon Jahr & Ingvild Broch, 107–22. Berlin: Mouton de Gruyter.

JAKOBSON, ROMAN. 1929/1962. *Remarques sur l'évolution du russe comparée à celle des autres langues slaves* (= *Travaux du Cercle Linguistique de Prague*, 2.) Reprinted in Roman Jakobson, *Selected writings, I. Phonological studies* (The Hague: Mouton).

JAKOBSON, ROMAN. 1936/1984. Contribution to the general theory of case: general meanings of the Russian cases. *Russian and Slavic grammar: studies 1931–1981*, ed. Linda R. Waugh & Morris Halle, 59–103. (Translation of 'Beitrag zur allgemeinen Kasuslehre', *Travaux du Cercle Linguistique de Prague* 6.240–88.)

JAKOBSON, ROMAN. 1960/1971. Linguistics and poetics. *Selected writings III*, 18–51. The Hague: Mouton. (Originally published in *Style in Language*, ed. Thomas A. Sebeok. Cambridge, MA: MIT Press.)

JANDA, RICHARD. 1980. On the decline of the declensional system: the overall loss of OE nominal case inflections and the ME reanalysis of *-es* as *his*. *Papers from the 4th International Conference on Historical Linguistics*, ed. Elizabeth C. Traugott, Rebecca LaBrum & Susan Shepherd, 243–52. Amsterdam: John Benjamins.

JANDA, RICHARD. 1981. A case of liberation from morphology into syntax: the fate of the English genitive marker *-(e)s*. *Syntactic change* (Natural Language Studies 25), ed. Brenda B. Johns & David R. Strong, 59–114. Ann Arbor: University of Michigan Department of Linguistics.

JESPERSEN, OTTO. 1917. *Negation in English and other languages*. Copenhagen: A. F. Høst.

JESPERSEN, OTTO. 1922. *Language, its nature, development and origin*. London. (Reprinted by W. W. Norton, 1966.)

JOCHNOWITZ, G. 1973. *Dialect boundaries and the question of Franco-Provençal*. Berlin: Mouton.

JOSEPH, BRIAN D. 1992. Diachronic explanation: putting speakers back into the picture. *Explanations in historical linguistics*, ed. Garry W. Davis & Gregory K. Iverson, 123–44. Amsterdam: John Benjamins.

JOSEPH, BRIAN D. & RICHARD D. JANDA. 1988. The how and why of diachronic morphologization and demorphologization. *Theoretical morphology*, ed. Michael Hammond & Michael Noonan, 193–210. San Diego: Academic Press.

KEIL, FRANK. 1989. *Concepts, kinds and cognitive development*. Cambridge, MA: MIT Press.

KELLER, R. E. 1978. *The German language*. New Jersey: Humanities Press.

KELLER, RUDI. 1990/1994. *On language change: the invisible hand in language*. London: Routledge. (Translation and expansion of *Sprachwandel: von der unsichtbaren Hand in der Sprache*. Tübingen: Francke.)

KERSWILL, PAUL. 1996. Children, adolescents, and language change. *Language Variation and Change* 8.177–202.

KIM, YOUNG-JOO. 1997. The acquisition of Korean. Slobin 1997, 335–443.

KIPARSKY, PAUL. 1968. Linguistic universals and linguistic change. *Universals in linguistic theory*, ed. Emmon Bach and Robert T. Harms, 170–210. New York: Holt, Rinehart and Winston.

KIRBY, SIMON. 1997. Competing motivations and emergence: explaining implicational hierarchies. *Linguistic Typology* 1.5–31.

KIRBY, SIMON. 1999. *Function, selection and innateness: the emergence of language universals.* Oxford: Oxford University Press.

KROCH, ANTHONY S. 1989. Reflexes of grammar in patterns of language change. *Language Variation and Change* 1.199–244.

LABOV, WILLIAM. 1963/1972. The social motivation of a sound change. Labov 1972b, 1–42. (Originally published in *Word* 19.273–309.)

LABOV, WILLIAM. 1966. *The social stratification of English in New York City.* Washington, DC: Center for Applied Linguistics.

LABOV, WILLIAM. 1972a. *Language in the inner city: studies in the Black English Vernacular.* Philadelphia: University of Pennsylvania Press.

LABOV, WILLIAM. 1972b. *Sociolinguistic patterns.* Philadelphia: University of Pennsylvania Press.

LABOV, WILLIAM. 1980. The social origins of sound change. *Locating language in time and space*, ed. William Labov, 251–66. New York: Academic Press.

LABOV, WILLIAM. 1981. Resolving the neogrammarian controversy. *Language* 57.267–309.

LABOV, WILLIAM. 1982. Building on empirical foundations. *Perspectives on historical linguistics*, ed. Winfrid P. Lehmann & Yakov Malkiel, 17–92. Amsterdam: John Benjamins.

LABOV, WILLIAM. 1994. *Principles of linguistic variation, Vol. I: Internal factors.* Oxford: Basil Blackwell.

LAFITTE, PIERRE. 1962. *Grammaire basque.* Bayonne: Editions des 'Amis du Musée Basque' et 'Ikas'.

LAKOFF, GEORGE. 1990. The Invariance Hypothesis: is abstract reason based on image-schemas? *Cognitive Linguistics* 1.39–74.

LAKOFF, GEORGE & MARK JOHNSON. 1980. *Metaphors we live by.* Chicago: University of Chicago Press.

LAKOFF, ROBIN. 1968. *Abstract syntax and Latin complementation.* Cambridge, MA: MIT Press.

LANGACKER, RONALD W. 1976. Semantic representations and the linguistic relativity hypothesis. *Foundations of Language* 14.307–57.

LANGACKER, RONALD W. 1977. Syntactic reanalysis. Li 1977, 57–139.

LANGACKER, RONALD W. 1987. *Foundations of cognitive grammar, Vol I: theoretical prerequisites.* Stanford: Stanford University Press.

LANGACKER, RONALD W. 1988. An overview of cognitive grammar. *Topics in cognitive linguistics*, ed. Brygida Rudzka-Ostyn, 3–48. Amsterdam: John Benjamins.

LANGACKER, RONALD W. 1991. *Foundations of cognitive grammar, Vol II: descriptive application.* Stanford: Stanford University Press.

LANHAM, L. W. & C. A. MACDONALD. 1979. *The standard in South African English and its social history.* Heidelberg: Groos.

LASS, ROGER. 1980. *On explaining language change.* Cambridge: Cambridge University Press.

LASS, ROGER. 1990. How to do things with junk: exaptation in language change. *Journal of Linguistics* 26: 79–102.

LASS, ROGER. 1992. Phonology and morphology. *The Cambridge history of the English language*, ed. Norman Blake, 23–155. Cambridge: Cambridge University Press.

LASS, ROGER. 1997. *Historical linguistics and language change*. Cambridge: Cambridge University Press.

LAWLER, JOHN. 1974. Ample negatives. *Papers from the Tenth Regional Meeting, Chicago Linguistic Society*, ed. Michael W. LaGaly, Robert A. Fox & Anthony Bruck, 357–77. Chicago: Chicago Linguistic Society.

LEHMANN, CHRISTIAN. 1982. *Thoughts on grammaticalization: a programmatic sketch, Vol. I.* (Arbeiten des Kölner Universalien-Projekts, 48.) Köln: Institut für Sprachwissenschaft.

LEHMANN, CHRISTIAN. 1985. Grammaticalization: synchronic variation and diachronic change. *Lingua e Stile* 20.303–18.

LEPAGE, ROBERT B. 1992. 'You can never tell where a word comes from': language contact in a diffuse setting. *Language contact and language change*, ed. Ernst Håkon Jahr, 71–101. Berlin: Mouton de Gruyter.

LEPAGE, ROBERT B. & ANDRÉE TABOURET-KELLER. 1985. *Acts of identity*. Cambridge: Cambridge University Press.

LEVINSON, STEPHEN C. 1983. *Pragmatics*. Cambridge: Cambridge University Press.

LEWIS, DAVID. 1969. *Convention*. Cambridge, MA: MIT Press.

LEWIS, G. L. 1967. *Turkish grammar*. Oxford: Oxford University Press.

LI, CHARLES (ed.). 1977. *Mechanisms of syntactic change*. Austin: University of Texas Press.

LI, CHARLES & SANDRA A. THOMPSON. 1981. *Mandarin Chinese: a functional reference grammar*. Berkeley & Los Angeles: University of California Press.

LICHTENBERK, FRANTISEK. 1983. *A grammar of Manam*. (Oceanic Linguistics Special Publication, 18.) Honolulu: University of Hawaii Press.

LIGHTFOOT, DAVID W. 1979. *Principles of diachronic syntax*. Cambridge: Cambridge University Press.

LIGHTFOOT, DAVID W. 1991. *How to set parameters: arguments from language change*. Cambridge, MA: MIT Press.

LINDBLOM, BJÖRN. 1983. Economy of speech gestures. *The production of speech*, ed. Peter F. MacNeilage, 217–45. New York: Springer-Verlag.

LINDBLOM, BJÖRN. 1986. Phonetic universals in vowel systems. *Experimental phonology*, ed. John J. Ohala & Jeri J. Jaeger, 13–44. New York: Academic Press.

LINGE, DAVID E. 1976. Translator's introduction. Hans-Georg Gadamer, *Philosophical hermeneutics*, xi–lviii. Berkeley: University of California Press.

LORD, CAROL. 1979. 'Don't you fall me down': children's generalizations regarding cause and transitivity. *Papers and Research on Child Language Development* 17.81–9. Stanford: Stanford University Department of Linguistics.

LÜDTKE, HELMUT. 1980. The place of morphology in a universal cybernetic theory of language change. *Historical morphology*, ed. Jacek Fisiak, 273–81. The Hague: Mouton.

LÜDTKE, HELMUT. 1985. Diachronic irreversibility in word-formation and semantics. *Historical semantics; historical word-formation*, ed. Jacek Fisiak, 355–66. Berlin: Mouton.

LÜDTKE, HELMUT. 1986. Esquisse d'une théorie du changement langagier. *La linguistique* 22.3–46.

MACAULAY, R. K. S. 1977. *Language, social class, and education: a Glasgow study*. Edinburgh: The University Press.

MADDIESON, IAN. 1984. *Patterns of sounds*. Cambridge: Cambridge University Press.

MAJOR, ROY C. 1993. Sociolinguistic factors in loss and acquisition of phonology. *Progression and regression in language: sociocultural, neuropsychological and linguistic perspectives*, ed. Kenneth Hyltenstam & Åke Viberg, 463–78. Cambridge: Cambridge University Press.

MAŃCZAK, WITOLD. 1988. Bartoli's second 'norm'. *Historical dialectology: regional and social*, ed. Jacek Fisiak, 349–55. Berlin: Mouton de Gruyter.

MARTINET, ANDRÉ. 1952/1972. Function, structure and sound change. *A reader in historical and comparative linguistics*, ed. Allan R. Keiler, 139–74. New York: Holt, Rinehart & Winston. (Originally appeared in *Word* 8.1–32, 1952.)

MATRAS, YARON. 1998. Utterance modifiers and universals of grammatical borrowing. *Linguistics* 36.281–331.

MATRAS, YARON. 2000. Mixed languages: a functional-communicative approach. *Bilingualism, Language, and Cognition* 3, to appear.

MAYR, ERNST. 1942. *Systematics and the origin of species*. Cambridge: Cambridge University Press.

MAYR, ERNST. 1978. Evolution. *Scientific American* 239.46–55.

MAYR, ERNST. 1982. *The growth of biological thought: diversity, evolution, inheritance*. Cambridge, MA: Belknap Press.

McMAHON, APRIL M. S. 1994. *Understanding language change*. Cambridge: Cambridge University Press.

MELTON, TERRY, RAYMOND PETERSON, ALAN J. REDD, N. SAHA, A. S. M. SOFRO, JEREMY MARTINSON & MARK STONEKING. 1995. Polynesian genetic affinities with Southeast Asian populations as identified by mtDNA analysis. *American Journal of Human Genetics* 57.403–14.

MENOVŠČIKOV, G. K. 1969. O nekotoryx social'nyx aspektax èvoljucii jazyka. *Voprosy social'noj lingvisitki*, 110–34. Leningrad: Nauka.

MERLEAU-PONTY, MAURICE. 1960/1964. On the phenomenology of language. *Signs* (transl. Richard C. McCleary), 84–97. Evanston: Northwestern University Press. (*Signes*, Librairie Gallimard, 1960.)

MERLEAU-PONTY, MAURICE. 1962/1964. An unpublished text by Maurice Merleau-Ponty: a prospectus of his work (transl. Arleen B. Dallery). *The primacy of perception*, 3–11. Evanston: Northwestern University Press. (Un inédit de Maurice Merleau-Ponty, *Revue de métaphysique et de morale* 4.401–9, 1962.)

MERLEAU-PONTY, MAURICE. 1964/1973. *Consciousness and the acquisition of language* (transl. Hugh J. Silverman). Evanston: Northwestern University Press. (La conscience et l'acquisition du langage, *Bulletin de psychologie* 236, XVIII 3–6, 226–59, 1964.)

MEYER-LÜBKE, W. 1923. *Grammaire des langues romanes*. New York: Stechert.

MILROY, JAMES. 1992a. A social model for the interpretation of language change. *History of Englishes: new methods and interpretation in historical linguistics*, ed. Matti Rissanen, Ossi Ihalainen, Terttu Nevalainen & Irma Taavitsainen, 72–91. Berlin: Mouton de Gruyter.

MILROY, JAMES. 1992b. *Linguistic variation and change*. Oxford: Blackwell.

MILROY, JAMES & LESLEY MILROY. 1985. Linguistic change, social network and speaker innovation. *Journal of Linguistics* 21.339–84.

MILROY, LESLEY. 1987. *Language and social networks* (2nd edn). Oxford: Blackwell.

MOORE, SAMUEL & ALBERT H. MARCKWARDT. 1968. *Historical outline of English sounds and inflections*. Ann Arbor: George Wahr Publishing Company.

MOUS, MAARTEN. 1994. Ma'a or Mbugu. *Mixed languages*, ed. Peter Bakker & Maarten Mous, 175–200. Amsterdam: Institute for Functional Research into Language and Language Use (IFOTT), University of Amsterdam.

MUFWENE, SALIKOKO. 1996a. The founder principle in creole genesis. *Diachronica* 13.83–134.

MUFWENE, SALIKOKO. 1996b. Creolization and grammaticalization: what creolistics could contribute to research on grammaticalization. *Changing meanings, changing functions*, ed. Philip Baker & Anand Syea, 5–28. London: University of Westminster Press.

MUFWENE, SALIKOKO. To appear. Language contact, evolution and death: how ecology rolls the dice. *Assessing ethnolinguistic vitality*, ed. Gloria E. Kindell & M. Paul Lewis. Dallas: Summer Institute of Linguistics.

MÜHLHÄUSLER, PETER. 1986. *Pidgin and Creole linguistics*. Oxford: Blackwell.

MURPHY, GREGORY L. & DOUGLAS L. MEDIN. 1985. The role of theories in conceptual coherence. *Psychological Review* 92.289–316.

MUYSKEN, PIETER. 1997. Media Lengua. *Contact languages: a wider perspective*, ed. Sarah G. Thomason, 365–426. Amsterdam: John Benamins.

NADZHIP, E. N. 1971. *Modern Uigur*. Moscow: Nauka Publishing House.

NETTLE, DANIEL. 1999. Functionalism and its difficulties in biology and linguistics. *Functionalism and formalism in linguistics, Vol. 1*, ed. Michael Darnell, Edith Moravcsik, Frederick Newmeyer, Michael Noonan & Kathleen Wheatley, 445–67. Amsterdam: John Benjamins.

NEWMEYER, FREDERICK J. 1992. Iconicity and generative grammar. *Language* 68.756–96.

NEWTON, BRIAN. 1964. An Arabic-Greek dialect. *Papers in memory of George C. Pappageotes* (supplement to *Word* 20), 43–52.

NORMAN, JERRY. 1988. *Chinese*. Cambridge: Cambridge University Press.

NUNBERG, GEOFFREY, IVAN A. SAG & THOMAS WASOW. 1994. Idioms. *Language* 70.491–538.

OHALA, JOHN J. 1981. The listener as a source of sound change. *Papers from the Parasession on Language and Behavior, Chicago Linguistic Society*, ed. Carrie S. Masek, Roberta A. Hendrick & Mary Frances Miller, 178–203. Chicago: Chicago Linguistic Society.

OHALA, JOHN. 1983. The origin of sound patterns in vocal tract constraints. *The production of speech*, ed. Peter F. MacNeilage, 189–216. New York: Springer.

OHALA, JOHN. 1989. Sound change is drawn from a pool of synchronic variation. *Language change: contributions to the study of its causes*, ed. Leiv Egil Breivik & Ernst Håkon Jahr, 173–98. Berlin: Mouton de Gruyter.

OHALA, JOHN. 1992. What's cognitive, what's not, in sound change. *Diachrony within synchrony: language history and cognition*, ed. Günter Kellermann & Michael D. Morrissey, 309–55.

OHALA, JOHN. 1993. The phonetics of sound change. *Historical linguistics: problems and perspectives*, ed. Charles Jones, 237–78. London: Longman.

PAUL, HERMANN. 1880. *Prinzipien der Sprachgeschichte*. Tübingen: Max Niemeyer.

PFAFF, CAROL W. 1979. Constraints on language mixing: intrasentential code-switching and borrowing in Spanish/English. *Language* 55.291–318.

PHILLIPS, BETTY S. 1984. Word frequency and the actuation of sound change. *Language* 60.320–42.

PINKER, STEVEN. 1989. *Learnability and cognition*. Cambridge, MA: MIT Press.

PINKER, STEVEN & PAUL BLOOM. 1990. Natural language and natural selection. *Behavioral and Brain Sciences* 13.707–84.

PLANK, FRANS. 1984. The modals story retold. *Studies in Language* 8.305–64.

PLUNKETT, KIM & SVEN STRÖMQVIST. 1992. The acquisition of Scandinavian languages. Slobin 1992, 457–556.

POLLARD, CARL & IVAN A. SAG. 1993. *Head-driven Phrase Structure Grammar.* Chicago and Stanford: University of Chicago Press and the Center for the Study of Language and Information.

PULKINA, I. & ZAXAVA-NEKRASOVA, E. (n.d.) *Russian.* Moscow: Progress.

QUINE, WILLARD VAN ORMAN. 1951/1961. Two dogmas of empiricism. *From a logical point of view* (2nd edn), 20–46. (Originally published in *Philosophical Review* 60.20–43, 1951.)

RAVID, DORIT DISKIN. 1995. *Language change in child and adult Hebrew: a psycholinguistic perspective.* Oxford: Oxford University Press.

REDD, ALAN J., NAOKO TAKEZAKI, STEPHEN T. SHERRY, STEPHEN T. MCGARVEY, A. S. M. SOFRO & MARK STONEKING. 1995. Evolutionary history of COII/tRNA^{Lys} intergenic 9 base pair deletion in human mitochondrial DNAs from the Pacific. *Molecular Biology and Evolution* 12.604–15.

REDDY, MICHAEL J. 1993. The conduit metaphor – a case of frame conflict in our language about language. *Metaphor and thought* (2nd edn), ed. Andrew Ortony, 164–201. Cambridge: Cambridge University Press.

RITT, NIKOLAUS. 1995. Language change as evolution: looking for linguistic 'genes'. *Vienna English Working Papers* 4:1.43–56.

ROGERS, E. M. & F. F. SHOEMAKER. 1971. *Communication of innovations* (2nd edn). New York: Free Press.

ROHDE, ADA, ANATOL STEFANOWITSCH & SUZANNE KEMMER. 1999. Loanwords in a usage-based model. To appear in the *Proceedings of the 35th Annual Meeting of the Chicago Linguistic Society.* Chicago: Chicago Linguistic Society.

ROMAINE, SUZANNE. 1982. *Sociohistorical linguistics.* Cambridge: Cambridge University Press.

ROMAINE, SUZANNE. 1995. *Bilingualism* (2nd edn). Oxford: Blackwell.

RONJAT, J. 1937. *Grammaire historique des parlers provençaux modernes, Vol. 3.* Montpellier: Société des langues romanes.

SAMARIN, WILLIAM J. 1962/1968. Lingua francas of the world. *Readings in the sociology of language,* ed. Joshua Fishman, 660–72. The Hague: Mouton. (Revised and expanded from original in *Study of the role of second languages in Asia, Africa, and Latin America,* ed. F. A. Rice, 54–64. Washington: Center for Applied Linguistics.)

SANKOFF, GILLIAN. 1972. Language use in multilingual societies: some alternative approaches. *Sociolinguistics: selected readings,* ed. J. B. Pride & J. Holmes, 33–51. Harmondsworth: Penguin Books.

SAPIR, EDWARD. 1921. *Language.* New York: Harcourt, Brace & World.

SAUSSURE, FERDINAND DE. 1916/1966. *Cours de linguistique générale,* ed. Charles Bally and Albert Sechehaye. (*Course in general linguistics,* transl. Wade Baskin. New York: McGraw-Hill, 1966.)

SCATTON, ERNEST A. 1983. *A reference grammar of Modern Bulgarian.* Columbus, OH: Slavica.

SCHELLING, THOMAS C. 1960. *The strategy of conflict.* Cambridge, Mass.: Harvard University Press.

SCHEVILL, ISABEL M. 1970. *Manual of basic Spanish constructions.* Stanford: Stanford University Press.

SCHLESINGER, IZCHAK M. 1979. Cognitive structures and semantic deep structure. *Journal of Linguistics* 15.307–24.

SCHMALSTIEG, WILLIAM R. 1976. *An introduction to Old Church Slavonic.* Columbus, OH: Slavica.

SCHWEGLER, ARMIN. 1988. Word-order changes in predicate negation strategies in Romance languages. *Diachronica* 5.21–58.

SEARLE, JOHN. 1979. Literal meaning. *Expression and meaning*, 117–36. Cambridge: Cambridge University Press.

SHIBATANI, MASAYOSHI. 1985. Passives and related constructions: a prototype analysis. *Language* 61.821–48.

SHNUKAL, ANNA. 1988. *Broken: an introduction to the Creole language of Torres Strait.* (Pacific Linguistics, Series C, No. 107.) Canberra: Australian National University.

SIEVERS, EDUARD. 1881. *Grundzüge der Phonetik: zur Einführung in das Studium der Lautlehre der indogermanischen Sprachen.* Leipzig: Bretikopf & Härtel.

SJOBERG, ANDRÉE F. 1963. *Uzbek structural grammar.* (Uralic and Altaic Series, 18.) Bloomington: Indiana University Press.

SLOBIN, DAN I. 1985. *The crosslinguistic study of language acquisition, Vol. 1: The data.* Hillsdale, NJ: Lawrence Erlbaum Associates.

SLOBIN, DAN I. 1992. *The crosslinguistic study of language acquisition, Vol. 3.* Hillsdale, NJ: Lawrence Erlbaum Associates.

SLOBIN, DAN I. 1997a. *The crosslinguistic study of language acquisition, Vol. 4.* Mahwah, NJ: Lawrence Erlbaum Associates.

SLOBIN, DAN I. 1997b. The origins of grammaticizable notions: beyond the individual mind. *The crosslinguistic study of language acquisition, Vol. 5: expanding the contexts,* ed. Dan I. Slobin, 265–323. Mahwah, NJ: Lawrence Erlbaum Associates.

SPERBER, DAN & DEIRDRE WILSON. 1995. *Relevance: communication and cognition* (2nd edn). Oxford: Blackwell.

STEPHANY, URSULA. 1997. The acquisition of Greek. Slobin 1997a, 183–333.

SUTCLIFFE, EDMUND F. 1936. *A grammar of the Maltese language.* Oxford: Oxford University Press.

TABOR, WHITNEY. 1993. The gradual development of degree modifier *sort of* and *kind of*: a corpus proximity model. *Papers from the 29th Regional Meeting of the Chicago Linguistic Society,* ed. Katharine Beals, Gina Cooke, David Kathman, Sotaro Kita, Karl-Erik McCullough & David Testen, 451–65. Chicago: Chicago Linguistic Society.

TABOR, WHITNEY & ELIZABETH C. TRAUGOTT. 1998. Structural scope expansion and grammaticalization. *The limits of grammaticalization,* ed. Anna Giacolone Ramat & Paul J. Hopper, 229–72. Amsterdam: John Benjamins.

TANNEN, DEBORAH. 1982. Oral and literate strategies in spoken and written narratives. *Language* 58.1–21.

TESLAR, J. A. 1957. *A new Polish grammar.* Edinburgh: Oliver & Boyd.

THELANDER, M. 1979. *Språkliga Variationsmodeller Tillämpade på Nutida Burträskal.* Uppsala: Uppsala University.

THOMASON, SARAH G. 1983. Chinook Jargon in areal and historical context. *Language* 59.820–70.

THOMASON, SARAH G. 1997. Ma'a (Mbugu). *Contact languages: a wider perspective,* ed. Sarah G. Thomason, 469–87. Amsterdam: John Benjamins.

THOMASON, SARAH G. & TERRENCE KAUFMAN. 1988. *Language contact, creolization and genetic linguistics.* Berkeley & Los Angeles: University of California Press.

TIMBERLAKE, ALAN. 1977. Reanalysis and actualization in syntactic change. Li 1977, 141–77.

TOMASELLO, MICHAEL. 1995. Joint attention as social cognition. *Joint attention: its origins and role in development,* ed. C. Moore & P. Dunham. Hillsdale, NJ: Lawrence Erlbaum Associates.

TRAUGOTT, ELIZABETH C. 1988. Pragmatic strengthening and grammaticalization. *Proceedings of the Fourteenth Annual Meeting of the Berkeley Linguistics Society and the Parasession on Grammaticalization*, ed. Shelley Axmaker, Annie Jaisser & Helen Singmaster, 406–16. Berkeley: Berkeley Linguistics Society.

TRAUGOTT, ELIZABETH C. 1989. On the rise of epistemic meanings in English: an example of subjectification in semantic change. *Language* 65.31–55.

TRAUGOTT, ELIZABETH C. 2000. Constructions in grammaticalization. To appear in *A handbook of historical linguistics*, ed. Brian Joseph & Richard Janda. Oxford: Blackwell.

TRAUGOTT, ELIZABETH C. & BERND HEINE. 1991. *Approaches to grammaticalization* (2 vols.). Amsterdam: John Benjamins.

TRAUGOTT, ELIZABETH C. & EKKEHART KÖNIG. 1991. The semantics-pragmatics of grammaticalization revisited. *Approaches to grammaticalization*, ed. Elizabeth C. Traugott & Bernd Heine, 189–218. Amsterdam: John Benjamins.

TRAUGOTT, ELIZABETH C. & HENRY SMITH. 1993. Arguments from language change (Review article on David Lightfoot, *How to set parameters: arguments from language change*). *Journal of Linguistics* 29.431–47.

TRUDGILL, PETER. 1972. Sex, covert prestige, and linguistic change in the urban British English of Norwich. *Language in Society* 1.179–96.

TRUDGILL, PETER. 1974/1983. Linguistic change and diffusion: description and explanation in geolinguistics. *On dialect*, 52–87. New York: New York University Press. (Revision of 'Linguistic change and diffusion: description and explanation in sociolinguistic dialect geography', *Language in society* 3, 1974.)

TRUDGILL, PETER. 1979/1983. Language contact and language change: on the rise of the creoloid. *On dialect*, 102–7. (Originally presented to the International Conference on Historical Linguistics, Stanford, California, 1979.)

TRUDGILL, PETER. 1986. *Dialects in contact*. Oxford: Blackwell.

TRUDGILL, PETER. 1988. Norwich revisited: recent linguistic changes in an English urban dialect. *English World-Wide* 9.33–49.

TRUDGILL, PETER. 1989. Contact and isolation in linguistic change. *Language change: contributions to the study of its causes*, ed. Leiv Egil Breivik & Ernst Håkon Jahr, 227–37. Berlin: Mouton de Gruyter.

TRUDGILL, PETER. 1990. *The dialects of England*. Oxford: Blackwell.

TRUDGILL, PETER. 1992. Dialect typology and social structure. *Language contact and language change*, ed. Ernst Håkon Jahr, 195–212. Berlin: Mouton de Gruyter.

TRUDGILL, PETER. 1996a. Dialect typology: isolation, social network and phonological structure. *Towards a social science of language, Vol. I: Variation and change in language and society*, ed. Gregory R. Guy, Crawford Feagin, Deborah Schiffrin & John Baugh, 3–21. Amsterdam: John Benjamins.

TRUDGILL, PETER. 1996b. Dual-source pidgins and reverse creoloids: northern perspectives on language contact. *Language contact in the Arctic: northern pidgins and contact languages*, ed. Ernst Håkon Jahr & Ingvild Broch, 5–14. Berlin: Mouton de Gruyter.

TRUDGILL, PETER. 1999. New-dialect formation and dedialectalisation: embryonic and vestigial variants. *Journal of English Linguistics* 27:319–27.

TRUDGILL, PETER & NINA FOXCROFT. 1978/1983. The sociolinguistics and geolinguistics of vowel mergers: transfer and approximation in East Anglia. *On dialect: social and geographic perspectives*, Peter Trudgill, 88–101. (Revised version of 'On the sociolinguistics of vocalic mergers: transfer and approximation in East Anglia', *Sociolinguistic patterns in British English*, ed. Peter Trudgill, 69–79. London: Edward Arnold.)

VAN RHEEDEN, HADEWYCH. 1994. Petjo: the mixed language of the Indos in Batavia. *Mixed languages*, ed. Peter Bakker & Maarten Mous, 223–37. Amsterdam: IFOTT.

VANDAME, CHARLES. 1963. *Le Ngambay-Moundou: phonologie, grammaire, textes.* (Mémoires de l'IFAN, 69.) Dakar: IFAN.

VENDRYÈS, JOSEPH. 1921. *Le langage.* Paris: Renaissance du livre.

VIHMAN, MARILYN MAY. 1980. Sound change and child language. *Papers from the 4th International Conference on Historical Linguistics*, ed. Elizabeth Closs Traugott, Rebecca Labrum & Susan Shepherd, 303–20. Amsterdam: John Benjamins.

VINCENT, NIGEL. 1978. Is sound change teleological? *Recent developments in historical phonology*, ed. Jacek Fisiak, 409–30. The Hague: Mouton.

VINCENT, NIGEL. 1993. Head- versus dependent-marking: the case of the clause. *Heads in grammatical theory*, ed. Greville G. Corbett, Norman M. Fraser & Scott McGlashan, 140–63.

VRBA, E. S. 1984. Why species selection? *Systematic Zoology* 33.318–28.

WANG, WILLIAM S.-Y. 1969. Competing changes as a cause of residue. *Language* 45.9–25.

WANG, WILLIAM S.-Y. (ed.). 1977. *The lexicon in phonological change.* The Hague: Mouton.

WARDHAUGH, RONALD. 1992. *An introduction to sociolinguistics* (2nd edn). Oxford: Blackwell.

WEINREICH, URIEL. 1968. *Languages in contact: findings and problems* (2nd edn). The Hague: Mouton.

WEINREICH, URIEL, WILLIAM LABOV & MARVIN I. HERZOG. 1968. Empirical foundations for a theory of language change. *Directions for historical linguistics*, ed. Winfrid P. Lehmann & Yakov Malkiel, 95–195. Austin: University of Texas Press.

WHINNOM, KEITH. 1971. Linguistic hybridization and the 'special case' of pidgins and creoles. *Pidginization and creolization of languages*, ed. Dell Hymes, 91–115. Cambridge: Cambridge University Press.

WILLIAMS, G. C. 1966. *Adaptation and natural selection.* Princeton: Princeton University Press.

WINOGRAD, TERRY. 1980. What does it mean to understand language? *Cognitive Science* 4.209–41.

ZAENEN, ANNIE, JOAN MALING & HÖSKILDUR THRÁINSSON. 1985. Case and grammatical functions: the Icelandic passive. *Natural Language and Linguistic Theory* 3.441–83.

ZIPF, GEORGE. 1935. *The psychobiology of language: an introduction to dynamic philology.* Cambridge, MA: MIT Press.

Index of authors

Index of populations (languages, communities and species)

This index also includes more inclusive populations, which may be defined phylogenetically or taxonomically (see pp. 15–16). Capitalized singular names refer to languages and capitalized plural names refer to communities unless otherwise indicated.

Index of subjects

Definitions and major explications are cited in boldface